Design Office Management

Design
Office
Management
Handbook

Fred A. Stitt
Editor

Arts & Architecture Press
Santa Monica, California

Library of Congress Catalog Card Number 85-061147

Cataloging in Publication Data

Design office management handbook.

    Includes index.
    1. Architectural practice—Management. 2. Engineering
practice—Management. 3. Design practice—Management.
I. Stitt, Fred A. II. Title.

ISBN 0-931228-10-7

Printed in the United States of America.
First Printing.

Designed by Joe Molloy.

Contents

Contributors

We are deeply grateful to the contributors to this anthology, and to the publications which originally published their articles, for allowing us to reprint them. There are several contributors not included on the list because we were unable to discover their current professional affiliation: David Burnstein, J. Douglas Dietrich, Andrew Loebelson, and Charles A. Parthum. We hope to rectify that in the next edition.

James Anderegg
Mr. Anderegg heads his own firm, Anderegg & Associates, which provides contract librarians to architectural and engineering firms, Detroit, MI.

Douglas Bevis, A.I.A.
Mr. Bevis is chief financial officer for The NBBJ Group in Seattle, WA.

Weld Coxe, Hon. A.I.A.
Mr. Coxe is chairman of The Coxe Group, a Philadelphia management consulting firm specializing in the design professions, and has written two books and numerous articles on all phases of design office management.

John Coyne
Mr. Coyne heads a marketing and public relations consulting firm specializing in assisting A/E firms since 1975, Minneapolis, MN.

Anthony F. Dannible
Mr. Dannible is senior partner of Dannible/McKee & Associates, a New York firm specializing in ownership transition and valuation.

Nick Despota
Mr. Despota is an independent television producer and consultant who can be reached through the Society for Marketing Professional Services, Alexandria, VA.

Donald P. Dillon
Mr. Dillon is vice president of Nelson Charlmers, Inc., an insurance agency specializing in professional liability insurance for designers.

Paul G. Dombroski
Mr. Dombroski is a specialist in the field of human resources for A/E firms.

Thomas Eyerman, F.A.I.A.
Mr. Eyerman is the partner in charge of firm-wide administration and finance at Skidmore, Owings & Merrill, Chicago.

Russell Faure-Brac
Mr. Faure-Brac is president of Environmental Impact Planning (EIP), San Francisco, CA.

Raymond L. Gaio, A.I.A.
Mr. Gaio, an architect and engineer, during 20 years has consulted to thousands of design firms on all aspects of marketing and most recently was vice-president in charge of corporate marketing for DMJM.

Lowell V. Getz
Mr. Getz is a financial and management consultant to design firms, Houston, TX.

Mardy Grothe
Dr. Grothe is a psychologist, management consultant, and partner in the consulting firm, Performance Improvement Associates, Brockport, NY.

Malcolm Heard, Jr., A.I.A.
Mr. Heard is a project architect at Perez Associates, New Orleans.

Michael R. Hough
Mr. Hough is publisher of *Professional Services Management Journal*, *A/E Marketing Journal*, and other design professional publications, P.O. Box 11316, Newington, CT 06111.

Edwin P. James
Mr. James is a consultant with Arthur Andersen & Co., specializing in design firm government contracting.

Gerre Jones
Mr. Jones is a marketing and public relations consultant to design firms and publisher of *Professional Marketing Report*, Washington, DC.

Marie Kovacic
Ms. Kovacic, a writer and editor for AIA continuing education programs, was formerly on the professional practice staff.

Barry B. LePatner
Mr. LePatner is a partner in LePatner, Gainen & Block, a New YorkCity law firm. Mr. LePatner is business and legal advisor to more than 200 design firms.

Paul Lurie
Mr. Lurie is a partner in the Chicago law firm of Fohrman, Lurie, Sklar and Simon.

William J. Mager
Mr. Mager is a consultant specializing in design firm management, Bethesda, MD.

Charles M. McReynolds
Mr. McReynolds is a human resources consultant to architects and engineers, installing compensation, benefit, retirement, and productivity plans, Sierra Madre, California.

Frank Munzer, A.I.A.
Mr. Munzer is president of the Eggers Group, a New York-based architectural firm.

Harry J. Orchard
Mr. Orchard specializes in employee stock ownership plan work with professional firms. He is with Private Capital Corporation, Larkspur, CA.

Bradford Perkins, A.I.A.
Mr. Perkins is a principal of Attia & Perkins Architects in New York and describes himself as "an architect trying to practice what he preaches."

Paul W. T. Pippin, A.I.A.
Mr. Pippin was an associate partner with Skidmore Owings & Merrill for 15 years and 27 years with the firm. He has taught project management at Yale and Columbia.

Richard Praeger
Mr. Praeger became chairman of the board of URS Corporation following his firm's acquisition by URS.

Nora Lea Reefe
Ms. Reefe is president of Consultant Management Services, Inc., Tampa, FL.

Frank W. Rees Jr.
Mr. Rees is president of Rees Associates, Inc., an Oklahoma City architectural firm.

Thomas R. Rohan
Mr. Rohan is a contributing editor of *Industry Week* magazine.

Clare Ross
Mr. Ross is executive vice president of Peter A. Lendrum Associates of Phoenix, AZ.

Marc Roth
Mr. Roth is an associate attorney with Fohrman, Lurie, Sklar and Simon.

George Schrohe
Mr. Schrohe is president of Management Design, a San Francisco consulting firm.

Maeve Slavin
Ms. Slavin is executive editor of *Interiors* magazine.

Frank H. Smith III, A.I.A.
Mr. Smith is an architect and marketing consultant, Atlanta, GA.

Margaret Spaulding
Ms. Spaulding is director of Management Design, design office marketing consultants, San Francisco, CA.

Frank A. Stasiowski
Mr. Stasiowski is editor of *Professional Services Management Journal*.

O. C. (Russ) Tirella
Mr. Tirella is financial and contracts officer for Moore, Gardinek & Associates, a consulting engineering firm in Asheboro, NC.

David Travers
Mr. Travers is a management consultant, author of *Preparing Design Office Brochures: a Handbook*, and president of Arts & Architecture Press.

B.A. Whitson
Mr. Whitson is project manager with the Bank of America.

C. Norton Wright
Mr. Wright is vice president and director of business planning and development for O'Donnell, Wicklund & Pigozzi, Northbrook, IL.

Peter Wylie
Dr. Wylie is a psychologist, management consultant, and partner in the consulting firm, Performance Improvement Associates, Brockport, NY.

Introduction

It hasn't been long since running a design office was strictly a gentlemen's game. It wasn't considered gentlemanly to give attention to productivity and efficiency, for example. Those were considered to be petty concerns suited to working class types who ran factories.

It wasn't gentlemanly to learn business skills. That was bourgeois.

And, above all, there could be no such thing as marketing or promotion. That was ultra-gross. It would encourage unbridled competition, which would lead to a business orientation, which would lead to greater efficiency and productivity. In some people's minds, such materialistic considerations would ruin the profession.

The design professions avoided such dilemmas for many years through custom and law.

A combination of cultural traditions and educational barriers blocked general admission to the gentlemanly profession. As backup, it was illegal to inform people on one's design skills, services, and competitive advantages. Where it wasn't illegal, you'd get booted out of the professional associations for violating their transparently self-serving codes of ethics.

There wasn't any information on how to market design services. Some well-established design practitioners seemed to know how to get work, but they insisted that their socializing, country club lunches, and civic activities were in no way to be considered marketing or advertising. After all, that was forbidden.

Then some people fought the system. There was a lawsuit here, another one there, a Justice Department brief, some court rulings....The traditions started unraveling.

It became legal to compete. It became "not unethical," according to a change of mind by the American Institute of Architects, to be an architect *and* a builder.

More changes. You could offer a different fee structure than your colleagues had agreed you should offer.

The ultimate for many was that you could advertise your services.

Something else was happening. People had started studying the profession—seriously studying it for the first time. It's hard to believe now, but for generations virtually nobody paid attention to the operations of this complex and fascinating profession.

When I did my first research in the mid-sixties on the problems of setting up an office, getting clients, and doing drawings in new ways, I found only three books and a handful of British articles that had been published on such matters. There were no manuals. The books that had been published were out of print. There were no newsletters.

Now there are a half-dozen newsletters; dozens of books; hundreds of articles, papers, audio- and videotapes; endless seminars, workshops, and conferences. A Niagara of ink, a deluge of advice on how to go about doing one's work, how to avoid problems, how to grow and prosper.

Which is why this book was created.

When David Travers described his idea for this book well over a year ago, I thought, "At last!"

At last! Here was the opportunity to salvage the best information published in these last ten or more years. This was information that might otherwise just go out of print and disappear. Information on every aspect of how to do things better, if not best, in a design practice.

Travers first described his concept of the book as an encyclopedic management handbook. Everything from forming an office to selling one. Have a problem with marketing? Here you go—advice from a whole bunch of experts on all areas of marketing. Having a problem with overhead? Look under Financial Management. Want your office to be more productive? Here are the tools and techniques.

Now it's done. The book is loaded with good stuff by all kinds of good people who are specialists in the areas on which they wrote. It's worth a lot of attention and will be for some time to come. So use it on that basis—as a source book.

Everything here is the best we could find on these subjects. The information covers most of what matters on the business side of creating a design career. If there's anything you'd like to see that isn't covered, let us know and we'll find a source for you and include it in the next edition.

Fred A. Stitt
Orinda, California
March 31, 1986

Organization and
General Management

1

Where Is the Practice Going?

Because of their different bottom lines, professional firms often have difficulty setting clear goals. Offices with a quantitative bottom line can usually set very concrete goals—for example, to realize a specific return or investment; to maintain a specified market share; to grow at X percent per year.

On the other hand, architects or engineers who have a qualitative bottom line tend to state goals more in terms of ideals: to do "good" work; to build a "better" environment. There is certainly nothing wrong with aspiring to "motherhood" ideals, but the difficult part comes when you try to define such a goal. It is impossible to manage a course toward a goal you cannot define. The navigator who sets a course for "London" has a much clearer management task than the one who wants to sail to a "bright new world."

Professional Goals

In terms of organization direction, it is necessary to understand the difference between goals, objectives, strategies, and tactics.

Goals, as used here, are the desired results—such as world peace.

Objectives, in this context, are the milestones en route to that goal—end the conflict in the Middle East, for example.

Strategies are the means to the objectives—get some of the adversaries talking.

Tactics are the actions taken to carry out the strategy—such as inviting two of the adversaries to Camp David.

At all levels on this ladder, the distinction between a manageable goal or objective and an unmanageable one is whether the end result is measurable. Thus the goal

"We want to be the best design firm in Indiana"

is difficult to work toward, because there are likely many different measurements of "best." A more manageable goal statement might be:

"We want to be recognized for the quality of our design work."

Such a goal could be measured in these terms:

"We want to be published at least _____ times a year in _____ magazine."

Weld Coxe

Reprinted from *Managing Architectural & Engineering Practice,* Van Nostrand Reinhold 1982. Copyright 1980 by Weld Coxe.

When a professional practice has its goals documented clearly, it is already on the way to being well-managed.

"We want to receive design awards in at least
two of every three annual awards programs of
the state (ACEC)(AIA), etc."

"We want our clients to talk about us as an
'award-winning' or 'innovative' firm."

Sometimes the goal can be measured in terms of the objective. For example, the goal

"We want to become a multidiscipline firm"

could be translated into the first objective:

"We will open an Interiors Department within
one year."

launched with the strategy:

"We will begin by recruiting an experienced interior
designer to head the department,"

and implemented by this tactical management step:

"Bill has the responsibility to locate the interior designer
and is authorized to agree to compensation
up to $_____." (Or it could say: "Bill is authorized
to search for at least two qualified candidates,
and to present them to the full partnership for interviews
and final decision.")

In practical terms, for architects and engineers, goals should state what you want your practice to be. There is nothing wrong with idealistic goals provided you know how you will measure the results. And there is also nothing wrong with concrete, quantitative goals for a professional firm (e.g., "We want to be the largest civil engineering firm in town") provided you have a handle on what you must be qualitatively—in terms of the quality of service you render your clients—in order to achieve the qualitative goals. Whatever the goals of the practice, once defined they must be translated into objectives for a number of very specific aspects of practice. For example:

Firm Capability(ies). What disciplines, expertise, and services will we offer?

Markets. Whom will we seek to serve? how far will we travel?

Firm Size. How large a staff will we need?

Volume. How much work will we need to support this organization?

Financial. What must we put up to make it happen? What do we expect in return?

Personal Goals of the Decision Group. What will each of us contribute through our roles and what does each of us want in return?

Don't wait to set goals until you know how to manage them. You have a right first to aspire to whatever you really want to be.

You have a right to aspire to whatever you really want to be.

Personal Goals

In practice, the area of personal goals, listed last above, should be the starting place for goal setting in a professional design firm. The common business management theory that sets organization goals ahead of personal goals derives from the business assumption of stockholder ownership, with managers as caretakers of some else's investment. (It further follows that since this investment is usually financial, the goals are financial.) This is not so in most professional firms. By usual definition—and many state laws—a professional firm is controlled by those in its active management, and thus their personal and professional goals are inseparable from the organization goals.

When the managers of an absentee-owned business get together to discuss sales, if Bill doesn't want to work as hard as the goals require, he can usually be replaced by someone who will agree to try. Conversely, when the partners in an engineering or architectural firm get together and Bill is one of those partners in the room, it is not a question of what he *ought to do* for the firm. Rather it is a matter of what Bill, in terms of his personal and professional goals, *will do* that sets the course of the organization.

Some design firm partners may say, "We want the firm to grow, but we don't personally want to work that hard; let's hire the talent to do it for us." Well and good if you can manage it, but generally as soon as that talent finds out the firm's success depends more on their efforts than on yours, they will demand to be your partners, or they will become your competitors. This is why so few of the engineering and architectural firms that were bought out by business in the late 1960s have remained successful. If the best professional talents in an organization don't control their own destiny, they quickly leave to go into practice for themselves – where they can set their own goals.

Risk Factor

Another personal factor that affects professional firm goals is risk. It has long been an axiom that the success of any new business is proportionate to the risk the founders are willing to take. This, for example, is why wise bankers require personal guarantees on real estate loans—because they know the entrepreneurs will work harder if their shirts are at stake. It is less recognized that, at least until recently, most practicing architects and engineers have come from the lower risk-taking cross section of our society. The design professions have attracted individuals of principle, dedication, and ideals, but these are not always qualities found in high risk takers. This behavioral profile is demonstrated in practice in such ways as the degree to which a design firm will challenge and lead its clients versus doing what it is told to do, and in the kind of lease the partners will sign for office space. (It is interesting to observe how many architects have office space inferior to that which they would consider designing for any client.)

The point to be made about the risk factor when setting goals is simply to recognize it. If the decision group in a practice is not risk ori-

When one partner or group of partners wants to take substantially different risks things get sticky.

ented, they will probably set goals that require limited personal exposure—both financially and professionally—and be comfortable with the results. It is when one partner or a group of partners want to take substantially different risks that things get sticky.

The process of goal setting may founder at such points if it is not well managed. The only valid goals for a design practice are those that are fully integrated with the personal goals and styles of those who set them. Thus goal setting must begin with free and open communication among the goal setters. Unstated differences or open conflicts in the group that are not managed will lead either to unrealistic goals (because not everyone is committed to them) or to no goals at all.

The Goal-Setting Process

Thus the process through which goals are set is the most important management process in a design firm. It should be done formally, in an atmosphere removed from day-to-day pressures. It must be given enough time.

In practice, the best format for goal setting is for the decision group to meet in a retreat environment—away from the office and, if possible, away overnight so the participants will not be distracted by at-home concerns each evening. The length of time required is a factor of past experience at goal-setting retreats, and the number of participants. If goal setting is to be truly participative, each person needs a certain amount of "air time" to have his point of view heard. As a general rule, groups of five or fewer members have a productive retreat in two days. Add an additional day for every three to five additional participants.

Often the most effective way to make such a retreat productive is to hire a behavioral facilitator trained in group process. The facilitator is not there to help set goals but to observe the communication process in the group and see that differences and conflicts are brought to the surface and effectively managed. Also, the presence of a third party can help (1) prevent deterioration of the agenda into a staff meeting, (2) domination by one or another participant, or (3) acceptance of inconclusive (nonmeasurable) objectives.

If you feel you must conduct the retreat yourself, keep in mind a few management processes that can help get things off on the right track.

One helpful device is to have each person, at the outset of the retreat, complete in writing the following statements:

1. The best things that could happen at this retreat, for me personally, would be _____.

2. The worst things that could happen at this retreat, for me personally, would be _____.

These statements should be prepared privately, then posted on a wall, read by all, and discussed to make certain that each person's starting points are understood.

It is sometimes helpful at this point to ask each participant to estimate on a scale of 0 to 10 the probability for a successful outcome of the retreat. These probability fore casts can be repeated once or twice a day

The process through which goals are set is the most important management process in a design firm.

throughout the retreat as a means of learning how the participants are feeling about the ongoing process.

Another device useful in integrating personal goals with professional goals and roles in the organization is to ask each participant to list personal wants by completing the following:

1. For me to be more effective in my role, I would like from the organization *more*_____.

2. For me to be more effective in my role, I would like from the organization *less*_____.

3. For me to continue to be effective in my role, I would like from the organization the *same*_____.

As before, each person should first prepare answers privately. Then the individual answers can be consolidated and displayed (at blackboard scale). As the retreat discussion focuses on how to achieve these, considerable progress can be made toward realistic goals.

The output from the goal-setting process, however it is conducted, should be a written list of goals and objectives with specific assignments of responsibility with due dates by which individuals will prepare detailed strategies for implementation.

How far ahead can you plan? This is a constant dilemma in design firms. Since they are service organizations, much of their destiny is shaped by the needs of the clients they serve. In recent years, the rate of social, economic, and technological changes that affect design firms has made it very difficult to plan in any detail more than three to five years ahead. But some of the larger engineering firms have been experimenting with longer-range goal setting—as far out as fifteen and twenty years. Only time will tell how practical this may be.

It is best to express goals in two time frames:

Long-Range Goals. What we want the practice to be in three to five years.

Short-Range Goals. What we want the practice to be in one year as we move toward the long-range goals.

When a professional practice has its goals clearly documented, it is already on the way to being well managed. With the destination of the practice set, day-to-day management can go to work monitoring the course.

Choosing Organization Structure

Weld Coxe

Reprinted from *Managing Architectural & Engineering Practice,* Van Nostrand Reinhold 1982. Copyright 1980 by Weld Coxe.

As a rule of thumb, the client will insist on as much principal attention from the architect's or engineer's organization as the client will give to the project in his or her organization.

Selecting an organization structure is the first—and often the most important—management choice to be made in implementing goals. The structure of a design firm determines how it will serve its clients, and what kind of roles by principals and staff will be needed to provide that service.

Selecting the right organization structure for a design practice involves considerations of client management, design process, and organization control. Each factor needs to be considered for its own implications, and they often conflict with one another. The final organization structure must be a parity of all three.

Client Management Considerations

There can be no design practice without a client, and the client must be an integral part of every design firm's organization structure. At the project level, this is usually accomplished in one of two ways.

In Figure 1 a principal takes charge of managing the client and the project and serves as the link between the client and the firm for the life of the job. This is the most common pattern in small and medium size firms.

The variation shown in Figure 2 is common in larger firms where the number of projects outgrows the number of principals. Each project is then delegated to a staff or project manager who provides continuity to the client for the life of the project.

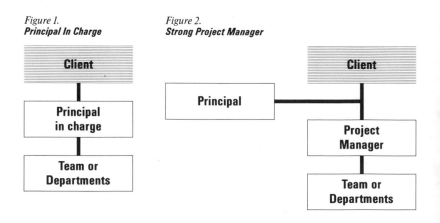

Figure 1.
Principal In Charge

Figure 2.
Strong Project Manager

Both structures are basically strong project manager formats, with the difference being whether or not the manager is a principal. Both work well once the client link with the project manager is adequately cemented. In practice, however, cementing that link is not always easy; as a consequence there are many variations in structure that creep into firms because of the nature of the professional service process. These can seriously weaken the organization if not effectively managed.

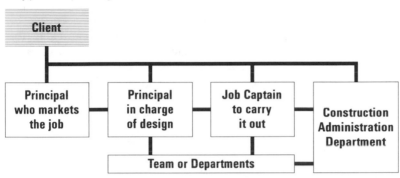

Figure 3.
Many (or No One) In Charge

Consider the client management structure shown in Figure 3. This is a project where the client established his or her initial relationship with the principal who marketed the job. That principal does not want to be involved in executing the project and therefore intends to hand the technical work to another principal or department head. This is fine in concept, except that in this case the client doesn't accept a complete handoff and keeps coming back to the marketing principal for some of the job communication. As the project continues, the principal in charge of design finishes the concept and wants to hand the execution to a job captain so he or she can go on to other work. When the job goes into the field, another handoff is supposed to occur as the job captain, usually a superior "inside" person, turns over day-to-day contact to an "outside" specialist. In this format, is it any wonder the marketing principal can never be extracted from the job?

Variations of the case shown in Figure 3 take place in virtually every design firm every day. The logic from the architect's or engineer's point of view is obvious: each person in the organization concentrates on what he does best, and the project is passed along the firm's "assembly line" until it is done.

The difficulty is that while assembly lines may be excellent organizations on which to build automobiles, the client for that automobile doesn't enter the auto company's organization until the product is finished. On the other hand, a professional service firm is always juggling a dichotomy: part of its product is service to the client and part of its product is the project result. Whereas some professional firms may be able to deal in an assembly-line fashion, most client don't like it at all. They engage a professional to design their project and then want/expect that professional to take them by the hand and lead them through the maze until the project is finished. This is an essential ingredient of the professional process. If the client wanted an assembly-line process, the client would buy stock-plan structures.

Thus the choice of organization structure in a professional firm has considerable influence on the type of clients who are comfortable in giving their work to that firm—or vice versa.

To choose an effective structure, it is first necessary to understand the difference between client management and project management. The starting point in professional service is managing the client. Doing this effectively takes as much time and attention as the client requires. For example, a client who hires an engineer and then delegates the project in the client's organization will generally accept delegation within the engineer's organization. But a client who wants to be intimately involved in every aspect of the design of the project will demand that the principal professional be equally involved.

As a rule of thumb, the client will insist on as much principal attention from the architect's or engineer's organization as the client will give to the project in his or her organization. This fundamental consideration of professional relationships explains why most private residential architecture is done by small firms, and why most governmental engineering is done by larger, more bureaucratically organized engineering firms.

Design Process Considerations

From a management standpoint, the choice of a structure for the design process is a matter of communication and coordination. Most architectural and engineering work today involves multiple disciplines and multiple functions, and the role of management in the design process is to keep projects moving among these functions and disciplines in an efficient and effective sequence.

There are two primary variations. Figure 4 illustrates a departmentalized structure where each major function (or discipline) of the design process is separately managed. The department head is responsible for both the function and the staff necessary to perform that function. Such a format usually provides tight, efficient control of each major segment of the design process and can accommodate various sizes of projects simultaneously within a department. Its limitations lie in coordinating and scheduling functions, and in the need to categorize staff within single functions, whereas many design professionals prefer a broader role in projects.

Figure 5 illustrates the so-called team approach structure, where a group of professionals, assembled for a specific project, performs all the functions required to execute it. Such a format focuses the team's attention on all aspects of the project or projects at hand, thus fostering close coordination. The format appeals to staff professionals with broader interest in

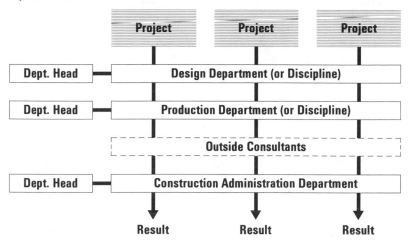

Figure 4.
Departmental Structure

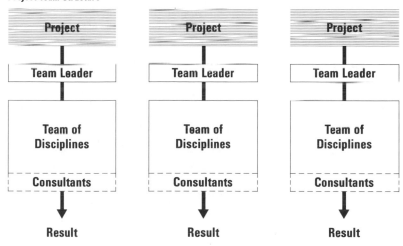

Figure 5.
Project Team Structure

the design process. The limitations of this format come in the difficulty of encouraging firm-wide standards for all teams; in the relative inflexibility of the teams to adapt to different size projects and/or schedule interruptions; in the personnel management, since the team leader tends to be task oriented and looks to someone else in the firm to provide human resources to the team. In practice, the team approach works best on larger projects in large firms. In smaller firms (or with smaller projects in a large firm) the team becomes a studio of people who work together as a team on a variety of simultaneous projects.

The team studio approach is often costlier to operate because of the difficulty of reassigning people between teams during short-term down periods. On the other hand, the departmentalized approach tends not to train from within the kind of staff needed for multifunction project management and firm management roles. In the long run the two costs may almost offset each other.

The choice of departmental vs. team approach is best made based on the format in which the specific people work best. This can often lead to hybrid structures, such as those shown in Figures 6 and 7.

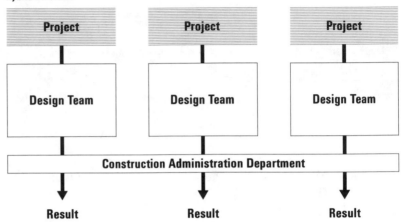

Figure 6.
Hybrid Structure

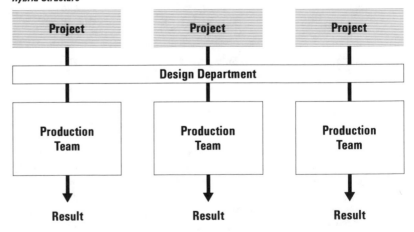

Figure 7.
Hybrid Structure

Organization Control Considerations

At the management center of every organization a number of functions must be performed to control the organization's progress en route to its goals. There are two approaches to fulfilling these functions, and it is important to understand their definition.

Leadership. The function of setting goals for where the firm will go and of establishing the major policies that will define the route to be taken to get there. Leadership can be vested in a strong individual or in a group of partners or directors. At the bottom line, the leadership sets the tone of the firm.

Management. The function of helping people steer the course set by a leader or group of owners. In design practice it involves managing the marketing to find the kind of clients the firm wants; managing the human resources to see that the necessary staff is attracted to do the work; and managing the assignments, schedules, budgets, and other factors that are necessary to make it all happen in a productive way.

Management Styles

There are several ways (styles) in which management can be performed. Management can be provided in a directive, autocratic manner, which is frequently the case when the leader and manager are one and the same. Or management can be provided in a facilitative manner, with the manager being an agent of leadership and entrusted with the role of seeing that the functions are performed by and throughout the organization.

The choice of management approach is often a function of the style of the leader(s). In small design organizations one person frequently wears all hats. In group practices the management functions are frequently divided, and several people wear dual hats as part-time organization manager and part-time functional/discipline/client manager. In terms of organization structure, however, the number of people involved in management is not as important as their management style. Directive management control has implications on the organization structure that are very different from those of facilitative management.

Generally, when people think of organization structures they tend to visualize the pyramidal format that is typical of organizations designed for hierarchical decision making. See Figure 8, for example.

While this organization pattern is sufficient for many business organizations, it is difficult for professional practice because it does not make clear where the client fits. Since the purpose of a structure is to define the routes of management control, a design firm structure that does not include the client defines only the internal management process—and this is only a small portion of the management that must go on in design practice.

To include the client in a design practice structure requires a format such as that shown in Figure 9.

What is missing from Figure 9 is an illustration of how the organization itself is managed. Nevertheless, many design firms—especially partnerships—operate very much like this and simply omit a structure for management. In its place a series of partnership/staff meetings serve the management function. This is inefficient at best, and usually leads to lowest-common-denominator decision making and a lot of individual autonomy at the expense of organization strength.

There are two basic ways to include management in the format in Figure 9, and the choice is defined by whether the control is to be directive or facilitative.

Figure 8.
Typical Business Organization Heirarchy

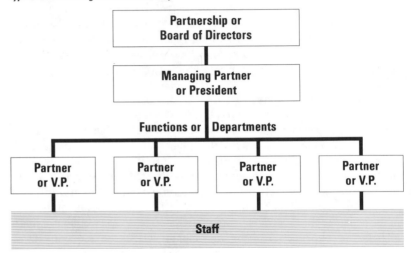

Figure 9.
Typical Service Organization Matrix

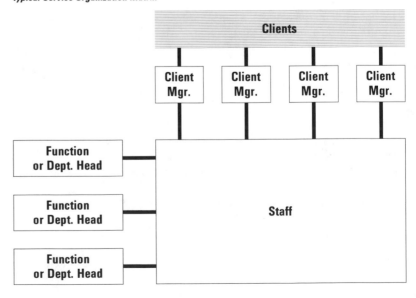

Figure 10 illustrates a strongly directive management, where decisions about product, marketing, personnel, and so on are decided at the top and fed down into the organization. This most closely parallels the pyramidal concept in Figure 8. The last word in the organization is closely held; clients know it, and most work comes in through or because of the principal manager. The strength of this structure is the clear, quick format for decision and the ability to deliver a strong, consistent quality of service. Its primary limitation is the physical inability of a single control source to do it all. Another limitation is the frequent difficulty of autocratic management to retain good talent in a design practice. The format works best in smaller organizations.

An alternative approach is that given in Figure 11. In this format the management functions are more facilitative and less autocratic. Management's role here is to coordinate and provide support and encouragement for a group of unit leaders, rather than to tell everyone autocratically what to do. Its strengths are in the way the collaborative format supports the multidiscipline, multifunction nature of today's practice and in its ability to grow, since the burdens of management are shared by a group. It also fosters growth of future leaders from within. The independence that it allows individuals, however, can lead to problems in maintaining a consistent organization process. There is also a very real shortage of management-inclined professionals who want to fill the central management role.

Architects and engineers are trained to control most of their decisions themselves, rather than manage a decision process involving others

Figure 10.
Directed Organization Structure

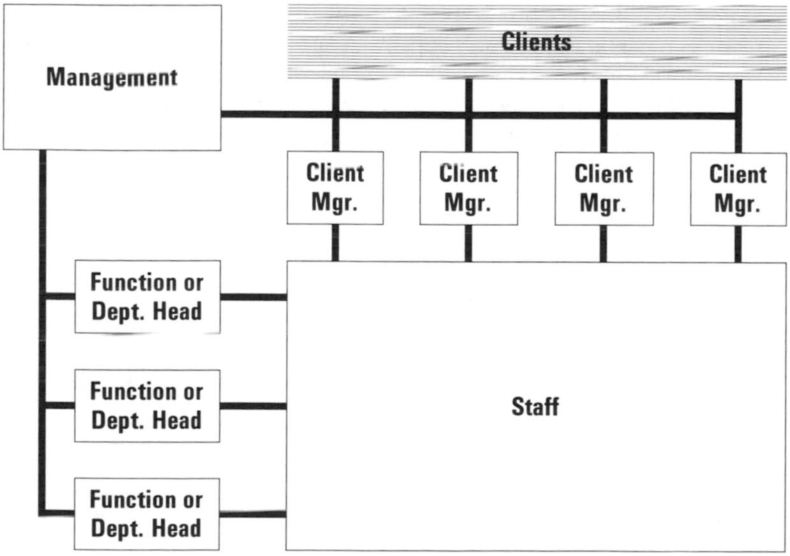

Figure 11.
Managed Organization Structure

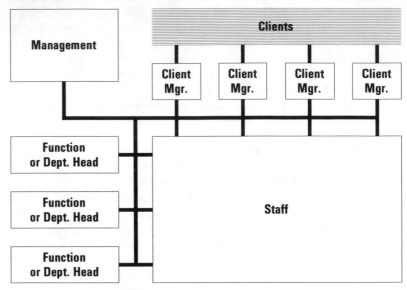

It is for this reason probably more than any other that so many design professionals practice in small organizations where they can do it all themselves. There is absolutely nothing wrong with this approach to practice, so long as it is a choice willingly made in the light of the implications and consequences.

In the end, the best structure is the one that is most effective for the people involved. Since no two people are alike, there is no reason why two structures must be alike. Don't copy someone else's structure just because it works for them. Find what works for you, while fulfilling the considerations of client management, design process, and organization control, and you will have the foundation for good practice.

Organization for Good Design

*Malcolm Heard,
Jr., AIA*

In 1976 Perez Associates (then called August Perez and Associates) enjoyed a well-established reputation as one of the largest and busiest firms in its part of the South. Its organization was loose and pragmatic. By the time August Perez III assumed control of the firm in 1976, there were forty employees with few clear demarcations of responsibility. Perez wanted a more manageable system.

During this same time of transition, a feeling grew that the quality of the firm's architectural design deserved more consistent emphasis. Through the years, the firm had done careful design work on selected projects but had, here again, no clear policy or standards. Spurred in part by the firm's united effort in winning the competition for New Orleans' Piazza d'Italia in 1975, optimism grew into a belief that consistently good design work was an attainable goal. The question became one of *how*. What shape of organization could give more order to a lively operation without cramping its style?

Neither Corporation nor Atelier

One step in reorganization was to set up a series of meetings within the office. Another step was to send a young architect in the firm to visit several architectural firms across the county. Each had evolved a finely tuned organization that was hierarchical in much the same way that a modern corporation is—chief executives at the top and a middle level of project managers, among whom all of the projects were divided. Below project managers there was either a system of project assistants or a division into design and production specialists. Again the question came up: is current architectural practice a matter of a group of specialists operating under managers after the corporate model, or would a system of more independent project architects performing a wider range of architectural activities make sense?

Gradually, a philosophy emerged. It focused on the individual project and on having each building attain a level of excellence. Organization became not an end but a means to further the quality of each project. Translating the idea from projects to people, the focus fell on the author of the individual project, the project architect. Latent in all of this is the conviction that the best architecture is ultimately a single vision (if not an individual act) sustained from conception through construction. The conditions of modern practice, however, and the complexities of construction require the participation of many people. The ideal solution,

There were forty employees with few clear demarcations of responsibility.

Organization became not an end but a means to further the quality of each project.

therefore, is the synthesis allowing the strongest individual conception to be advanced by the most supportive infrastructure—something akin to a classical balance between the individual and the group.

Project Architect: The Key Figure

The project architect becomes the continuity in a project. Perez Associates' organizational structure has no project managers as such, no equivalent to the corporate middle management level. On smaller jobs the project architect performs as wide a range of activities as possible: he deals with the client, designs the project, supervises construction documents, and works with the construction administration department on design questions and change orders. On larger jobs the project architect delegates more authority, sometimes in areas of design, sometimes in administration, according to his personal bent. The person delegating tasks on one project may be performing delegated tasks on another.

With this system, the quality of the project architect is ultimately the quality of the firm. It is necessary to attract and keep the best project architects. It is also essential to support and educate the less experienced project architect and give him the benefit of the firm's total experience. Perez Associates has developed mechanisms to accomplish this.

Technical and Design Support

Two positions have been created: the technical advocate for technical support and the architectural advocate for design support. Instead of management from above, the architect receives support from his peers. The term "advocate" is intended to imply the championing of a cause within the office.

The technical advocate has established a systematic approach to contract documents and has written a detailed contract checklist for office use. He works with each project architect, establishing the format for drawings, raising and answering questions throughout the project's development, and checking the finished set of construction documents. He recommends corrections and refinements to the project architect. His job is a chance to learn as well as teach. He researches new techniques in both construction practices and construction documents, maintains the technical library, and is in the process of developing a file of standard details.

The position of architectural advocate rotates annually. The architectural advocate organizes the peer review, a process by which each project architect presents his project to a group of his peers for discussion. The emphasis is on the advocacy of ideas which might otherwise be dismissed in favor of something more expeditious.

From one viewpoint, the Perez organization looks like a cluster of architectural offices under a single ownership sharing common support facilities. The complex task of orchestrating the whole belongs to the president and manager of the firm. He handles assignment of support to projects, financial monitoring, and contracts.

With this system, the quality of the project architect is ultimately the quality of the firm.

Positive Reaction from Within and Without

Support for the system has become increasingly strong within the firm. A recent meeting to discuss the need for uniformity in handling details of project administration caused the group to adopt a program to educate project architects in the fine points of project administration. Such a program has just started under the direction of a project architect with a special interest in project administration.

Clients respond well to the new system in which they maintain direct contact both with the firm's owner and with the specific architect who is designing their project. On several occasions clients have returned to the firm with new work and stipulated that they want the same project architect they had before. What better tribute to the project architect and to the system?

Planning a New Architectural Practice

Marie Kovacic

For a new architectural firm to succeed, design talent and architectural vision must be tempered with realistic planning and a sound business management foundation.

The first steps in setting up an architectural firm are deciding which method of organization will best serve one's situation and goals and engaging an attorney to help set up the firm. The three basic alternatives of organization are proprietorship, partnership, or corporation. Proprietorship is the simplest form, giving one person complete control as well as complete legal responsibility. Partnership, the most common form chosen by architects, lets several people share both ownership and liability. The corporation, a relatively new option in several forms, is a separate legal, taxable entity, and under it the principals become employees eligible for employee benefits and possibly reduced liability.

The choice will be largely determined by whether the new firm will be a one person operation or larger. Small firms are the rule in today's architectural practice. A 1977 survey of AIA firms showed that a fifth were composed of one person, and more than half of four or fewer. If the firm is to be composed of more than one person, partners or principals should be chosen for their complementary skills to provide the greatest possible range of services without resorting to outside help.

The architect's choice should take into account several other factors as well. The long-range goals of the principals should be considered, including the type and size of projects desired and areas of specialization anticipated. The architect's age is a factor, for as a practicing architect grows older, it becomes increasingly apparent that less cash value can be obtained from a firm in which he is the main asset. Liability consequences are minimized through corporations, but maximized in proprietorships. A tax advantage may be gained through one form over another, depending on the number of principals and volume of work. AIA's *Current Techniques in Architectural Practice* provides a more thorough discussion of all these factors.

Initial Capitalization

Before the firm can be established, sufficient financial resources must be amassed to assure that the firm can survive the first lean year. Initial capitalization is needed to set up the firm and sustain it during the nonincome period before projects can be completed and billed. *Current Techniques* suggests that a firm have a minimum of 25 to 30 percent of

Sufficient financial resources must be amassed to assure that the firm can survive the first lean year.

anticipated annual billings to operate comfortably. Initial capital can be obtained as investment from the firm's founders, and/or borrowed from banks or friends or family. Establishing a good relationship with a bank and a banker at this time is prudent, for they can provide valuable financial advice as well as money. Financial planning should include establishing a line of credit which can be used to cover the payroll and any unexpected needs that arise, and establishing a credit record for future loans by borrowing and paying back. The firm should start to accumulate assets, which include signed contracts as well as money in the bank.

Before the firm begins operation, a financial management system must be set up with help from an accountant to handle money effectively in a way that will complement the firm's objectives. The AIA's financial management system offers components such as the computer-based financial management service rendered rather than the traditional percentage-of-construction-cost basis.

Location Is Important

Where the architect establishes a practice depends on personal preference as well as basic market considerations. The locale must have demonstrated growth opportunities if the firm is to avoid stagnation. The practitioner should look specifically for sustained population growth, growth of nonagricultural employment, and a healthy local building industry. The area in which the architect grew up or went to school can offer contacts that are valuable for gaining business. However, if such an area is in a no-growth or slow-growth period due to regulatory or economic considerations, no amount of contacts will foster a successful architectural firm.

Good surroundings contribute to a firm's credibility. Even a one-person firm should have office space, if only for meeting clients, because working out of one's home conveys an unsuccessful, not very professional impression. Office space should be chosen for appealing surroundings and accessibility for both clients and employees. There should be sufficient space for all functional requirements, including reception, management, and production. However, investment in the office should be kept to a minimum to avoid tying up precious capital. The firm should endeavor to meet equipment needs adequately with the least possible initial investment by renting rather than buying.

Effective operation demands a variety of information resources. As in other fields, the amount of information on architecture is expanding exponentially, and sifting through the immense quantity to find pertinent data absorbs time. Consequently, the most frequently used data should be available in-house in an organized, easily accessible arrangement. Principals should know where to obtain infrequently used materials, making use of the closest architectural school library or the in-house library of another firm willing to share its resources and information services. A basic resource on products and materials is Sweet's yearly catalog, which qualified firms (chosen by the quality and quantity of their projects) can obtain free through application to Sweet's Division of McGraw-Hill Infor-

Working out of one's home conveys an unsuccessful, not very professional impression.

obtain free through application to Sweet's Division of McGraw-Hill Information Systems Co. Most important, the firm should set up an organized, easily accessible filing system to accommodate resources, office business, and projects. Chapter 14 of *Current Techniques* enlarges on this issue.

Seek Outside Counsel

Since there are many areas in which the principals of a new firm lack expertise, it is wise to seek outside counsel. Legal advice is needed to set up the firm and provide guidance in a variety of ensuing circumstances. Financial and insurance advisers can help set up the necessary safeguards to protect the firm and keep it running smoothly. An accountant is invaluable in the firm's early months to help determine such matters as whether the firm would profit from using cash basis for tax purposes while maintaining accrual basis for internal information. Management consultants can help with firm organization and related matters.

Consultants are also valuable in expanding the range of services that a firm can offer. As a rule, the smaller the firm, the more important it becomes to anticipate varied needs and seek out consultants who will be willing and able to provide services that cannot be met in-house.

In most offices, personnel policies evolve in response to pressure rather than according to plan. Whenever an office consisting of more than one person operates without a written statement of firm policies, problems typically arise in matters such as tardiness, paid time off, and unclear areas of responsibility. To avoid conflict, every firm should begin with its own written statement of personnel practices that clearly defines firm policy on such subjects as absence, illness, holidays, overtime, dress, and office supplies. The policy should also establish a regular review of employee benefits and encourage strong communications to promote a smoothly functioning office. AIA's *Personnel Practices Handbook* offers a guide which architectural offices can use to develop an individualized office manual. (See also the Employee Relations section of this book for office manual and related information.)

Since operating an office exposes the architect to every imaginable hazard, prudence demands an early analysis of all the risks and a recognition of what coverage is needed to protect the architect and the firm. There are four basic types of insurance which every firm should have: legal liability, including professional liability insurance; property damage; crime coverage, including bonding; and employee benefits, which include life insurance, disability protection, medical coverage, and retirement benefits. A detailed examination of architects' specific insurance needs is contained in *Current Techniques*.

To minimize risks and misunderstandings in client relations, every agreement to provide service should be put into writing. Independent architects should know what kinds of agreement are required for various contracts with clients, consultants, and contractors/owners. Volume 2 of *Architect's Handbook of Professional Practice* is a handy reference to the easy-to-use AIA documents, with all of the standard forms of agreement.

Each project that the firm undertakes should be a step forward in developing the firm's goals.

Identify Your Goals

The ultimate test of every firm is obtaining the type and amount of work to make the firm succeed. From the beginning, the architect should identify areas of interest and focus on selected markets. The firm's long-term plans should include identifiable goals that recognize the firm's capabilities and possibilities. In setting those goals, the architect should carefully consider how he wants the firm to develop: is a large firm desired, or will a small staff be better suited to the firm's individualistic approach? What margin of profit is desired, and what timetable is there for achieving that profit? Are there specific design achievements and awards that are particularly important in the architect's aspirations? Each project that the firm undertakes should be a step forward in developing the firm's goals. Generally, finding the first few clients is the most difficult step in establishing the firm. Effective marketing of a firm's service is a manifold process that requires persistent effort and daily attention. As mentioned earlier, an architect's friends, family, and former business associates can be excellent sources of business, serving as referrals as well. The architect should work to gradually increase visibility through membership in civic, religious, and other social organizations.

Market Aggressively

Since personal contact rarely provides sufficient initial business, the architect must be prepared to be aggressive in marketing the firm. Realistic economic and geographical market research should be followed by a concentrated marketing effort. Business development aids such as brochures and slides of the firm's previous work can be persuasive marketing tools. Offering an unusually broad base of services such as construction management or design/build can be an excellent selling feature, but the architect must be sure that he has the necessary skills, know-how, and any extra liability coverage that might be needed. Most important, clients are best won through the architect's communicating an effective approach to solve the client's problem rather than a recitation of qualifications.

Because a neophyte firm is eager to find work, there is a tendency to take any project that comes along. This dooms the firm to failure, or at best mediocrity. An architect must know when to turn down a project. A small firm will lose money on a project for which the bill for services rendered is less than $1,000, and the only reason for accepting such a project is in the hope of gaining further work through that client or through a referral.

Once an architect lands a project, his most important marketing tool is good work. Surveys indicate that 60 to 80 percent of the dollar volume for a typical firm comes from satisfied clients and referrals. Strategy for ensuring project success should include communicating with the client regularly and encouraging client participation. Perhaps the most important achievement in any project is to keep within the budget and keep the client informed if his demands cannot be met within the budget. The most critical step for continuing success is to go after a second project before the first project is completed, for that is the only way to provide a steady

An architect must know when to turn down a project.

flow of work.

As the firm begins to take shape, there is one last step that is too often overlooked: the continuing education of the architect. The prevailing tendency is to become immersed in the day-to-day details of making the office function, but the architect needs to find time to maintain himself as a professional.

In the architectural firm, whether new or well established, success is a continuing effort, requiring a good balance of business sense, design ability, and professional knowledge.

The Business Plan

A major problem that most professional services firms have is the lack of a formal business plan. Such a plan gives direction to the firm and ensures that its scarce resources (mainly time) are spent where the greatest return will result. Most A/Es firms do not plan because they are usually rather small and because they lack a management awareness that would dictate this elemental first step in conducting a business. The majority of executives in this business are up-from-the-ranks technical types who live day-to-day, in many cases minute-to-minute.

The Plan Elements

The business plan includes several elements: an overall strategic look at the firm and its environment; a marketing plan; a financial or profit plan; and a human resources or personnel plan. Each element is an integral and complementary part of the unified business plan. In preparing the plan there are two horizons: the long-range look five years out and the short-range, immediate action plan or budget for the next year.

The strategic portion of the plan is the classic management school approach to analyzing your firm. First decide on goals and objectives, such as profitability, size, type of work or clients, and desired reputation. Next, take a brutally frank look at the firm's strengths and weaknesses—remember that you are not selling yourself to a client. Look at what the outside world is doing that is impacting your business—remember that almost every problem can be turned into an opportunity for the firm. Finally, select those opportunities that are right for the firm in its environment.

The strategic plan is implemented by means of the marketing, financial, and human resources plans. The marketing plan lists in detail exactly what has to be done to penetrate the marketing niches that were identified in the strategic plan. Included are such items as specific goals, assigned responsibilities, organization, budgets, and marketing tools such as public relations and brochures.

The financial plan establishes a profit goal and the required billings and level of expenses necessary to attain that goal. Thus, the following items are included: target profit goals; required billings; a firm multiplier and billing rates for all staff; programmed staff utilization rates; a budget for overhead expenses; and a cash-flow plan.

The human resources plan, which very few firms prepare, recognizes that the only way to achieve the marketing and financial plans

Michael R. Hough

The firms that will succeed in this constantly changing business are those that follow a formal business planning process.

is by effectively utilizing the firm's only assets—its people. The following items are included: a skills inventory; an equitable employee evaluation system; an effective wage and salary administration program; and relevant staff training and development.

How to Do It

Those few professional services firms with a successful business plan do it on a continuing basis. However, the concentrated effort is in the fall when the plan for the next year is formulated. All employees are involved, right from the junior draftsman level on up. Key staff members get together off by themselves to thrash out the critical questions. Where does the firm really want to be in 1990? What internal and external obstacles will prevent the firm from getting there? What specific steps must be taken each year to overcome these obstacles? It should be emphasized that this is a total plan involving all elements of the firm and not just the marketing staff or the financial types.

Outside consultants are sometimes retained to help prepare a firm's first business plan. However, to make it work the firm itself must be committed to the process and must contribute the bulk of the effort.

The firms that will succeed in this constantly changing business are those that follow a formal business planning process. These firms are positively charting their course rather than just drifting with the current, as so many A/Es seem to do.

Management Efficiency

Fred A. Stitt

There are vast differences in the performance of design firms. For example:
  • Most firms do well to earn $3,000 to $4,000 net pretax profit per technical employee. Others earn $7,000 to $8,000.
  • Most drafters spend from forty to one hundred and fifty hours per working drawing sheet. Others spend from eight to thirty hours on drawings of the same size, type, and complexity.
  • A/E firms of all types earn an average of 5 percent to 6 percent net profit on gross revenue (before taxes and profit distributions). But there are others that almost always earn 15 percent and more.
  • Most offices are happy to win 10 percent to 20 percent of the contracts they pursue. A few firms consistently win 80 percent to 90 percent.

While the differences are large and obvious, the causes are not. Many of the most successful firms don't follow the "success" rules. Some who follow all the rules only show average performance, or less than average. For example, long-term growth plans are a must according to most management consultants. But many of the most successful and fastest growing design firms have no plan whatsoever.

Other success policies that are in question include the use of management by objectives, goal reviews, policy manuals, and organization charts. The results from a survey of 500 architectural offices, published on page 77 of the Spring 1984 issue of *Architectural Technology*, name a number of such policies that make no measurable difference in office performance.

Many office principals believe long work hours make the difference. Our own surveys find that principals who put in fifty- and sixty-hour or more work weeks take home substantial income. But the long hours don't seem to affect their net output compared to other, higher paid principals who stick to forty- to forty-five-hour weeks.

So what makes the difference between low, average, and high performance? Of all the things A/E firms can do to rise above the norm, which are the most effective?

Success Rules
Studying the most successful A/E practices, we find one aspect stands out: successful firms don't do everything they're supposed to do for superior performance, but they do a few things extremely conscientiously.

Many of the most successful design firms have no plan whatsoever.

Those few "right things" are usually expressions of strong personal interests, convictions, or talents of principals and managers. Here are some examples:

1. The most productive and profitable firms commonly use systems drafting and systems graphics, but that's only part of their success in employee productivity. With or without the systems approach, three management policies are common to the high production firms: good pay with profit sharing, clarity in information and feedback from supervisors to drafting staff ("clarity" includes speed), and project planning that keeps false starts and design revisions to an absolute minimum during working drawing production.

2. If these firms collect financial statistics, or use management by objectives, policy manuals, etc., they truly use them. Most offices that claim to use such tools only go through the motions. They may gather financial statistics, but the reports are not read. If they read and analyze the statistics, nothing comes from it, no decisions are made or action taken. If they prepare and distribute policy manuals, job descriptions, and organization charts, the documents are put aside and ignored. The most effective managers use only a few such tools that they think are necessary to meet specific needs, but they use them actively as working documents and not as background reference material.

3. The simple secret of a large number of top-performing firms is that they find and keep a limited, high-quality, repeat clientele. They know that single-building clients will come and go and are consistently the worst money losers and troublemakers. These firms pursue sophisticated, multibuilding clients and work with them, and grow with them, for many years. This approach has an extremely high payoff, even for offices that are not particularly noteworthy in any other way.

4. They commonly give extra care and attention to select, narrow aspects of their work and management. For example, a partner in one high-profit Atlanta office insists on charging fees that are 20 percent to 30 percent higher than the norm. He goes to great lengths to cost out projects, provide comprehensive services, and show clients what they get for their money. Then he makes sure the office performs in ways that matter most to the clients, mainly meeting deadlines and bringing bids in on budget. Ninety percent of his clients are repeat clients who follow the "you get what you pay for" school. The office does little else that is exceptional but net income is nearly double that of most comparable firms.

5. They maintain clear-cut divisions of management. The triumvirate partnership—design/management/production, with perhaps shared marketing functions or a separate marketing director—is characteristic of design offices that enjoy the largest and most stable practices. Partners in smaller firms tend to get involved in one another's work and decision making so that ultimately no one person is in charge of any particular office function. At that point no one is managing any aspect of the office in the directed way commonly found in the strong-performance firms. (Architectural firms with no dedicated production management by a partner, or with more than one design partner, often exhibit the worst managerial and

Decisive aspects, such as work flow and income, should get daily no-nonsense monitoring.

production confusion and mishaps.)

6. They focus on what counts. The most important work gets the first attention each day. Decisive aspects of the company, such as work flow and income, get daily no-nonsense monitoring. It's reversed in the worst-managed offices. There the bosses and managers often find nonpriority items to be "more interesting." In these firms there's obvious conflict between the needs of running a company and the personal needs and interest of those in charge.

7. They stop doing what they don't do well. In a typical case, a design firm owner who "just wanted to do beautiful buildings" teetered from financial crisis to crisis for years in a vain effort to run a full-service A/E office. The architect finally saw the light and let his production and engineering departments spin off as a separate company. Now he just does what he does best—design beautiful buildings—and his clients pay others to do the technical work under his direction.

One lesson emerges over and over: doing everything well isn't possible and most likely is not even a desirable idea. The realizable and profitable route is to identify a few aspects of work that really matter and that fit the principal's best talents. Then give these aspects undivided attention and care.

Identify a few aspects of work that really matter and that fit the principal's best talents. Give these undivided attention and care.

Managing Change

Weld Coxe

It is universally accepted that a shift to computerized design and production systems is inevitable, meaning change in virtually every role in a design firm.

It is clear that among the challenges which design firm management must tackle, the one that will involve more changes in the next few years will be the management of change itself. It is one thing to project all the marvelous new things design firms will face in the 1980s: matrix quality control, human resource departments, computerized design and production systems, hot new markets, etc. For most of these there are already seminars, newsletters, textbooks, and consultants to tell us what the new world expects or requires of management.

It is an entirely different matter, however, to take these new systems into existing organizations and effect the changes necessary to make them happen. It seems that each time firms have tried to make significant changes, more often than not they have gone outside for experienced people to bring in the needed skills. Lacking those people, they have muddled along with the resources (people) already on board and have achieved only a fraction of the potential benefit of their actions.

There are symptoms of this historic pattern everywhere:

1. It is reported that computer-trained young architects and engineers are commanding salaries 50 percent above those with similar experience but without computer skills. There is no equivalent differential reported for computer-trained older architects and engineers.

2. A major engineering firm that led the parade in establishing a top-level human resources department is finding only one of its seven divisions is taking seriously the department's efforts at personnel development. Why? That department is headed by the youngest manager in the firm. All the older managers give lip service to measuring the performance of their staff, but they are still refusing to evaluate each other.

3. A 150-person A/E firm which has just installed a CAD system reports proudly that as many as twenty-five of its people have been staying late at the office on their own time to experiment and play with the new toy. When asked the age of these motivated staff members, the manager replied, "Oh, it's all the younger people—most of them in their twenties."

These examples illustrate the prevalent notion that change only occurs in generational cycles. The reality is that the changes which must be made in design firms can't be accomplished by writing off everyone over thirty-five or forty and by leaving it to a younger generation to implement the new ways. There aren't enough young people to do it all; the senior people have too much experience that must be retained; and the marketplace won't wait twenty years for the torch to pass by evolution.

We must learn to change ourselves in this generation.

The Changes

What are these changes? Firm by firm the simple answer is: whatever changes are necessary to stay competitive. The most widespread change will be in three areas:

1. Quality control and coordination. The client is not satisfied to simply receive the best effort of the people assigned to the project. Efforts to make firmwide quality control effective are going to require major changes in the way technical teams are organized, operate, and are supervised.

2. Key personnel development. The "hiring hall" no longer assures firms an adequate supply of people skilled in the tasks needed, and firms are recognizing the need to develop their own future key personnel. This sounds simple on paper but in practice will require enormous change in attitude, responsibility, and roles by those with the experience to develop new leaders.

3. Adoption of new systems. It is universally accepted that a shift to computerized design and production systems is inevitable, meaning change in virtually every role in a design firm.

These areas are interrelated and involve the learning of new skills and processes by people at all levels of the firm. The question for management is: how to make this learning (change) occur? There are no experts who can show us how it has been done before. The design professions are not alone in facing the need to make wholesale internal change in how they go about what they do. All U.S. industry is facing the same challenge in different clothing as it acts to recapture its competitive edge from currently more productive cultures, such as the Japanese. Change such as design firms face is going on throughout U.S. society. The Census Bureau estimates that 40 million Americans between the ages of sixteen and sixty-five are in career transition. Adult education is the fastest growing phase of education today. Thus, design firm management can expect to find a new national attitude toward change as they grapple with their own piece of it.

The historic American approach to productivity and excellence has been to encourage individuals to compete for personal achievement.

Three Principles

Although there are no experts with easy answers, there are some principles which are gaining acceptance as foundations from which to begin managing change.

Principle #1. Collaboration is more effective than competition. The historic American approach to productivity and excellence has been to encourage individuals to compete for personal achievement. The Japanese approach that is fascinating the industrial world (and has come to be called Theory Z) is to encourage results through collective, collaborative effort. Their success with participative decision making, their "quality circle" approach to quality control, and similar interactive processes open a new horizon that is worth exploring.

Principle #2. People prefer to learn by practical, hands-on experience rather than through lectures where they are told what to do. There is a quiet revolution going on in educational theory that is pointing in the direction of experiential learning which offers the opportunity to build training for change into the ongoing, hands-on activities of the firm.

Principle #3. Teaching is not the same as learning. In the end it matters little how wise and intelligent is the teacher if the student does not learn. Thus, a good way to manage progress toward change is to put control of the pace in the hands of the learners. Ask them what they need to effect change—don't just tell them.

If these principles are accepted, following are some suggestions for the manager(s) interested in implementing change in a design practice:

1. Learn interpersonal skills. The behavioral scientists are teaching us successful processes for interpersonal communication, conflict resolutions, and team building. These techniques work. If managers become comfortable with their own interpersonal skills, the process of dealing with change throughout the organization will be more comfortable for the organization.

2. Learn to manage teams, not just individuals.

3. Manage decisions to go forward with change as a group. If you involve everyone who will be affected—the departments, project teams, specialists, and even outside consultants—in the original decisions about how to proceed with change, they will all own a piece of responsibility for the result. It cannot be decreed from above.

4. Put teams (not individuals) in charge of implementing each change, and don't limit their authority to determine who will be involved. If they ask management to participate in learning, be prepared to commit the people, time, and effort requested.

5. Encourage "change groups" to use case study approaches to learning—perhaps by doing (or redoing) actual tasks parallel with existing methods. Involve everyone who would have a part in the real case.

6. Expect the learning/training/changing to cost money – lots of it. Budget and track the investment so you are sure to set realistic goals for payback. Don't stop the change effort until you are getting the results you and the team expect.

Finally, keep your peers in other firms informed of your progress, and ask them to share what they are learning about managing change. Since everyone will be tackling the same problem, there will be much to learn from each other.

Begin now. In a real sense the recession may be timely because it is giving many firms breathing room from project pressures of the recent past and near future. Those with confidence in the future could find this the best time to begin investing in the changes that the future will certainly require.

You have to make people partners in change rather than objects of change.

A good way to manage progress toward change is to put control of the pace in the hands of the learners. Ask them what they need to effect change—don't just tell them.

Management Pathologies: Biopsies

The architectural press almost invariably describes how design firms have risen from obscurity to prominence. But few articles address the equally instructive, if less popular, subject of why firms fail. There are, of course, many types of failure: failure to achieve the principals' major objectives; failure to achieve a firm's full potential; failure in the form of complete organizational collapse; or just plain going broke. Applying the techniques of management pathology, it is possible to trace the causes of most failures to one or more flaws in the leadership of a firm. Some of these flaws are noble ones, worthy of a Greek tragedy, but most are petty or avoidable. Both the noble and the petty are discussed in the following article, with examples of the basic pitfalls presented as a series of brief case studies. All are composites of real situations—sufficiently disguised, it is hoped, as to be unrecognizable.

Bradford Perkins, AIA

Probably the commonest failure is the firm that has a brief run of luck and then disappears.

Case One: Halley's Comet

Probably the commonest failure is the firm that has a brief run of luck and then disappears. Firm A spent ten years building a reputation for consistent quality on a series of small commissions. The three principals all worked directly on each project and developed a growing list of happy former clients. Then they obtained a dream commission: a major project for a client willing to support an innovative design solution. The architects made the most of the job and, with the resulting favorable publicity, rapidly became a hot firm. As more big projects came their way, the office grew from ten to sixty people in two years—but then the problems began.

Too soon the principals began believing their own publicity and playing the role of gurus. At the same time, they spread themselves too thin—a problem that was aggravated by their lessening interest in the details of new projects. More and more time was spent enjoying the fruits of their prosperity. Quality became inconsistent and client loyalty weakened. No organized business development program was created. As a result, when a recession hit, their work dried up, they shrank quickly back to a ten-person firm, and eventually faded into obscurity.

Case Two: Buggy Whips and Pharoah's Dream

Architecture is a cyclical business which never lets a firm rest on its laurels. Firm B built a strong practice in educational and other public building types. The principals were confident of their continuing prosperity and regularly spent the firm's profits. Unfortunately, school populations began to decline, the economy slumped, and Proposition 13 applied the coup de grace to their traditional markets. The firm suddenly found itself without work and without the financial staying power to rebuild in another area of practice.

Case Three: The Grass is Always Greener

Unlike Firm B, many firms are never satisfied with their current areas of practice. This too can lead to problems. Firm C acquired a strong reputation for planning studies, which occasionally led to architectural commissions. Even though the firm's finished buildings never matched the quality of their predesign studies, the principals felt that they wanted to be architects, not planners; so they ignored their study work and put their efforts into getting design commissions. The basis of their reputation soon shifted from excellent planning to mediocre architecture. With this shift came the beginning of their decline.

Case Four: Cannon Fodder

It is good advice to anyone who thinks himself irreplaceable to observe what happens when he withdraws his finger from a bucket of water. Unfortunately, this lesson has often been translated into blind belief that no one is irreplaceable—a statement which, in the short term, is not necessarily true. Firm D prospered for years under the leadership of a man who made it clear that he believed in this "no one is irreplaceable" axiom. As is generally the case today, the firm's reputation became more and more dependent on the principals who were actually carrying out the projects. But when a crisis came, the key principals felt no loyalty to the top man and left the firm, taking their clients with them.

Case Five: Joseph's Brothers and the Captainless Ship

A variant on the loss of key personnel is the forcing out or failure to replace the person or persons who built the firm. Firm E's younger partners breathed a sigh of relief when their concerted efforts finally compelled the domineering founding principal to retire. In reaction to his autocratic approach, they decided to manage by committee. All of the committee members were "inside" men who frowned on the founder's "egomaniacal" and "wasteful" interest in speeches, parties, travel, and other "nonproductive" efforts. Eventually, though, the committee found that, in the name of prudent management, they had performed a lobotomy on the firm. Devoid of its personality and constipated in its decision making, the office muddled its way into mediocrity.

Case Six: Peter Principle by Primogeniture

Like many parents, architects often want to pass on what they build to their children. The desire to hand down the leadership of a firm is understandable, but often a disservice to both the child and the parent-architect's colleagues who helped create the legacy. Firm F—with the insistence of its founder—promoted the founder's son to fill his father's place upon retirement. The merit of this promotion was not convincing to either clients or key staff, and both soon departed.

Case Seven: Swollen Heads, Upturned Noses, and Feet of Clay

"No one person is a complete architect" is far truer than "no one is irreplaceable." Firm G, for example, built itself upon the sales skills of its principals. Unfortunately, it never matched sales ability with comparable skills in design, production, and the many other capabilities necessary to serve a client properly. The principals ultimately ran out of new people to sell to. Firm H, in contrast, built its reputation on design expertise, but, like Firm G, never balanced its forte with other requisite skills. Tough competition and bad references cut short their moment of success.

Achieving balance has never been easy for most architectural firms, because of big egos and misguided snobbishness. Too many firms have been led by individuals who could not tolerate equals—or, when they could, had too little respect for skills other than their own to tolerate full partners in balancing capability areas.

Case Eight: Financial Management New York City Style

The financial rewards of the design professions are rarely comparable to those of other professions and businesses. Regrettably, this fact is not recognized by many architects. Firm I grew and prospered—and its principals' ability to spend grew with it. Staff was hired in advance of need, offices were outfitted in a manner consistent with the firm's design tastes, and personal spending by the principals began turning to slow whisky and fast cars, sailboats, and women. This expensive lifestyle was financed with borrowed money and a failure to pass on funds owed to consultants. In time, Firm I's credit ran out; its creditors forced it into near bankruptcy, and it suffered a general dissolution of its reputation and practice.

Generic Causes of Decline

A full list would require a book, but the more important ones and their management implications can be summarized as follows:

1. For a firm to achieve and maintain success it must recognize that it has to be good at every component of both the profession and the business of architecture. Put in the simplest terms, a firm has to sell well, provide consistently good service on the projects it sells, and manage both the projects and its own office in a way that generates a profit. There is no significant margin for error in today's competitive, demanding-client, low-profit-margin world.

2. To do all basics well, the firm should have a plan that establishes goals, realistically assesses its own strengths and weaknesses, and then outlines logical steps to build on those strengths and overcome the weaknesses in the pursuit of the goals. This is not as easy as it sounds because it requires honest self-appraisal—an unusual gift.

3. Successful business development is usually directly related to a realistic plan, a strong reputation in a good market or markets, and constant efforts to develop new leads and sales. It is important to remember that once reputation or momentum has been achieved, it must never be lost. Few firms are ever given a second chance. In addition, as illustrated in Case Three, a firm should not abandon an area of strength or even dilute its impact. Any expansion into new areas must be governed, as already

Few firms are ever given a second chance.

35

noted, by a realistic plan to eliminate weaknesses while building on existing strengths.

4. A realistic plan and effective business development program must also recognize that the market is not static. No firm can depend on one building type or a long-standing reputation to carry it through the future. Today, the pace of change in all things is accelerating and firms must change, too, if they are to stay viable.

5. The firm's organization must be structured to respond to the new work produced by business development. This means not only having the full range of technical skills required for excellent service, but also an organizational structure that permits these skills to be focused on the right problems. In Case One, for example, the firm did not build a structure—one with new partners or a strong middle management—capable of accommodating the additional load created by growth. The one- or two-leader firm is particularly vulnerable today as clients become increasingly demanding of personal and error-free service.

6. Any firm seeking to grow must create a structure that can attract and hold the best available person in every key position. Somehow the principals of the typical architectural firm are going to have to take a lesson from leading attorneys, accountants, advertising agencies, investment bankers, and other service firms. In such firms there is room for more than one "star," and in the best of them each major position is held by a specialist whose reward and status are based more on his contributions to the firm's success than on some arbitrary professional caste system.

There should be no fear about taking on additional partners, officers, or principals. As service firms in other professions have repeatedly shown, the proper choice of additional partners to fill leadership openings can expand both the financial pie and the quality of the service. Any partner in any category who pulls his weight costs nothing.

Partnerships and other principal ties are primarily business relationships—hopefully, but not necessarily, strengthened by personal ties of friendship and respect. Because they are business relationships, they can be severed with far more ease than most people assume. But these relationships should be made or severed principally for business, not personal reasons. When personal jealousies, father-son loyalty, or other emotions interfere in such decisions, the results rarely benefit any of the parties involved. As a result, one of the primary roles of the leader(s) of a firm must be to minimize the inevitable jealousies and petty personal differences that can sow the seeds of destruction.

7. Probably the most dangerous period for any existing firm occurs during the transition of leadership from the founder(s) to the next generation. It is at this point—more than at any other—that a realistic plan and assessment of strengths and weaknesses must be made. What should be identified are the real holes left by the departing leaders, and the actions necessary to fill these holes.

8. The principle of "why not the best" should be applied to all positions. Failure to weed out deadwood is almost as serious an error as

Probably the most dangerous period for any existing firm occurs during the transition of leadership.

neglecting to keep staff levels closely related to the volume of work available. Given the limited fees which architects receive, it is imperative that funds be spent on productive personnel. This does not mean, however, that a hire-and-fire philosophy should apply. With such policies it is impossible to form the mutual bond of loyalty and respect between principals and staff that is essential to the building and maintenance of a productive, stable staff of quality personnel. It should always be remembered that the best staff have the most options and, without some bond to their present office, will be the first to exercise them.

9. Because salaries constitute almost two-thirds (and the most readily adjustable segment) of most design firms' expenses, they must be the focus of financial control. Most firms—with or without such controls—make money during periods of rapid growth because personnel and other expenses usually do not catch up with volume. With controls applied to personnel, however, the other easy time to make money is when month-to-month volume remains steady and relatively little effort is required to keep all technical personnel billable. Unfortunately, few firms ever enjoy such conditions. Most experience wild swings in volume and need to expend a growing percentage of their resources on securing new work. These conditions, combined with narrow profit margins, leave no room for error or waste.

Now more than ever, it is essential that design firms observe the most basic principals of financial control:

• Above all, a firm must make money to grow and prosper.

• To make a profit, the first effort must always be directed to keeping volume and expenses in balance. This requires coordination of business development, project scheduling, and staffing. The closer a firm comes to achieving a consistent balance, the more likely it is to make a profit.

• Financial management must, of necessity, be conservative. Owing to the cyclical nature of the building industry, it is essential that a firm accumulate cash reserves to weather the inevitable crises. There is no room for "big shop-itis" that wastes the firm's (and its creditors') resources on personal expenses. Too many people are hurt by such actions.

• Effective financial management is impossible without some formal controls on volume, expenses, and cash flow.

Of course, even the strictest adherence to all of the above precepts cannot guarantee that a firm will either achieve success or avoid failure. After all, management alone is hardly the raison d'etre of a design firm. As the case studies illustrate, a weakness in any management area can cause failure but only superior professional capability can ensure success.

38

Manpower Planning

David Burstein

One of the most difficult tasks for the manager in an A/E/P firm is manpower planning. Unlike his counterpart in industry or government where work loads are generally planned at least a year in advance, the manager in a consulting firm must contend with changes in workload that can occur on almost a daily basis. Yet in spite of the enormous difficulty of accurate manpower planning, this is an activity that must be done in order for the firm to operate efficiently and profitably. The single most commonly observed failure in manpower planning is excessive sophistication and complexity in approach. Given the many demands on the manager's time, manpower planning is often delegated a low priority, especially if the amount of time demanded by a complex system is great. The result is that projections are seldom updated and manpower planning is done by "gut feel." The key to successful manpower planning, therefore, is to select a simple approach and keep projections updated on a regular basis. Leave the sophisticated systems to managers who can forecast workloads accurately over a relatively long period of time. In consulting firms, the poor quality of the input data does not justify the use of complex systems.

The Four Requirements
Proper manpower planning answers four basic questions:
1. Is there a manpower shortage or surplus?
2. Is the shortage (or surplus) temporary or long term?
3. Which kinds of people are needed (or not needed)?
4. How can the shortage (or surplus) be alleviated?

Answering the first question requires a simple, yet systematic, way of comparing the work backlog with manpower availability. In a small, single discipline office, it may be perfectly adequate to combine all labor categories into a single projection. A slightly refined version would consist of making separate projections of engineers and draftsmen. In a large, multidisciplinary firm, it may be necessary to prepare separate forecasts for each discipline. It can therefore be seen that the level of detail varies with the size and diversity of the firm even when the same basic forecasting system is used. However, efforts should be made to minimize the number of separate projections that are made.

The results of this work load projection can also be used to determine whether the shortage or surplus will be short term or long term. A plot can be made showing the total manpower availability over an

If the workload curve drops off sharply, it means that any current manpower shortage is probable short term.

extended period of time. If the work load curve drops off sharply, it means that any current manpower shortage is probably short term; if it decreases gradually, the shortage is probably long term. (Note that this curve rarely increases. This is because the current backlog is being continuously reduced, while new jobs have not yet been sold.)

The third question—which kinds of people are needed or surplus—can best be answered by talking directly to the individuals who have the needs, the project managers. They can advise the manager in detail about the deficiencies or surpluses on their jobs. In a consulting firm, this communicative approach is far better than pigeonholing each person into a category and relying on a computer to mate the personnel needs and availabilities. Not only does it provide more accurate results, but also tends to treat people like individuals rather than machines.

Answering the final question—how the shortage or surplus can be alleviated—requires long-range planning. A few suggestions as to how this can be done effectively are presented below.

Resolving Short-Term Work Load Problems

If there is a temporary increase in work load, a number of alternatives exist which can solve the problem without hiring people who will have to be laid off when the workload returns to normal. These include:

- overtime;
- use of temporary employees;
- subcontracting;
- joint venturing;
- use of individuals normally assigned to overhead functions.

The key to successfully implementing these measures is to lay the groundwork before the crisis is at hand. For example, many universities have programs through which students can be hired on a temporary or part-time basis. However, the way to get the best possible help when you need it is to avoid these programs. Rather, individual professors should be contacted to find out which are the really outstanding students. These students can then be called when the crunch arrives. Another approach is to develop a list of retired professionals living in the community. These individuals can also be called upon when experienced help is needed on a short-term basis.

One of the best approaches to solving both temporary shortages and surpluses is to enter into reciprocal agreements with other firms, preferably firms which do similar work but are not direct competitors. Such arrangements can include joint ventures, subcontracting, and/or temporary transfer of employees. Temporary employee transfers are generally made at a multiplier which is less than the normal overhead charged to outside clients. They also often include agreements that the firm to which the employee is being temporarily transferred will not try to hire that employee without permission from the other firm.

Many other examples could be cited for alleviating temporary manpower shortages or surpluses. The important thing is to make plans ahead of time so that quick, effective action can be taken when the crisis

The important thing is to make plans ahead of time so that quick, effective action can be taken when the crisis arrives.

arrives.

Long-Range Recruiting and Training

If it is determined that the long-term workload justifies the hiring of more full-time personnel, it must be realized that it generally takes one to two months from the time a decision is made until a person is hired. In the case of disciplines which are in demand (e.g., chemical engineers or hydrogeologists), it could take much longer. What is therefore needed is a long-range recruiting and training program. Such a program should answer the following questions:

1. What kinds of people will we probably need over the next few years?

2. What mix of experience levels do we want?

3. Which individuals on our present staff should be groomed for positions of greater responsibility?

4. Where should we recruit additional staff?

5. What criteria should we use to judge potential employees?

6. How will the hiring of new personnel affect our existing staff?

Work overloads can sometimes be alleviated by establishing priorities and simply delaying work on the lowest priority items. This is fine as long as it is confined to overhead activities, e.g., keeping the office library up-to-date. However, this practice can lead to problems if certain projects are assigned low priorities. Remember that each client considers his project to be number one priority and will be most unhappy if you do not treat it as such. In planning and design firms, the outstanding manager is the one who can arrange to meet all project commitments.

Outside Board Members

George Schrohe

Two years after an architectural firm appointed an advisory board of outsiders, it had contracts for three medical clinics, a building type the firm never before had been able to capture.

An engineering firm introduced two outsiders to its board of directors. In spite of a recession the firm saw a 9 percent increase in profitability the next year.

What produced these improvements and similar results in other design firms was the sudden availability of new information, wisdom, and contacts. In this article, I will outline the advantages of having outsiders participate in directing a firm's decisions, and how to bring such a group into an operation.

A firm's own circumstances determine whether it is preferable to add decision-making outsider members to its board, or whether to appoint a board which is strictly advisory. Many roles of the two types of boards are similar—both advise on and critique current policies and performance; both review future plans and budgets.

Board responsibilities differ in their power to implement change. Advisory boards recommend. Conventional boards of directors decide. The number of nonshareholders on an advisory board is generally higher than on a board of directors. The following discussion does not distinguish between the two types of board except where their authority and liability differ significantly.

Outsiders bring information and experience from fields not otherwise represented.

Benefits of Outside Members

The benefits of having outsiders involved can be considerable:

1. Outsiders bring information and experience from fields not otherwise represented in high-level decision making. For example, designers may be well versed in production, but lack up-to-date knowledge of finance, marketing, management, and personnel matters.

2. Outsiders offer insights and contacts on diversifying a firm's work, or in capitalizing on the organization's established expertise.

3. They can provide healing advice in dealing with internal disagreements and tension, and support ways of channeling human resources to greater effect.

4. As nondesigners, outsiders can loosen up ingrained patterns of thinking and established operating procedures.

5. Whether or not they have the power actually to influence management, the presence of outsiders asking questions can increase

management efficiency and effectiveness.

6. In times of management changes, the reassurances and counsel of outsiders can provide stability and continuity.

7. Pressures on a CEO are reduced when responsibility for policy is shared by the board.

Benefits to Outside Members

The benefits of having outsiders on a board are not one-sided. Board members win, too:

1. They are exposed to a new industry and can learn from it.

2. They, too, make new contacts which can enhance their own careers, firms, or industries.

3. Prestige is gained in being asked to join a board.

4. Compensation is appealing, whether in the form of fees or, in the case of directors, through opportunities for part ownership.

5. Finally, more important than compensation is the sense of being involved with a team that is going somewhere.

Criteria for Selection

Criteria for selecting outside board members focus on two apparently contradictory qualities: being different, yet fitting in.

1. Outside board members broaden the scope of the board. Some professionals to consider are bankers, accountants, attorneys, psychologists, professors, management consultants, marketing strategists, financial analysts, or others with special expertise not already represented on the board.

2. Outsiders should definitely be outsiders; they should not have existing contractual ties with the firm.

3. They should understand the evolutionary concerns of a professional design business experiencing growth.

4. While from outside the design profession, board members should have an understanding of the profession and building industry.

5. They should be sympathetic to your firm's style—your mode of operation and the kinds of markets you want to address.

6. Finally, outsiders can be used to correct imbalances in your existing board—for example, an absence of women or minority group members in the firm's leadership.

In more general terms, a new board member should be a team worker, a listener, optimistic, decisive, an independent thinker, and a doer. In selecting board members avoid those who say "yes" to everything, egotists and heavy socializers, and those who cannot distinguish between formulating policies and ordering more pencils.

Responsibilities

Responsibilities of outside board members include:

1. Evaluating management performance and recommending improvements.

2. Establishing and critiquing policies, objectives, responsibilities,

Board members should have an understanding of the profession and the building industry.

and strategies.

3. Approving and reviewing budgets and identifying fiscal problem areas.

4. Monitoring financial, personnel, marketing, and production areas.

5. Ensuring legal compliance for the firm.

6. Representing shareholders' positions.

7. Mediating disagreements.

8. Providing useful contacts.

How much a particular board does depends on the authority assigned to it. At a minimum, a board will help with long-range planning and will guide changes in the firm's focus, organization, and operating procedures.

The mechanics of setting up a board and making it effective vary from firm to firm. Yet there are a few rules of thumb to keep in mind:

Size: five to seven members.

Composition: for a conventional board, 30-60 percent shareholders; for an advisory board, a majority of nonshareholders.

Selection: solicited, nominated and elected, or appointed.

Term: overlapping terms of two or years. Keep in mind that it takes a year to get to know the firm.

Frequency of meetings: monthly, quarterly, or bimonthly.

Remuneration: $100-$1,500 a meeting plus expenses.

Overcoming Objections

Some firms resist including nonshareholders because they are reluctant to divulge confidential information to outsiders. However, this is a negligible concern because most information employed in board deliberations is not truly confidential. Furthermore, directors typically take an oath of confidentiality.

Indentifying and interviewing potential board members is a major undertaking.

The logistics of coordinating a group of outsiders for meetings and of keeping them informed might seem an obstacle. In fact, the incentive to keep information up-to-date and in credible form increases management efficiency. Outsider professionals cannot work productively with crisis management.

Identifying and interviewing potential board members is a major undertaking. Yet the process itself can be used to help focus the firm's goals and organization.

For their part, outsiders sometimes decline membership, fearing liability for the actions of others. Directors' liability insurance obviates this concern.

These challenges are negligible when measured against potential benefits of having outside board members. Consider the impact on a firm of suddenly having more diversified talents and information to support management decisions; of the infusion of experienced individuals to evaluate the firm's policies and procedures; of regular, thoughtful contact with a group of business and professional leaders.

An Outside Board

Do we practice what we preach? Or do we tend to expend our planning and design energies on our client's needs and fail to complete the planning process within our own firms? This sort of tunnel vision, if not corrected, can create a myopic top management that simply reacts to events, and is incapable of either anticipating change or planning for it.

Many corporations have addressed this problem by establishing a board of directors controlled by persons outside the organization. Outside boards of directors, however, are rare within the planning and design profession. This is unfortunate because, besides exerting the discipline necessary for long-range planning, an outside board can provide a myriad of benefits to a firm.

Benefits of an Outside Board

To begin with, an outside board of directors will require annual business plans of high quality on which to base many of its most important decisions. The development of these plans forces management to immerse itself in issues affecting the long-range direction of the firm. And by putting pet projects on the back burner in order to complete this task, management often develops a better understanding of the firm's overall situation. Such an overview, which is critical to successful planning, usually follows the creation of an outside board as a matter of course.

A viable long-range plan, updated annually, can also serve as an effective management guide. If, in addition, the board is properly selected and does its job, management of the firm will improve substantially. And as the management team grows stronger, profits will increase.

Another benefit is that when it comes to fairly distributing the profits, outside board members can afford to be objective, and act in the firm's best interest. This fact being plainly evident to each owner, the chances are good that the method of distribution suggested by the board will meet the approval of all owners.

Finally, outside board members can speak without fear of intimidation, freely discussing issues that might be unpopular with the strong personality at the head of the firm. Such issues might never be dealt with otherwise, and—depending upon their nature—could present unnecessary impediments to growth. On the other hand, when a chief executive officer receives a positive appraisal from the board, he can be certain the assessment is objective and well deserved.

Frank W. Rees, Jr.

An outside board will require annual business plans of high quality.

Selection of the Board

Obviously, the selection of board members will depend to a great extent upon the unique strengths and weaknesses of each firm. Nevertheless, there are a few general statements that can be made concerning the make up of the board.

The first of these concerns its size. Five to nine persons has proven to be an excellent working number in most situations. Of this number, a majority should come from outside the firm. To ease the initial transition, members should be added slowly, at the rate of one or two per year, until the optimum number has been reached.

If members are elected on a rotating basis to three- or four-year terms, there will be a steady supply of new members questioning the status quo, as well as a healthy contingent of experienced members familiar with the functions of the firm. If, additionally, each member is required to exit the board for a minimum of one year at the end of his term, there will be fewer confrontations during the periods of changeover in the board.

An outside board of directors is not for everyone. The firm must be managed by mature, secure people who can handle constructive and sometimes stinging criticism. It can also be difficult for top management to accept the fact that outside board members are called upon to provide knowledge and wisdom that is evidently not present within the firm. In a sense, it seems like a slap to the ego; in reality, it is only good business sense: outside members can supply specialized knowledge from a range of backgrounds that would otherwise not be available.

Summary

In the final analysis then, establishing an outside board of directors involves four main steps. First, a CEO who is considering such a move must decide that an outside board is needed, and that he is personally willing to put up with the criticism that will follow. Next, he and his management team must evaluate the firm's strong and weak points and determine the makeup of the future board. New members should then be selected, at a fairly slow rate, with the overriding concern being to meet specific needs within the firm. Finally, and perhaps most importantly, the owners must give the board full authority to act, including authority to hire and fire the CEO. Also, the firm must reward outside board members for the time and experience they are providing to the firm.

> **The firm must be managed by mature, secure people who can handle sometimes stinging criticism.**

Managing Branch Offices

Frank A. Stasiowski

Sooner or later most growth-minded firms consider the question of whether or not to develop a branch office. Many of the management problems that arise in branch office management occur because of the way in which offices were set up in the first place.

We have found that planning for the branch office is the most important step in determining your success or failure at managing it once it is established. Consider the following questions given to us by principals in large firms:

1. Have you truly evaluated the market for your services in the new branch office with statistical clarity or is your reason for opening the office merely responsive to some immediate pressure?

2. Have you decided how to compensate the branch office manager?

3. Will the branch office be a "profit center" or will you continue to manage on the basis of centralized financial control in the main office?

4. How will one office handle the charging of transfer time on work performed for another office?

5. Does the branch office have a marketing plan for developing its own work?

6. How will recruiting of new people be handled in the branch office?

7. What overhead controls will be placed on the new operation?

8. Is a predetermined process established for accurately measuring success or failure in the new branch office?

9. How will quality control be handled?

Each branch office as it grows is now competing against another for work.

Profit Center or Not

In talking with six firms with multiple offices, the question as to whether or not a branch office should be a profit center and how to manage it appears to be the most significant management problem faced by firms with many offices.

Case #1. One multidisciplined midwestern firm in four locations has operated on a purely profit center concept for several years. Although the overall profits of the firm are not bad as compared to industry averages, the firm has three major problems:

1. Each branch office as it grows is now competing against another branch office for work.

2. It is almost impossible to get one office to work on projects for another office unless fees are actually paid amongst offices.

3. Each office is competing for personnel and handles its own payroll and overhead expenses through its own checking account.

Case #2. A major A/E firm in the Southeast is on a discipline profit center basis in which each discipline (architecture, engineering, planning) is expected to achieve profit goals. Finance for the firm is centralized as is personnel administration and recruiting. The total firm's profitability has been very good over the past two years. Each division head is responsible for achieving both manpower utilization goals and dollar profit goals.

One potentially serious problem is that project profits are not closely monitored either by the division/discipline heads or by project managers. Thus, a very good project manager who is able to bring in a project under budget on schedule is carrying a poor project manager unable to achieve such results.

Case #3. A firm in the Far West which has five offices within a radius of 200 miles has found that as a 200-person firm, it still cannot compete and is not competing successfully for large projects. Its image is that of several small offices operating together, but not of a 200-person-total organization. Thus, its work is a multitude of small projects on which it is difficult to maintain a consistent level of quality control. Since each branch office is primarily responsible to support itself in the marketplace, the firm has no overall marketing plan. The strength of this approach is that as long as geographical competition isn't a factor through growth, each branch office has an incentive to survive as if it were an independent firm. Also, having local offices in very politically sensitive communities has proven beneficial toward obtaining local work since the firm is heavily dependent on community contacts for that work.

The Preferred Direction

The following advice comes from a large engineering firm which has attempted several different approaches to branch office management:

1. Profit centers must be established on a geographic basis which reflect both a commitment to marketing and a responsibility for overhead control of an office.

2. Branch office managers' compensation should not be totally dependent on branch office profits, but should reflect a measurement of staff utilization, office overhead relationship to corporate budgets, new market penetration, and corporate growth goals. All office managers should participate in corporate profits, and all branch office profits should be pooled before corporate profits are divided.

This particular firm has a profit distribution plan which recognizes five categories of performance and assigns each category a budgeted point rating per manager. The five categories are gross sales, overhead control, branch office profits, staff utilization, and corporate business development. Each branch manager is rated annually in each category and awarded a number of points for that category based on performance. Then all managers are placed in ascending order according to the point totals.

Reward branch office managers on achieving corporate goals as well as branch office goals.

Starting with the lowest manager, each manager's point total is compared against his normal budget of points. The lowest individual is given his share of the profits based on his actual percentage of the total points awarded. The difference between his budgeted amount and his actual amount is added back to the pool before the next individual percentage is calculated. If the total pool of bonuses is not spent, it goes back into retained earnings.

If you are considering a branch office, take the advice given to us by several firms:

1. Have some project work in a location before going. Otherwise, expect a minimum expenditure even for one person in a marketing capacity of $75,000 to $100,000 per year for at least two years before you get your first job.

2. Avoid cutthroat competition by not setting up strict profit centers in each branch. Instead, be certain that all branch office managers are rewarded on achieving corporate goals as well as branch office goals.

3. Retain centralized financial controls such as payroll and project cost accounting.

4. Retain centralized personnel recruiting and human resource functions to reinforce corporate personnel policies.

5. Have a corporate marketing plan which reflects all market goals based on a companywide evaluation of strengths and weaknesses instead of individual branch office market plans.

Finally, proceed cautiously and not in haste. It is much easier to open a branch office than to close one.

Improve Your Partnership

Dr. Mardy Grothe
Dr. Peter Wylie

Most design firm principals, like most married couples, never seek outside help to improve the way they work with each other. Even when they do seek help, it's usually too late, but mostly they never get help, even when their relationship is a major source of dissatisfaction for them.

Ask yourself if this quote could be from one of your partners: "I've got a fairly good idea about how to deal with problem employees, but that's not my biggest concern. What I'm wondering about is me and my partners. We hardly ever talk frankly about our own performance. Or even about how we're getting along with each other. We're not unhappy, but we're not happy either. We're successful, but we're not happy. And I don't think we're alone either. What can we do to deal with this kind of problem and maybe even improve the quality of our partnership?"

It Takes Work

Let's say that you, like the person who posed this question, want to improve the quality of your relationship with your partners. What can you do? Here are some immediate suggestions:

1. Make the improvement of your relationship with your partners a top priority. Like a marriage, a partnership is a relationship between people. If any relationship between people is going to succeed, it's going to take work. Too many partners pay lip service to the amount of work that a relationship requires. Like gardeners who plant the seeds but forget to tend the garden, they get out of it what they put into it: not very much.

What does "making a commitment to improve our partnership" really mean? Well, it certainly means putting time, effort, and energy into the relationship. It also means other things like:

• accepting your partners as having a right to be different from you and not trying to make them be more like you;

• being willing to sit down periodically and talk openly about your relationship with each other;

• being able to listen to the other person's point of view, especially when it's different from your own;

• talking openly about your own thoughts and feelings, especially when there are problems;

• taking responsibility for the contribution you're making to problems in the relationship, rather than laying it all off on the others;

• being willing to look for solutions to problems that everyone can live with rather than trying to have it all your own way.

Too many partners pay lip service to the amount of work the relationship requires.

This stuff sounds good in theory, but almost everyone knows how hard it is to put into practice. That's why it's important to make a strong personal commitment right up front.

Examine the Partnership

2. Reflect about your relationship with your partners. Each partner should think independently about the quality of the relationship between the partners, any problems that exist, and suggestions for making it a less frustrating and more satisfying partnership for everyone. This thinking should be done with a pen in hand so that important thoughts can be captured for later discussion. Use these questions to stimulate your thinking:

• What are things you really value in your partners, ways they've really helped the firm and enriched your life; and things about them that frustrate you and have gotten in the way of the firm's growth or your personal satisfaction?

• How has your relationship with your partners evolved over the years? How are problems between you and your partners dealt with—out in the open (maybe even too openly), under the table, or swept under the rug?

• What are some of the sensitive, touchy subjects that should get talked about but are never even mentioned? What topics have you ducked? What do you suppose your partners haven't mentioned to you?

• How are you and your partners viewed by other key people, like clients, junior partners (including those who have left the firm), and employees?

Talk to Each Other

3. Get everybody together to talk about how to improve your relationships with each other. Do this for at least a day at a quiet, secluded spot where there are no telephones and people beating down the door to get your attention. Bring a flip chart along to record main points that are discussed.

Start by asking each person to focus on a good, thought-provoking question, like: "On a day-by-day basis, how satisfied or dissatisfied are you with your relationship with each of your partners? What are the major sources of frustration and dissatisfaction? What could we—your partners—do to make your life less frustrating and more satisfying?"

Give each person the best opportunity to respond fully and completely. We suggest the following ground rules:

• When the first person starts talking, everybody else should listen attentively. Particularly avoid such ineffective things as interrupting when you disagree, rolling your eyes to the sky when you have a completely different view, or disparaging the ideas of the person who's doing the talking.

• When the first person finishes talking, the rest of the group should encourage him or her to talk even more, saying things like, "What else would you like to add?" or "What you're saying is very interesting. Keep

Touchy subjects that should get talked about never even get mentioned.

talking."

    • When the first person finishes building on original remarks, the ball should be tossed to the next person.

    • After everybody has responded to the first question, move on to a second question and recycle through the entire process.

    4. Get the group working immediately on a couple of ideas that everybody can get behind. By the time everybody responds to all of the questions, the group will have amassed an enormous amount of information. The important next step is to start working on a few things everybody can agree to even if they don't seem like the most important things to you. Don't worry at this point if touchy subjects have not surfaced, or what to do about areas of disagreement. Get the group started working on joint efforts. More difficult projects can be tackled later, and some will even take care of themselves.

    5. Don't be ashamed to ask for help if you need it. If for any reason you can't do what we've suggested or you try and find that you couldn't do it on your own, don't be afraid to ask for outside help. Rather than see it as a failure on your part, asking for help when it's needed is a sign of maturity and effectiveness.

       There are many reasons to improve the quality of your relationship with partners, some of which have to do with things like productivity and profits. However, the most important reason is that you will get more satisfaction and fulfillment out of your working life, and speaking very personally as partners for many years, that's what it's all about.

Asking for help when it's needed is a sign of maturity and effectiveness.

Design Quality: A Central Management Issue

Bradford Perkins, AIA

Management and design cannot be separated in offices that aspire to consistent quality.

According to most of what is written, great architectural design is created by individual artists. While it is true that most significant works of architecture are usually developed under the guidance of a single strong design leader, there must be some credit given to the role played by the many other participants in the design. Few significant projects have less than ten people (architects, engineers, interior designers, specialist consultants, construction managers, and, of course, clients) involved in the design decision making, and many have fifty or more. Even when my grandfather was starting his practice and sharing office space with Frank Lloyd Wright in the 1890s, this was the case.

Thus, the truth is—as any experienced architect with a reasonably controlled ego will admit—that design excellence is, in part, a result of management of a complex team, all of whose members contribute to the quality of the final result.

Good Design Needs Effective Management

Effective management can help achieve the goal of consistent design excellence. I do not, however, try to contend that design excellence can be achieved by management alone, or even that it is the most important factor.

Management skill cannot substitute for design worth managing, but it can make design ability more effective. Thus, design quality—and the ways to help achieve it—must be a central management issue in any firm concerned with design excellence.

To say that design quality should be a central management concern appears, at first, to be a muddling of the traditional separation of design and management in architectural firms. In fact, most architects make a careful distinction between management and design. One has to do with finance, administration, and other related matters, while the other is the core of an architectural practice. This may be the way some approach these two interrelated subjects but, as this article argues, management and design cannot be separated in offices that aspire to consistent quality.

Typical design/management situations emphasize the need to face the issue. Some examples of these situations might be:

• The established firm with a solid—but dull—reputation, that is losing an increasing number of the best jobs and staff members to other firms with hotter design reputations. How does the firm meet this challenge?

• A firm that—due to the design skills and reputations of the founding principals—has grown rapidly to fifty people. The principals no longer can find the time to design, the work is assigned to a changing group of associates, and the consistent quality of design is lost. How do the principals regain control over quality?

• The firm that finds itself expected to compete on a design basis for an increasing number of jobs, but never seems to win. The losses are expensive and demoralizing. Can the firm be structured to compete effectively? Should it make the effort to compete at all?

• The firm that has done a great deal of good, small work but cannot break into larger, more professionally challenging projects. How does the firm obtain the design opportunities it wants and needs?

• The firm that is organized into departments (design, production, construction) where the project is run by a project manager. The designs produced by the design departments are often unrecognizable by the time they are built. How can design control be combined with management efficiency?

• The firm that always seems to encounter some project problem—budget, schedule, client dictates—that prevents it from achieving the quality of design it seeks. How does one control the process of designing and building a building?

All of these firms must address the interaction of design and management, because not addressing it has created the situations they now face. Thus, wherever design is carried out by a team (as in almost all major projects today), wherever design depends upon having and guiding a receptive client (as almost all good architecture does), or wherever the process of doing a project has an impact on the result (as almost all processes do), management is a factor in producing quality design.

If effectively planned and controlled, this interaction—I hope we have just agreed—can significantly help achieve what should be a central objective of all firms: the highest possible design quality within the inherent constraints of each project.

Setting goals means recognizing what you want to achieve.

Interaction of Design and Management

Let's explore how this interaction of management and design should take place. Consistent design quality depends most of all on the skill and force of the firm's design leadership, remembering that leadership is a quality of a person and cannot be conferred. It is also dependent on at least the following other items:

• How the firm defines its goals for design alongside other aspects of its practice.

• What type of projects the firm secures.

• How the firm defines the design process, allocates resources to each phase of this process, and monitors this process as the project is executed.

• How the firm is organized.

• How the firm relates to its clients.

• How, in this media-influenced period, the firm builds its design reputation so that it attracts the clients and staff to perpetuate both the image and substance of design excellence.

• And, of course, the talent, experience, energy, and will of the entire project team.

As the way these factors can affect design quality will vary with the firm, its composition, and temperament, etc., I do not claim to have the answer in any area—and I am struggling with the same issues in my own practice—but it seems clear to me that the search for the right framework in each of the above areas is an essential step toward each firm's approaching and eventually achieving consistent design quality. This article merely tries to outline the issues that must be addressed within the framework.

Setting goals means recognizing what you want to achieve. The principals' values and objectives—no matter how loosely they have been expressed—set a framework. To state that the overriding goal of most architectural practices is to provide the client top-quality service resulting in building solutions that are esthetically, technically, and functionally advanced, as well as of consistently high quality, is not enough. Every goal set by a firm and its principals has some impact on the firm's response to the design quality factors just listed.

Firm targets for size, profitability, growth, type of projects, ownership, control, and other areas all have a direct or indirect impact on design quality.

For example, a firm that wishes to grow into a 100-person office with a practice based on hospitals and laboratories will have to pursue design excellence within a different set of constraints than a firm that pursues housing and office projects and does not want to expand beyond the number of projects that can be personally directed by the firm's founding principals. The former will have to develop more than one principal designer as well as a core of senior technical specialists who share project leadership, while the latter can maintain centralized control in the hands of a single design principal.

How the principals define design quality can have the most direct impact.

How the principals define design quality and set goals for its achievement, however, can have the most direct impact. In this area it is particularly important to add another dimension to the tendency to use only quantitative values as the basis for a firm's goals. Without some kind of tangible policy to the contrary, those who are primarily involved in design will find the going rough in a time that measures success mainly in terms of optimized revenues and minimized expenses.

Creativity, taste and problem-solving skill—terms that defy quantitative measure—must be given equal weight in the final structure of a firm's objectives.

Today, the diversity of design-quality definitions has multiplied, as more firms question traditional modernist dogma. For example, whether explicitly stated or not, some firms' objectives include one or more of the following:

• To do something innovative or newsworthy on each project—a common goal of firms trying to establish a reputation.

• To define the traditional design response to a particular building type—a goal for many firms with specialized institutional (schools, hospitals, etc.) practices.

• To design buildings that emphasize the functional, maintenance, cost, and other performance objectives of the owner rather than esthetic criteria—perhaps the objective of several of the office, hospital, and housing specialists.

• To consistently impose on each project a single design theory—a goal of some firms dominated by a single, strong design personality.

No matter how the design goals are defined, if they are defined, they will influence how a firm approaches its work, allocates its resources to a project, guides and judges its own design efforts as the projects develop, selects and develops its staff, and many other central design quality actions.

Practice mix is a strong determinant of design goals. Design goals are, of course, directly affected by a firm's projects. The type of projects a firm has is usually a function of what the firm seeks. If a firm wants to establish a strong design reputation, it must find a way to obtain work from clients with the desire, budget, and program to generate public interest and make design excellence possible.

It is obviously far harder to build an image with small additions to proprietary nursing homes, small industrial buildings, or low-income housing than it is with a corporate headquarters or a college's performing arts building. How a firm selects the type of work it wants and then secures it has already been covered in many other articles and books. The point here is that the realism, and even the definition, of the firm's design goals are in large part dependent upon the direction and success of the firm's marketing efforts.

Moreover, the design goals must address the needs of the building and client type. Different building types generate very different design constraints. These differences must be reflected in the continual regeneration of a firm's design philosophy and process. High technology, code-constrained, and programmatic buildings such as hospitals and laboratories, often present more difficult esthetic challenges than a development office building or luxury condominium where a different combination of a client's decision-making, program, budget, and technical priorities governs.

More than one solid old-line firm has been hurt by turning away from its own practice's roots to design philosophies and processes incompatible with its traditional projects' needs. This is usually done in a misguided attempt to rapidly upgrade design quality and image. A typical sequence is:

1. Firm loses several projects, in part because of a reputation for dull design.

2. Principals decide they must upgrade their image and skills.

3. Principals hire a designer from a "design firm" and try to import a new process as well.

4. Firm turns its back on the skills that still brought in clients.

Design excellence is not imported but instead requires a long-term effort.

5. Firm image does not change and clients and old-time staff are alienated.

6. Design "savior" is fired and the firm reverts to its former ways—often in a weakened condition.

To avoid midlife crisis, it is important to remember that design excellence is not imported but instead requires a long-term effort directed from the top in a way that integrates its pursuit into every aspect of the firm's activities. Not only a firm's real goals, but the work it gets to do, help set the context for the development of a design process.

Copyright March 1984 by *Architectural Record*.

To Grow or Not to Grow

Frank A. Stasiowski

Most design firms struggle with the issue of growth. Growth can be defined in terms of staff size, in terms of dollars and cents, or in terms of the quality of design that a firm produces. Because of the perception in the 1960s and 1970s that a firm that did not grow could not survive, many struggle with the issue of growth even today.

There are a few firms who have decided not to grow in number of employees, but who continue to grow in annual sales. Many firms grow only by a percentage margin each year to cover a cost of living increase for all employees. Whatever your goal for growth, there are particular stages through which firms go when they grow. Each of these stages can be characterized by the activities of the principals, the owners, and the managers within the firm.

Stages of Growth

During the past ten years we have found that growing design firms pass through several unique and well-defined stages of growth. Ask yourself where you are in the following series of stages.

Stage 1. Most firms are started through the efforts of one or two people who have secured a project. All of the firm's energy is centered around the promotion of a single design service. The entire organization is an informal one in which all employees tend to be jacks of all trades rather than specialists. Owners and founders are personally involved in the design and carry out most other activities within the firm resulting in an intensive work effort to produce service for the client. All decisions are made quickly, and are based on an intimate knowledge of the firm's environment and the people that work within it. There is little complexity because there are few projects, and clients are served well because there is sufficient time to meet their every need.

Stage 2. Because of the energy and enthusiasm displayed by the owner/founders, the firm begins to grow. Word of mouth sparks interest among other clients. As the firm grows, more structured organization and control procedures become necessary to keep track of all operations. Specialized business expertise such as financial and marketing management becomes necessary. When the firm reaches a twenty- to thirty-person size, the owner/founders are no longer able to maintain personal involvement in the day-to-day supervision of each employee. At approximately forty people, business managers are brought in and tasks become specialized with lines of communication being formalized into monthly management procedures and reporting. Overhead begins to go up.

Stage 3. To maintain growth, authority must be shared with lower levels of management. The third stage of management growth in a design firm is the development of project management systems within the firm which encourage lower-level employees to become involved in the authority/responsibility chain and to take on client responsibilities in the marketplace. At this stage, we observe many design firm CEOs who are unhappy with their own role as managers because they are far removed from day-to-day work "on the boards" and are in professional management positions that they were untrained for. In many firms, this stage is characterized by increased specialization in particular design markets which leads to further penetration and the beginning of a defined image for the firm.

Stage 4. As a firm continues to grow, Stage 4 is exemplified by the development of strong departments in coordination with a project management system. Many managers begin to lose sight of overall company goals in favor of personal or departmental ambitions. Because corporate management has not yet become totally professional, the interpersonal relationships among managers are not dealt with expeditiously thus resulting in a lowering of morale and in the hiring of outside specialists to improve areas such as personal management, marketing management, and operations. This stage is often the most traumatic stage in the growth of a design firm because the CEO must face the question of whether or not professional outside management is needed to help the firm continue to grow.

Stage 5. Formalized long-range planning and budget procedures become the cornerstone of a design firm that has grown to Stage 5. Generally these procedures are put into place after the firm has gone beyond the 100-person mark and realizes that its future depends on a coordinated plan/direction which requires input from various levels of management in a cohesive team framework to achieve well-thought-out goals. We observe at this stage a desire by many in top management to re-create an environment similar to the one expressed in Stage 1 above, in which the personal interest in company goals is re-created and a personal awareness of firm-wide activities is shared to contribute to the overall firm success. Cornerstone activities of a Stage 5 firm are: long-range planning, market planning, and financial planning.

The CEO must face the question of whether professional outside management is needed to help the firm continue to grow.

Growth Considerations

As a design firm moves through the five growth stages, it can undergo a tremendous amount of financial and design stress. Many firms have gone bankrupt because they have grown too fast while others have been put out of business because of a lack of control on the quality of their design work. There are a number of significant benefits that are lost with growth, which you should consider before plunging into a growth mode:

Flexibility. The larger a firm is the more it is weighted down with high overhead and more rigid operating procedures. These procedures reduce the firm's ability to respond quickly to changing markets and changing technology. The classic example is a firm which forms a committee to study a decision that could have been made in a small firm in a matter of days, and takes the committee a matter of months.

Employee Motivation. Employees of small firms can see the firm's success as a result of their own efforts. Every day they must produce and continue to produce while they are directly involved in projects, meeting clients, and seeing the results of their efforts in the built environment. As the firm grows, however, employees may lose sight of the efforts that their work contributes to the overall project and with this is a loss of personal interest in the success of the firm.

Creativity. Small firms are innovative in meeting market demands because of the close contact among marketing, design, and management personnel. As the firm grows this intermingling contact is lost and with it goes much of the company's competitive creative edge. Ask yourself when was the last time that your firm had a true design review in which the entire team was present to criticize a project.

Decision Making. Growth dictates that top management become more and more removed from day-to-day operations on the board. Information must be formalized through reports and procedures, and channels of communication become cluttered with paper. As top management becomes less familiar with many of the firm's activities, it is less able to interpret information that is received. Thus, decisions may not be made quickly enough or correctly enough in the marketplace. The perception of those in the marketplace may be that the quality of your work is slipping because effective decision making is slowing down.

Management Ability. Young, aggressive design professionals are able to manage one or two projects effectively as the owner/founders of a new design firm. However, as a firm begins to grow, demands for improved sophistication in management capability increase exponentially. Design professionals are simply not equipped in most cases to meet the demands of high-level management placed upon them by the growth of their own practices. Additionally, as a firm grows, most entrepreneurial managers may not wish to join a large organization. Because large organizations have "bureaucratic environments," aggressive young project managers may choose to join a small, intimate firm which would allow them to express their creativity in management.

Think Before You Grow

If your firm struggles with the issue of growth today, consider the five stages outlined above and try to take advantage of some of the mistakes made by firms that have gone through the growth stages. Long-range, financial, and market planning are subjects which are not privy to large firms alone. Even a small firm should take the time to structure a long-range plan for itself which includes an effective market plan and financial plan. It is not written that you must grow if you have a long-range plan. However, it may be written that you will never grow without a plan.

Do not plunge headlong into the struggle to grow without thinking

Employees in small firms can see the firms' success as a result of their own efforts.

Design professionals are simply not equipped in most cases to meet the demands of high level management.

about the problems and the changes that growth brings. You may find that being larger does not bring happiness or increased profitability, but instead brings with it a series of headaches that you would have never encountered had you not decided to grow.

Liability Insurance Tips

Frank A. Stasiowski

We collected sixty-four ideas on professional liability insurance for architects and engineers to use when considering the crisis in errors and omissions insurance.

Use the following checklist to examine your current status on professional liability insurance. Remember that each item may not of itself solve your problem, but by combining items you could go a long way to reducing your premiums or at least gain comfort in the current crisis.

The items are listed in no order of importance since each is important in itself.

1. Talk to your clients about the errors and omissions problem. Most clients are unaware that architects and engineers are in a crisis regarding liability insurance. By talking to them you at least get them on your side before signing a contract.

2. Buy "pay per project" insurance from your carrier and pass it along to your clients.

3. Pass liability for hazardous waste or asbestos use on to the sellers of property for any preexisting problem, instead of having your client accept the problem upon purchase of a site to be renovated. Doing so requires that your client negotiate this clause into the purchase and sale agreement when acquiring property.

4. Carefully evaluate the stability of your current carrier. Many insurance companies have been wracked by severe losses in the past year due to natural catastrophes and airline disasters. Some are in financial straits. Before renewing with a company, check the financial stability of the carrier.

5. Evaluate the claims procedure of your carrier. Be certain that your current carrier has not modified its claims procedure to reduce its exposure. Also, be sure that any required procedure is strictly followed by your personnel to avoid an excuse for the company to drop coverage on a claim.

6. Find out the qualifications of the attorney who will defend your claim. If possible specify an attorney prior to the rise of any claim. Often you will be handed a junior attorney who has no knowledge of the A/E industry. To avoid this, identify by name the defender of your choice.

Paperwork Is Subject to Subpoena

7. Redo all internal forms such as telephone memos and project meeting minutes to be certain they reflect the increased importance of

Most clients are unaware that architects and engineers are in a crisis regarding liability insurance.

liability insurance. Remember that any correspondence or communication between your client, your contractor, and yourself is subject to subpoena in a court case. Assure yourself that all your forms have been reviewed in light of the current crisis.

8. Turn down work. That's right! Turn down work on which the fee is bid or the liability exposure is greater than you wish to take.

9. Have a contractor review your drawings and specifications before you put them out to bid. One design firm in the Midwest started paying a fee to an independent contractor to review drawings for "buildability" and thereby eliminated or reduced his liability exposure on the job site.

10. Go bare. Eliminate professional liability insurance entirely and avoid many lawsuits which are aimed at those who have the deepest pockets.

11. Don't switch carriers just for price. Now is not the time to shop price for liability insurance. Instead, ensure that every term in the proposed contract is the way you want it.

12. Tighten all language in your contracts. Have your insurance carrier review every contract now on the books, and have him give you a course in how to write contracts for future work. Much language in contracts could be tightened to protect you from many frivolous claims.

13. Be sure your project managers are licensed. Licensed design professionals should be running all projects in your firm. Anyone running a project who is not licensed should be required to obtain one within a specific period of time. Doing so will reduce your errors and omissions.

14. Go back to clients and find out about problems early. Rather than hiding problems in a closet, talk to your clients about the nature of any problems that could arise. No one is perfect, including you. By doing this you may avoid the necessity of a claim.

Licensed design professionals should be running all projects in your firm.

All Insurance with One Broker

15. Buy all your firm's insurance from one carrier. Rather than buying E & O insurance from one carrier and general liability insurance and health insurance from another, combine all your insurance with one broker or carrier thereby giving you a "bigger stick."

16. Always address liability in negotiations. Unlike many design firms, you should bring up the subject of liability and indemnification at every negotiation with a client.

17. Deal only with brokers who specialize in A/E insurance. It is vital during this liability crisis that you deal exclusively with an insurance broker who understands our architecture and engineering business. Do not go to your local neighborhood insurance broker and expect that he will understand E & O insurance as it is today.

18. Raise your deductible to three years' worth of your profits. According to industry statistics a deductible equal to three years of your firm's accrual profits is as high as you should go.

19. Move the firm away from pollution liability projects. Rather than taking on hazardous waste or asbestos projects, move the firm to other marketplaces which avoid this type of liability.

20. Assess a carrier's loss prevention program. Before taking on a new insurance carrier, find out what he will do for your firm to help you with loss prevention. Many carriers run elaborate seminar programs for your personnel; others do nothing.

21. Ask for a list of A/Es insured by a carrier before insuring your firm with them. Many firms are just entering this marketplace; others have been in it for years.

22. Put your details on a CADD-secured system so they cannot be changed. By assuring yourself that every detail going out of your office is of the highest quality, you will begin to reduce liability claims involving your details.

23. Be certain that defense is not terminated without notice when funds are depleted on your case. Many architects and engineers have found that their defense had been halted by the attorney assigned to their case simply because insurance funds had run out. Whenever a claim occurs, find out how much legal defense you have and know where you stand at all times.

24. Check out the track record of clients and their financial credit. Ask how often clients sue. Do they have in-house counsel? Checking your clients before signing a contract is prudent business—never more so than now in light of the liability crisis.

25. Avoid clients who use bidding for selection. Any client who is that price-sensitive will be the first to file a claim for the most minor financial inconvenience.

26. Avoid nontraditional approaches to design work. Whenever you are asked to enter into a new form of contract with partners who are contractors or developers, beware.

27. Avoid equity positions in projects. While equity positions may seem to give you a better profit potential on a project, they also increase the potential for liability claims from third parties. Remember, as an owner you may be asked to defend both your A/E practice and your equity position simultaneously.

Don't do projects outside your expertise.

28. Be certain to operate legally in the state where the project is located. If you are not licensed in a state or have not taken the proper steps to operate your business there, you may be liable for a claim.

29. Don't do projects outside your expertise. We hear over and over of firms taking on brand new projects in areas they are totally unfamiliar with.

30. Keep clients happy. Happy clients don't sue. At all costs communicate with your clients. Keep them happy at every step during the project.

Insist on Construction Services

31. Insist on construction phase services as part of every project. The worst of all possible scenarios is the design professional eliminated from the construction scene, thereby allowing the owner and contractor to construct the project as they see fit.

32. Use standard form agreements prepared by national societies that

have been thoroughly examined from a liability standpoint and will protect you better than any mongrel form of agreement.

33. Have a precise method to calculate the fee. While this may not seem a major liability insurance problem, uncertain fee arrangements lead to claims, especially when a dissatisfied owner cannot figure how a fee was calculated.

34. Always retain ownership and control of drawings and specifications. The drawings and specs are instruments of service, not products.

35. Always delineate specific owner's responsibilities and schedules for delivery of what the owner is to provide on the project. Be certain to outline, in writing, exact due dates and level of quality for each item the owner will deliver to you.

36. Never sign indemnification agreements, guarantees, or warranties.

37. Never use "upon completion of" clauses for payment. These clauses leave open to dispute the subjective matter as to what is complete or not complete.

38. Keep objective project records—just facts, not opinions. Whenever opinions are rendered in project meeting minutes they make the minutes almost invalid in a court of law. Be certain to cite facts only.

39. Keep current with billings and collections. This good management procedure also can alert you when a client is thinking about making a claim. Clients who have not paid bills for a long time may be getting ready to file a suit against you.

40. Involve all of your staff in loss-prevention seminars. Remember that secretaries can make mistakes as well as project managers or principals. Every person in your firm should be exposed to loss prevention education.

Transfer Assets

41. Minimize assets held within your corporation. Transfer your assets to your spouse or your children to minimize available target for a liability claim.

42. Put in an excess fee if a client won't limit liability. Offer a client a specific amount of liability coverage; if the client will not limit your liability to that coverage, put in an amount above your normal fee.

43. Have all owners agree to pass on your limit of liability to others in contracts. While this is a difficult clause to include in many contracts, if the owner agrees to do so, it may save you a major claim by a third party.

44. Set up a separate corporation for high-risk work. For instance, if you are now doing high-risk asbestos or hazardous waste work, develop a separate corporation and be sure to include other owners so the corporation will be legally at arm's length.

45. Deal only with legal counsel who has specific A/E experience. Many firms have legal counsel who serve no other architects or engineers. Ask your legal counsel how many other firms they worked with prior to your dealing with them.

46. Refuse to indemnify anyone for their risk or their work. By in-

demnifying someone you accept 100 percent of their liability.

47. Don't do work on purchase orders. Design work is service; it is not a product. By using purchase orders you accept product liability in those cases.

48. Structure a peer review program in your geographic area. Have member firms review each other's liability and quality control programs to spot weaknesses.

49. Be sure to have signed contracts on all projects before starting work. One of the surest ways to lose a claim is to be doing work without a contract.

50. Run the firm so as to disburse most assets annually. Do not seek to build a capital intensive firm; instead pay most profits out to partners or principals each year.

51. Go bare and fund losses as they hit. According to insurance company statistics it takes an average of four years from claim to settlement on most liability cases. This means you could potentially fund a loss with tax-deductible dollars after a claim is made.

52. Have all subconsultants contract directly with owners. If you do not contract with a subconsultant, the liability arm is further away.

53. Find out if your insurance is on the "claims made" or "occurrence" basis. And understand the difference.

54. Be aware of pollution exclusions for preexisting hazardous materials such as oil, water, vinyl/asbestos tile, or asbestos in ceilings.

55. Make a list of potential hazardous materials such as vinyl/ asbestos tile, sand-blasting residue, coal tar roofs, or electrical transfer and teach your staff to be aware of them, especially on renovation work.

56. Don't do hazardous waste work without indemnification from the client. Even the Corps of Engineers provides indemnification.

57. Before working in other states, investigate specific new liability laws which bind A/Es under certain circumstances. Be certain that a state has not recently passed a law in light of the current liability crisis.

Don't Volunteer

58. Don't volunteer help on any issue not in your contract, or you will be held accountable. There are many stories concerning architects and engineers who simply stop by to observe a site and are wrapped into liability claims by a third party who happens to observe an architect or engineer on the site.

59. Consider hiring a special A/E attorney on your staff to negotiate all your contracts.

60. Never start work until a contract is signed, and require all staff working on the job to read the contract and understand all its provisions before working on any aspect of the project.

61. Limit liability on any project to the amount of your fee. And have the client agree to it.

62. Resist politically motivated work. Politicians have a way of reversing allegiances and attacking a design firm if anything goes wrong.

63. When making assumptions on certifications, state what they are.

Go bare and fund losses as they hit.

In fact, don't do certification if at all possible.

64. Always limit what certifications can be used for specifically, in writing between you and your client. Never do a blanket certification without understanding clearly its purpose and knowing exactly what you are certifying.

We recommend that you take this list and pass it around to every member of your firm. Add to it specific ideas from your firm's practices. Every little bit can help you avoid the liability crisis.

Liability Insurance

Donald P. Dillon

Property and casualty companies have been experiencing such adverse loss experience in the last four years (i.e., for every dollar in premiums collected, they have paid out $1.20 or more in claims and related expenses), that all businesses can expect increasing insurance premiums on their property and casualty policies.

Until late 1984, insurance companies were still willing to reduce premiums to compete with each other for property and casualty business. This has all changed, and insurance companies are offering renewal policies on all types of insurance at substantially higher premiums.

The reason for this change is twofold. Insurers essentially make money in two ways: by underwriting insurance risk, and by investing the premiums.

The insurance companies' underwriting losses and overhead expenses have more than wiped out their premium income for several years; but these losses have been more than offset by investment profits, partly because interest rates have been high. As long as investment yield was high, insurance companies competed with each other to retain market share and keep cash flowing for investment.

Despite warnings by financial analysts that losses were outpacing investment returns and interest earnings, the insurance industry continued its fierce price competition. However, by the end of 1984, the party was over. Insurance companies as a group lost $9.6 billion on underwriting and made only $8.2 billion in investment income.

Many companies did much worse than average.

By the end of 1984, the party was over.

Impact on Architects and Engineers

Professional liability insurance companies were also affected by an intensity of competition from new insurance companies that entered the professional liability field.

These new companies assumed that they would be able to take advantage of the premium cash flow and the long delay in settling professional liability claims, which stretches the investment horizon of the premium dollar to many years.

The long-term providers of professional liability insurance were frequently forced to reduce premiums to retain market share despite worsening loss ratios. The new companies often justified their low prices as the cost of entry into the professional liability business.

When the insurance industry posted their large underwriting losses for 1984, the honeymoon was over for most of the new professional liability companies. Many of these companies have suddenly pulled out of the marketplace and are issuing nonrenewal notices on their policies. Any new insurance company that uses aggressive price discounting to obtain professional liability business will now find that as they are forced to raise their premiums, they will lose large blocks of policyholders who bought their policies strictly on the basis of price. This may accelerate the remaining new companies' withdrawal from the professional liability marketplace.

What Should the Architect and Engineer Do?

Never has it been more important to have your professional liability coverage with one of the veteran long-term providers of professional liability policies. For the last five years, these companies continued to put great emphasis on the quality of a potential insured, loss prevention, and effective claim service capabilities. Unless your policy is with one of the long-term providers of this coverage, you could be faced with the following decisions: if you have an outstanding claim and your insurance company withdraws from writing professional liability coverage, what will be the quality of their defense of your claim in the years to come? You could be caught in a "Catch 22" situation on a potential claim where neither your current insurance company that is withdrawing from insurance nor the replacement insurance company will take responsibility for a potential claim.

You should use a professional liability insurance specialist. Throughout the United States, there are insurance brokers and agents who specialize in this type of insurance. These people can be a valuable resource to your firm. The agent should have access to most, if not all, insurance companies offering professional liability insurance. The agent will be able to point out the different terms and conditions between the policies; e.g., some companies define "claim" in a very narrow sense; some policies exclude cost estimating; some exclude claims arising from late delivery of plans and specifications; and some do not cover legal fees. The experienced agent will be able to look past a mere comparison of premium cost to guide you on stability of the insurance company as well as policy conditions.

An excellent method for you to determine if an insurance agent is knowledgeable in professional liability is to request from the agent evidence that his office will be able to review your client contracts and respond in writing on the agent's stationery that the documents you are signing are covered under your policy. Carrying a professional liability policy does not automatically cover the design professional for every client contract, hold harmless agreement, certification form, etc. An experienced professional liability agency will screen your contracts and respond in writing as to where the contract conflicts with your policy. Experienced insurance agents know that there is more to buying professional liability insurance than a low premium.

Many companies are issuing nonrenewal notices on their policies.

You could be caught in a "Catch 22" situation on a potential claim.

Managing Information: The CIC

The typical professional services firm has an insatiable need for timely and accurate information. Whether it is the latest version of a city's building code or the name of the ambassador to Nigeria, information is the lifeblood of private consulting firms.

Unfortunately, most firms have a very poor process for getting information. Usually one wall in the conference room serves as the unsupervised "library," with each technical professional keeping his own set of codes and catalogs. It takes all morning and a dozen phone calls to get the exact wording of the proposed energy bill. Marketing has to poll the engineers to see if the firm has ever done a curved girder bridge. No one can find a copy of the feasibility study for the telephone company project done last year. The firm's mailing list has not been updated since 1977. And so on.

More and more firms are overcoming these problems by establishing a central information center (CIC). The library is the nucleus of the operation but also included, as one firm put it, is "everything having to do with the collection, storage, and retrieval of information."

Function of the CIC

As a library, the CIC performs the following functions:

1. Acquiring and maintaining general interest, reference, and technical books relating to the firm's practice.

2. Ordering and controlling subscriptions to various magazines, periodicals, and information services.

3. Providing liaison with other information centers such as the university library and government agencies.

4. Researching questions, using its own resources or those of the other information centers.

In addition, the typical CIC gets involved in a lot more activities, such as:

1. Being the central repository for design-related reference materials such as the firm's master specification and typical details; building and other regulatory codes, including government design manuals; Sweets and other manufacturer's catalogs; and interiors samples.

2. Storing all marketing and promotion materials such as past proposals, capsule descriptions of all present and past projects, project sheets and other components of the flexible brochure system, personnel resumes, master slides of the firm's work, and even the audio visual

Michael R. Hough

Most firms have a very poor process for getting information.

equipment itself.

3. Maintaining information on clients such as annual reports, Moodys, government organization manuals, and *Who's Who*.

4. Being the central source for all government documents such as the *Federal Register*, *Commerce Business Daily*, and various technical publications.

One firm has the CIC handle all its central files. Another has it act as the central archives for all file material over five years old. In this case, the CIC discards all extraneous information and binds what is left into compact books. Another CIC is handling the microfilming of all plans and file material.

Advantages of the CIC

The list is endless because the purpose of the CIC is to become involved with all information gathering and disseminating for the firm. When this is the case, the following advantages occur:

1. Time is saved because one individual is responsible for the information function.

2. Better technical work results because everyone is using the latest manuals and catalogs.

3. Money is saved because the firm does not pay for needless duplication in technical publications or periodical subscriptions.

Setting Up the CIC

To set up a CIC, first you need one person to be the information centroid. If you are a smaller firm under twenty-five, this person will probably have other duties such as clerical, or it could be a professional librarian part-time. But even in smaller firms, all the functions we discussed would be performed.

Larger firms should have someone with a background in library science.

The larger firms should have someone with a background in library science. This person knows what to have within your library and— more important—what information can be obtained outside and where.

When first establishing a formal CIC, start slowly and acquire only what is needed for your particular type of firm. One firm suggested $150 a month as an initial budget for books and periodicals.

One recommendation is to pull back all the reference material bought by the firm in the past but now squirreled away in the employee's book shelves. It may be all right for them to keep the material, after it has been catalogued.

Speaking of cataloguing, that is the most important function of the new librarian. Know what you have and require a sign-out system to know where everything is. Note it is not necessary to have one central library; one firm has satellite libraries in each department but the sign-out system is still enforced.

Have all books and periodical purchases made by or cleared through the CIC. The book can be permanently lent to an individual but at least the CIC will know the firm owns it. You can avoid many purchases of costly reference books by having working relationships with other nearby libraries.

Help is available if you need it. The Special Libraries Association offers a one-day consultation visit that is free except for travel expenses. Contact their executive director at 235 Park Avenue South, New York, NY 10003 (212) 777-8136, and ask for the consultation packet.

The American Institute of Architects offers advice and assistance to the fledgling architectural librarian. For more information, contact the AIA, 1735 New York Ave. NW, Washington, DC 20006 (202) 785-7300. Another source is the librarian at one of the larger firms near you.

Two excellent articles on the subject both appeared in *Consulting Engineer*: "Does Your Firm Need a Technical Library" in the December 1974 issue and "Launching Your Own Library" in the August 1975 issue.

Internal Information Systems

James Anderegg

Most professionals prefer to concentrate on their profession and leave the nitty-gritty housekeeping chores that relate to records and data bases to others, and the less expensive the others the better. How many times have you seen an architect who puts untold hours and intense care into the planning, programing, and design, give the same attention to the correspondence and calculations records after the job is done and paid for? And yet in today's world of increasingly litigious clients, it is more and more necessary to be involved in these aspects of practice. The data base underlying the design decisions must be up-to-date at the start of a project and the records must be complete at the end.

This article will try to outline the scope of the problem and suggest some ways to think about its solution. It will also offer some rules of thumb that have been learned in the past twenty-five years.

Rule. Don't try to simplify the system by merging its parts. Sources of information in an office are comprised of a number of distinctive, indissoluble components. They should not be merged. In some cases this is obvious, in others the boundaries are more subtle.

Library Contents

Starting at the library end, the parts are:

1. Catalogs. Most practitioners, and especially those in large firms, feel that product manufacturers do a good job for them with catalogs. I have always found just the opposite. My own studies, consisting entirely of surveys of catalogs selected randomly from the shelves of firms without libraries, show an average age of three-and-a-half to four years. Some time ago, Sweets did a very careful study of the coverage of fifty offices by fifty manufacturers. On average, the results were very discouraging. Most manufacturers were spotty in their coverage and, from the professional's side, comprehensiveness of collections did not reflect the size of the firm. Some small firms did much better than some of the large ones, but on the whole, nobody was well served. I think that the confusion stems from the fact that in every market there are a handful of representatives who do a superb job and are very visible doing it. Everyone else shares the credit.

The reality is frequently a situation where the individuals and key people gather their own collections of personal favorites. With the pressures on time, these are not kept up-to-date and are finally subject to all of the faults of any voluntary, unmanaged nonorganization. At the

When a need arises, the oldest information is the most available. The new is in someone's drawer.

same time, there are usually open shelves where departmental catalogs reside. These suffer from Gresham's Law of Untended Catalogs where the old and out-of-date (read valueless) drive the new and current (read valuable) out of circulation and into someone's private collection. The problem, of course, is that when a need arises, the oldest information is the most available. The new is in someone's drawer and he's out.

The general breakdown of catalogs is: architectural (Uniform System Divisions 2-14), mechanical (Division 15), and electrical (Division 16). For planning purposes, architectural and mechanical need about the same shelf space (100' to 135') and electrical needs about half as much. Ordinarily, one would expect to group them by division number, but it must always be kept in mind that every office is different.

2. Codes. The importance of up-to-date codes is obvious as are the current amendments tacked on to national codes by many local political jurisdictions. It is also essential to have the full array that prevails on a specific project. A few years ago, a handful were sufficient. Recently, I saw a project with twenty-seven different codes.

They are usually grouped by federal, state, and cities under appropriate states. It is a minor point, but large projects should have their own codes and those codes should be filed with and become part of the project record.

3. References. There are essentially two classes of data here. One is commercially published material such as *Architectural Graphic Standards*, *Means Cost Data*, etc. The other is association literature produced by national manufacturer associations. Both are needed. There are also a number of government-published items that belong here such as weather data. ASTM can also go here or with codes.

4. Books. Hardcover books on design, theory, history, planning, etc., are usually grouped by subject and in most architectural or engineering firms they do not make up a large collection. Planning firms, on the other hand, may have 10,000 or more items here. It should be noted that the index of this material should be firmwide and include the items in the partners' offices. These latter items should carry blind addresses.

5. Periodicals. The library should have its own subscriptions for these are extremely helpful if research is called for on contemporary work. One helpful thought is to bind past issues. Society and association transactions and EPA literature fall into this area and seem to form an ever-expanding monster that takes on a life of its own. This is especially true in civil engineering.

6. Reports. They go by many names, but what I'm referring to here are the plastic-bound, in-house published "Feasibility Study" or "Program for...," etc. They are a product of past work by the firm, or sometimes were generated by some other professional office. They can be very valuable, if indexed properly, both to save professional time and to produce new business. And yet frequently they are tossed aside, lost, or simply filed with past work.

7. Specs of past jobs. As a library collection, these should not be confused with the copies filed with the project records. Those are essen-

Know what you have and require a sign-out system to know where it is.

tial records; these are a source of data from past work for future work and as such are occasionally cut. They can be very helpful and are usually filed by project number.

Archives

1. Drawings of past work. These should be handled with great care to preserve a record of what was conceived and what was done on the completed work. The record should include sketches, mylars, bid sets, changes, and bulletins to produce as complete a record as possible. Aperture cards offer a way to keep track of the myriad changes on individual sheets during the course of the work and shop drawings may, in some cases, substitute for "as builts." This material is essential if one goes to court over a past project and it also can be a source of new work.

2. Project files. This material divides itself into two broad categories of test reports and correspondence, but also includes contracts and permits, etc. These are necessary to get the job done and a sine qua non for any defense later if problems arise. I have a friend who discovered early on in a project that those genial and charming contractor types he was dealing with on a large hospital had bid a bare bones price and then later sued the architect, among others, to make a profit on the nine preceding jobs that they had done. My friend discovered "defensive architecture" on the spot and has practiced it ever since.

Special thought should be given to including the calculations as part of this record. Civil calculations can be taken at bid date; structural when the building tops out; mechanical both at bid date and when the project is complete; and electrical when the project is completed.

3. Photos. Progress photos probably should be filed with the project records but seem to gravitate to the slide room.

4. Slides. These are usually kept in the promotion department and their major use seems to be new business. Filed by project, it is possible to group them in several ways to make their use much easier. (See the article "Order From Chaos" in the Marketing section for more on slide and photo care.)

Product Information Management

Maeve Slavin

The essence of a designer's mind-set and training is the ability to make order. Yet, in one critical area, disorder frequently prevails. That is in the researching, storing, and communication of product literature and sample information. It is no exaggeration that many design offices still rely on haphazard and outmoded systems, if indeed system is the word for a handy bottom drawer, a convenient shelf, the floor? Habit and the crisis of the charrette lead to repeated specification of familiar products that worked well in successful prior jobs.

Today, increased professionalism in the delivery of design services is mandatory. Product awareness is directly related to design excellence and profitable business. But keeping on top of the latest news of the marketplace is time consuming and highly specialized. Busy offices do not, typically, have the personnel to spare for the degree of effort required to stay up with the proliferating surge of constantly changing catalog listings, be they hardware, furniture, construction material, flooring, textiles, or finishes. Smaller firms believe that they can in no way meet the cost of maintaining either the services of an on-staff specialist or the space to house an information support system.

The way to sustain top-level product quality and state-of-the-art specification is to know precisely what is happening in the industry. And the way to accomplish this is to recognize the value of a functioning resource center or library, appropriately staffed. The role of the library specialist is to keep constant vigilance on the marketplace by reading, research, monitoring, and establishing friendly contact with vendors and manufacturers' representatives. In this way, the librarian becomes the clearinghouse for a two-directional flow of information which ultimately benefits the design firm itself, the end user, and by process of feedback, the entire industry.

So, there is a better way. But is there a One Better Way? The answer is, probably not, given the differing philosophies, structures, and goals of individual design firms. Even among offices where product and materials centers have been instituted, there is no agreed across-the-board methodology that they all subscribe to. There is division of opinion on both nomenclature and function. Should there be a design library, staffed by a library science specialist, or should there be a resource center run by a color and materials expert? To what degree should the librarian or color/materials specialist interact with the design staff? How much space should be allocated to the library/resource center? Should samples and literature

Centralizing the flow of information can be measured in increased efficiency and productivity.

be stored separately in adjacent or even removed locations? To what extent can available electronic communication technology be utilized?

There are no definitive answers to these questions. What is agreed is this: centralizing and streamlining the flow of information brings paybacks that can be measured in increased efficiency and productivity; higher standards and quality of design; and expanded expertise in specification of finishes, furnishings, and detailing. Time is saved through reduction of research duplication. The firm and its clients benefit from more effective cost analysis. The client receives long-term satisfaction from materials and products that will survive the wear and tear of time. The reputation of the design firm is enhanced. Investment in the services of a full-time professional can, moreover, advance the depth and range of services offered. It is an investment that every firm, large or small, should consider worthwhile.

What follows is a how-to-do-it survey of three significant design firms. They share commitment to knowledgeable design decision making, based on the most current information, and can be considered pioneers in the comparatively new, still inexact, and fast-evolving field of product and materials information processing. Together they represent the cutting edge.

Trained Expertise

Environmental Planning & Research, Inc. (EPR), headquartered in San Francisco, ranks sixth in interior design volume in the country. William Van Erp is in charge of its design library. A librarian in the classic sense, he holds a Master of Library Science degree. He advocates the application of library science principles to the tangled web of samples and product literature, and encourages design firms to hire library experts. Recognizing the trend toward specialization of skills in design offices, he maintains that designers do not have the time to research product options themselves. Hence the librarian's function as information gatherer and educator is as vital to a firm's success as is the traditional function of designer. Without the librarian's input, he says, "There is no variety of design. Designers get locked into deeper and deeper ruts."

Working System

Van Erp's system is an example of exceptionally efficient, centralized organization. The library itself reflects the firm's work: 70 percent interior design and 30 percent architecture. Of the 600 catalogs on file, those on architectural subjects are ordered according to Sweet's numbering system, then alphabetized by manufacturer in each category. Interiors catalogs on furniture, accessories, etc., are alphabetized by manufacturer. Product samples are organized by type, fabrics in master binders, peg boards, and boxed samples—all alphabetized by manufacturer. Carpet samples are organized either in books or boxes. Laminates, metals, paints, and floor coverings are all shelved in groups. The system is simple and effective. Designers can seek out their own information, but when stumped they can refer to Van Erp for help.

Van Erp's system is an example of exceptionally efficient, centralized organization.

Designer Librarians

Skidmore Owings & Merrill, Chicago, a component of a nine-city, nationwide organization with $1.4 billion worth of construction annually, is an obvious giant. Four color/materials specialists man the material resource center, interacting with architects and interior designers as members of project design teams. In contrast to EPR, SOM takes the position that design professionals, with interior design or art major backgrounds, prove effective in the dual role of information gatherers and design decision makers where color, texture, and materials are concerned. This combination places the resource center as a direct intermediary between vendors and suppliers on the outside and the in-house design staff, and permits active participation in projects.

Although the centralized product library is available to all SOM personnel, members of the color/materials group act basically as much as designers as librarians. Sandra Fandre, an interior designer, heads the department, backed up by Vicky Lidman, Cecelia Mitchell, and David Stankey. However, information gathering is pursued consistently, to the degree that new product samples frequently show up on file even before announcements appear in the press. Problems of obsolete price lists and infrequent updatings are eliminated. Samples are stored in what is known as "the sample room" in spanking white drawers and shelves. Catalogs and brochures are kept in shelving in the area immediately outside the sample room. The SOM system is a valuable prototype of highly design-motivated research and information processing.

On a Smaller Scale

GN Associates, New York, is a young (established in 1979), small (twenty on staff) firm, specializing in interior design, graphics, and materials and finishes services to architects and developers. In 1981, 1 million square feet of interior design space was put in place, with 3.5 million square feet of materials and finishes services in addition. Its founding partners, K. Robert Najarian and Carol Groh, were formerly associates of SOM, New York. From its inception, the firm was committed to incorporating a research center into its overall management planning strategy, and Mary Montray was brought on board very early on. Montray, an interior designer, works in similar fashion to the SOM model, acting as an integrated member of design teams as a specialist in color, texture, materials, and finishes. At the same time she interfaces with vendors, keeps totally current with developments in the markets, and organizes and maintains the sample library. Literature, brochures, and catalogs are stored in a separate section of the office and do not fall under her responsibility.

We do not consider our resource center to be even slightly a luxury.

"We consider the service Mary provides to our design staff and to our clients to be an integral part of our business," Groh said. "She is an absolutely key figure in our firm. We do not consider our resource center to be even slightly a luxury." She did allow that the extent of GN's commitment is unique for a firm of its size. GN's example should inspire other firms in its size category to implement resource specialization.

Networking

For small firms in particular, but big firms also, the possibilities of electronic data systems offer computerized techniques for product information processing. Networking is soon to come on-line, bringing the option of linking office-based computers with centralized data banks. Right now, the Xetron Contract Design Furnishings Library, introduced at Neocon 1981, is an affordable service. An automatic microfiche system, containing the complete catalogs of more than 350 contract office furniture manufacturers, the library works on a subscription basis. Information is updated weekly. The system can be obtained at the annual rate of $495. For further information, contact Xetron, One IBM Plaza, Chicago, IL 60611.

Xetron and down-the-road electronic networking, however, solve the problem only of reducing the space occupied by catalogs and other literature in systematized, current form. There still remains the necessity to house product and materials samples, and to assign a staff member responsibility for their organization and updating, and to act as the contact point with the industry. This person is a vital element in the library matrix. Whether via the librarian or the resource specialist/designer, the contemporary design office absolutely requires the latest news of the current marketplace. And the industry needs feedback from and contact with the inner workings and needs of design firms. Upgraded communication, sharpened design excellence, and increased productivity is what it's about.

Financial Management

2

Controlling Financial Management

W hen I took over the administration of the Eggers Group a few years ago, during a period of architectural recession, the firm was saddled with severe cash-flow problems. Moreover, no one had a method for forecasting what our future financial needs would be even three or four months down the road. This led me to establish management reporting systems that would serve as accurate indicators of the overall financial status and future of the office, as well as prospects for individual projects. These systems work so well today that I can monitor the firm's standing on a daily basis, project future needs well in advance, gauge the profitability of each project, and set future goals. Since many architects, regardless of the size of their offices, face the same problems we confronted, an explanation of our management systems and how they work may prove generally useful. Essentially, the systems furnish two kinds of information: a record of what actually occurs, and a forecast. The following reports help monitor the pulse of our practice: a cash-flow report, an "aged accounts receivable" report (i.e., a report of all outstanding uncollected billings, showing the length of time they have been due), a marketing report, a new contract awards report, and a project management report.

A new cash-flow report is generated every six months, and updated every three months, on the basis of billing forecasts, manpower projections and estimates of extraordinary expenses (Figure 1). In conjunction with the principals-in-charge, I personally prepare the billing forecast, which helps keep me abreast of every project in the office. I also inform the controller of any anticipated extraordinary expenses, such as bonuses, speculative work, and competition expenses. The manpower projection is prepared by the chief of production. On the basis of these estimates, the controller prepares a report that contains actual targets for expenditures.

The first thing I look for when I get this draft report is the bottom line—the amount of money left at the end of each month to be carried over to the start of the next month. Depending on whether we have come up short or even, we either borrow or plan our short- and long-term investments. After review and adjustment, a final six-month cash-flow report is completed, to be reviewed within three months.

At the end of each month, actual figures for that period are added to the original cash-flow report. In addition, we are able to extract a profit or loss estimate for the coming month, based on the income we know we

Frank Munzer, AIA

No one had a method for forecasting what our future financial needs would be, even three or four months down the road.

Figure 1

```
                    C A S H   F L O W   R E P O R T

                         J U L Y   1 9 8 1
```

	ESTIMATE	ACTUAL	VARIABLE FAVORABLE (UNFAVORABLE)
RECEIPTS:			
Opening Balance			
Securities Due (and $ from Saveway MC)			
Income from Billings (incl. Reimbursables)			
Income from Loan (Bank)			
Extraordinary Income			
Joint Venture Distributions			
Cash Contributions (Directors)			
Other Income			
Balance in Cairo Office Accounts			
TOTAL RECEIPTS:			
DISBURSEMENTS:			
Gross Payroll (Staff)			
Directors Payroll			
Consultants Fees			
Branch Office Expenses - Trenton, NJ			
Branch Office Expenses - Cairo			
Profit Participation - Contract Holders			
Payroll Taxes; Quarterly Taxes			
Directors Taxes			
Insurance Premiums (and loan repayment)			
Insurance Claims - Deductible			
Distribution to Directors			
Retired Officers			
Loan Payable to Bank			
Securities (and $ transfers to Saveway MC)			
Accounts Payable - Trade			
Accounts Payable - Rent			
Misc. Items - New WP Machines			
Office Alterations			
TOTAL DISBURSEMENTS:			
BALANCE:			
Operating Balance - End of Month			
+ Saveway A/C and Securities Held			
TOTAL BALANCE:			
BILLINGS: (Forecast vs. Actual)			
PERSONNEL:			

need in order to break even. With this monthly report in hand, I am able to determine the month's profit or loss; the amount of monthly billing (and whether we made or exceeded our target); the amount of cash that came in; the number of personnel on the payroll; the amount of cash available to meet the next month's expenses; what money we have invested; and how much we still owe consultants.

At the end of each month I also receive an aged accounts receivable report listing all jobs, billing amounts, dates, and payments. In this way, I know which clients are becoming delinquent and can initiate whatever proceedings are necessary for collection, having first discussed the situation with the principal-in-charge. Many architects complain that they are victims of slow payment, but thanks to our follow-up system, most of our bills are paid within thirty to forty-five days.

We bill monthly, based on the percentage of work completed the previous month, unless our contract specifically ties payments to project phases. We accustom our clients to a monthly payment structure as soon as work begins. This creates a steady cash income and balances cash expenditures.

New Contracts and Marketing

Monthly reports prepared by the marketing coordinator reflect activity by officers of the firm involved in business development. Each principal prepares a report outlining what action has been taken with each potential client and when future action is planned. We include an additional sheet that reports pending proposals and gives a breakdown of the firm's marketing activities. A report on pending projects that have been inactive that month is also included. This report enables the marketing coordinator, who annually presents the firm with a detailed marketing plan, to check the month's activities reports against the targets established in the yearly plan. This system keeps individual principals in touch with the marketing effort on a continuing basis. It also helps maintain momentum in the pursuit of new work by reminding all of us that every month we must obtain commissions equal to monthly billings if we are to stay in business for the next year.

A report on new contract awards is issued quarterly. The marketing plan establishes targets—broken down into six-month and quarterly increments—so that we know how much new work we need to meet our marketing goals. Once a job is awarded, the billing forecast is revised. The aim of this report is to keep a continuing check on our marketing effort (is it producing the business needed?) and to give us an accurate picture of forthcoming personnel needs.

We accustom our clients to a monthly payment structure as soon as work begins.

Taking the Office Pulse

While I keep my finger directly on the pulse of the general organization, our vice presidents maintain close control of individual projects by means of a computerized project management system. At the beginning of each project we draw up a schedule of tasks broken down into fourteen work categories with biweekly personnel allocations for each (Figure 2). The categories are: programming, schematics, design development, working drawings, specifications, interior design, color work, construction administration, field construction administration, owners' changes, model, preliminary, master planning, shop drawings. To encourage pulse monitoring at all levels of the organization, this information is entered on a form that is available to all managers.

Every other week, managers receive an automatic computer printout that compares time and money estimates to actual output, show-

Figure 2

PROJECT MANPOWER BUDGET

Project ———
No. ———
Principal ———
Data ———

Work Type #		Salary budget		Bi-Weekly Pay Periods										
		Hrs.	Amount											
Programming	1													
Schematics	2													
Design Devel.	3													
Wrkg. Drwgs.	4													
Specifications	5													
Interior Design	6													
Color Work	7													
Const. Admin.	8													
Field Const. Admin.	9													
Owners' Changes	10													
Model	11													
Preliminary	12													
Master Planning	13													
Shop Drawings	14													

The key to the success of our project management reporting system is that we make it realistic and as simple as possible.

ing the current status of the job in terms of hours, dollars, and percentage of the budget expended to date (Figure 3). This becomes a quick reference that enables us to gauge where we are on every job in the office, so that problems can be worked out before they escalate. Now that managers are used to the system, we find that they actually monitor their jobs on a weekly basis, verifying their results against the biweekly printout. The principal in charge and the contract officer also get copies of the computer printout and refer any major problems to me. This means that action can be taken before the difficulties get out of hand. The percentage of work completed is not included on these printouts because we have found this information so difficult to garner. If we waited until we received it, the reports would never get out at all. When managers present their reports in person, we ask them how far their projects have progressed.

The key to the success of our project management reporting system is that we make it realistic and as simple as possible. We don't include information we don't need and we break down the paperwork into brief segments, so that a number of people can share the preparation of target figures. Beware of overzealous accountants, bookkeepers, and computer programmers who, if let loose, can destroy the system by cluttering it with too much information.

Our system also gives employees in the firm a feeling of confidence and direction that offsets the time and effort they have to spend on

Figure 3

ADP MANAGEMENT REPORT

COMPANY NO. DTK — RPT. NO.1 — PROJECT STATUS REPORT 05/03/81

	TOTAL HOURS	TOTAL DOLLARS
COLOR WORK 21870-0-07		
CURRENT	.00	.00
JOB TO DATE	73.00	749.19
ESTIMATE	103.00	750.00
DIFFERENCE	30.00	.81
PERCENT DIFF.	29.13	.11
PCNT.EXPENDED	70.87	99.89
CNSTRCTN ADMIN 21870-0-08		
CURRENT	.00	.00
JOB TO DATE	3533.50	32545.87
ESTIMATE	2604.00	30000.00
DIFFERENCE	929.50-	2545.87-
PERCENT DIFF.	35.70-	8.49-
PCNT.EXPENDED	135.70	108.49
FLD CNSTRC ADM 21870-0-09		
CURRENT	.00	.00
JOB TO DATE	600.00	5725.44
ESTIMATE	556.00	6000.00
DIFFERENCE	44.00-	274.56
PERCENT DIFF.	7.91-	4.58
PCNT.EXPENDED	107.91	95.42
MODEL 21870-0-11		
CURRENT	.00	.00
JOB TO DATE	.00	.00
ESTIMATE	97.00	500.00
DIFFERENCE	97.00	500.00
PERCENT DIFF.	100.00	100.00
PCNT.EXPENDED		
21870-0-**		
CURRENT	.00	.00
JOB TO DATE	9087.00	82209.54
ESTIMATE	8516.00	90500.00
DIFFERENCE	571.00-	8290.46
PERCENT DIFF.	6.71-	9.16
PCNT.EXPENDED	106.71	90.84

making and checking the reports. It enables us to set realistic goals and reward those who strive to reach them. It also leaves my partners free to design and manage the work of the firm without getting involved in day-to-day financial management. Because we are frank with our employees—holding regular meetings with key personnel to show them where the firm is going—they see the value of these systems, and know that profits made on their jobs are not going to turn into someone else's losses.

When our project management system was initiated, the Eggers Group had been experiencing unwarranted losses on several projects that totaled as much as $100,000 a year, or 1.5 percent of earnings, simply because of sloppy management. Using the new system, we have found that both income and profits have increased substantially over the last few years, even though we have hired only two new employees. When my partner Bern Kurtz heard this he said, "Find me those two people, Frank, I want to hire more like them."

Myths and Truths about Compensation

Weld Coxe

Ｈow many architects believe these myths: (a) that architecture is not a remunerative profession? (b) that the only way architects can hope to be economically successful is to run their practices like a business? Both are false—by a wide margin.

The facts are that a great many architects are earning compensation more than adequate to maintain highly satisfactory professional lifestyles. And a great many architectural firms are doing more than well enough to finance their growth and evolution while paying their top people very well, all without having to compromise their architectural standards in favor of inappropriate business values.

These are facts. Convincing the profession they are so is an entirely different matter.

Ever since the first studies of architectural firm profitability were published in the mid-1960s, the profession has been bombarded year after year by statistics that reveal low average profitability. The original studies pegged average architectural firm profitability at 5-7 percent and average principal compensation at less than half the compensation of lawyers, doctors, and other leading professions. The most recent Financial Statistics Survey published by *Professional Services Management Journal* reports average pretax, prebonus profit of architectural and engineering firms at 6.05 percent. Published reports lamented that most of the averages were worse than the totals given a year or two earlier.

All the data are true—as far as averages go. The problem is that over the last two decades the constant repetition of these figures has made it almost an article of faith in architectural circles that the profession is poor and unrewarded. The litany has become so pervasive that many of those who do well feel almost guilty and are inclined to keep their success to themselves. Perhaps worst of all, word of the dark economic picture is trumpeted loudest in the architectural schools, producing class after class of entry-level professionals who have no confidence in the economic future of their careers.

The Statistics Reexamined

It is time to look at the other, sunnier side of the coin. A deeper examination of the same statistics makes it abundantly clear that many architects and architectural firms are doing quite well. Table A, drawn from the same *PSMJ* Financial Statistics Survey, shows that the upper 25 percent of architectural firms report pretax, prebonus profits of 14.49

The same statistics make it abundantly clear that many architects and architectural firms are doing quite well.

Table A
Firm Profitability (Pre-bonus Pre-tax Profit on Net Revenue)

All Architects and Engineers	6.05%
Top 25% of Architects and Engineers	12.72%
Top 25% of Architects Only	14.49%
Top 10% of Architects and Engineers	19.21%
Top 10% of Architects Only	22.19%

Source: PSMJ Financial Statistics Survey

Table B
Compensation (Of Proprietor, Managing Principal or President)

	Base Salary	Bonus	Combined*
Top 25% A & E	86,000	26,500	115,000
Top 10% A & E	120,000	50,000	160,000
Top 25% A's only	75,000	26,900	99,480
Top 10% A's only	100,000	40,000	134,500

*Do not total due to statistical averaging
Source: PSMJ Financial Statistics Survey

The real key to success of financially successful firms: they expect to do well.

percent—more than double the average. Profitability of the top 10 percent is 22.195! In both these percentile groups the architectural firms are out-performing engineering firms, despite the widely held belief that engineers are more businesslike than architects.

Table B compares similar data for the top principals in firms. Instead of the widely reported average salary and bonus of about $60,000, the top 25 percent of architect principals take home just short of $100,000, and the top 10 percent report earnings of $134,500. Neither of these figures takes into account the accruing value of the principals' equity in their firms, or substantial contributions to pension plans and other perquisites.

Practice and Business Defined

How are these results achieved? Is it, as the MBAs would have us believe, only those firms that are most "businesslike" that do well? In order to answer this question it is first necessary to look at the difference between "practice" and "business."

"Business," as defined by Webster, is '…a commercial or mercantile activity customarily engaged in as a means of livelihood'. "Practice," on the other hand, is defined as 'the carrying on or exercise of a profession or occupation….To follow a profession as a way of life'.

In this light, it becomes clear that while some architects may give first priority to their need for "a means of livelihood," the great majority are dedicated to architecture as "a way of life." What needs to be recognized is that dedication to architecture does not mean that one cannot be rewarded for it.

If one were to conduct a survey of all the firms that have won national, state, and local AIA (or *Progressive Architecture*) design awards over the past ten years, it would undoubtedly prove that the great majority of the award-winning firms are also in the upper 25th percentile in financial performance. (It is also probable that many of the remainder may be among those with the worst financial performance.) But the conclusion of such a study would be inescapable: good firms, doing good work, can also do very well.

The question is: do those firms that provide "good" service and produce "good" work have to put their practices into strict business envelopes in order to do well financially? Not at all. Business skills help, but they are by no means the key to success. Put another way: all the business practices in the world will not help an average, mediocre firm do better architecture, and unless a firm does good work it will not for long do well monetarily.

What the profession needs to focus on—and teach students—is not business per se but a new definition of "good" architectural practice, based on what is being demonstrated every day by the firms that are doing well. That would take a book to describe in full, but if the book had twenty chapters, only one or two would need to focus on the purely business aspects of practice.

The other eighteen chapters would deal with the characteristics of the good, successful firms that are often lacking in those firms that do poorly, including:

• A superior ability to communicate with clients, understand and relate to their needs, and design buildings that respond to those needs, while also achieving and maintaining excellent architecture.

• A superior understanding of their own architectural process—how a job is carried through from beginning to end—and a belief that process is every bit as important a contribution to design excellence.

• A superior ability to challenge, train, and develop their talented people so that everyone in the firm shares the understanding that good work will bring good rewards.

This is perhaps the real key to the success of financially successful firms—they expect to do well. Those firms that may do good design but don't do well financially always seem ready to prove their own point. But those firms that raise their expectations usually achieve them.

As a simple example, consider the potential impact on performance in the firm where, if goals are met, principals will receive incentive compensation equal to 100 percent of their salaries, and middle managers will receive bonuses of 50 percent of their salaries. The performance of a project designer or project manager at, say, $40,000, who is promised an incentive bonus of 50 percent of salary if profits reach 15 percent, is totally different from that of a similar $40,000 person in a firm that believes the best he or she can do is 5 percent profit and a $2,000 bonus at Christmas. This is not an example of running an architectural practice like a business. It simply illustrates that good people are likely to perform to the expectations that surround them. A principal architect with three children in college, who believes the best he or she can do is $55,000 per year, will very likely do no better.

How do firms get to pay incentive compensation of 50-100 percent of salaries? By achieving profitability of 14-15 percent or more. It is becoming clear that firms with profits no better than 6-7 percent cannot, at the same time, finance their own needs and also pay handsome salaries. Firms that achieve profitability of 14 percent or more can easily do both. It is as simple as that!

None of the above is intended to denigrate the value of good business practices in the architectural firm. They definitely help. But all the business skills in the world will not make an "average" architectural firm more successful.

The conclusion? It can be demonstrated without question that: (a) architecture can be and is in fact a fully remunerative profession for many; (b) the easiest way for architects to achieve economic success is to be good architects—in the fullest sense of the word.

End of myth.

Isn't it time to stop thinking poor and start focusing on the qualities that really produce professional success?

All the business skills in the world will not make an "average" architectural firm more successful.

Reprinted from the April 1985 issue of *Progressive Architecture*, copyright 1985 Penton/IPC.

Profit Illusions

Clare Ross

It is possible for a firm to lose money on almost every project and still show a profit. Sounds impossible? It is not impossible; in fact, it can happen and has happened in many design firms in recent years.

As long as new work continues to come in at a rate in excess of the production going out the door, you can, in fact, be inefficient, lose money on all projects, and continue to show profit as a firm on a cash basis. But, this is only an illusionary profit, or in another sense, a deferred loss coming due at some future date. It is characteristic in firms that experience rapid growth in a very short period of time. When this growth exceeds the firm's capacity to staff projects adequately with experienced people, project control is lost. This erodes quality and the major emphasis shifts to getting the work out and putting out fires.

This is a "going out of business mode" because the cyclical nature of the design profession ensures that deferred losses eventually come due. As soon as the incoming work load levels out, or begins to decline, losses that were hidden, or deferred, or covered by the cash flow of growth, go right to the bottom line and can spell disaster for the firm. It is still necessary to be charging time to complete those bankrupt projects while there are no remaining fee dollars to be billed to the project. This means that you must absorb the direct and indirect costs without being able to recoup by billing to the client.

As soon as the incoming workload levels out, losses that were hidden can spell disaster for the firm.

In addition, you are locked in contractually and must complete the job, but financially, you can't afford to. If you try to reduce your direct labor line to improve financial profitability, it can further aggravate your ability to complete the job. The cycle goes on and on.

Sound like a "Catch 22"? It can be, but it doesn't have to be. Let's take a look at how to work out of this kind of a problem, and better still, how to prevent it from happening in the first place.

Bankrupt Projects

The immediate problem is establishing a program to work out from under the current bankrupt projects, minimizing the losses on those projects, and protecting the newer projects from the same fate.

1. Ensure accountability by tying the project manager's job security, growth, and equity participation to each project performance both financially and technically. The next step is then to measure each project manager's performance, holding each accountable and isolating any basic reasons for nonperformance. Nonperformance resulting from

nonaccountability can be rectified by instituting regular review criteria, timetables, and guidelines by top management. But, if the project manager does not have the necessary skills or ability to perform, the firm should either train and upgrade him or replace him. The project manager is the key to the success of any design firm and should represent the best technical and management talents of the firm.

2. Rebudget all existing over budget projects to insure satisfactory completion while minimizing the loss exposure of the firm. This budget should be translated into a project work plan outlining tasks, manpower allocations, and schedules.

3. Establish budget control mechanisms and monitor all projects on a weekly basis. Biweekly or monthly financial reports may not be timely enough at the functional level.

4. Crank up the marketing effort to generate new income. This is essential. Cash flow must be generated to cover the losing projects until you work out of the hole. This is absolutely necessary to prevent serious cash problems or reductions in the net worth of the firm.

How to Prevent It

Let's take a look at what could and should be done to prevent this kind of scenario from creeping into your firm, either in whole or in part.

1. Manage growth and be as selective as possible regarding the project size and type that you pursue. Don't exceed your staff's capacity to produce these projects. Try to gear yourself and your firm's capabilities for a digestible level of growth. When you hit the peaks, farm out the excess work to consultants or associations. Let them pick up the overflow while you use this growth to build a solidorganizational structure to meet the project demands that are happening today.

As you build your organizational structure, become more project oriented and work hard at developing strong project managers with strong project teams.

2. Get top management involved. Management must communicate to the firm that successful project performance is the key to the growth of the firm and is the central factor in the performance review of every technical employee. Not only must this be communicated, but it must be scrupulously followed through and implemented to get the message across.

3. Staff projects properly. The project manager is the key to your success. Have only strong project managers and department heads. This can be done by improving skills through training, upgrading, and careful hiring practices. The project manager is the one person who makes it all happen. If the PM is weak, the team is weak, and the project and client will suffer. Develop strong project managers. Give them authority and hold them accountable.

4. Develop a responsive management information system for projects and use this tool to measure the PM/team performance on a regular basis. Regular project budget information is essential for the PMs and their teams to stay on top of the project.

The project manager is the key to the success of any design firm.

Competitive Pricing

Even though we may not agree with it, competitive pricing of professional services is already with us and there is no doubt that it will become much more prevalent in the future. The tide of consumerism and antibusiness public opinion is simply too strong for NSPE, AIA, or any of the other professional societies to overturn. The NSPE case is a laudable effort to uphold the principle of professionalism, but the only one that will probably benefit from all the effort is the law firm that is getting $200,000 a year to defend the case.

We are not talking about clients selecting professionals by opening sealed envelopes and taking the lowest bid. Though some misguided clients will do this, the more usual form of competitive pricing will be to select three or four firms that are equally qualified to do a project and then ask each to submit a detailed scope of services and fee estimate. The selection will not be made solely on the basis of lowest fee, but fee will definitely play an important part in who is selected.

Many public clients, particularly from the large federal agencies, believe that a lower price for professional services does not always mean lower quality, nor does higher price necessarily mean higher quality. A lower fee could simply mean that the firm is better managed by using its staff more effectively and by eliminating the frills in its overhead. In their opinion many firms hide behind the no-fee-competition curtain, not for professional reasons, but because they are poorly managed.

Competing on Quality

Whether or not you agree with competitive pricing, you should have a strategy to respond to it. If you do not want to submit price information for a project in competition with others, there are a few things you should do beforehand.

The primary thing is to create a desire among clients to select you solely on the basis of your quality of service. This presupposes your selection of the type of work and client that can and does choose for quality alone. Normally very specialized, high-value-added work for private clients falls into this category (corporate headquarters, complex HVAC systems, etc.). Such project types as elementary schools and sewer-main design are not in this category.

The key sales pitch to this type of client is the benefit that you and only you can provide him. Naturally this benefit has to be what he really wants and you have to be able to actually provide it. In addition you have to

Professional Services Management Journal

Many public clients believe that a lower price for professional services does not always mean lower quality.

have an excellent track record and high-quality (and probably highly paid) people. Finally, just because you do not compete on a price basis does not mean you do not have to watch your costs; there are limits to what a client will pay, even for the greatest expert in the world.

Competing on Price

What if you decide to compete on the basis of price? First, this does not mean you start submitting sealed bids for every project that comes down. Stay away from sealed bids altogether because there is no way everyone can be bidding on the same scope of services. Instead always tie your fee estimate to a very specific scope of services which you write yourself.

Always tie your fee estimate to a very specific scope of services which you write yourself.

Next, it is especially important in price-competitive work to stick with what you are good at. Remember, the idea is to come out with something left over at the end and this seldom happens when you are using the project for on-the-job training. So carefully select the projects you go for.

Price competition will mean changes to your internal management. Contrary to popular opinion, you will need more experienced (rather than less experienced) people who can do the work the first time with less wheel spinning. Your overhead costs will have to be kept down by making sure your people are chargeable more of the time, by eliminating the frills such as individual secretaries for each executive, and by fine tuning your marketing program so that you are not wasting money chasing rainbows.

Finally, your project management will have to improve. A good place to start is with the client by making sure he does his share to make the project run smoothly and efficiently. This is much easier to do where you have gotten the project on a price-competitive basis. Your project manager and the firm's project management controls will both have to be very efficient to make sure no wasteful tangents are pursued and that any deviation from plan is immediately detected and corrected.

Professional Fee Estimating

Charles A. Parthum

Let's briefly look at the methods of fee payment before we discuss fee estimating, because a knowledge of how a firm is to be paid may well determine the detail the firm will have to go into to estimate a fee that returns to the firm the cost for doing the work plus a reasonable profit.

1. Per diem fee. Per diem fees, familiar to all of us, are simply dollar amounts per day for the different grades of individuals working on the job. Per diem fees (which include on a daily basis the unit measure of all costs plus profit) are used in many types of professional work where the scope of work cannot be well defined. Report work, investigative work, or preliminary design work may be done on a per diem basis, often with an upper limit. If an upper limit is required, the firm uses its experience and judgment and track record on previous similar undertakings to determine a reasonable upper limit, keeping in mind that whether or not the upper limit is high enough, the firm will have to do a complete job or run the risk of losing its client and perhaps even its reputation. A per diem type of arrangement should be flexible enough so that, if halfway through an investigation other aspects should be investigated or more emphasis put on other parts of the study, it can be equitably done. If a special project, such as expert testimony, will involve senior people in a firm, per diem fees are sometimes higher than standard because the people involved are "tied up" and their normal duties are interfered with.

2. Multiple of salary fee. In many ways, this type of fee is the same (and equals) a per diem fee except that instead of spelling out a certain dollar amount per day per grade, a multiplier of basic wages (or salary cost plus a multiplier of salary cost) is indicated. This method is more flexible because increases in wages and fringe benefits are automatically passed on to the client (as long as the upper limit, if there is one, is not exceeded).

3. Cost Plus a fixed fee and cost plus a percentage fee. These two types of fees are similar and are the sum of salary costs, normal overhead, and various reimbursables, plus a fixed fee for profit in the one instance or plus a percentage of cost for profit in the other. When a cost plus a fixed fee or a cost plus a percentage is used as the basis of compensation, reimbursable costs must be carefully defined in advance so that there is no misunderstanding about whether these are additional costs for which the client should reimburse the firm, with or without a separate markup, or whether they are considered to be included in the normal overhead.

The agreed upon fee should return to the firm the costs of doing the work plus a reasonable profit.

4. Lump sum. Where the scope of work can be well defined, and the client and A/E agree, this method of payment is sometimes used. It provides both parties a definite figure at the beginning of the work.

Costs of Doing the Work

As stated above, the agreed upon fee for providing professional services should return to the firm the costs of doing the work plus a reasonable profit. What are included in the costs of doing the work?

1. Salary cost. One of the most important costs is the basic wage that is paid the employee. In addition to the basic wage, what is known as salary burden or fringes becomes a cost to the firm. The salary burden includes the employee's salary when he is sick, on vacation, and holidays, plus unemployment insurance costs, excise (or franchise taxes) and payroll taxes, contributions for social security, workmen's compensation insurance, and such fringe benefits as retirement and pension plan coverage, and medical and other insurance benefits. As a percentage of direct wages paid, salary burden may range up to 30 percent or more. Basic wages plus salary burden equals what is commonly known as salary cost or direct personnel expense.

Other costs in addition to salary cost that apply to a professional firm include the various overhead costs and consist of physical plant costs, support costs, professional costs, business development costs, and miscellaneous costs.

2. Physical plant costs. The cost of maintaining an office, whether it be a rented office in the downtown part of a city or a building which the firm owns in the suburbs, is a physical plant cost. The cost of the office includes rent, heat, light, telephone, air conditioning, maintenance, insurance, and other applicable costs.

3. Support costs. Professional offices usually have secretaries, typists, telephone operators, administrative and personnel people, a library, and a librarian. Many now also have computers. All the above plus professional liability insurance, office and drafting supplies, printing, legal and audit work, furniture, laboratory, employment advertising, interest, transportation, subscriptions, etc., can be described as essential support costs.

Firms must have enough reserve to absorb losses and to pay for unexpected expenses.

4. Professional costs. The cost of keeping up with the profession is also a cost which the firm must recognize if it is to grow. These costs vary with the firm, but include such items as the payment of professional dues, preparing articles for publication, and the cost of sending people to committee and society meetings, including the cost of the man-days as well as the expenses of travel and attendance at such functions. The cost of the man-days that the firm gives up by sending people to various meetings, plus the expenses, are costs that must be figured in the professional overhead if the firm is to have an accurate idea of how much it takes to stay in business.

5. Business development costs. The coost of travel, man-days, printing, consulting, meetings, investigations, etc., necessary to prepare technical submittals for new or prospective work is a real cost whether or

not the prospective job is obtained. Also, small services to long-time clients are often done when needed, regardless of whether funds are available for payment at that time, because professional firms frequently feel they have a professional obligation to keep their clients advised of what or what not to do.

6. Miscellaneous costs. Not all jobs, unfortunately, make money. Firms must have enough reserve to absorb losses and to pay for unexpected expenses and for such items as Christmas parties, employee outings, and a host of other miscellaneous costs not already mentioned.

All of the above costs, obviously, must be paid by the firm regardless of whether all its people are working full-time on jobs (in which case all the basic wages paid can be classed as billable wages), or whether some employees are administrators, etc., or are marking time or tying up loose ends on jobs (in which case their wages are not billable). Simply stated, all costs (and profit) must be applied and received from projects for which wages are paid for productive (billable or chargeable) time.

The overhead costs described above may add up to 130 percent or more of billable wages paid. In other words, the overhead costs may run more than the actual billable wages paid. This is perhaps a bit difficult to understand, but it is so, and it is one of the facts that clients may not readily appreciate.

If all of the above costs (plus a reasonable profit) for the firm over a period of time, say a year, are divided by the billable wages paid out over the same period of time, the firm can determine the multiplier of basic wages (billable) that must be realized in order to stay in business. It's not unusual for this multiplier to approach or exceed 3.0.

Smaller firms with less overhead may be able to make a reasonable profit at less than a 2.0 markup. Many larger firms with more fixed costs (the fact that a firm has more fixed costs doesn't mean it is more inefficient; on the contrary, the firm may be spending more to improve itself in the field) may require that the fee be more than three times basic wages.

This is one reason why professionals should not bid competitively on the basis of cost for projects. A cost may be obtained from a firm that is not proficient in the work expected to be done, mainly because it has not spent the money necessary to keep itself, its employees, or its office abreast of the developments in the profession. What any client wants is the best work done; the client should therefore select a professional firm on the basis of experience, qualifications, and reputation, and then negotiate a reasonable scope of work and fee. Obviously, a professional firm must have an adequate financial accounting system in order to know where and what its costs are and how to apply them.

Fee Estimating
Fee estimating for any project then is dependent on the professional who is experienced in the types of alternative solutions possible in the work to be estimated, knowledgeable as to the capacity of and availability of his individual personnel, and aware of what hidden problems arose on similar jobs in the past. The various parts of the project, if it is a design

Overhead costs may add up to 130 percent or more of billable wages paid.

project, should be estimated by the teams or disciplines involved, and by outside consultants if their services are to be utilized.

Arriving at a confident fee estimate "simply" results from an estimate of man-hours or man-days, multiplied by the costs per unit, adding other costs peculiar to the project, adding the profit, plus a contingency for unknowns and to cover the firm's experience or impression of client involvement or requirements. The length of the job and the fee should usually be tied to a completion time so any delays beyond the firm's control will allow for renegotiation if costs increase; possible escalation in costs and wages must be considered also.

Because professional service is a labor intensive business and the major cost element in a fee is labor cost, it is critical that the labor estimates be as reliable as possible.

Estimates of labor effort can be developed by two approaches. One approach, which I will refer to as the rational approach, involves defining the scope of the project in sufficient detail to identify each task to be accomplished by type of talent (e.g., selection of pump characteristics requires two man-days of Grade III engineer at $xx direct cost per man-day). A buildup of the cost by the rational approach can result in additional information besides the fee estimate. Time sequencing of the manpower demands can contribute to the firm's understanding of projected manpower utilization.

The Parametric Approach

The second approach to estimating labor, which I will refer to as the parametric approach, can be used on repeat-type projects for which sufficient statistical cost data is available in the firm's files. For example, if the labor effort required for the design of several wastewater treatment plants is a matter of record, one finds that the man-hours of drafting work per drawing is a function of the number of drawings. Further, the total man-hours applied to the design effort will correlate with the construction cost. Over a period of several years a firm can build a very reliable parametric base.

One word of caution: the parametric base should be used only to test the reliability of the rational approach. Errors in the parameters (e.g., construction cost estimate or drawings estimates) are magnified in the labor estimates. The advantage of applying this approach is that the construction cost estimate, the drawings estimate, and the labor estimate should correlate, thus serving as a check on the three independently developed estimates.

Some firms require the prospective project personnel for the job, wherever possible, to assist in preparation of the proposed agreement and fee. In this manner, they have more involvement with the fee with which they will have to work. It also gives them experience in determining where the costs are and all of the things that might be involved.

Finally, the writing of a professional agreement is just as important as the fee. The fee should cover what the agreement says will be done. The agreement must be clear about payment not only for items directly con-

A professional firm must have an adequate financial accounting system

nected with the work, but also for necessary work to be done by others, surveying, borings, material testing, printing, etc., and should specify whether they are included in the fee or whether they are extra items that will be paid for separately, or whether the client will furnish them. That's only logical. But, if this is forgotten, the least that will happen is that relations with the client will deteriorate, and many times money will be lost. Clients are looking to the professional to guide them, to advise them, and to do all that is necessary to get the job done. There is good faith involved, and if the agreement does not spell out and make it entirely clear as to who pays for what all the way through, everyone concerned will wish it had.

It is difficult to arrive at a fair fee that returns to the professional all the costs for doing best quality work plus a reasonable profit, but it is essential.

Cost Plus Fixed Fee

O. C. Tirella

The accounting procedures of consulting engineering firms have come under criticism by federal agencies. Specific criticisms have arisen in regard to 201 and 208 Planning programs and their conduct. These programs have a number of intrinsic problems. The scope of work cannot be clearly defined and feasibility studies are hampered by the lack of legal knowledge of EPA technical personnel. Legal ramifications cause lengthy delays, and authorizations for a change order are a lengthy process. With these difficulties in mind, a cost plus fixed fee (CPFF) contract seems to be the most equitable method of compensation.

Pricing a Project

We recommend that in the overall pricing of a project, the following points should be adhered to:

1. The best engineering judgment should be utilized in determining the job classifications required to accomplish the proposed scope. Start-up labor and improvement curves should be utilized whenever applicable. Careful consideration should be given to the length of the project, and forward pricing techniques should be utilized to determine the average actual hourly rate. Based upon the cost accounting guidelines that were published in the ACEC report entitled "Uniform Cost Accounting," the actual hourly rate should be determined by dividing the annual compensation by 2,080 hours. An average for each job classification should be determined.

2. The overhead computations should include all necessary and reasonable business expenses. It is impossible for computations to adhere to cost principles outlined in the Federal Procurement Regulations because such necessary costs as interest, key-man insurance, business promotional costs, and bad debts are not allowable under these rules. When an overhead determination is made, prior history, the current year's actual overhead, and forward pricing mechanisms should be used. Government auditors generally try to utilize an optimum working condition that would result in the lowest overhead rate. A provisional overhead rate could be negotiated on a more fair and equitable basis.

3. All other direct costs charged to all clients, i.e., travel, per diem, reproduction costs, subcontracts, should be determined as accurately as possible. It should be pointed out that a per diem rate should not be used. Instead, an estimate of the actual subsistence and lodging should be made. With the escalation of costs, if the subsistence and lodging

are not estimated, the application of a standard per diem rate could result in a nonrecoupment of travel costs.

If this type of contract is employed, there should be no excess profits of any sort. The maximum profit attainable would be the 15 percent fee (assuming that the total estimated cost equalled the actual incurred cost). If the actual incurred cost, including an increase in overhead rates due to escalation, does not amount to the original estimated cost, a proportionate reduction in the fee should be employed. In essence, it would be a 15 percent fee on the total actual incurred cost up to a maximum. If the actual overhead costs and rates exceed the total estimated cost because of business conditions, the consultant would be reimbursed for the excess; however, there would be no fee factor applied to this overhead cost growth. This method would ensure that the agency received qualified services and that the consultant would be reimbursed for his cost of doing business. It would also yield a lower overall profit on that particular project. The contract should be carefully administered and any type of change in scope, no matter how minor, should be clearly identified. An equitable adjustment should be promptly made in order to compensate the engineer for work outside of the scope. Please note this would also include any change in the term of the contract.

"Buying into" a Contract

Under the normal type of CPFF contract, the contractor does not have a financial responsibility to complete the contract. The government's only direct recourse is to adjust the fee based upon the percentage of completion. This system is not to the advantage of the agency or consultant. Conceivably, there could be considerable delay in projects and contracts that will not be completed. Therefore, the agency and government should also carefully administer the contract. However, if the negotiated labor effort is insufficient to accomplish all tasks, the engineer should be compensated for these costs but should not receive a fee for it. This would encourage the engineering firm to make a careful estimate of the labor effort required. This system would also reduce the chance of any firm "buying into" a contract by underestimating their labor requirements and later demanding a contract modification.

If the scope of work is clearly defined and an agreement is made as to the level of effort, labor rates, 15 percent fee factor, and other direct costs, and assuming there was adequate cost and pricing data and forward pricing, a fixed price contract could be employed, thus placing the risk completely on the consulting engineer. Absolutely no adjustment would be made either upward or downward for the actual cost incurred versus fixed price. Again this assumes that cost and pricing were submitted and an adequate preaward audit was made. It there is a change in the scope under a fixed price contract, the same estimating techniques should be utilized in order to arrive at a fair level of compensation. These methods would properly reflect an adequate price, coupled with an incentive for qualified work.

Chargeable Ratio

*Professional
Services
Management
Journal*

Chargeable ratio (or utilization rate) is one of the most critical financial controls in a professional services firm. You are selling your time and the time of your staff and any time not sold is just poured down the drain.

You should know what your chargeable ratio was last year and what it is running right now. It is simple to compute: hours or raw payroll dollars charged directly to projects (whether billable or not) divided by the total paid hours or raw payroll dollars in the firm (excluding vacation, sick,and holiday but including paid overtime). Principals and support staff must be included in this computation.

Most firms that compute chargeable ratio as we have described say that their ratio has to be at least 65 percent in order for the firm to be profitable. However, your firm may be unique so you should compute your own break-even ratio.

There is a tremendous leverage on bottom line profit when you start improving your chargeable ratio. Management consultant Kenneth Barlow says that a firm's gross profit can be doubled or even tripled by a 10 percent improvement in utilization. Figure out the effect on your own firm by doing a pro forma income statement with your chargeable time increased by just 5 percent.

There is a tremendous leverage on bottom line profit when you start improving your chargeable ratio

Chargeable Ratio Goal

Your firm should have an overall chargeable ratio goal. Every subunit such as departments and branch offices should also have a goal. Typically a production unit such as the drafting department would have a higher goal than the rest of the firm while the accounting department would have a much lower goal.

Next, all individual employees should have their own goals. This goal should reflect the relative responsibility of the employee and it should be part of his overall evaluation. It is not possible for everyone to be 100 percent chargeable because there is always some downtime and, besides, you should be investing a certain number of hours each year to further develop each employee. One firm we know has the following chargeable ratio goals for its employee classifications:

Draftsman, 95 percent
Entering professional, 90 percent
Intermediate and senior professional, 85 percent
Project manager, 80 percent

Technical principal, 75 percent
Nontechnical principal, 25 percent
Administrative and clerical staff, 20 percent

They do not always hit these targets, but they are always trying.

Here are some suggestions on how to keep your chargeable ratio as high as possible:

1. Make sure everyone understands the importance of keeping the ratio above a certain level. Periodically post the ratio for the firm as a whole and for each subunit.

2. When principals and other administrative staff work on a project, this time should be charged to the job—whether or not they "produce" anything. Examples would include taking the client to lunch, billing the project, and typing a progress report. All of these activities are legitimate charges to the project even if the time cannot be billed. The next step is to get this time into the original fee estimate and approved by the client as billable time charges.

3. Start-up time in the morning, coffee breaks, and so forth should be charged to the major work effort that day (hopefully a project). The rationale is that this break or short downtime makes the employee more effective on that effort.

4. Lower your unit of time measure to fifteen minutes and make sure to charge the project for phone calls (just like your lawyer charges you).

Many firms do not push chargeable ratio because they say most of their work is done lump sum and therefore there is no advantage to charging every possible hour to the project. We believe this is false reasoning due to the following:

1. Each project should be fully burdened with its costs so that you can tell the winners from the losers. Projects that take an inordinate amount of administrative time (such as those for the government) should be charged their true costs.

2. As we have said before, you should be doing everything to lower your overhead rate and one of the ways to do this is to charge everything directly to projects.

Each project should be fully burdened with its costs so that you can tell the winners from the losers.

Using a Multiplier

*Professional
Services
Management
Journal*

Despite the current emphasis on CADD and other computer oriented procedures for practice, the provision of an hour of labor to clients remains the primary business of the professional service organization. Until such time as the design professions become even more computer service-oriented (as they inevitably will) any key indicators of performance will be based on labor cost statistics.

Some firms have found themselves able to successfully operate by examining two figures: effective multiplier and overhead multiplier. The assumption is that direct project costs other than labor and revenue from sources other than labor are equal. The client reimburses the firm at close to a one-to-one basis for any costs other than labor. A firm's profitability depends upon maintaining the margin between its revenue from services rendered and its total labor and overhead costs.

Effective Multiplier

Effective multiplier is calculated by dividing revenue from services rendered (revenue earned from labor only) by direct labor (the cost of labor provided to revenue-earning projects). The effective multiplier is the firm's "real" multiplier as opposed to a "standard" multiplier which may be listed as the billing rate on a schedule of fees. Comparing the real to the standard is a good way of evaluating the firm's fee discounting practices.

Overhead Multiplier

**Architects typically have
higher effective and
overhead multipliers than
engineering organizations.**

Overhead multiplier is determined by dividing the firm's total overhead (costs not assignable to specific projects) by direct labor. Overhead includes indirect labor and fringe benefits. Looking at overhead as a multiplier instead of an absolute number allows examination of overhead despite growth or other changes in a firm's operations.

Profit is analyzed as a changing percentage of direct labor, direct labor being the real resource which is "sold" to the client. The goal of any organization is to increase or at least maintain the margin between the two multipliers. Various statistical studies show typical multipliers for design firms in different markets. In most markets, as achievable effective multipliers go up, so do the overhead costs necessary to operate in those markets. It is possible to examine effective and overhead multipliers from three perspectives.

Practice. Multipliers differ statistically according to the discipline practiced. Architects typically have higher effective and overhead multipliers than engineering organizations. Multidiscipline organizations fall statistically into the middle range. This is reasonable when one considers that architectural organizations typically have higher occupancy and marketing costs than engineering firms and that architectural firms are also subject to more fluctuations in activity.

Governmental/nongovernmental. Firms which have a considerable governmental client base typically have lower overhead and lower effective multipliers. Governmental audit considerations and price examination policies stress low overhead. Increasingly, governmental units place artificial limits on an overhead multiplier which will be reimbursed. In order to maintain a margin between the multipliers, "governmental" firms need to maintain overhead expenditures below restricted levels. Price policies are a function of cost so that as overhead goes down in response to governmental requirements, so do effective multipliers.

Price/nonprice competitive. There is now a significant segment of the design services market which is price competitive. Stated another way, there are now a large number of clients for whom price is an important part of the selection process. Firms which must compete on the basis of price (i.e., submit a proposal with a lower effective multiplier) must also maintain lower overhead in order to be able to compete profitably.

Statistically, architectural firms with an entirely private client base who do not select on the basis of price have the highest effective multipliers and also the highest overhead multipliers. On the other hand, the lowest effective and overhead multipliers were found in engineering firms operating heavily in the governmental and price-competitive markets.

There are now a large number of clients for whom price is an important part of the selection process.

Calculate Your Personal Multiple

Andrew Loebelson

The multiple—the factor which relates the billable salary of each professional to the income the firm needs to satisfy the client and make a profit—may be one of the most useful tools an architecture or design firm has to plan and manage its business. The reason: correctly determining the multiple forces one to project all the aspects of running one's firm for the coming year.

You must forecast all the costs of running the business, decide on the profits you wish to aim for, and estimate the number of professional hours that will be utilized on income-producing work. The rewards for doing this successfully will be a better managed firm which can purposefully respond to the vicissitudes of the business environment.

While the multiple is most often thought of as a billing tool, it is really a planning tool. Many firms bill for their services by charging clients, say, three times the hourly wages; or perhaps two and one-half times the direct personnel expense (wages, plus fringes) expended on any project. Too often this multiple is chosen just because so many other firms are using one or another nice round number. Don't confuse that number with your actual multiple. Each firm has (or should have) a multiple based on its own unique operating characteristics. The derivation of its own true multiple allows a firm to know its actual costs for doing each and every job.

Even when billing is done by other means, such as a percentage of construction costs or furnishings, the most accurate method of figuring out true costs is by determining the number of hours of each staff member required. The proper use of the multiple in this instance correctly covers the overhead and builds in the appropriate profits.

Conversely, when you are forced to meet a fee set by other parties, divisions by your multiple will give you the maximum amount of billable time that can be spent on this project without eating into one's planned profits.

A Simple Formula for the Multiple

One determines what one's income goal is for the coming year, and divides that by the total cost to the firm of the professional time of your staff that will be available to earn that income:

$$\text{Multiple} = \frac{\text{Your income goal for the year}}{\text{Total cost of professional time}}$$

> **The "multiple" is most often thought of as a billing tool; it is really a planning tool.**

To expand those concepts slightly: your "income goal" should be the amount of money you need to earn to pay all your people their salaries and fringes, cover all overhead and sales costs, and have enough profit left over to allocate properly for benefit of the owners, the staff, and the firm.

Determining what to divide the income goal by is easier. One starts with the total of the salaries of staff whose work is billed to the client. Do not include overtime since that would be an undesirable long-term commitment. Subtract a proportion of that for unproductive or unbillable time—for design firms it is typically about 15 percent. For principles involved in sales or other unproductive services, subtract an additional percentage of their salaries appropriate to their jobs. Make sure support staff are not included unless you actually bill out their time. Now add the costs of fringe benefits for these people and divide. Fringe benefits typically total 20 to 35 percent of salaries.

Two Kinds of Multiplier

Note that there are two forms of the multiple. If one divides just by salaries, and does not include fringes, the multiple is a larger number which is applied to the salary. When one divides by the direct personnel expense the multiple is a smaller number applied to direct personnel expense. Mathematically, the two numbers result in identical fees. Example: If fringes are 20 percent and the multiple times salary is 3, the multiple times DPE (1.2) will be 2.5. A $10 salary hour times 3 equals $30. A $10 salary hour plus 20 percent fringes ($2) times 2.5 also equals $30.

The latter is probably more palatable to clients, since it is a smaller number, while the former is easier to work with in-house since it deals with the straight salary figures.

This seems more complicated than it is. Take a fictional example—a twenty-six-person design firm in the New York area called FR/SL Inc. Figure 1 is a worksheet like one that Frank Right, one of the two principals, might have used to figure out their multiple. This one sheet lays out most of the strategic planning for the year. Figures that aren't here, such as the targets of the promotional budget or the types of people to be hired later, must nevertheless have been considered in order to arrive at the budgets for those areas. As you can see, it is not all that complicated. However, there are a few points worth touching on.

1. The expected yearly costs should include all the costs one can think of. Fringes should be refigured each year and budgets should be planned for each item as temporary help, bad debts, etc. Promotion also can be roughly allocated.

2. The profit goal should not be set simply as a percentage of income. Profits should be allocated to four different groups: to federal, state, and local governments through taxes; to the employees through bonuses, profit sharing, and pension plans; to stockholders as dividends; and to the firm as retained earnings. These goals, above all, should be set well in advance.

3. Having determined the correct multiple, one needn't tell the client what it is. If this firm can round its billing multiple up to 3, more power

to it—that's $34,000 more in profit. But for use in-house, or to determine straight billing rate, the correct multiple should be used. The multiple can also be used to determine billing rate categories, e.g., project managers = $45/hr, etc. This requires averaging the salaries in each category and applying the multiple to the average hourly rate.

4. The billable direct personnel expense is simply determined and does not include overtime. Otherwise, the firm would be committed to a year in advance to work overtime just to meet its objectives. Each overtime hour adds a disproportionate amount of profit, but excess overtime will result in subtle costs—matching time off, inefficient work habits, extra fringe expenses, etc. It is best not to plan on any major amounts of overtime.

The proper use of the multiple, whether or not the client even sees it, can help a firm to bid properly, schedule realistically, and profit.

Overhead Pitfalls

Overhead controls are essential to operate a profitable design firm, whether the work is government or commercial. Forward overhead budgets are part of those controls, as is the control of and elimination of unnecessary costs.

When a cost breakdown is required on a price proposal, the overhead rate often becomes a bone of contention with the firm. Much of the controversy derives from government contract cost principles as covered by Defense Acquisition Regulation (DAR) Section 15 (formerly ASPR) and Federal Procurement Regulations (FPR) Part 15. There are also other agency cost regulations such as NASA, EPA, and DOE, which flow over into commercial work. In process is the Federal Acquisition Regulation (FAR) which will govern all other government regulations.

Government auditors are ringleaders in attempting to disallow various items of overhead. Regulations ban certain costs as unallowable on government contracts; however, auditors tend to stretch the rules in an effort to throw out as many costs as possible. There are many gray areas in the cost principles which become the battleground between the contractor, the auditor, and the firm in resolving the overhead rate. Because an auditor often misinterprets the intent of the cost principles, remember that an audit report is only advisory and can be overturned by the firm if sufficient rebuttal data are provided to the contracting officer. However, it is best to attempt to get the audit report cleaned up either via a reply to a draft audit report or at an exit conference with the auditor. A firm should not hesitate to oppose an audit finding which it thinks is wrong based on interpretation of the cost regulations. An unallowable cost is a loss of profit.

The base to which to apply the overhead expense to determine a rate sometimes becomes a dispute. Auditors like to move items from indirect to direct cost (decrease the pool and increase the base) which has a "double whammy" effect in lowering the overhead rate. They may further question the base the firm has used in an effort to reduce the rate. A firm should stand ready to defend whatever base it has proposed.

Unallowable Costs

Most of the unallowable costs cited by the regulations are in the overhead and G&A expense areas. Thus, auditors concentrate on those pools in their audits of annual rates or of contract price proposals, change orders, and claims.

The following examples of costs are often improperly questioned

Edwin P. James

A firm should not hesitate to oppose an audit finding which it thinks is wrong.

by the auditor.

Reasonableness and allocability. This catch-all phrase is based on the auditor's judgment vs. the firm's judgment. It should be opposed unless the evidence supports the auditor.

Advertising, entertainment, and donations. Although unallowable per the regulations, the auditor tends to question items beyond the scope of the wording in the regulations. Design firms should establish separate accounts for each cost and not include items that are actually allowable.

Business lunches, dinners, and meetings. The auditor likes to question these costs as entertainment. They are only unallowable if the basic purpose of the event is entertainment and not business development.

Excessive executive compensation. The Environmental Protection Agency (EPA) in particular has this item high on their priority list. The regulations under Compensation for Personal Services provide the following rebuttals to audits:

- approval by IRS;
- for services rendered and not a return of profit;
- comparison with similar companies;
- reasonable under an established policy.

Compensation surveys may be used to compare with executive compensation at similar companies. EPA's own survey may often be turned against them by averaging the top three executives and factoring their data up for an inflation factor.

Rental costs of property. The DAR has been revised to tie into the Financial Accounting Standards Board (FASB) Directive No. 13 covering leases. It requires capitalization of leases under certain circumstances, with a showing on the books of a breakdown between depreciation and interest in the lease cost. That interest is allowable as it is not interest on borrowings but interest charged by the lessor.

On rent between organizations under common control, the auditor will try to prove it is cheaper to own than to rent. A firm must assemble data to overcome this matter, including current market prices if it were to own the property. Rental costs of personal property and of real property where the lease is not capitalized are allowable if reasonable in the community.

The FPR does not tie into the FASB rule. It allows costs under short-term leasing (five years or less for real property; two years or less for personal property) if reasonable in the community.

On long-term leases, the firm must prove it is cheaper to rent than to own. The same holds true for rent between organizations under common control. The FPR allows the cost where the lessor is also the manufacturer of the personal property.

On rent between closely held companies, the auditor usually disallows interest and profit in the rental cost. Profit on profit within a company is unallowable on government contracts. One rebuttal on interest is to prove it is cheaper to rent than if the lessee (not the lessor) is the owner of the property. All government agencies now recognize facilities capital cost of money (imputed interest) as a cost. This helps offset the interest

On long-term leases, the firm must prove it is cheaper to rent than to own.

included in closely held leases if the firm cannot prove it is cheaper to rent than to own. The lease would have to be capitalized to get into the interest base.

Making Money at Design:
A Case Study

David Travers

Designers with even a solid grasp of the business end of their profession are at least uncommon.

Losing money is easy in the design fields. The ways are infinite. Designers, however, have several favorite ways of going broke: (1) not getting enough work to stay in business; (2) not charging enough for the work they do get; (3) not controlling indirect costs; and (4) not collecting what is owed to them. Any one of these can do the job. But you can go under quicker by combining any two of them.

The first, not getting enough work, translates into not marketing effectively. There are two general categories of selling: direct and indirect. Direct selling means going after jobs, knocking on doors, looking under every rock for a prospect, taking "no" as a positive response, ferreting out new business possibilities, and following them up assiduously.

Indirect selling I define as inducing the prospective client to initiate the contact. This doesn't mean that a firm can be any less aggressive promotionally than is the firm marketing itself more directly. To be successful, you must be aggressive. It's just that your promotion takes a different tack. Public relations in one of its many forms is usually the keystone of the indirect selling strategy. A client can't come to you if he doesn't know you exist.

Michael Graves, Gwathmey and Siegal, Stanley Tigerman, Eisenman, Robert Stern—you may consider them entertainers rather than successful architects, but they are extremely aggressive promotionally. You can't turn around without seeing them, their names, their work. The same has been true over the years about Kevin Roche, Pei, Saarinen, Kahn, Neutra. Those books and magazine issues on them and their work didn't happen by chance. They made them happen. Promotion—direct and indirect—is addressed in another section of this volume.

Fee collection, the accounts receivable problem, is also considered elsewhere. What will be described and explained here is a simple method of operational and financial control for a design firm which will take care of problems 2 and 3 above—if it is accepted and used. A big if. Designers with a gift for or even a solid grasp of the business end of their profession are perhaps not unknown or even rare, but they are at least uncommon. Witness the annual mortality rate among new design firms which has hovered at 70 percent for years.

Let's examine a real but disguised office, Design Associates, analyze its financial problems, and then devise a program that will make it profitable.

Design Associates: An Analysis

Design Associates, a thirteen-man Kansas City firm, had experienced a gratifying eight-year history of uninterrupted growth until last year when business leveled off with net billings of just over $700,000. During this formative period, the firm developed structurally in an ad hoc manner, organizing in response to client and project needs. But there had been no corresponding effort to organize the firm as a business, to superimpose any kind of management structure over the project-oriented organization.

This unstructured growth has resulted in a current crisis, which in many ways is a textbook case study of the evolution of a growing company, where the founders are absorbed in the selling and producing of their services and indifferent to or ignorant of management activities.

Fred, founder and owner of Design Associates, has been floundering around trying to solve the problems that paradoxically seem to be arising out of his very success, but are actually the result of the firm's lack of firm, decisive business leadership at a stage when that is precisely what is needed.

The firm has marketed itself well during the formative period. According to a survey run by a management consultant called in by Fred to help solve his problems, client satisfaction with its design and service is extraordinarily high. Fred has gathered together with some care a staff of capable and talented professionals and technicians.

Those are formidable strengths: aggressive and able marketing, design skill, technical proficiency, and a list of pleased clients. In addition, Fred has provided a fine working environment for his people and a generous and competitive wage and benefit package to keep them. Just how generous will be seen in a moment.

DA Is Losing Money Despite Its Strengths

The consultant found that despite these strengths, DA lost money last year. Indeed, the loss was so great that without the offsetting profits of a furniture dealership that Fred is operating as an adjunct to his design services, DA could quite easily have gone under.

It is interesting to note that no one in the firm, not even Fred, was aware of the extent of the losses. Indeed, the staff can be excused for believing that the firm was very profitable. It had grown in size and volume continually over the years; it owns and remodeled at considerable expense the small office building it inhabits; and it has the handsome wage and benefit package, including bonuses. All testified to a successful, profitable practice. Although suspecting that all was not as it should be, Fred himself was unaware of the rate at which design was losing money. Analysis uncovered a loss in the design practice last year of more than $185,000 (Figure 1). A contributing factor was the fact that the overhead of the furniture business was loaded onto the design practice. (The loss would have been "only" $85,000 if a fair share of the overhead had been properly allocated to furniture.)

Overhead controls are essential to a profitable design firm.

Figure 1.
1986 Income & Expense

		Without Furniture Overhead
Direct Personnel Expense (DPE)	250793	250793
Overhead	652727	553191
Total Expense	903520	803984
Net Billings	718161	718161
Net Income (Loss)	(185359)	(85823)

Oddly enough, in the face of these depressing figures, a quick analysis of 1986 DPE and Billings in the following table (Figure 2) tells a very encouraging story about the operation. The Staff Utilization Rate (the ratio between billable time and total hours) is very high at an average of 70 percent. This measure of productivity compares more than just favorably with the industry average which was 63.5 percent (this and all subsequent industry average figures are from ASPM studies), down from 1985 but still high enough to return an average profit of 3-4 percent before taxes and discretionary distributions (bonuses, pension plans, etc.)

Figure 2.
Direct Personnel Expense and Billings for 1986

Average Multiplier: 3.37

Employee	Hourly Rate	Hours Worked	DPE	Util Rate	Billing Rate	Earned Billable
Junior Draftsman	8.92	1144	10204	.55	35.00	40040
Draftsman	11.28	1681	18962	.81	50.00	84050
Draftsman	11.69	1728	20200	.83	40.00	69120
Designer	12.15	1201	14592	.58	50.00	60050
Senior Draftsman	13.13	1467	19262	.71	60.00	88020
Project Director	16.36	1321	21612	.64	60.00	79260
Senior Designer	17.23	1405	24208	.68	60.00	84300
Project Director	18.46	1821	33616	.88	55.00	100155
Project Director	18.46	2017	37234	.97	60.00	121020
Director of Design	20.51	700	14357	.61	70.00	49000
Principal	35.90	1018	36546	.49	80.00	81440
			250793	.70		856455

Actual 1986 Billings: 718161

Unbillable Because Over Contract Maximum: 138294

Figure 3.
Overhead (Fixed and Variable)

Item		Without Furniture
Rent	52261	42000
Utilities	5349	5349
Insurance	16434	16434
Office Supplies	15919	15919
Adm./Cler. Salaries	84087	37087
Duplicating	8070	3500
Telephone	14017	9000
Auto Allowance	32846	32846
Travel/Entertain.	8319	8319
Promotion		
Business Develop.	33847	33847
Public Relations	11403	11403
Dues & Subscript.	1310	1310
Legal/Acct. Fees	6731	6731
Interest	33901	33901
Payroll Taxes	30693	27316
Group Insurance	15544	12953
Bonus Plan	90966	80960
Non-Billed Labor	109316	109316
Other	81714	65000
	652727	553191
Overhead: DPE ratio	2.63	2.23

Thus Design Associates would seem to have been very efficient in manpower use with a high volume of work and a high ratio of earned billable time. One could assume from that indicator alone that DA amassed huge profits during the year. This impression is reinforced by the firm's average multiplier of 3.4 times direct, which is also high compared to the industry average of 2.77 in 1986. Further strengthening the look of high volume and profits is the 1986 billings-per-staff figure of more than $60,000 as against the design profession average of $41,415. With figures like these, how could the firm have lost money?

Lack of Financial Controls

The consultant found the problem without much trouble. The factor upsetting all of the favorable indicators was overhead. DA spent far too much in indirect expense. Where the industry average in overhead expense was 1.55 times direct expenses (up from 1.45 in 1985), DA's ratio was 2.63—2.23 with furniture's share of the overhead removed (Figure 3).

The primary cause of this departure from the norm is that there has been no serious budgeting and control of expenses. The generous bonus plan contributed heavily. Still, as Fred told his consultant, "Overhead just seems to grow."

Fred is not unusual in this respect. Designers tend to look upon client-imposed budgets as a threat to quality and a burden on creativity. Cost control is viewed with the same hostility. This attitude toward client budgeting and control often causes designers to avoid imposing their own internal budgets and controls. This is costly. As Edwin James of Arthur Andersen & Co. said, "Overhead controls are essential to operate a profitable design firm."

Lack of Project Controls

Most of what the consultant found to be true about the firm's casual attitude toward indirect costs held for design as well, that is for direct costs on projects. Although there was an attempt to estimate the number of hours it would take to complete a project, it was not done for control purposes but for pricing. Fred and his director of design would estimate the hours needed to complete a project and base the fee on the estimate. The problem was that the hours assigned to each task were arrived at without consulting those who were to perform the tasks. The project designer may or may not even have been told the number of hours allocated, but in any case there was no serious attempt to make him adhere to the estimate. All were free to set their own pace and schedule, so long as they completed the job by a date which satisfied the client.

As a result, the consultant found, actual hours exceeded the estimates on almost every job by an average of about 15 percent. The Figure 4 shows billable time compared to time actually billed. If the billable time had been billed and paid for, that is if it had not exceeded the contract maximums, the firm would have lost far less money. In fact, if furniture overhead had not been carried by design, the firm would have made a profit of some $55,000 in 1986.

Figure 4
1986 Income & Expense

	Allowed Billings	Total Billable	Total Billable Without Furniture Overhead
DPE	247989	247989	247989
Overhead	652727	652727	553191
Total Expense	900716	900716	801180
Billings	718161 (actual)	856455	856455
Net Profit (Loss)	(181565)	(43271)	55275

The consultant told Fred that he had to separate furniture dealership costs from the design practice costs and institute project controls immediately. As an interim step, while a control system was being developed, he recommended that budgeted hours for each current job be reviewed with the project manager and the project designer. If they don't accept the estimates made by management, then compromise budgets must be developed that are acceptable. It is essential that the people performing the project tasks feel that it is their budget. Only then will they feel a commitment to it and make the effort to hold to it.

According to the consultant, it is precisely this commitment that has been lacking, not because the staff was uncooperative or incapable but because project personnel had not participated in the planning of the project and the hours estimated were either unrealistic or considered so. Secondly, there was no real effort by Fred to foster adherence to the estimates.

To remedy this feckless attitude, the consultant recommended that Fred manifest his concern openly by checking frequently on the progress of a job. In addition, the manager of a project was to check all timecards and initial the hours charged to his project, and the director of design was told to check them to make certain that they had been signed off by the project managers.

At Fred's request the consultant set about preparing a financial plan which would include

1. a reduced overhead budget for 1987 with no furniture business load, budgeted overhead accounts, and a monitoring and control system;

2. project controls and a system for monitoring and controlling schedule and expenses;

3. realistic profit targets.

Because it is difficult to improve on a report that is already concisely and effectively written, the rest of this piece is taken directly from the report and program the consultant designed for Fred and Design Associates.

The Financial Plan

Corporate Objectives

Since all else in planning for the future of a design practice derives from what it wants to achieve, where it wants to go, the first step is to formulate a set of clear, well-defined goals and objectives. We here offer several, some of which were voiced in one form or another by management during the course of our study.

1. Earn pretax profit of 8-10 percent of net billings.

Ordinarily this objective would not be placed at the top of the list for a professional design firm, but Design Associates needs to put an immediate stop to the losses incurred last year and presumably in previous years which were covered by furniture sales profits.

Strategy: Institute financial planning, budgeting, and controls in all areas of the operation.

2. Effect controlled growth over the next three years
    a. Increase billings to $1 million in 1987 and $1.5 million by 1990;
    b. Increase staff to twenty-five.
Strategy: Prepare and implement a marketing plan.

3. Do interesting, challenging, and profitable work and be able to turn down the opposite kinds.

Strategy: Pursue work selectively as far as is permitted objective 2, which is to grow.

4. Attract and keep the highest caliber staff.

Strategy: (a) Achieve the first three objectives so as to be able to pay top wages and offer interesting work; (b) institute an effective employee relations program.

While it is our only task to deal with the first two of these objectives by creating a sound business plan, we urge DA management not to neglect the others. We would be remiss if we didn't point out the particular need for a marketing plan. Although the office seems to have sufficient work in hand to satisfy its billing target for the year, there is still next year—and the years beyond. It is fruitless to prepare a business plan without at the same time developing a marketing plan to support it. An automobile without fuel might be an appropriate simile.

It is fruitless to prepare a business plan without at the same time developing a marketing plan to support it.

Income Projection

Based upon the information provided by management about jobs under contract (shown in Figure 5 as having 100 percent probability) and others with a high probability of coming under contract, we can project with some confidence that the 1987 billing target of $1 million will be achieved.

Figure 5
Projected Billings

Project Name	Total Est. Fee	Percent Probable	Portion to be Billed This Year	Projected This Year
Bank Building 1	45000	100	45000	45000
Industrial Building 1	60000	90	60000	54000
Office Building 1	75000	100	75000	75000
Office Building 2	50000	100	50000	50000
Bank Building 2				
Space Planning	155000	100	150000	150000
Design	200000	100	200000	200000
Drawings	100000	100	50000	50000
Office Building 3	60000	50	30000	15000
Savings & Loan	200000	100	100000	100000
Univ. Admin. Bldg.	130000	50	50000	25000
Manufacturing Cntr.	1400000	75	300000	225000
Miscellaneous	75000	100	50000	50000
Total Projected Billings:				1044000

The total exceeds the target, which means that if all goes as expected, there will be no need to capture additional work during the year. Although it is our experience that some jobs are inevitably delayed, some even abandoned, DA management is confident that other work is sure to materialize. Based on the firm's history, we concur.

Profit Objective

The profit objective of 8 to 10 percent of net billings is a reasonable one—if the projects under contract were correctly estimated and negotiated. The losses suffered by the design practice in previous years are attributable to lack of planning, budgeting, and control of the firm as a whole and of individual projects. If the control systems which are the heart of this submittal are conscientiously used, the pretax profit objective is quite feasible.

Operational Budgets

1. Direct Personnel Expense (DPE)

Like the above projections, our estimates of 1987 DPE and Billing Targets (shown below with 1986 DPE for comparison, Figure 6) are conservative and realistic. As are the overhead figures which follow. Both are based upon 1986 actual figures modified by DA's accounting department estimates, including two new employees already on board and a third expected to be hired this year. Last year was a nongrowth year for DA, so basing this year's estimates on 1986 is conservative. The projected figures have been made even more reasonable by being brought into line with the national averages. For example, the Staff Utilization Rate, which is the ratio of DPE to Total Technical Salaries, is 68 percent in our projection, less than the 70 percent attained by DA last year. The national average in 1986 was 63.5 percent, which is well below the projection, but DA has more work under contract already in 1987 than in all of 1986 and scored well above the national average, both indicating that the numbers in the DPE table are reasonable. Note also that the multiplier (discussed in more detail below) required to return the billing target is only 3.0 times DPE, which is lower than the 3.37 averaged by the firm last year.

In computing the DPE and billing figures, we have allowed for a new construction man in addition to the two new people hired the first of this year. The construction man is factored in for the last six months of the year (Figure 6).

2. Overhead

We have prepared two alternative overhead budgets for 1987 (Figure 7). One contains no bonus plan contribution; the other has a contribution of $52,000. Below the table the overhead total is shown as a percent of DPE. This is a ratio carefully watched by many firms as an indicator of efficiency and prudence, or the lack thereof. The industry average for this ratio last year was 1.55, extremely high. Design Associates' ratio was even higher at 2.23 (with furniture overhead burden removed; see Figure 1).

With the help of DA's accounting person, we have been able to reduce overhead targets to 1.80 with the bonus contribution included and 1.63 with no bonus. Both of these are high and a strong effort should be made to reduce the level of spending in 1987 or to increase DPE and billings...or both.

If billings hold as targeted, then the budgeted DPE and multiplier will return the profit objective and permit the bonus plan contribution. If billings falter, then DA can shift to the no-contribution alternative. The break-even analysis set forth later in this plan illustrates the use of these alternative overhead budgets.

Note that we have tried to remove all trace of the furniture operation from the design practice overhead.

Multiplier

DA's multiplier in 1986 exceeded the industry average by a considerable amount—3.37 times DPE as compared to 2.77. The targeted multiplier we have used in this plan is 3.0. It should make the firm more competitive yet still return the desired profit.

The formula for establishing the multiplier is simply stated:

$$\frac{DPE + Overhead + Profit\ Objective}{DPE} = Multiplier$$

Figure 6
1987 Direct Personnel Expense and Billing Targets

Employee	Hourly Rate	Hours Worked	DPE	Util Rate	Billing Rate	Billing Target
Junior Draftsman	9.00	1560	14040	.75	30.00	46800
Draftsman	11.25	1560	17550	.75	35.00	54600
Draftsman	12.50	1560	19500	.75	35.00	54600
Designer	12.50	1460	18250	.70	35.00	51100
Senior Draftsman	13.00	1460	18980	.70	40.00	58400
Senior Draftsman	13.50	1460	19710	.70	40.00	58400
Senior Designer	16.50	1460	24090	.70	50.00	73000
*Construction Supervisor	17.00	780	13260	.75	50.00	39000
Project Director	17.50	1460	25550	.70	55.00	80300
Project Director	18.00	1460	26280	.70	55.00	80300
Project Director	18.50	1460	27010	.70	55.00	80300
Project Director	18.50	1460	27010	.70	55.00	80300
Director of Design	21.00	1375	28875	.61	65.00	89375
Department Head	21.00	1375	28875	.66	65.00	89375
Principal	35.00	700	24500	.34	100.00	70000
			321328	.68		1055850

*For six months only

Average Multiplier: 3.00
Average Utilization Rate: 68%

Comparable figures for 1986 (see Fig. 2) were DPE: $250,328; Utilization Rate: 70 percent; Billable: $856,455; Multiplier: 3.37

The figures for DPE, overhead, and profit are inserted in the equation to arrive at the multiplier which is then multiplied times the hourly wages of the technical staff and rounded off. These then become the billing rates. We have modified only slightly the rates DA has been using, down to an average of 3.0 as compared with last year's 3.37. Here again we have followed conservative and accepted practice: working with DA's existing conditions modified by the norms of the industry.

$$\frac{321328(\text{DPE}) + 5248506(\text{OH}) + 105585\ (10\%\ \text{Profit})}{321328(\text{DPE})} = 3.00\ (2.96)$$

We have followed conservative and accepted practice: working with DA's existing conditions modified by the norms of the industry.

Figure 7.
Overhead Targets for 1987

Item	Last Year	Target This Year No Bonus	Target This Year With Bonus
Adm./Clerical Salaries	37087	34000	34000
Amortization/Depreciation	15170	20500	20500
Auto Allowance	32846	39500	39500
Bonus Plan[1]	80960	0	52000
Contributions	296	400	400
Dues & Subscriptions	1310	1000	1000
Duplicating	3500	3000	3000
Group Insurance[2]	14554	19000	19000
Insurance	16434	16000	16000
Interest	33901	10000	10000
Legal/Accounting Fees	6731	14000	14000
Maintenance/Repairs	4810	6500	6500
Miscellaneous	222	300	300
Non-Billed Labor[2]	109316	130000	130000
Office Supplies	15919	11000	11000
Outside Services	38850	52500	52500
Payroll Taxes[2]	30693	40000	40000
Postage	1400	2000	2000
Promotion[3]	45250	50500	50500
Rent	42000	47000	47000
Security	481	650	650
Tax/Licenses	3700	5000	5000
Telephone	9000	8000	8000
Travel & Entertainment	8319	9000	9000
Utilities	5349	5000	5000
	558098	524850	576850
Overhead: DPE ratio	2.25	1.63	1.80

1. Adjusted for no bonus and reduced bonus this year.
2. Adjusted for two new people recently hired and the first six months of a new construction supervisor during this year.
3. Promotion has been given a budget of 5 percent of Billing Target, including 50 percent of the principal's non-billable time.

The multiplier should be refigured from time to time, inserting actual figures as they become available during the year. The multiplier can be changed at any time to meet changing conditions, e.g., lowering it on a particular job to be more price competitive. But profit will be directly affected.

Break-even Analysis

A break-even analysis is more than a method for determining a firm's theoretical break-even point. It is also a management tool which can demonstrate graphically the probable effects of future events, assisting management to control profit and loss and to be flexible, adaptable, and fast on its feet when external conditions require it...which is most of the time.

Important to the break-even analysis concept is the fact that all expenses do not change at the same rate or proportion to billing volume. They range from those which increase or decrease in direct relationship to

Figure 8
Break Even Analysis—Current Year Without Profit

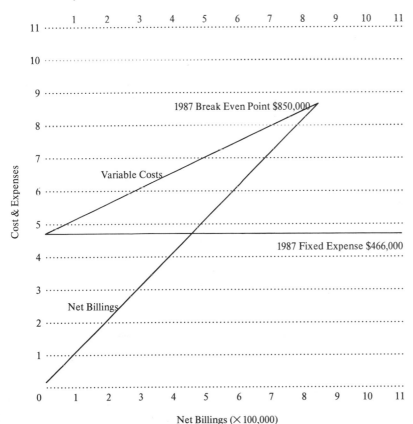

1987 Break Even Targets:

Net Billings	850000	100%
Variable Costs (incl. DPE @ 38%)	384000	45%
Margin Contribution	466000	55%
Fixed Costs	466000	55%
Net Profit	-0-	-0-

billings (e.g., DPE) to those expenses which are fixed and do not change at all with fluctuations in billings (e.g., rent, depreciation). There are some which contain both variable and fixed elements (e.g., DPE's share of fringe benefits).

We analyzed DA's 1986 overhead to develop fixed and variable cost data, and the accompanying break-even analysis for 1987 is based upon this data (Figure 8). The study period covered is not as long as one would like, but any inaccuracies should be insignificant.

We used DPE costs equal to 38 percent of net billings with 7 percent added as the direct portion of DPE (vacation, sick leave, payroll tax, etc.). In 1986 the actual figures were 35 percent and 6.2 percent. Variations in overhead and DPE account for the difference. Any deviation from the ratio of DPE to billings will directly affect the break-even volume. If the factor increases, so does the break-even point.

Margin contribution is the key to profitability. It is the difference between net billings and the total of variable costs and expenses. The

Figure 9
Break Even Analysis—Current Year With Profit Forecast

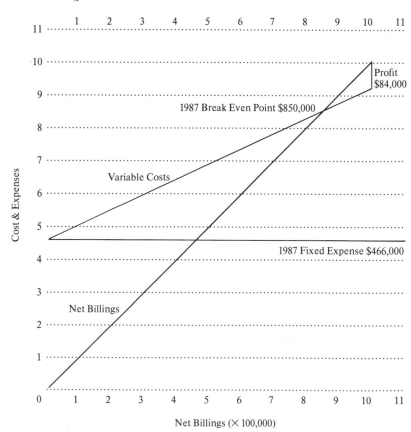

Profit Forecast at $1 Million Billings:

Net Billings	1000000	100%
Variable Costs (incl. DPE @ 38%)	450000	45%
Margin Contribution	550000	55%
Fixed Costs	466000	46.6%
Net Profit	84000	8.4%
Retirement Contribution	52000	5.2%
Net Net Profit	32000	3.2%

largest element of variable cost is DPE. Using the mentioned DPE to billings ratio of 38 percent, the margin contribution and variable cost percentages compute as follows:

Net Billings	100%	
Direct Labor (DPE)		38%
Indirect Portion of DPE	7%	
Total Variable Costs	45%	45%
Margin Contribution		55%

DA's fixed costs in 1987 should be, in round numbers, $466,000. With a margin contribution of 55 percent, the firm needs about $850,000 in net billings to break even. At this break-even volume, no bonuses would be paid. Such discretionary distributions as pension plans and bonuses should come out of profits as shown in the break-even analysis with projected net billings of $1 million (Figure 9).

Figure 10
Break Even Analysis—Last Year

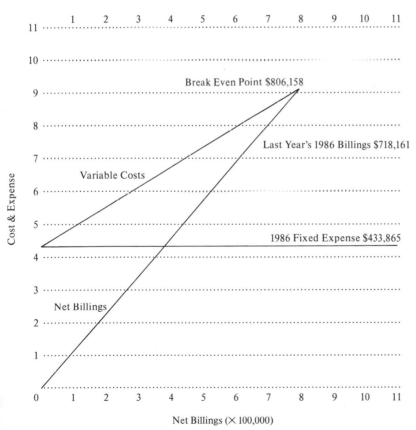

Cost & Expense

Break Even Point $806,158

Variable Costs

Last Year's 1986 Billings $718,161

1986 Fixed Expense $433,865

Net Billings

Net Billings (× 100,000)

1986 Break Even Analysis:

Net Billings	718161	100%
Variable Costs (incl. DPE @ 35%)	291333	41%
Margin Contribution	426828	59%
Fixed Costs	433865	60%
Net Profit	−7037	−1%
Retirement Contribution	−80960	−11%
Net Net	−87997	−12%

Since fixed costs are basically constant, the concept is that they must first be recovered by the margin contribution portion of net billings before there can be a profit. After they are recovered, the firm will make a profit of 55 percent on all subsequent billings—if the DPE ratio of 38 percent holds.

Herein lies one of the major values of the break-even exercise. If DPE begins to increase in relation to billings, as would happen if billings fell below projections, then the proportion can be rebalanced by reducing DPE through more efficient production and/or layoffs.

Using fixed costs and a target margin contribution, we can forecast the net profit for any volume of net billings. Figure 9 shows a break-even model based on projected billings of $1 million and a bonus plan of $52,000. The net profit is within the Financial Plan objective of 8-10 percent of net billings. The bonus plan contribution will reduce this to a net net profit of about $32,000.

Controls

We have developed several monitoring and control forms and systems to help DA management guide the firm to its targets and objectives. The first three monitoring systems—for overhead expense, nonchargeable labor expense, and billings—are self-explanatory. To know where you

Figure 11
Overhead Expense for (Month)

Item	Monthly Budget	This Month	Year To Date	Same Period Last Year	Over/Under Budget
Adm./Clerical Salaries	2833				
Amortization/Depreciation	1708				
Auto Allowance	3292				
Contributions	33				
Dues & Subscriptions	83				
Duplicating	250				
Group Insurance	1583				
Insurance	1333				
Interest	833				
Legal/Accounting Fees	1167				
Maintenance/Repairs	542				
Miscellaneous	25				
Non-Billed Labor	10833				
Office Supplies	917				
Outside Services	4375				
Payroll Taxes	3333				
Postage	167				
Promotion	4958				
Rent	3917				
Security	54				
Tax/License	417				
Telephone	667				
Utilities	417				
	43737				

are, you need to be able to compare budgeted figures with what is actually occurring. It is also valuable to compare actual with what has happened in past periods (and whenever possible with what your competitors are experiencing). This information should be made available to management in a timely manner so that corrective action can be taken whenever the firm is deviating from the desired path in any of these crucial expense and income areas.

The monthly billing target is an artificial number gotten by dividing the annual target by twelve. Jobs don't progress with such convenient symmetry, and some deviation from the monthly target is inevitable. But after a few months the monthly average should begin to bear some resemblance to the target.

You need to be able to compare budgeted figures with what is actually occurring.

Figure 12
Promotion Expense for (Month)

Item	Monthly Budget	This Month	Year To Date	Same Period Last Year	Over/Under Budget
Salaries					
Travel					
Entertainment					
Photography					
Printing					
Special Projects Labor					

Figure 13
Billings Report

Billings for Month of: _____

	Actual Billings (or To Be Billed)	Billable (but over Proj. Max.)
Monthly Target	87988	
This month		
Monthly Average		
Year to Date		
Same Period Last Year		
Over (Under) Target		

Marketing

3

Developing a Marketing Plan

There are five requirements for successful marketing:

1. You must find suitable prospective clients. "Suitable" means those you have a reasonable chance of selling and whose jobs you can do successfully.

2. You must understand the needs and uncertainties of those prospects in order to plan an effective strategy for winning the commissions.

3. You must have the actual capability to service those needs. That is, your skills must match the client's needs.

4. You must be able to convince the prospective client that you understand his design problems and can solve them.

5. You must do the job to the client's satisfaction.

Historically, designers have marketed themselves in an indirect manner. The definition of *indirect* here is the pursuance of a strategy which induces the prospective client to initiate contact with you when he has a project in mind. Some designers have been extraordinarily successful marketing indirectly, becoming active in the community, involving themselves in professional, civic, social, charitable, and local governmental affairs. This has brought them friends, contacts, respect, and work. In terms of the five requirements listed above, indirect marketing has fulfilled the first, bringing "suitable" prospects to the designer who has then been able to capture them by fulfillment of the other requirements.

It can be a winning combination. The ability to induce clients to come to you through friendship, influence, reputation, and then be able to persuade them through the effective presentation of your abilities is a formidable marketing approach.

Factors commonly encountered which undermine this strength include:

• Business inefficiency. While not primarily a marketing weakness, it can cause a firm to be unable to compete effectively, particularly where price is one of the deciding factors. Development of a sound business plan is essential. The financial and management sections of this book offer guidance here.

• Lack of skill and experience with the kind of projects sought, that is, going after unsuitable clients and projects. See the article, "Avoiding a Hopeless Chase after the Wrong Job," in this section. It discusses "lines of strength" a firm must develop, special expertise to supplement its general

David Travers

The market plan should, of course, derive from and support the professional and business objectives of the firm.

professional competence.

Left unremedied these two viruses, which can cripple even the largest office, are fatal to the small office.

With that minatory preamble, let me outline my recommendations for a marketing plan containing objectives, strategies, organization, and budget. The market plan should, of course, derive from and support the professional and business objectives of the firm, which we will assume are already in place. (See "PR Planning" for more discussion of promotional planning in relation to corporate and professional goals.)

Objectives

A. Achieve 1986/87 billings of $_____ .

B. Sell interiors as well as architectural services.

C. Increase our share of the local market.

D. Expand into other market (geographic, building type) areas.

You must set specific objectives. That is, based on your business goals and on market research, you should establish dollar target volumes for each of the above and specify the other market areas.

You should also make decisions about the building and project types you mean to emphasize under B, C, and D, based on research that has told you the market is opportune for those kinds of projects or will be. The finer grained your marketing objectives, the more focused your efforts can be.

Strategy

1. Local Marketing Strategy

The firm's strategy should be a more intensive cultivation and effective use of clients, friends, and contacts to:

- get additional and better information about market conditions;
- increase the number of leads;
- broaden the firm's network of friends and contacts.

Continuity of effort is the key to success in any kind of long-term program.

By more effective and intensive use, I don't mean arm twisting or suede-shoe selling. Rather, contacting should be on a regular, planned, and organized basis. Continuity of effort is the key to success in any kind of long-term program. There should be an increase in the frequency of contact with the most important of your friends, clients, past clients, and others belonging to or close to the local power structures. There should be a strengthening of relationships by regular, purposeful business and social entertaining.

Broadening of the network can be achieved by asking friends and clients to introduce you to influential people that they know but you don't, people who are involved with the future of the community, who know of contemplated building projects before others do. Examples: industrial real estate brokers; developers; economic consultants; mortgage investment brokers and lenders; bank loan officers; directors, presidents, and managers of local, state, and national banks; city, county, state, and federal agencies.

Don't go after every job indiscriminately. Assess your chances on the basis of the five requirements for successful marketing listed at the beginning of this piece. Work out the probabilities according to your experience in that kind of project and your influence (and those of the competition).

Create a publicity campaign to reinforce your marketing strategies and objectives. See the articles in the Public Relations section.

2. Strategy for Expansion into Other Areas

If you have not had much success in getting work outside your geographic area, it may not be because you are incapable of doing so, only that you have not followed the right strategy. Most firms fail here because they have gone after too many jobs which they had no chance of getting: they lacked experience with that kind of project and had no offsetting strength compelling enough for the prospect to overlook this most important of all criteria.

In terms of the five basic requirements, you must select "suitable" prospective clients. The inability of so many designers to match their real, existing, proven skills and experience to the needs of the client is the reason they have difficulty selling their services.

The strategy for getting work outside of the local area should begin, then, with a hard, cold look at your chances of getting that job. Remember, a prospective client with any intelligence looks for experience, experience, and more experience in the designers who ask for consideration.

Once convinced that you have sufficient experience and qualifications to win the job, all other things being equal, remember that all others things are not equal. Remind yourself that there are designers in that other city or area who enjoy the kind of influence and friendships there that you do in your bailiwick. To offset this, look at your list of friends and contacts to see if there are any that can help you, introduce you in the new territory. Influential friends and contacts are a major marketing strength too little used.

Consider an association or joint venture in cases where

• you have everything needed for the job except local influence;

• you have the inside track because of influence but lack the appropriate skills, experience, size, or whatever the client feels you need to qualify. (See the articles on joint venturing elsewhere in this section.)

Organization

A principal in the firm should be in charge of marketing. In a small firm he would also act as director of the activity. The rule of thumb is firms of thirty professionals or more can afford and should have a professional marketing manager. He or she should be the single point of contact for leads and inquiries, identifying prospects, developing the marketing plan and marketing tools, deciding how much effort should go into the pursuit of individual prospects, and making certain the effort is made.

In other words, the marketing manager or director should be given complete responsibility and authority under the control of the principal in charge, who in turn is responsible to his partners, if any.

The inability of so many designers to match their real, existing, proven skills and experience to the needs of the client is the reason they have difficulty selling their services.

Once convinced that you can win the job, all other things being equal, remember that all others things are not equal.

See other articles in this section for detailed, specific methods for organizing and implementing the marketing plan and the kinds of marketing activities engaged in by other firms.

Marketing Budget and Controls

Let me quote here from the budget section of the article "PR Planning."

"The following guidelines for the PR budget are based upon three factors:

"1. It is generally accepted that on the average design firms spend about 6 percent of gross billings for promotion, i.e., marketing and public relations.

"2. How this figure is divided between the two depends on the nature and intensity of a firm's marketing activities. That is, what the balance is between direct (selling) and indirect (PR) promotional activities. For the sake of simplicity, we will assume an even balance.

"3. It seems to be the rule that the percentage of gross billings (the 6 percent average) is applied to the previous year's billings. It makes more sense to base marketing expenditures on what they are supposed to produce. Thus, the total promotional budget here should be based on Corporate Goal 1, a 15 percent increase over last year's billings. Assuming for the moment a firm of 100 people with billings last year of $4 million gives us a $4.6 million projection for this year. Six percent for total promotion is $276,000 and half of that for PR is $138,000..."

The promotional budget for design firms can range from 3 percent of billings for the A/E juggernaut with astronomical billings, great momentum, and well-oiled promotional machinery, to 10 percent or more for the tiny office trying to get moving. Add to that the infinite variety of combinations of direct and indirect selling techniques which should be tailored individually to the thousands of design offices with differing thoughts about marketing—from disdain for aggressive marketing to complete acceptance, even enjoyment of selling and all its nonprofessional (not "unprofessional") aspects and challenges. What you have is a complexity that makes it impossible to create one single matrix of plan and budget to fit all offices and conditions.

Marketing costs will largely be an indirect labor expense.

It can safely be said, however, that, unlike PR expense, marketing costs will largely be an indirect labor expense. It will consist of up to 50 percent of the time of a principal in a small office. Or the salary of a marketing director (who is also PR director in a middle-sized office) plus the time required of the principals and others in the firm who play a part in marketing.

Whatever the balance a firm strikes between direct or indirect marketing, the cost in "nonproductive" time will be considerable. Proposal and presentation materials can be expensive, but time charges will far outweigh them. A brochure can cost $30,000 and more to print, but the time in planning, assembling the contents, and preparing it for printing can equal or exceed that. And remember a brochure can be amortized over its several years of use. Labor cannot.

To control these costs, budgets should be set. That we cannot give you here a budget that fits your unique conditions doesn't mean that you shouldn't create one. The sundry articles in this section offer a menu of marketing methods and techniques for you to draw upon. Be sure the mix is suited to your resources, to you, and to the others in your office who will be involved.

Marketing too should be given an account number and as many subaccount numbers as are needed to provide management with a clear picture of how much is being spent and for what. Actual expenditures should be monitored and compared to budgeted figures on a monthly basis.

A caveat. Project managers and, yes, even principals have been known to treat the promotional budget as a slush fund for salvaging bankrupt projects.

The Marketing Audit

Gerre Jones

Due to the dynamic nature of marketing, any marketing plan is outdated before it is fully implemented. A variety of external factors can and do alter perceived marketing opportunities, and the successful firm must be able to adapt quickly and adjust to all such shifts and changes.

An "audit" implies an appraisal and review of a business activity or function and usually is made at the end of a specific phase or time period—a season, fiscal year, and the like. Audits traditionally are made to review and judge the accuracy of accounting and financial operations and most dictionaries follow this usage.

The Marketing Audit Defined

For our purposes, consider the marketing audit to be a programed evaluation of all activities included in the marketing function of your firm. The audit, properly planned and carried out, becomes both diagnostic and prognostic, concerned equally with the future and the present. Its focus is on identifying existing program weaknesses and potential weaknesses which may arise down the line. On a less negative note, the marketing audit is a future-oriented examination of a firm's marketing position. Success should also be analyzed so a firm can capitalize on the plan's strong points.

An American Management Association report on the nature, purposes, and problems of the marketing audit describes the process:

> "…[T]he term 'marketing audit' is used here to denote a systematic, critical, and unbiased review and appraisal of the basic objectives and policies of the marketing functions and of the organization, methods, procedures, and personnel employed to implement the policies and achieve the objectives. Note that this definition identifies six separate aspects of the marketing activities which should be appraised: objectives, policies, organization, methods, procedures, and personnel."

Six separate aspects of the marketing activities which should be appraised: objectives, policies, organization, methods, procedures, and personnel.

Timing of Audits

And audits are for good times as well as bad. Technically, marketers won't know their plans have gone off track until the audit is made. Environmental changes can rather quickly have a disastrous impact on the best of plans. The AMA report cited above makes the case elsewhere for auditing apparently successful marketing activities:

"Success tends to foster complacency, laxity, and carelessness. It permits tradition and habit to become the dominant shapers of marketing programs. It allows dry rot and excessive costs to develop and spread. It leads some marketing executives to become so deeply involved with existing policies and methods that they never bother to examine the possibility of performing the marketing tasks in other ways—ways which, although once inappropriate, now may be more closely in tune with the company's needs.

"The dangers of success clearly suggest that in marketing as in home maintenance the time to fix the roof is when the sun is shining. They point clearly to the need for continual, systematic, critical, and objective appraisal of even the mostsuccessful marketing operation, *while it is successful* ."

Ideally, periodic audits of a marketing plan should not be necessary, because conscientious marketers should continually monitor the effectiveness of their operations. In fact, however, as the preceding citation suggests, marketing executives become identified with certain strategies, electing to pursue them bindly when other courses may be more effective. No plan or program is perfect or far-seeing enough to be engraved in stone. Use the audit approach to spot coordination shortfalls, misdirected efforts, outdated strategies, and unrealistic goals.

Management Evaluation
The evaluation process is a three-staged one for management:

1. Find out what happened—get the facts; compare actual results with planned ones to determine variations.

2. Find out why it happened—which specific factors in the marketing program accounted for the results.

3. Decide what to do about it—plan the next period's program and activities so as to improve on unsatisfactory results and to capitalize on favorable ones.

Control Point Selection
To initiate the marketing audit, several control points or yardsticks are selected. These are from the marketing variables with the greatest potential for influencing the success of the marketing plan and are usually set out in the plan. For each control point used the plan should give a definition of significant deviation from the point necessary to trigger an alarm in the marketing department.

When a significant deviation is found and the causes isolated, adjustments to the marketing plan are in order. It is axiomatic that only a continuing review of opportunities and performances will enable a firm to recognize deviations and other changes as they occur.

The number and type of control points will depend on the particular objectives, strategies, and programs of a given marketing plan. Our purpose here is not to suggest all possible control points, only some that most plans include.

Some audit yardsticks:
• total fee volume;
• fee volume by market segments;

• fee volume by sales territories.

These figures should be compared against past performance, firm goals (as set out in the marketing plan), and the total fee volume for your selling area. If your marketing is on a country-wide basis, the last comparison would be made against total construction nationally for the time period under consideration. A market share analysis for a design firm might take the form shown in Figure 1.

Figure 1

Year	Your Fee Volume	Total Fee Volume in Your Market Area	Your % Share of the Market
1980	$3,750,000	$600,000,000	0.625
1979	4,000,000	610,000,000	0.656
1978	3,450,000	600,000,000	0.575
1977	3,100,000	580,000,000	0.534
1976	3,850,000	530,000,000	0.726

Another audit section deals with fee goals versus fees actually realized. This analysis is particularly important when a firm has several sales territories or branch offices charged with marketing. A firm with four offices, for example, might use the type of evaluation in Figure 2.

Figure 2

Office	Fee Goals	Actual Sales	Performance Percentage	$ Variation from Goals
A	$750,000	$810,000	108.0	+$ 60,000
B	610,000	600,000	98.4	− 10,000
C	375,000	475,000	126.7	+ 100,000
D	890,000	810,000	91.0	− 80,000
	$2,625,000	$2,695,000	102.7	+$ 70,000

This chart demonstrates the pitfalls of dealing only with total sales or costs. Totals often are misleading and inconclusive and will seldom uncover signs of trouble or serious weaknesses. On the face of it, office C, with a 26.7 percent increase over its fee dollar goal, might appear to be doing an outstanding marketing job. Deeper analysis, on the other hand, may show that office C should have been charged with a $550,000 fee target for the year instead of $375,000. Office D, which appears to be doing a less than satisfactory job of marketing, may have been tasked too heavily for the market conditions in its area.

Mark Stern, in his "Marketing Planning: A Systems Approach," lists several possibilities for controls, in addition to the obvious control point of profit. Adapted to professional services marketing, Stern's control points include:

1. Sales expense to fee revenue. The expense-to-revenue ratio is a reasonable measure of the efficiency of your sales organization.

2. Promotion expense to fee revenue. These are indirect costs, such as for public relations, advertising, and printed marketing tools.

3. Sales force productivity. This ratio may be in terms of personal selling hours expended per dollar of fee revenue. Or it can be in terms of the fee dollar volume realized by the average sales person per week, month, or year.

Another point for ratio analysis is the total marketing return rate. This is the product of project dollar volume divided by total marketing expenditures—and it gives a quick picture of how much fee bang a firm is really getting from its marketing bucks.

Performance Evaluation

The most difficult problem with the majority of marketing audits is in performance evaluation of those in marketing. Many firms do not have standards by which to judge marketing performance. In such cases the auditors must develop standards as they go—either operational standards, which focus on specific activities, or appraisal standards, which involve personal performance judgments.

Since the marketing audit is such a powerful tool for the marketing planner, many firms turn to outside consultants for assistance with their first audit or two. A greater element of objectivity theoretically is assured, but consultants must spend at least several days familiarizing themselves with the firm's management, its operation, the marketing staff, the current marketing plan, and, of course, reviewing and fine-tuning the established control points. The consultant's productivity is thus somewhat diminished.

The most difficult problem with the majority of marketing audits is in performance evaluation of those in marketing.

What You Do—
Order from Chaos

*A/E Marketing
Handbook*

T his article takes you through the basics of organizing your work as a marketer. We discuss from our own experience what and how things can be organized rather than delving too deeply into specific systems.

Start with the premise that you alone are responsible for organizing the marketing effort. The reasons you need to get organized are simple, important, and will cover both active and reactive tasks:

Active. Good organization enables you to initiate more creative approaches to marketing your firm (a fire-prevention campaign).

Reactive. Good organization enables you to respond quickly to emergencies (a fire-fighting campaign).

Putting Order into Your Organizing

It is difficult to say which activities must be handled first or what exact order is most fitting for your firm. We know professional marketers who were hired to support firm principals in direct day-to-day selling. Each firm is different, and you will want to direct your energies to the most pressing needs first. That may mean a lot of knee-jerk reactions to emergencies, but at some point you want to start planning and stop merely reacting. Our approach to solving organizational problems and arranging priorities begins with determining how other tasks will be accomplished.

The ideal way to get organized would be to shut down your firm for about three months and remake or patch the systems.

The ideal way to get organized would be to shut down your firm for about three months and remake or patch the systems. But you can't. Many of your attempts to get organized will be frustrated by the day-to-day responsibilities placed on you. Our advice is simply to respond to the daily crisis while spending whatever time you can in the effort to get organized.

Much of getting organized is time management and organization of priorities. Time management is basically rescheduling what you do so that you can attend to number one priorities first. Two books that can help you in this area are *The Time Trap* by R. Alec Mackenzie and *How to Get Control of Your Time and Your Life* by Alan Lakein.

Goals and Understanding: Organizing Your Thoughts

The organization process may have begun before you assumed the marketing position. Research your firm to know what your priorities are:

• Read everything available to you about your firm: articles, pamphlets, existing brochures, any and all publications concerning the work of your firm or its people.

• Search out and read memos regarding projects, budget analyses of the firm in general and of specific projects, correspondence with consultants and with friends of the firm.

• Get to know the people, the personalities, their capabilities, how they work (or do not work) together.

This process will give you an overview of your firm, its strengths and weaknesses, what you can build upon, and what (or whom) you must overcome in order to realize the goals set forth in the marketing plan (which at this time may only be a hazily defined vision). Evaluate what in business development has worked in the past and what has failed in order to see what may continue to work, what must be changed, and what new approaches may be appropriate. Materials and systems that worked in the past may not continue to be effective, especially if the marketing plan directs the firm to enter new markets.

Try to avoid allowing the direct sales effort (e.g., writing proposals, preparing for presentations, pulling slides) to divert you from your goal of organizing the marketing program resources. We have spent literally years cranking out successful proposals, while our marketing resources drifted closer and closer to a state of chaos. The resulting level of disorganization increased the difficulty of responding quickly to daily sales needs.

While meeting your firm's immediate selling needs, do not lose track of your need to organize the overall marketing effort.

Analyze the Marketing Plan

A prime factor in getting organized is understanding your firm's plans and the expectations of others regarding your position. Knowing these will help you establish priorities (according to the plan) and know where major long-range efforts must be placed. It is impossible to analyze your marketing tools without first understanding the overall framework in which they are to be used.

In his book, *How to Market Professional Design Services*, Gerre Jones devoted the entire chapter, "Getting Organized," to the writing of a marketing plan. The point here is obvious; without some written plan, it is very difficult to get organized.

Interview Key People

Contact key people in the firm to cull their views on marketing needs and on the firm in general.

These interviews will show you ways in which key people in the firm are involved (or not involved) in marketing. The interviews will allow you to get to know the key people in the firm as well as giving them the opportunity to come to know you and to see you in action.

Your interview should include questions like those shown below as well as others more directly related to the work and personality of the person being interviewed. Do not be afraid to deviate from your format or follow an unexpected train of conversation.

Keep the interview professional, serious, and short. Good organization means fewer surprises for you. You must gain the trust of these key people so that they will share responsibility and information with you, not withhold it from you. Remember also that truly key people have little time to chat and have probably been interviewed by a marketing person before, with very little resulting from it. Therefore, be brief and to the point, but do it! Use the following questions as a general guide:

1. What types of projects does the firm intend to pursue? Are there major differences from what is being done presently or different geographic areas of interest?

2. What are the special talents of the firm? What are the firm's drawbacks?

3. Are there any special talents among the staff that are currently being promoted by the firm? (Remember to follow this up with a staffing survey, explained below.)

4. How were existing projects brought into the office?

5. What, if any, have been recent breakthroughs in the marketing effort? Who initiated them?

6. What, specifically, can be done to improve the marketing effort?

7. How should the firm handle public relations and indirect marketing, publishing, awards programs, seminars, group participation, press relationships?

8. What growth or change should take place in the direction or nature of the firm?

9. What intelligence on relevant markets already exists within the firm, and who is responsible for this information?

10. What talents for marketing are available in-house, and for which must consultants be used?

11. Lastly, some questions on money to be asked, particularly of principals in the firm:
- What type of support will the marketing effort be given?
- Is there a marketing budget?
- To what extent will marketing ideas be funded?
- What type of staff expertise will be available to marketing?
- How is this staff time accounted for when spent on marketing?

Analyze Your Own Role

When you feel you understand your firm, its goals, its position in desired marketplaces, how it is seen by the outside world, and its ability to produce in its intended markets, it is time to look inward for a moment. To be well organized in your marketing efforts, determine what is expected of

You should write your job description for yourself, including the goals you and others have for this position.

you. This simple analysis of your own role in the firm will help define your priorities.

We think you should write your job description for yourself, including the goals you and others have for this position. Pass this description around and get a general agreement on it from those in charge. Differentiate tasks between the first six months (background organization and definition of needs—while responding to selling demands) and your function thereafter (e.g., continue to improve systems, do market research, write proposals, organize sales materials).

The Network

Some marketers posit that the most important element in their lead-finding efforts is an effective network (reflecting the "ole-boy" network). This network provides information about your markets, your competition, prices, and services, and who is looking for work or just found a job. The best information usually comes directly from people in your network. You will learn in time from whose mouths (both within and outside the firm) the best information is derived.

Much of getting organized is time management and the setting of priorities. Time management is rescheduling what you do so that you can attend to number one priorities first. Two books that may help you in this area are *The Time Trap* by R. Alan Mackenzie and *How to Get Control of Your Time and Your Life* by Alan Lakein..

The network is a system of "live wires" connected to the key marketing people in your firm, yourself especially. There are many ways to organize a network. Ideally you have an active card file or printout from a word processor (or computer) on which are printed (updated constantly!!) the names of people who are in the network. These names should be cross-referenced and described as much as possible, and may even be subdivided by type or rated as to relative value to the firm. We offer here some simple methods for organizing the network once you have begun to put it in print. Remember always that the network is not a dead file or a telephone directory; it is a living hot line and a spontaneous reference system.

If you use a card file, either one that rotates or the old recipe box type, you may want to organize by names only, remembering that, if the network is active, the people who use it will know the people in it. However, you may also want to cross-reference by firm, so that, when you need to know who are your contacts at Glutz Land Development, you can quickly see that someone there knows you. Another method is simply to break down the network into its basic types and organize these separately, though still by name within the given type. This method may yield groupings such as:
- consultant;
- prospective client;
- existing and/or past client;
- agents, writers, public figures;
- special friends (of the firm or its principals);
- by project type (health care, retail centers).

The network is a system of "live wires" connected to the key marketing people in your firm.

However, remember that the more filing cubbyholes you create, the more nooks and crannies there are in which information you need can hide. Therefore, whatever approach you use, keep it simple.

A warning: the names on a list such as this are usually personal contacts developed by people in your firm over many years. Note whose contact within your firm this person is.

• Colleagues within your firm may feel proprietary about sharing these contacts with you.

• People whose contacts form the network must stay in touch with them until they hand them over to you (along with a personal introduction).

The point is, really, that these contacts must be nurtured and used, not stuffed into a "dead" file.

Your job is to see that the network is used and that it grows, not to sit on it until it hatches of its own accord. People will use the network more efficiently if you get in and organize it, help evaluate it, and see to it that people really do use it.

Information about the Firm: Written and Graphic

The undertakings described so far will help you organize your basic approach to marketing. You must now inventory and evaluate your marketing tools and personnel.

Information about your firm can be quickly grouped into two major subheadings: words and pictures. This material should be complete and up to date, and appropriate in style and content to the firm and its marketing goals. Following is a quick overview of methods we have used for organizing this material.

Boilerplate. The stock statements about the firm—its people, history, design philosophy, and significant projects, ad nauseam (though only at times)—constitute what we commonly refer to as boilerplate. This is generally off-the-shelf information used in proposals or statements of qualification, sent only with introductory letters or stuffed in with a brochure sent to a prospective client. This material should be written in such a way that it can be assembled to apply to general audiences or can be manipulated to contain variations applicable to more specific audiences. Firms having word processors can easily fine-tune their boilerplate to address a specific audience's perceived interests. Whatever your firm's capabilities for producing this material, creating, maintaining, and updating the boilerplate is a primary activity of marketing.

A marketing database of text would include:
• U.S. Government Standard Form 254 and 255 data;
• standard form letters of interest, letters of intent, letters of inquiry;
• standard outline proposals;
• resumes of all firm staff and management;
• variations of all the resumes to emphasize particular skills clients will be concerned about for particular jobs;
• varied text for custom proposal-type submittals;
• office newsletters, bulletins, reports, client information manuals,

and checklists;
- standard background information to include with press releases;
- mailing lists;
- logs of client contacts with reminders of future contact points;
- ongoing work histories and evaluations of best and worst client types, best and worst building types, etc.

In some firms the information gets divided into:
- material about our firm for our clients;
- material about our clients for our use.

You should have a file for boilerplate to keep this material organized by how you use it. The file index for this may read something like this:

I Introductions
  A. General introduction to the firm
  B. Introduction to the firm (industrial manufacturing facilities)
  C. Introduction to the firm (health care facilities)
II Resumes
  A. By personnel (general/alphabetically)
  B. By project type (alphabetically by personnel)
III Project Descriptions
  A. General
  B. Industrial manufacturing facilities
  C. Health care facilities

Project Descriptions. We have found that project descriptions are used in a number of ways, from attachments to letters to pages in a statement of qualifications. Project description sheets can be developed in a number of styles, including printed sheets with a picture of the project. In organizing project descriptions, as in all other boilerplate, keep a supply at hand while the originals are kept in a more secure location. Whether stored on a computer or in a separate file, always keep originals in a secure place under your control. We usually organize project descriptions alphabetically within project type subheadings.

Evaluate how your written material is being used, then develop a style that reflects your firm and is properly geared to the intended market.

Printed information is not as adaptable as that which is created in-house, and the use of this type of boilerplate may call for the creation of many series of somewhat similar information.
- Establish a consistent graphic style that reflects that of the firm.
- Keep the files up to date, and always have enough boilerplate information on hand in a finished form so that something professional in appearance can be assembled in less than fifteen minutes should the need arise. (We can assure you it will.)

Reprinted Articles. Magazine articles or other published descriptions of your work, not written by your firm, are always good marketing tools and should be kept in reasonable quantities. Unlike boilerplate, this printed material is usually not altered. For this reason, you can have many copies printed in the best quality you can afford. File this type of written information, organized to reflect its subject matter and placed close enough to your boilerplate so it may be pieced together quickly for a general or a specific audience. Again, our experience has led us to organize all information by project type or market.

Brochures. Your responsibility will be to oversee production of brochures and to keep them up to date and organized so that they are handy for anyone in a responsible position to give one away. But, you should know when they are given out. You may want to treat brochures like stock in a store and log them out as they are used, noting who is using them and for what purpose. One marketer we know placed a numbered sticky-back label on each brochure. When people took brochures, they peeled off the labels and placed them in a log book next to the person's name.

Proposals. The proposals you write when pursuing work should also be filed in such a way that you can reference those which are still active and can easily retrieve or reuse information from those which are old or inactive. Though you may be duplicating information filed elsewhere, it makes sense to file copies, not only of the proposals, but of all associated material such as notes, letters, and important phone numbers. When you open the file eight months after submitting a proposal, you should be able to replicate the proposal or get critical information from it without running all over. One firm we know keeps two separate files on every proposal submitted: one for all original text, letters, and memos and another for two or more copies of completed proposals.

Graphics. The rule is simple: all original art and first-quality negatives should be kept out of the hands of anyone other than yourself or your designate. This prohibition includes principals in your firm. Organize and file your originals by project and by type (e.g., Project: Newark Office Park. Type: color negatives, or original prints, or transparencies). These only leave the office when you need prints to be made from them or when *Architectural Record* calls, in which case you make duplicates for yourself and send the originals by special handling. But you will send originals, albeit nervously, to magazine editors because you want, in print, the best quality graphics possible.

As for prints from these precious originals—whether of models, renderings, completed projects, or charts and graphs—our experience indicates it is better to have many prints of a few agreed-upon favorites than to have a few prints of everything. Spend all the time you need editing and reducing graphic material to that which is really first rate.

Prints are expensive, and giving them away should be a serious undertaking. A good brochure will reduce your need to mail prints to prospective clients. However, brochures fall out of date quicker than Italian furniture, and prints of active projects (usually not in the brochure) will tell an audience where your firm is now.

Filing your photographs. File photos and other graphics by project or description (e.g., construction management, medical office buildings) to reflect the organization of your written material. If you have boilerplate on a particular subject with charts, photos, and graphs to illustrate the text, file the charts, photos, and graphs under the same title as the text, but not in the same place. This way you maintain the elemental difference between graphic and written information. Cross-reference projects that fit into two or more categories. Filing and organizing your graphics is not as difficult as keeping track of them once they are filed.

Slides. It is a simple fact of life that slides disappear. They "walk," are left on airplanes, or find their way into portfolios when people leave the firm.

Slide organization is much like the organization of graphics outlined above, only more so. Some firms use slides frequently, making them prone to destruction and loss. Periodically review all new slides; cull them to a reasonable number, retaining those that are commonly liked; and make several duplicates of each. Then lock up the originals and throw away the key. Organize slides by project type, type of slide, its quality level, and/or by how it may be used.

Whatever you do, keep the slide-filing system simple by avoiding complex numbering, indexing, and cross-referencing. Follow these simple rules when filing slides:

• Weed out bad or useless slides before they even find their way into the system.

• Organize slides according to basic divisions of how they are used, such as "presentation" slides and "historical" or "record" slides. Within these basic divisions, organize slides by project type or in some way that reflects how you market the firm.

• Assign one person to maintain order in the slide system.

• As said before, keep the master slides safe from everyday use.

A System Described
In a firm we know, the slides are filed alphabetically by project within overall categories of project type. The system also contains two separate groups of slides: "first" slides (the best, most used) and "second" slides (ones of less quality, unique or special topics, and ones which are less frequently used). The first set contains three or four copies of less than twenty slides per project. The second set contains fewer copies of a larger variety of shots. In addition, each principal or project architect who makes presentations has his or her own slide show arranged in a carousel tray ready to be used on a moment's notice or adapted for a special presentation. Every slide itself is labeled as to where it should be filed and marked to show how it should be placed in the carousel.

Let us quickly review this particular system, bearing in mind that it is only an example of how you might organize slides without purchasing a manufactured system.

In a drawer or drawers of a filing cabinet (we used large lateral files) were sections labeled "First Quality":

1.1 City Planning
1.2 Health Care
1.3 Housing
1.4 Renovation
1.5 Hotels/Restaurants

In another separate drawer labeled "Second Quality: Special

Weed out bad or useless slides before they even find their way into the system.

Slides," we filed them under the same subheadings:

2.1 City Planning

2.2 Health Care

2.3 Housing

In a separate, literally fireproof room (you may consider a safe deposit box), we filed, with the same numeric system, the original slides, transparencies, and negatives (for prints).

What we had in this system were two file drawers (or more) which duplicated themselves but were of different quality. A third system consisted of the prepackaged shows mentioned above.

Slides were filed in plastic slide holders, labeled for the project with each slide labeled in turn. So within the file drawer you would find dividers for each project type (1.2 Health Care) with sheets for each project (St. Mary's Hospital Medical Office Building).

As we mentioned before, this is just one example of how slides may be filed in-house. There are a number of manufactured slide-filing systems on the market; and though we cannot recommend one brand over another, if you decide to purchase a system, rather than creating your own, you should ask questions such as the following:

• What is the capacity?

• Can I add on to the system for a reasonable cost?

• Does it protect the slides from the elements and (very important) from handling?

• Can it be secured?

• Can I view the slides without touching them?

• Can the system be organized with enough individuality to work with my other filing systems?

• Does it require a lot of space or special ventilation?

• For the cost, is it worth more than some other item I could use (like a word processor)?

Evaluation of Material

Once you have reviewed and organized the items outlined above, it is time to evaluate this material to see that all the pieces work together. This evaluation will give you a good idea of what you have to work with and how good it is in order to move your firm to up-grade, infill, and create new material as necessary.

1. Begin by noting the material that really is first rate.

2. Make up a simple code for yourself that will tell you what quality certain pieces of material are (say grades A, B, C, and D).

3. Take the material that is first rate, whether it consists of slides, brochures, written boilerplate, or well-designed fact sheets, and review it with key marketing people in the firm for consistency of style:

• Are the headings or titles shown on each piece in a similar or complementary manner?

• Is the type face the same?

• Is the paper on which graphics, text, or offset photos are printed similar in color and texture?

• Could you take something from each area or a description of each job, randomly throw them together, bind them, and have it look as if it were produced as a coherent package?

• Does the material meet your current marketing needs, i.e., are subjects relevant?

The answer to at least some of these questions will probably be *no*, and, if it is, your work is cut out. We suggest that you take the best material and make sure that the quality is good and that the style meets standards set by principals and senior marketing staff. Then use these pieces as a standard by which you and perhaps one or two others will judge all marketing material.

Secure a budget for upgrading marketing material. This budget may be lumped in with your budget for creating new material, in which case you will decide whether it is more important to create something new or upgrade something already in use.

Let the second- and third-rate stuff just fall out of use as you create new, better material.

In addition to using your own in-house top quality material as a standard, research other material from other firms within and outside your field. See what large corporations are presenting as well as what the competition is using. When it comes to setting a style, review work that is common to your intended market. A corporate chief executive officer (CEO) will respond well to a different graphic style than that which appeals to a superintendent of schools. Do not be afraid to adapt (not steal) from other sources. Remember that Mies van der Rohe said: "I don't want to be original, I want to be good."

Staffing Survey

People are surely the most important resource you have in marketing your firm's services. People ultimately sell the service, produce the project, and create your relationships with clients. Organizing a file of project descriptions is a lot less complex than organizing the people you will rely on in your marketing efforts. Determine who in your firm will carry out certain tasks, and make sure that these people can and will contribute to the marketing effort. Review the entire staff to see who is most saleable.

There are always hidden talents and useful experience represented by the staff in your firm. One fairly easy but important job is to conduct a staffing survey. Information to include in this survey:

• types of projects worked on by people in your firm while employed elsewhere;

• the amount of time and number of projects on which these people have experience;

• their responsibility on the given projects.

This information can go into a matrix which will show you at a glance the type and levels of experience you have represented in your firm. You can assemble a typical project team, based on past experience and position, that can be used in presenting your capabilities to potential clients in a variety of markets. Create an 'experience' file on each member of your firm and use this to make resumes and complete your staffing survey.

Evaluating the Effort

Whether or not you evaluate your own performance, others will be doing it. Evaluation is a key aspect of organization; it will tell you where you need to place more effort, hence time, money, and which personalities are not contributing to the marketing program.

Evaluation should cover the material described above, general performance, written proposals, special marketing efforts, and presentations to clients. Evaluation should cover ongoing and specific efforts. Know, for example:

- the number of cold calls it takes to hit a live client;
- how many live clients it takes to make one job occur.

You should keep statistics for evaluating these efforts and use them as a basis for showing improvement. Always request a debriefing from a client on any major effort to obtain a project.

Evaluate the performance of those with whom you work, including senior staff. Anytime there is a meeting with potential clients (from a formal interview to a casual lunch), you should get a briefing or debriefing.

High on a Hill

So far we have discussed organizing operations, material, and personnel, all of which should be under the marketer's full-time control. Much of the marketing effort is carried out by people whose actions you don't know about and cannot control. This lack of knowledge can hurt your desire to get organized, but what can you do about a senior staffer who just does not play ball?

No matter how the marketing effort is organized, you will work closely with people who carry heavy burdens of project management along with their marketing roles. These key people help with market research, serve as resources for proposals and other written material, make presentations, and are the all-important "closer-doers." Often these people have little understanding of the team effort involved in marketing.

Involving Senior Staff in Marketing

By creating useful support systems and by sheer effort, you can break through this communication barrier. You cannot organize a successful marketing program without the involvement of key senior people. To conclude, we'll give a few hints on how to involve senior staff in your marketing efforts.

1. In one firm we know, the marketing coordinator gave a series of lunchtime seminars to describe marketing activities in general and his role in particular. The turnout was good and the response very positive. Most people were not aware of all he did for the firm, and, when the technical people realized how busy he was ("Hey, he's just like us—overworked"), they were much more interested in assisting in any way they could.

2. Another way to get senior staff involved in the marketing effort

is simply to ask for their assistance and tell people directly how they can help you and what the incentives are for getting involved. Incentives should, of course, be worked out first with principals in your firm but may include expanded responsibilities on projects they assist in obtaining or recognition in published articles. Try to find out what the senior technical people need to improve their professional lives, and then see if there is a way that helping your marketing effort can help them achieve this.

3. Some senior staff people are threatened by the power that surrounds marketing and are put off by marketers. We have, in certain instances, overcome this prejudice by emphasizing the support nature of our work, reminding those sensitive souls that the marketing effort supports them in producing the kind of work they have dedicated their careers to.

4. Finally, you can gain the support you need from technical staff by creating tools these people will want to use. Go to the extra effort (always beware of the expense) of designing a really distinctive cover for the latest proposal, and make sure your good products are circulated so that people see what you do. This visibility and openness will attract people who can add a dynamic force to your marketing effort.

You cannot organize a successful marketing program without the involvement of key senior people.

Marketing Training

*A/E Marketing
Journal*

"A year and a half ago we had no formal marketing program," says Nancy Elder, the marketing manager for McNamee Porter & Seeley, consulting engineers based in Ann Arbor, MI. In initiating the program, Elder remembers, "people felt very uncomfortable—they didn't want to do it. There were all kinds of psychological blocks to get over."

The first step was to improve the proposals. Elder organized a team for each opportunity and worked with assigned individuals to put the pieces together. After two months, they submitted a proposal for a big job that everyone wanted—and got the job. Credibility for both Elder and the process she installed shot up.

Over time, the hit rate went from about 5 percent to 83 percent in short lists made. "But then we found out," notes Elder, "that when we were shortlisted we were losing at an alarming rate in the presentations."

She developed, with the approval of managing partner John Holland, an intense three-day educational program for fifteen people. It was held out of the office.

On the first day, starting at 7:30 a.m., a person from University Microfilms gave a general talk on presentation techniques, covering such things as the use of audiovisuals and effective speaking.

The presentations were videotaped. "People were horrified," recalls Elder.

Use Outside Experts

Elder feels it's important to have outside experts for such talks to get the attention of the listeners. She also involved a local management consultant, Ron Phillips, who helped in the design ("He made it tougher on people than I would have") and who facilitated the three days. "He was integral to the success," says Elder. At nine o'clock the participants broke into small groups; each was given a different past proposal submitted by the firm and four hours to develop a ten-minute presentation. Slides and graphic materials were made available for their optional use.

The presentations were videotaped and made without interruption or comment. Then the tapes were shown. "People were horrified," recalls Elder. The group critiqued the performances.

At the end of the afternoon, Elder shared the findings of some research she had conducted with clients of the firm on what they like to see in presentations. These had been tape-recorded and selections were played back. What they said they liked was the exact opposite of what the participants had just done—e.g., more participation by the project manager and less talking by the PIC, and attention to the project at hand rather than general capabilities of the firm.

That evening the attendees had another assignment—to individually develop a five-minute introductory presentation on the 140-person firm. These were delivered the morning of the second day. Without much comment necessary, says Elder, it "clearly identified what worked best." The remainder of the morning featured another outside talk, this one on speech habits.

The Presentation Charrette

Then came the big test. Again divided into groups of four, each team was given the proposal that was the first major victory of the new marketing program. They had the remainder of the day to prepare twenty-minute presentations.

"The pressure was enormous," comments Elder. "Everyone wanted to prove they could be good at marketing." Many stayed up until two in the morning finishing their work.

On the third morning, dressed as instructed in what they would actually wear for such an event, the teams, one by one and without seeing the others, made their presentations. The "selection committee" was composed of a client who had just retired, the marketing person from another engineering firm, and a former state government selector. They were allowed ten minutes to ask questions after each presentation. Again the whole thing was videotaped.

"The improvement was unbelievable," exclaims Elder. When all were finished, the entire group listened in as the selection committee discussed its views and made its decision. Everyone adjourned to a long and suitably celebrative lunch.

The afternoon concluded with a viewing of the tapes. As they departed, Elder handed out copies of *How to Dress for Success*."

Soon after this seminar, the firm had an opportunity to make a presentation before a real prospect. Not only did they win, but the client said it was one of the best presentations he had ever seen.

Since the event, the firm's former presentation hit rate of 12 percent has improved more than seven-fold to 85 percent.

"My only regret," says Elder, "is that we didn't have more people at the seminar. It is very expensive and a big interruption. But the payoff is enormous."

My only regret is that we didn't have more people at the seminar. The payoff is enormous.

Client Complaints
and Problems

Fred A. Stitt

A/E managers are often appalled by the indifference of job applicants. They show up late; they are unprepared; they display little interest in the firm or its needs. Some are defensive, aloof, and play hard to get.

Not so commonly known is that clients have the same complaints about many of the design firms they interview. Clients anticipate that A/Es will run their jobs the same way they approach getting the commission. The firm's behavior during the screening and selection process is a literal audition of reliability, competence, and enthusiasm. Many A/Es bomb out because of trivial but—to the client—glaring oversights.

The screening and selection of A/Es becomes mainly a search for negatives. Often, the winning firm is not all that superior to the others, but they have made fewer mistakes. Usually, it's that. Perhaps plus some positive element, but many jobs are won by default by reasonably conscientious—not outstanding—firms.

Common Failings

Here are some of the most common negatives reported by clients:

• A client or client committee sends a prequalification form to contending firms. Many responders will ignore one or more items on the form. The items are part of a weighted point criteria system for comparing the offices under consideration (see "Evaluation by Clients"). Anyone who fails to fill in all the blanks is throwing away points and telling the client "I'm not interested enough to respond to this."

• The client's design program won't normally include all relevant design data. Drawing out such data is considered part of the design professional's role. Clients are surprised at how few architects have a procedure for systematically examining and diagnosing client needs.

• Clients need to know who the project manager will be, his or her qualifications, and whether s/he will be on the job from beginning to end. Some architectural firms don't even volunteer the names of the office principals in their first submittals.

• Clients are not impressed by overly glamorous displays, but most designer presentations are so alike that clients can't recall who was who. They like unique factors, "tie breakers," that they will remember when making their choice. They like unusual qualifications applicable to the job at hand. Clients have been hooked by good job documentation systems, good prototype systems, and advanced design/production systems that

The screening and selection of A/Es becomes mainly a search for negatives.

promise to save time and money. They want specifics, not generalities, about advantages they gain from A/Es' systems.

More on What Clients Want vs. What They Get

Another common client gripe: "A/Es don't listen to what we ask them to do." Clients say their questionnaires are rarely filled completely. Clear statements and rules in their requests for proposals are ignored. Checklists and time limits are provided to guide presentations, but many presenters are shocked when reminded to abide by them.

Clients say they ask for rough schematics and get mounted presentation boards and scale models. They ask for preliminaries to show to banks for financing and get working drawings. One client asked for feasibility and code studies and received a complete building design—with model—before the architect discovered that the lot was unbuildable because of zoning restrictions.

These stories are not exceptional. Clients we have talked with all say the same thing: A/Es—especially architects—don't listen. Or if they do listen, they don't respond.

One client asked for feasibility and code studies and received a complete building design—with model.

The Solution

The solution is plain and simple. It entails making a systematic checklist diagnosis of the client's needs and wants. These are translated into a complete list of services and tasks connected with those services. The checklist is completed with estimated time and costs for each service. Then, when a client asks for a fire code study or a quick look at the site or some data for a county commission, that is what is written down and that is what is delivered.

The diagnostic checklist and tasks/services checklist have many values. They protect the designer from client memory lapses and from demands for additional, noncontract, and nonreimbursable services. What has been agreed to is checked and noted. When new services are requested, out comes the list and they are negotiated by time and cost on the spot.

"Most A/E brochures and newsletters I see are embarrassing. It's pathetic!" says a national store chain's facilities VP. The most glaring flaw, according to him and others: an unbelievable number of misspellings and typos in headlines, titles, and text. Second most obvious problem: A/E writing is self-serving, disorganized, abstract, and empty of content. Clients want facts and figures. They want quantities in the text and qualities expressed in the illustrations. Third most common complaint: A/E graphics are amateurish and often copied directly from competitors.

There's a very useful tip for you in the above complaints. We're told, and we've observed, that one out of ten or twenty A/E brochures or newsletters is truly professional in appearance and content. A firm that produces absolutely top quality materials says the extra time and care adds no more than 5 to 10 percent to the cost.

The Worst Problem

What's the worst A/E problem from the standpoint of management and finance? Financial and business consultants who serve the profession give consistent opinions on A/E lapses: no long-range planning or management by objectives; slow fee collection processes; inaccurate or no timecards from principals and associates; no ongoing, weekly monitoring of time, costs, or other financial indicators on the firm's projects. Any of these can spell eventual disaster.

The overall solution: contemporary, systematic, financial management techniques. They're all built around everyone keeping accurate time records. One office switched to financial management and discovered they had been losing $20,000 a year in reimbursables. Principals had been lax in keeping records on calls, meetings, research, and a multitude of other petty but reimbursable tasks completed for clients.

Another architectural firm took a close look at its financial data and discovered virtually all its losses occurred with one type of client. So it dropped that type of client—the 10 percent of its work responsible for 90 percent of its problems—and gained by giving more attention to the most beneficial types of clients. (The loser for the firm was the "single building" client. Other offices have stopped working for government agencies after a similar analysis of costs.)

Another mystery solved by financial management analysis: a firm doubles and redoubles work load and staff over several years, but earns fewer after-tax dollars than before. A new timecard system and analysis of past records pinpoint the problems: a slow fee collection process and a guesswork approach in establishing their multiplier and their fees.

All advanced financial management begins with timecards. Everyone fills them in on an ongoing, daily basis. Without the ongoing feature and daily pickup of completed cards, no accounting system can be accurate. So says every office that has switched from informal to more rigorous financial systems.

A large engineering firm tells us their worst clients are, beyond a doubt, architects. A principal engineer says: "Architects are the most demanding, least cooperative, most arbitrary, and the slowest paying of any client group we have." His company's solution has been to become a primary design agent and hire architects only when absolutely necessary.

Other major complaints from consulting engineers: architects revise buildings, send progress prints, and fail to show by memo or red lining where the revisions are. Engineers have to waste time hunting down changes the architects could easily make clear. Another common problem in recent years: architects insist on going to overlay pin registered drafting, provide no training in procedures, create numerous disruptions in drafting and interim printings, and expect consultants to reduce their fees in the process.

There's a large bright spot: through all the complaints about and among A/Es, each of these problems suggests a simple and rewarding solution. A little extra care with brochures/newsletters moves a firm way

Another architectural firm discovered virtually all its losses occurred with one type of client.

ahead of the pack in marketing. As does attention and objectification of client wants and needs. Systematic use of timecards and enhancement of traditional bookkeeping practices isn't revolutionary, but it's saved failing firms and helped others leap from a survival level to high profitability. Some candid meetings between architects and engineers and the switch to overlay tightens up project coordination and scheduling immensely.

Evaluation by Clients

Fred A. Stitt

Here are standards and scales of evaluation used by some private clients and public agencies in their consultant selection process. They can serve as a guide to what and what not to convey to a prospect.

State Checklist

Firms short-listed by one state are evaluated according to the following items, each of which is scaled from one to ten points:

1. Depth of organization, including qualifications of personnel and consultants.
2. Size of organization relative to the project's work load.
3. Room within the current work load and project time schedule to handle the project.
4. Record of past work for the state in meeting the budget.
5. Record of past work for the state in meeting schedules.
6. Record of past work for the state in errors, claims, extras.
7. Special competence/experience relative to the project.
8. Location of the firm—in-state is ten points, out-of-state is five.
9. Overall design and planning quality.

Municipal Client Checklist

Here is a city's rating system for a design competition:

1. Total organization's evident ability to meet the program: 50 percent.
2. Experience and qualifications of project staff and management: 20 percent.
3. Breadth and success of experience with similar projects with emphasis on budget: 10 percent.

Private Client Checklist

Here is a corporate client's checklist:

1. What is the firm's history with similar projects in time and cost?
2. What unique, special skills or experience does the firm bring to the project?
3. Is this firm making an assertive effort to understand our needs?
4. Does the firm respond accurately to requests for information?
5. Will the firm keep the same management team in charge of the project?
6. Will other projects and deadlines take precedence over ours?

What is the firm's history with similar project in time and cost?

7. Is there genuine rapport between all who will have to work together on the project?

Comprehensive Rating System

Here is a comprehensive rating system used by a number of clients and agencies. Some use a one to five score system for each item, some use one to ten. Some weigh the more important items and multiply the evaluation times the weights to get final tallies.

1. Relevant prior experience of the total firm.
2. Relevant prior experience of proposed project team members.
3. Relevant prior experience of proposed consultants.
4. Depth and diversity of the firm's skills.
5. Number of staff available for the project.
6. Firm's experience with energy conservation.
7. Firm's experience with preventive maintenance.
8. Quality of management procedures.
9. Quality of planning analysis and design methodologies.
10. Previous experience in time and cost with similar projects.
    Bonus Factors:

11. Extent of computerization of design, scheduling, and documentation.

12. Office proximity to the project or previous experience in the locale.

13. Number, percentage, and pay equality of minority and women employees.

14. Experience with public officials, civic organizations, etc., who are in a position to influence regulatory approvals.

Motivating the Prospect

Fred A. Stitt

What moves a prospective client? How is it some people know how to zero in on what's most important to a particular buyer? The ability has been called sales instinct, but—as with most "instincts"—there are tricks to it.

One device, well known to top professional sales people but not so much to A/Es, is to work with a mental check list of key questions most clients want to have answered without having to ask them. They are called prime mover questions.

These prime mover questions are 1) Will you help me make more money? 2) Will you help make me famous? 3) Will you help me feel secure? 4) Will you make life easier and more pleasant? 5) Will you help me gain power or prestige or influence? (Readers may notice that these are the kinds of questions that hover in the back of one's mind when interviewing job applicants.)

A/Es who are adept at marketing touch all bases in the preliminary approach to prospective clients. Then they go a step further. A particular client or client group usually ranks one of the unspoken questions as most important. The A/E marketer's job is to find out which is most important and give it priority emphasis in the presentation or interview.

A client concern these days: does the A/E have good relationships with people in the public planning or zoning boards?

Profiling a Client

A number of offices, both large and small, do comprehensive profiles on prospects' personalities. Profiling includes gathering data on the subject's likes and dislikes. It's a search for specifics on what the client will respond to and what will turn him or her off. Most important, it leads to an understanding of deeper personal motivations that will influence decision making.

Many clients are perfectly open, even adamant, about their motivations. Certain developers, for example, insist before a formal presentation on knowing cost details on an architect's past work. They want a list of former clients, and they want to know if those clients made money or not. Architects ignore such requests at their own peril.

An increasingly common client concern these days: does the A/E have good relationships with people in the public planning or zoning boards? A good record of approvals is worth gold and deserves emphasis in brochures and presentations. Another worry: is the A/E business-minded and solvent? One office reassures prospects by providing copies of its financial statements.

Profiling is expedited through informal personal contact. One architect, after a phone call to clarify details of a company's building needs, came away with the following items: the client is looking forward to retirement; he's badgered by subordinates who can't do things for themselves; he's worried about crime and wants a stronger central government. Trivial items, but they add up to a comfort- and security-minded client—one who wants a smooth sailing job, minimum participation, and responsibilities taken off his shoulders.

Influential members of a college planning committee were profiled to reveal these items: two members were art collectors and had unusually strong interest in design values; one powerful member was a local history enthusiast. These data guided the winning presentation, which focused on design and methods of integrating new work with the town and campus architectural heritage. The losing presentations were generalized exposition on education, social values, and building technology.

Profiling at long distance is trickier but possible. Some firms use reports on client prospects from Retail Credit Co. or Dun & Bradstreet. Background information may be found in national or regional editions of *Who's Who* and various business and professional directories. Corporate annual reports are widely used sources. Local newspaper morgues sometimes have useful items on executives and their companies. Often adequate profiles of top executives appear in personality articles published in trade papers and journals.

Client research has its pitfalls. Some users of profiles have tripped up badly on insignificant or erroneous data. Important profile material is sometimes locked up and fails to reach people who put presentations together. And too often the information isn't integrated within a broader idea framework to guide action. The prime mover questions above provide such a framework.

Hooking Prospects into Appointments

Some sales representatives are artists when it comes to progressing from cold initial contact to meetings. Their methods are useful to anyone trying to meet with prospective clients. For instance:

• When making preliminary contact by letter, name a date and time when you will call to exchange further information. People tend to be available and prepared for calls prearranged in this fashion. Houston sales expert John Wolfe offers this rule: "Use the letter to sell the call, use the call to sell the appointment."

• Use the phone call to emphasize the importance of a face-to-face interview. Don't get into detail. Responses to questions made off the top of the head often have to be retracted or modified later. Premature answers to questions can also lead to premature "no, thanks" from the prospect. Respond to questions with "that depends" answers, e.g., "That depends on a more detailed examination of your needs. Let's get together Monday morning..."

• Give reasons for having an appointment right away. You'll be in the prospect's building or neighborhood on other business; you're going out of town soon; you have some timely and exciting new information and you want the prospect to be the first to get it. Mainly, set limits on the time you have available.

• Plan the telephone call. Use a checklist of points to cover. This avoids oversights and embarrassing callbacks to clear up some forgotten point. A list also keeps a conversation moving and prevents long pauses, fumbling for words, and talking too much. Make points, get the appointment, and get off the phone.

More on Unspoken Client Needs and Questions

Clients won't often tell architects what's exactly on their minds. There are things they want, but they don't say them. Members of a church building committee, for example, wanted their bell tower to be higher than another denomination's church spire down the street. But they were afraid to say so explicitly. Their architect was forced into long arguments on the issue. He argued on aesthetic grounds for a lower tower, but the arguments had nothing to do with the real, unspoken desire of the clients.

Unexpressed and undiscerned needs and desires lead to endless confusions. A school board agreed that they wanted participation and input from students and faculty. But they consistently ignored or rejected all such input the architect conveyed to them. Board members wanted to seem up-to-date and democratic, but they had other concerns. Their overriding concern was personal prestige. They feared erosion of their power if students and teachers had any real influence over the project.

Another confusing situation experienced by many architects: the custom home client works very cooperatively throughout the project, then suddenly begins to reject the architect's authority. The client doesn't say so, but sees the house becoming the "spiritual" property of the architect. He reasserts ownership by pushing the architect out of the picture. It often takes the form of personal rejection, which the architect finds painful and inexplicable.

Negotiations with prospective clients break down when unspoken requests aren't heard.

Why Negotiations Break Down

Psychologists have isolated some simple rules that clarify these murky waters. One primary rule that can help untangle all communications: people talk and act almost entirely to enhance self-protection, self-interest, or self-esteem. This means that most statements, no matter how carefully disguised, are really requests of one sort or another. Negotiations with prospective clients break down when the unspoken requests aren't heard. Examples:

• A prospective client spoke frequently about skiing; the architect responded with comments on the previous winter's snow conditions. The prospect was actually wondering about the architect's willingness to give his project priority status and push it into construction before winter. The architect didn't hear this and negotiations faded away.

• A corporate real estate manager told an architect, upon first meeting, about his handling of a difficult business situation. The architect responded with a better story. The manager came back with another. The architect one-upped him again. The manager was asking for personal recognition and didn't get it. The architect's one-upmanship effectively terminated the relationship.

Aside from personal validation, there are hard business questions every prospective client wants answered. What's the A/E's record on meeting deadlines and keeping costs within budget? How reliable are the employees and consultants? Does the A/E really have the capabilities to do the job competently? Will other work get more attention? Is the A/E financially sound? Can the A/E's word be trusted?

Some A/Es keep a mental file of stories to tell that answer questions before they are asked. Such stories show the A/E's capabilities and integrity through specific examples.

Listen for unstated requests and concerns in all the casual remarks made by people you deal with. You'll uncover some very helpful surprises beneath the small talk and between the lines of seemingly straightforward business talk.

Maintaining Contact

Many newly formed relationships with clients die from inertia. When both the A/E and client are passive, for certain nothing will happen. If the client is action-oriented but the A/E is slow on the uptake, the client looks around for someone with more drive.

We've found one usually effective method for keeping the spark alive. The goal of the method is sustained positive contact. Sustained contact keeps the A/E involved with the client thinking about a new project. A way to maintain contact is to become the client's information service.

Some firms are quite methodical about this, seeking out problems the prospect may be wrestling with. These then become links for the next stage of contact. "I can get cost data on that to you first thing Monday morning." Come Monday, more detailed questions are sought and a date to deliver the next bit of information is set. If the client doesn't know what questions to ask, the A/E helps find some. There's a pitfall to avoid here: there is no point in finding negative questions that throw the contemplated project into doubt. Instead of "I'd better check the zoning; they may block you on that," it should be "I'll check zoning and the batting average on variances to see what your options are."

There are other pitfalls to watch out for. It's usually a mistake to answer a technical question off the top of your head. It's better to promise speedy delivery of reliable data. Such promises have to be scrupulously followed up. Clients cut loose in a hurry when A/Es have memory problems or take forever to deliver.

The fact-finding approach is augmented by use of the psychological tip cited above, that almost every statement is a request in disguise. For example, a client who complains about heavy responsibilities and time demands can be asking, "Can you carry the ball on this thing and leave me free to take care of other business?" A clue is offered when certain statements are repeated. The repeats indicate that the special implicit meaning of the statement has not been satisfactorily received and

A way to maintain contact is to become the client's information service.

acknowledged.

Advice from Clients about Sales Contact

Corporate facilities executives who frequently deal with A/Es have some good advice on how to improve client contact:

• Don't be shy about initiating contact by phone or letter. One manager points out that his job depends on finding capable and experienced consultants who can perform well for his company. If you have it, he wants to hear about it.

• Make contact, but don't just drop in. It may seem obvious, but managers say it happens frequently. It is inconvenient, and it makes a lousy impression.

• Do homework and rehearse, even when going for a quick, informal interview. Clients say A/Es who are not well prepared often dig holes for themselves. They get nervous under questioning, get carried away talking, make transparent misrepresentations, and sometimes flatly contradict themselves. One airline facilities manager says he likes to encourage A/Es to ramble. It lets the most woefully unprepared and incompetent design professionals quickly weed themselves out.

• Clients commonly complain about offices that change project managers in the middle of a job. It creates confusion. The client almost invariably feels shortchanged, like he is receiving second class treatment.

• Tell what you can do better for the client than your competition can. That's the main thing the client wants to hear about. If there are no advantages to your service, then there's no reason to use it.

What Is Most on Clients' Minds

What is usually most on a client's mind when he interviews design professionals? Two words cover it: cost and time.

Forty-four percent of owners rate the design firm's ability to complete a building on time and within budget as the most important consideration. Twenty-five percent express the same concern by ranking experience with the type of building to be constructed as most important. That is from a survey of clients published by a leading building magazine.

Other points from the survey: 19 percent of clients give top ranking consideration to past dealings with the design firm; 15 percent say ability to produce projects with a minimum of problems is most important. Again, these highest-ranking client considerations are basically the same. Clients look most of all for evidence of care in handling cost, time, and quality control.

The same client needs were reflected in *Fortune* magazine some time back. Fifty-six percent of corporate clients rated experience with the same building type as their most important concern in selecting design firms. Second was excellence of design capability. Third was satisfactory previous work.

Clients are clear about their needs, but the presentations they see often are not. "Irrelevant" is the word we hear most often from clients about design firm presentations. One leading design firm has taken the

Clients say A/Es who are not well prepared often dig holes for themselves.

Irrelevant is the word we hear most often from clients about design firm presentations.

hint and has named "Relevance and Competence" as the guiding themes in all presentation planning.

Government and Politics

Fred A. Stitt

There are lots of minuses in doing work for the federal government. Not only are the regulations and red tape horrendous, but you might try for thirty to forty advertised jobs before landing one. Then, when all is said and done, there's little or no profit, especially the first few times through the process.

Still, there is work available, and the feds are anxious to spread it as widely as possible. A/E selection procedures have been reformed and are reasonably clear and objective. The client won't default on you. If you do the work properly, you get paid for sure. And, after learning the ropes, some A/Es make out just fine with government projects.

Federal officials give A/Es a good look at the current situation during periodic COFPAES Federal Programs conferences. Here's a summary from a previous major conference:

• If you're new to government work, it's desirable to start with smaller jobs. The agencies are more likely to try newcomers on the smaller work, and they're anxious to bring in new, smaller offices. If you perform well, it greatly improves your chances of getting larger jobs later. The checking-out process goes both ways. If you can't stand the paperwork, you'll find out soon enough on a small job without getting swamped by it.

• Many agencies, especially the Department of Defense, have lots of small jobs, remodelings and additions. Procurement procedures are often simpler on these projects. If your office is located near job sites, and if you keep in close touch with the local contracting officers, you may find minimum competition to contend with. Form 254 is fairly simple and often all that's required for consideration for jobs with moderate fees, depending on the agency. But besides submitting the 254 to place on file, you have to let the agency know you are interested in specific jobs.

• For medium- and large-size jobs, you have to deal with two forms, the 254 and the 255. They're available from any of the regional offices of the GSA (no charge). The 254 is a general questionnaire of qualifications. It puts you on the list. Then, when a specific job is advertised, you submit the more detailed Form 255 as your "letter of intent" for the job at hand. You have to submit the 254 to any and all agencies you might be interested in working for. You will not be considered for any particular job just because you've filed a 254.

Important Points about Using the Forms

1. You don't have to fill out the 254 in the same way for each agency. Tailor the record to suit the agency involved. The VA, for example, wants to know about your medical building experience.

2. Agencies want to know what you do best. You save everyone's time and improve your chances by submitting data only on work categories where you have outstanding abilities. Out of the many categories listed on Form 254, stick to about six to eight of your best, and cite three or four examples of each.

3. It's very important to emphasize the experience of your people. It doesn't matter if your office hasn't done a particular building type, so long as you have people who have had the experience. You can cite jobs done by your people for other firms, so long as you avoid implying having done them yourself.

4. Some offices send 255s in response to every job advertisement. The agencies say this dilutes the offices' reputations, and they won't be taken seriously. Be specific—aim for the jobs you're most qualified to do.

5. Keep track of the dates you send in the 254 forms. Updates have to go in every year to keep you in the file—and the agencies won't tell you when your time is up.

6. There's something wrong with nearly three out of four forms submitted. Most errors can be overlooked, but some things—like the large number that are sent in without dates and signatures—can't be accepted. So watch the details.

The old Form 251 wasn't used all that much in A/E selections in years past. Influence and political pressures were important factors—decisive in many cases. This changed radically during the 1970s, but favoritism and corruption problems never go away entirely, and there are hints things may deteriorate badly again. Agency heads generally resented having to bow to political favoritism and welcomed the new procedures. Part of the procedural reform entitles you to be told why, with documentation, you did not receive a job you were running for. (Some agency chiefs say that any undue political pressure on your behalf will propel your 255 right into the reject file no matter how good your qualifications.)

Government jobs are good bread-and-butter for some firms, but neophytes are warned not to expect windfalls. A commission on government procurement study shows most offices make little or no profit on such work. The situation reportedly improves after an office has had some practice in handling the red tape.

Gerre Jones' *Professional Marketing Report* says that 65 percent of all government contracts are issued in October. That's the last month of the federal fiscal year and the last chance for agencies to spend money before it reverts to the U.S. Treasury.

If you work for the feds, don't rely on prompt payments. A Senate hearing disclosed GSA, HEW, DOT, etc., all pay about 70 percent of their invoices late.

Professional Marketing Report says that 65 percent of all government contracts are issued in October.

Avoiding a Hopeless Chase

David Travers

Decisions about what jobs to pursue and how much time and money to spend on the effort should be made on the basis of a well thought out business development program.

How to select jobs to pursue and how much time to spend on the effort are problems totally ignored by the several textbooks on marketing professional services. The books are valuable, no question. They outline sales programs, tell how to marshall forces into an efficient sales machine, how to get leads, and how to follow them as aggressively as conscience and professional objectives will allow. But none mentions an even more basic problem: how to avoid a hopeless chase.

The inclination is to go after anything and everything, especially if you are a worried practitioner who is winding up drawings on the last job in the shop. The theory is: "Buy chances on enough lotteries, and you're bound to win one." Even the A/E juggernauts, who should know better, frequently base their decision on what work to pursue on something other than a hard appraisal of their chances to get the job and the costs of trying. A juicy commission on the horizon can cloud the judgment. For example, a Midwest firm with no hospital experience—not so much as an outpatient clinic to its credit—made a costly effort to get three large hospital projects, pitting itself against firms which had done thousands of beds. This is an instructive example of hope subduing reason, and we'll examine it more closely later.

More and more, architects are being selected on the basis of a rather formal system of comparative analysis and interviewing. A result is that even the most innocent letter expressing interest in providing consultant services can have unpleasant consequences if you ask for a more ambitious bite than you can chew.

First of all, presentations to a search committee can be expensive propositions if done properly. Done badly, they can be even more expensive, costing you where you are most vulnerable: in your reputation. Selection committees don't like their time wasted, and word gets around. And finally, losing out on jobs where you have a good competitive position is bad enough. To reduce your average by repeatedly going after commissions where your chances are at best small can paralyze a firm, draining its morale as well as its finances.

Assess Your Chances Realistically

Decisions about what jobs to pursue and how much time and money to spend on the effort and what to spend the time and money on should be made on the basis of a well thought out business development program that is derived from professional goals, profit objectives, and—

most importantly—a realistic evaluation of a firm's chances compared with competing firms.

Let's take a look at the Midwest firm's unfortunate decision to try to break into hospital work without any hospital experience. Firstly, it was anxious to get into a new and fruitful field. Enthusiasm had ebbed for its bread-and-butter work—hotels and other commercial buildings. It felt fettered by its own specialized capabilities. Two of the firm's proposals, for mammoth federal medical centers, were made in association with a small regional office that had some forty- to ninety-bed community hospital experience. The smaller office asked the larger one to associate, needing its substance and believing it to have political influence (which it didn't) and to know its way around the federal labyrinth (which it also didn't. The aura of business ability that clings to the largest of the A/E firms is as persistent as it is false. The view might be understandable if it were just the small looking at the large, but even large firms believe their peers to be free of their own faults and inefficiencies.).

The larger firm carelessly agreed, thinking it had nothing to lose. But, because of its greater manpower and graphics capabilities, preparation of the proposals and combined 255 form fell to it. The cost in time and materials was on the order of $5,000. The result: 0 for 2.

The third job, a 350-bed hospital, was brought to the large firm by a friendly and influential hospital planner who asked if the firm wanted to be included in a select list of A/Es to be considered for the project. There would be an expensive out-of-state interview requiring the attendance of the proposed project team. The partners huddled. They had a few medical office buildings and a psychiatric nursing home to their credit. On top of that was their hotel experience. And what the hell, hospitals are just hotels for the sick, aren't they? The decision was to accept the invitation.

The air around the partner assigned to the job became unpleasantly charged as he researched hospital design. He suddenly found himself in a strange new world with foreign technologies and a language that only resembled English—intensive care, acute care, extended care, nuclear medicine, multiphasic screening. Another huddle and a sober reconsideration by the partners. They were now caught between two stools: attend the interview, show their ignorance, humiliate the firm, and embarrass the friendly planner; or not attend and also embarrass the planner, but perhaps less so. They chose to withdraw.

They were now 0 for 3 and the cost of their folly: one friendly and influential consultant and the earlier $5,000.

Deal from Strength

The competition for every commission is getting stiffer. This calls for dealing from your greatest strength, not exposing your weaknesses. Let's take a moment to analyze what constitutes the general strengths of an office and then look at specifics. Viewed from the marketplace, the design office has shaken down into three major types of operation. Classified by business strength and strategy, they are:

The competition for every commission is getting stiffer.

The Design Office. Relatively small, elite, and exclusive, this category produces high profit-margin design. Preeminent design talent—real or illusory—is its competitive edge. In a price-conscious world, these offices are not competitive in terms of cost. The most successful of them can pick and choose among the limited number of institutional and corporate clients for whom cost is, at most, of incidental concern.

The Volume Office. In its purest form, this category is the polar opposite of the design office. Highly competitive and market oriented, it deals in a large volume of diversified services and uses the sophisticated selling and promotional techniques of big business—which it is—including the exploitation of bigness itself. To maintain a high volume of work, this office follows a strategy of growth in capacity and in capabilities by acquisition of talent and skills. It may go public, invest in its own projects, merge with like-minded aggressive firms in related fields, etc. It rapidly discovers and penetrates new markets as they open up, acquiring existing regional practices rather than associating or joint venturing with them. (This may seem to be reinforcing the myth of infallibility which surrounds the big firm, but this is a description of its strategies, not its successes.)

The "*Line of Strength*" Office. This is a catchall category. Firms in this third and by far the largest classification have achieved whatever measure of success is theirs by developing and following their own lines of strength. The competitive advantage of this office is the result of a resourceful pursuit of at least one—but usually more than one—of the following strategies: specialization (building types); design skill (solid but unspectacular); efficiency of operation (lower fees); geographical specialization (local influence); ideas (better mousetraps); and promotional skill (aggressive sales).

Evaluating Your Strengths

A fifth element that can completely upset what would otherwise be a very simple equation: influence.

The ability of a firm to capture a particular commission is related to the sum of its relevant experience, its capabilities, reputation, and ability to present these qualities effectively—plus a fifth element that can completely upset what would otherwise be a very simple equation: influence. Each of these factors has component elements. Below, I have broken out what I consider to be the most important from the client's point of view and I have assigned values to them corresponding to their importance. In this manner, the designer can assess his and his competitors' strengths in specific prospecting situations.

1. Experience
   • Experience with projects of the same type and equal or larger size. Same type means exactly that. If the job in question is a hospital, don't count clinics, medical office buildings, or pharmacies—only hospitals, and they must be of comparable size (same number of beds minus 10 percent OK). If it's a forty-story corporate monument, no ten-, fifteen- or even thirty-story spec office buildings.

Values:

Ten or more projects $= 100$ points each
Six to ten $= n^2$
One to five $= n \times 2$

• Experience with the same project type but smaller in size. Still no pharmacies, etc., for hospitals; no motels for hotels. If it's an 800- room downtown convention hotel and your or the competitor's experience is with 150- or 200-room motels, don't count them here. They're in the next category.

Value:

Ten or more projects $= 20$ points each
Six to ten $= n \times 2$
One to five $= n$

• Experience with projects of related type. Examples: motels for hotels; five- and ten-story speculative office buildings for twenty-five- and thirty-story office buildings; neighborhood shopping centers for regional shopping centers, etc.

Value: $n/2$

2. Capabilities

• Size of firm. Given an important project, generally the larger the firm, the greater the competitive advantage. Smallness is suspect, even (especially?) when it's deliberately maintained. Bigness, on the other hand, connotes strength and stability. Unless, then, you know that the client is an exception to the rule: Value equals staff size.

• In-house disciplines. Although special circumstances, including local custom, vary the rule, generally clients prefer to deal with one design consultant, and it is a decided advantage to have in-house all of the disciplines that the client will require for the project at hand.

Value:

All services required	$= 50$ points
Architectural & structural only	$= 25$ points
Architectural only	$= 10$ points
Design only	$= 1$ point

If less than full A/E services are required, scale all categories upward; e.g., if only architectural and structural are asked for by the client, then that level of service becomes worth 50 points, Architectural $= 25$, Design $= 10$.

3. Reputation

The importance of a good professional reputation is manifest. The chances are that good general repute is what got you and the others on the list. Now you need specific references—impressive and persuasive third-party recommendations. The range of points allows you to scale yourself and your competition according to:

• The importance of the person or company giving the recommendation. The closer he is to being a respected peer of the prospective client, the greater his influence will be.

• The enthusiasm of his recommendation, which is a function of his satisfaction with the building(s) you or your competitor did for him, adherence of the project(s) to budget, quality of the services rendered, fees charged. The prospective client will also factor in the relevance of the project(s) done for the recommender to his own. Value: 0 to 100 per reference up to a limit of 200 points.

Usually you will be familiar enough with the reputations of your competitors to be able to quantify them. Finding out who they are may take some digging. You don't have to know the name of every firm being considered, however, to come up with a reasonable estimate of your odds.

Look out for the anomaly on the list, the one you can't understand being considered. There's probably a very good reason that he is there, and it is also probably not favorable to your cause.

4. Presentation Technique

There are two theories about the role and importance of client presentations and interviews. One is that they are the big opportunity to sell your firm and clinch the job. The selection committee, in this view, has gone over the brochures and qualifications materials of all the candidates and is eagerly waiting to have questions answered and doubts resolved. The firms that don't shine will be sent packing. In short, this theory holds that it's during the interview that a commission is won or lost.

The other theory maintains that the presentation-interview process is actually one of elimination. The task of the committee is to reduce the number of firms qualified to undertake the job at hand to three or two or even one. It is looking for flaws in the candidates' experience, abilities, character. The differences for which the committee is looking are negative ones. According to this view, most candidates will blow it somehow, and if a firm can just make it through the interview without doing anything wrong, it will find that it has made the cut.

I subscribe to the second theory that there is more to be lost than gained in the interview and suggest you put an upper limit of twenty points on presentation ability. I also suggest you keep your presentations simple and idiot-proof.

5. Influence

Even if you've been honest in the appraisal of your experience, capabilities, reputation, and presentation ability, the influence wielded by you or your competitors can play havoc with the calculations. It's possible to get a job with only influence and a license (remember the anomaly on the list I warned you about). Not only can influence be the most powerful of the five factors, it is the most elusive. In a philosophically egalitarian society, favoritism—whether from friendship or darker motives—is not advertised. It's private in nature, but it exists.

Start with an assessment of your own direct and indirect influence. Have you ever done a project for a respected competitor of the prospective client? Do you know the prospect? Do you know anyone close to him? (One firm's librarian does profiles on important prospects, finding out where he and his key people went to school, what clubs they belong to, and the like. A search of alumni lists and membership rosters reveals useful names often enough to be worthwhile.)

In evaluating the competition's influence, you should assume that

This theory holds that it's during the interview that a commission is won or lost.

It's possible to get a job with only influence and a license.

if they have been in business locally for any length of time, they will at least know someone who knows the client. The more active a competitor is in the community—socially, professionally, philanthropically—the more influence he is likely to wield. Influence can be of such titanic importance that you should do your utmost to uncover any that may exist on your part or that of the competition.

The point range here is large; the depth and warmth of the relationship are the controlling factors:

• Previous project designed for the same client. Considerations: client satisfaction and relevance of the project to the present one. If you've done a good job of a relevant nature for this client and none of the others has, the commission is yours—providing there has not been a catastrophic change in your firm or the client's. Value: 0 to 500

• Previous project designed for a member of the client's selection committee or, if there is no committee, then for a member of the client's board of directors. Same considerations as above. Also consider the strength of the particular committee or board member in the client's scheme of things. In other words, what is *his* influence? Value: 0 to 200

• Prospect is a friend or acquaintance. You tend to run in the same or touching circles, and the prospect has had a chance to appraise you, but in nonprofessional circumstances. Value: 0 to 100

• Prospect is a friend of a friend. This is a three-way relationship and difficult to give value to with any certainty. To be safe, be conservative in your own behalf and liberal with the competition. Value: 0 to 50

• Know a key man in the client's organization who is assigned to the project. Value: 0 to 50

• Know key executives in the client's organization. Value: 0 to 15 each

• Know members of the selection board or board of directors. Value: 0 to 20 each

In each of the categories, I have listed the obvious kinds of qualities and relationships. You should not take the list as definitive; add to it, refine it in any way that you can. The more inclusive and finer grained it is, the more accurate will be your forecasting.

Let's work out the probabilities on a hypothetical project (see Evaluation Table). It is a twelve-story, 170,000-square-foot headquarters office building for a growing company, located in a suburban population center of a large metropolitan area. The building will have more space than the client now needs, but he plans to grow into it. Meanwhile, about half the building will be rented out. The client is president, chairman, CEO, and founder of his company. He has appointed four of his board members and his operations chief to a search committee. The client will make the final selection from the top three firms out of a field of ten. The architectural firm in which we are interested is a thirty-five-man office, down fifteen people from last year when it billed $2 million (including engineering, which it bought). It has been in business about ten years, growing sufficiently in the good times to weather the bad. Its largest volume has been in low-rise apartment developments, which led it into planned unit development. In the last three years, the office has done several low- and medium-rise apartment buildings in conjunction with PUDs, but now is looking desperately for another market. The principal has never had much time for a social life, which probably means that he prefers not to have one. He has a reputation as a competent practitioner.

1. Experience
   • Projects of the same type and size: the office has done two twelve-story office buildings of about the same square footage and one fifteen-story office structure.

   Value = 9 points (n2)

   • Projects of the same type but smaller: the firm has completed seven office buildings in the two- to five-story range.

   Value = 14 points

   • Projects of a related type: none.

2. Capabilities
   • Size of firm: 35 people
   Value = 35 points.
   • In-house disciplines: architectural, but that is all that is required.
   Value = 50 points.

3. Reputation

   This is a judgment call, so no self-delusion allowed. The firm has done only three buildings of the same type and size or larger. The last one was the fifteen-story structure for a savings and loan, whose president is on the board of the client's company and also on his selection committee. That's why the firm is on the list. He got the earlier building because the savings and loan had financed two of the residential developments designed by the firm, and the savings and loan president was favorably impressed.

   The firm's performance on the S&L building was good. Our friend the architect had decided wisely to please the client at all costs, believing that he would or could be of future help. Question: should the good will of the S&L president be counted both here and under "influence," where it should certainly be counted? In the interest of a conservative evaluation, I suggest not.

   The prior building was published in one of the professional journals, and this should be considered here. Also the good references from the clients of the smaller office buildings, who were pleased with the firm's performance.

   Value = 50 points.

4. Presentation Technique

   Although the principal of the firm is effective when talking about residential development, he is still learning about office buildings and hasn't much in the way of visuals.

   Value = 0.

5. Influence

   The firm's strength here is its relationship with the S&L president on the committee. Everything depends upon how steadfastly he will fight for the firm during the initial elimination process. And then, if it makes the cut, how effective he is with the client. His S&L is considering financing the project, which should count heavily with the client.

Value = 200 points.

EVALUATION TABLE

	Our Firm	1	2	3	4	5	6	7	8	9
1. Experience										
a. Projects of same type/size										
Values: ten or more = 100 points each		1100			1300					
six to ten = n^2			36	64						
one to five = n times 2	6					4				
b. Projects of same type/smaller										
Values: ten or more = 20 points each										
six to ten = n times 2	14									
one to five = n						3				
c. Projects of a related type										
Value: n/2	35	230	70	80	100	10				
2. Capabilities										
a. Size of firm										
Value: number of employees										
b. In-house disciplines*										
all required services offered = 50 points										
architectural and structural only = 25 points										
architectural only = 10 points	50	50	50	50	50					
design only = 1 point						25				

Note that "all required services offered = 50 points. Thus, if architectural and structural are all required, it is worth 50. Architectural only becomes 25, design only 10.

	Our Firm	1	2	3	4	5	6	7	8	9
3. Reputation										
Considerations are:										
a. Importance of references to client										
b. Enthusiasm of recommendations (a function of satisfaction with services, fees, adherence to time and budget schedules, etc.)										
c. Relevance of projects done for references										
Value: 0 to 100 points	50	90	75	75	90	25				
4. Presentation Effectiveness										
Value: 0 to 20 points	0	15	5	10	10	0				
5. Influence										
a. Designed prior project for prospect										
Value: 0 to 500 points										
b. Know prospect nonprofessionally										
Value: 0 to 100 points		50	80	25		20				
c. Prospect is a friend of a friend										
Value: 0 to 50 points						50				
d. Know key man assigned to the project										
Value: 0 to 50 points		25								
e. Know key executives in client organization										
Value: 0 to 15 points		30								
f. Designed prior projects for a member of selection committee or board of directors										
Value: 0 to 250 points	200									
g. Know member of selection committee or board of directors										
Value: 0 to 50 points each		60	30		30					
A. Individual Totals	355	1650	346	304	1580	137	?	?	?	?
B. Total of All On List					4372					
C. Probabilities (A/B)	.08	.38	.08	.07	.36	.03				

The combined chances of competitors 1 and 4 getting the commission are 74 percent.

Figuring the Chances

Our friend's total is 355 points. Those allotted to the competition are self-explanatory now that we've gone through one tabulation. Let's say that our architect is familiar with five of the firms on the list, those that are in his area. The other four are out of town and unknown quantities. (If the picture is not clear using the firms with which you are familiar, you should call any contacts you may have in the home towns of the unknowns to get a line on them.)

By taking the grand total of all points, dividing that total into the individual totals, we can get a percentage of probability for each firm. Bear in mind that the four firms not figured into the total lessen the chances of all the others to some unknown degree, i.e., the 8 percent probability of our friend is inflated.

In addition to providing an estimate of a firm's chances, the percentages indicate how much time and money should reasonably be spent in the attempt to get the job:

1. The building will be about 170,000 square feet. At $70 a foot, that amounts to $11,900,000 in construction.

2. The fee should be about 5 percent, but half of that will go to the engineering consultants, leaving 2.5 percent or about $300,000 for the architect.

3. A reasonable ratio of promotional direct labor and expense to fee is 5 percent, in this case $15,000. Since the chances of the firm getting the project are only 8 percent (actually less than that because of the four unknown competitors), we should discount the expenditures accordingly. That is, the actual expenditure on going after the job should be in line with the probabilities of getting it. In this case that would be 8 percent of $15,000 or $1,200.

That is the absolute maximum. In reality, the firm should only spend that much if it will later have good use for the presentation materials developed and the experience gained in pursuit of the project.

The times call for prudence and self-control in all aspects of your operation. Plan, and then adhere to the plan, deviating only after a hard appraisal of the situation and a skeptical look at your own motives. Keep records of the costs of pursuing work; build up information on your successes and failures, and evaluate. You may find yourself winning more commissions—you certainly will lose fewer.

The times call for prudence and self-control in all aspects of you operation.

Follow Up—Win or Lose

There are several important follow-up points in professional services marketing. They include:

1. After the initial telephone qualification call (or other type of first prospect contact), when you've decided to pursue the job.
2. Following the first face-to-face meeting with the prospect.
3. After the formal presentation.
4. Following the submission of a written proposal.
5. After the award of a project—particularly if you lost!

The method of follow-up in any given situation will be dictated by your current reading of the prospective client and the information you've amassed through intelligence gathering. The follow-up might be in the form of a telephone call, a memo, a handwritten note, a formal letter, a reprint, or a relevant news clipping on almost any subject related to identified interests of the prospect.

It's Easy for the Winner

This discussion will concentrate on follow-up point number five; after project award. If your firm was selected, the follow-up is a much more pleasant, upbeat task. For all of the losers, it is a sometimes difficult, but always necessary, windup to the whole marketing process. There are, incidentally, no other numbers involved in selection beyond number one. Marketing people are prone to try to take some of the sting out of being passed over by references to finishing second or third. In selling there is number one, the winner, and all of the others (the losers), and any attempt to camouflage the true situation serves absolutely no useful purpose.

When your firm has been selected we recommend an occasional check back with the client to find out what tipped the scale in your favor. The answers could be helpful in planning future presentations—at least to the same type of client. The approach might be along the lines that you know the client had a difficult choice to make, and for the potential mutual benefit of your future relationship could they tell you some of the areas of consideration in which your firm seemed to stand out in their final evaluation.

You should make it very clear that your interest is not in why the others lost—that's a negative approach and usually will be counterproductive. A little logic applied to the answers should give you most of these reasons anyway.

Gerre Jones

There are no other numbers involved in selection beyond number one.

Always Follow Up a Loss

When the job goes to someone else, which will be 75 to 90 percent of the time, try to find out why—particularly if several cuts were survived before the final interview. Unbelievable as it sounds, many offices drop all further contact with potential clients as soon as they learn that they were passed over for a particular project. It is only simple courtesy to thank the client for his consideration and visit, if there was an interview, and it is good basic public relations for future consideration by the client and his associates. If it can be learned from the client or other sources which firm was selected, assure the client that he made an excellent choice, preferably in writing with a copy to the principal of the firm that was selected. Such a gesture costs nothing, it is a sign of professionalism, shows that you are a good sport to the prospective client—for whatever that could be worth when another job comes along in his organization—and is bound to leave a lasting, favorable impression on the winning designer.

Finally, maintain contact with all clients and potential clients, regardless of the outcome of any one presentation. If the approaches are kept open to bridges which were painstakingly built over the weeks and months leading up to a presentation, the possibilities for consideration for future projects should be excellent.

The two preceding paragraphs appear on pages 163-164 of *How to Market Professional Design Services* and furnish a kind of introduction to the remainder of this article.

Client Constraints and Concerns

When you've lost and extend yourself to congratulate clients on their selection it can have a reassuring side effect. The buyer of a service is at a distinct disadvantage vis-a-vis the buyer of most products. Where product buyers have an opportunity to apply the five senses to their tangible purchase—to squeeze, smell, taste, kick, heft, observe, and listen—before making a commitment to buy, the purchasers of services are forced to make commitments long before "production." They have only unfulfilled promises of performance by the seller, presenting a much more difficult buying decision for most people.

Any client who has just made a decision to entrust X thousand or million dollars (usually of someone else's money) to a design firm is understandably nervous—no matter how many times he or she has been through the process. A little encouragement from another design professional about the choice can be an important psychological boost. And the client is not apt to forget where the needed encouragement came from.

Some (too many) design professionals are loathe to go back to the client for a debriefing, feeling it is somehow unprofessional or an imposition on the client. Neither supposition is true. It is unprofessional not to attempt to improve your marketing efforts and the image of the firm they project to clients and other outsiders. And as for the client, debriefing research is justified on the basis of the investment made by a design firm in presenting to the client. The client owes you the information.

Too many design professionals are loathe to go back to the client for a debriefing.

Ask for Help

When going back to a lost client, attitude is important, whether the follow-up is by phone or in person. What must come through to the client is "We need your help," rather than "Why didn't we get the job?" (or, worst of all, "Why did XYZ Associates get the job?") Strive for an atmosphere of the client assisting your firm to do a better job the next time around. You are looking for information about symbols (the presentation as a communications exercise) as well as substance (where and how did it come through to the client that you were less able or experienced than the competition?). Don't confine your postpresentation research to just the presentation itself. Some or all of your graphic tools (brochures, proposals, reprints) may have fallen short of the mark in conveying the proper professional image and your experience to the prospect. Perhaps a personality conflict developed during the presentation, but went unnoticed or unreported by any of the presenting team. Perhaps the presenters or the presentation did not come through as an organized and relevant exposition. Take the follow-up questions as far as you feel you can.

Clients Expect a Follow-up

Many federal agencies make it a point to offer debriefings to losing firms following a presentation. One of these is the Postal Service. In a conversation several years ago, Todd Kite of the Postal Service estimated that fewer than 10 percent of the firms interviewed contacted him later for a debriefing on the selection.

The Veterans Administration is another agency that attempts to give every break to firms interviewed for VA projects—both before and after presentations. Mike Schaller, chairman of the agency's A/E evaluation board, in addition to being very available for face-to-face meetings in his office, furnishes copies of the VA evaluation board's criteria and scoring sheets (VA Form 08-3375) and a list of all firms to be interviewed to each firm selected to make a presentation.

It is discouraging to note that many short-listed firms choose to ignore this kind of assistance. The evaluation sheet should tell a design office quite a lot about structure and points of emphasis for the presentation. A review of the competition should give a marketing director certain guidance on the same points. According to the VA, perhaps 20 percent of the presentations made appear to have taken any note of the material furnished by Schaller's office.

As for follow-up, the record is little better, in spite of an expressed official willingness to provide feedback to those firms not selected. While a personal visit is probably the most productive, telephone calls are readily accepted and letters of inquiry promptly answered by Mike Schaller.

Imaginary Rules

Most corporate representatives we have dealt with recognize the importance of feedback to design firms following a series of presentations. While they may not go to the lengths to offer follow-up debriefings as some government agencies, I have never experienced a refusal from a corporate client to discuss the matter.

Management consultant Dr. Richard E. Byrd suggests that most design professionals tend to be very careful about breaking real or imaginary rules set up by clients. And most of the time the "rule" turns out to be an assumption made by design professionals—or it is a silly or unnecessary rule that they are not willing to test.

While Dr. Byrd's original reference dealt primarily with preinterview activities, it is just as applicable to postpresentation activities. Somehow a feeling becomes established that a prospect shouldn't be bothered after a selection is announced. Earlier we suggested that such ideas might be based on misplaced concerns about unprofessionalism or "bothering" a client—to which we added, "Not true!"

In summary, keep in mind that postinterview debriefings are an important part of intelligence gathering—a logical continuation of the total marketing process. There is nothing demeaning about going back to lost prospects to ask for their help in making your future marketing more responsive (and productive).

The economics of the situation make it imperative for a firm to engage in such follow-back work. Odds are that the lost client will have at least one more project in the reasonably near future. By having made one shortlist, your firm is already prequalified in the client's mind. Thus, much of the front-end marketing costs will not have to be incurred again the next time around with the client—if you maintain contact—and those costs can be amortized, in a sense, in future project pursuit.

Finally, make all information obtained in follow-ups available to others in the firm for their general guidance in future interviews and in dealings with that client. A memo to the file on the follow-up, with copies to those involved, is one way of disseminating the information. Over a period of time certain specifics may begin to emerge from this kind of research. One presenter may generate more personality conflicts with client interview teams than anyone else in the firm. Or other presenters may just not be able to project themselves as being comfortable and at ease in front of a client group. In such cases early and radical surgery is indicated. Retraining may be the answer, but you cannot allow anyone to represent your firm in a presentation who consistently alienates the prospective client—for whatever reason.

Post-interview debriefings are an important part of intelligence gathering—a logical continuation of the total marketing process.

Market Research

One of the least understood, least used, yet valuable tools of marketing that is coming more into use is research—market research. For architects and engineers, market research is an effective means of gauging the type and extent of project design work anticipated in a given territory or specialty.

The successful use of market research for large and small A/E firms alike can help in the following ways:

1. Determine whether the kinds of project work they are strong in will likely be available over the next year or so.

2. Allow firms to develop a planned strategy for going after work (the marketing plan).

3. From market research feedback, enable firms to match up and adjust projected work to the strengths of their staffs.

4. In the long run, market research helps to smooth out the peaks and valleys of operation that so many architects and engineers go through. In essence, it works against two philosophies that unfortunately are all too prevalent: a) turn on selling effort when production schedules are down and turn off selling effort when the pipeline is full; and b) we can design anything, so we go after everything (as opposed to capitalizing on firm strengths by project types and being selective in selling effort).

We have found in consulting to A/E firms that those firms that develop more formalized marketing plans and use market research to gauge work and for projections generally produce dramatically more proposal opportunities than those firms that trust strictly to a cold-call, selling activity.

As indicated, both large and small firms can use and afford market research. The form of research can be simple and self-conducted. I often recommend to firms when putting their first formal marketing plans together that they do their own, what I call, "50¢ market research." It is a learning experience; they see how it fits into marketing strategy; and when these firms eventually do turn to more involved and advanced forms of research by using research consultants, they better understand what can and cannot be accomplished; how to organize the approach; and how to interpret feedback.

Steps to Follow

What follows is an example of how a small firm can conduct its own 50¢ market research:

John Coyne

Both large and small firms can use and afford market research.

1. Look over the firm's past year to two-year workload and determine the percent mix—the break out of project work by type. Example—hospitals versus classroom buildings versus municipal facilities (fire halls, jails, maintenance garages) versus commercial or industrial projects, etc., if yours is an architectural firm. For engineers, measure mix of waste water treatment plants, versus bridges, streets and highways, piping, energy, etc.

2. Based on project-type mix and location of work over the year or two, identify, if you are an architect in health care, let's say ten to twenty hospital administrator clients, prospects, or source people that you feel can share with you their knowledge of projected design work for a given territory, county, etc., over the next year. If you were to identify ten such people in a county, you might have three past clients; three prospects you tried to win but didn't; three potential clients you haven't met but who can fill out the geographical county spread or representation; and possibly one banker or attorney who either has a good handle on building design activity in an area and/or has clients in building ownership, real estate, and planning (therefore privy to the contemplated market).

Of course, the larger the lineup of people you have (known as the "sample"), the better chance you have of gaining a reliable fix on anticipated work. The above example is for hospitals. Repeat the process if you want industrial, commercial, or municipal feedback.

Some other people you might add to your list for firsthand research input include client board members, zoning commission members, research staff of companies and utilities, chamber of commerce/industrial commission development people, stockbrokers, commercial real estate brokers, public relations people (private and public sectors); the list can go on and on.

3. Next, create an outline of what you are going to say when you telephone each person on your client research lineup. That's right, I suggest you telephone these people...don't go see them (to save time and to lessen embarrassment your first time into this task). On what to say, it is suggested that you

- introduce yourself and the firm right off;
- indicate the purpose of the call is to help develop your firm's marketing plan; ask for five minutes of their time, that you would appreciate their help/appraisal of projected hospital design work (or whatever) over the next year or so;

Assure them you are not calling to determine their specific plans or to gain leads.

- assure them you are not calling to determine their specific plans or to gain leads (this is true, although you may end up with some);
- ask if you are calling at a good time or if a better time should be scheduled;
- indicate that more and more architects and engineers are turning to planned, formalized marketing, so you, like others, are attempting to develop good market research and can use their help.

Open-Ended Questions
4. If given the go-ahead, proceed to ask open-ended questions such

as: "How do you perceive the amount and kind of hospital (or whatever) design work over the next year?...What is your appraisal, best guess for work—new beds, replacement, renovation, conversion to outpatient, or what?...What do you see for auxiliary facilities, for elderly housing, etc.?" While you're talking, you might ask, "From a hospital administrator's standpoint, what are the main services or benefits architects in this area should be offering hospital clients?"

5. Then, listen carefully to feedback and make notes. Where I have seen variations of this research approach used, it has: (a) given firms a good and legitimate reason for calling—also made some feel more comfortable; (b) turned up good input; (c) turned off maybe one in twenty or thirty people called (generally these probably wouldn't make good clients anyway); (d) frequently flattered the people called who respond willingly with information; often they think more highly of A/Es who plan their marketing effort and seek advice; sometimes they refer you to other good sources for information.

6. After your calls, set up a rating scale based on feedback. An example might be as follows:

If eight of ten people called favorably appraise the type of work, rate the potential of the area Excellent.

If six are favorable, rate Good to Very Good.

If four are favorable, rate Average.

If three or less are favorable, rate Poor.

Such a rating per county, section of county, state, etc., will help you decide where to put your selling, staff, and travel effort in priority against rated potential. You will be on your way toward being more selective. The exercise will make your strategy and new business projections more realistic in your marketing plan.

In summary, what has been described is a simple, unsophisticated, informal research approach that can be used by large or small firms. The approach has most of the ingredients of advanced interview research techniques. Using it and adapting it to your firm will help you increase the odds of a successfully planned marketing effort. Try it and I believe you will find value in 50¢ market research.

Prospecting for New Business

Raymond L. Gaio,
AIA

Those responsible for business development frequently overlook two prime client sources: past clients and previously lost prospects.

Past Clients

An analysis of the client mix of design firms shows that repeat business from past clients ranges can range up to 75 percent of the total current work load when there is a planned, purposeful, aggressive program aimed at recapturing them. Without an organized effort, past clients usually remain past clients.

One of our architect clients recently sent out announcements of a name change and incorporation. The mailing included all current and past clients, including those for whom the firm had worked in its first years of operation. A few days later, there was a call from a client the firm had done a small project for a decade before. Not having had any contact with the firm in the intervening years, the past client had felt that the design firm wasn't interested in his business. The simple announcement card resulted in the past client giving the firm a $500,000 construction project, large enough to more than pay for the cost of the announcement.

This was no isolated case. We have all heard past clients say, "I thought you had outgrown us," or "I decided you didn't want anymore business from us," or express some similar sentiment after reestablishing contact after years of neglect.

There are endless ways of maintaining contact with a past client for whom you want to do continuing work.

Another immediate step in organizing a productive business development program is an analysis of jobs lost in recent years.

Lost Prospects

Another immediate step in organizing a productive business development program is an analysis of jobs lost in recent years. Usually the purpose of lost-job analysis is to pick up weaknesses in your marketing

Project	Client	Date	Reason Lost, & to Whom
City Center Community College, Centerville	Indiana Comm. Coll. Board	May 1979	Didn't make final cut. XYZ selected. They had 3 completed CCs to our 1.
Interstate Bank Bldg.	Weston Development	Jan 1980	Bid too high. ABC selected (influence).

techniques, but the same information can be used for cultivating lost clients. It is a particularly useful source of continuing contacts when the firm has survived several cuts and was in the final three to five firms under consideration by the lost client. The assumption is that the client must have liked some things about the firm, and there should be no reluctance in calling him about future projects.

An important point to keep in mind about both past and lost clients is that much of the qualification work, information gathering, and contact cultivation done for the earlier presentation will still be valid if not left to languish too long. This means saving marketing time and money.

Marketing Rules of Thumb

• Out of every ten contacts (potential clients), one solid prospect should result.

• Out of every five presentations to live and solid prospects, one job can be expected.

• This means that out of 100 contacts, there should be ten good prospects. Presentations to them should result in two jobs.

• Lead time for results in a business development program is about nine months.

On the average each contact will take two hours, including intelligence gathering and contact, so that you have an investment in time of some 100 hours per job won. If the business developer's time is valued at $30 per hour (DPE), the cost is about $3,000 per job. For a $2 million project with a 6 percent fee of $120,000, that is 2.5 percent of the fee for direct sales costs, which accords well with the normal range of promotion costs of 5-7 percent of net billings, including marketing tools and support costs.

Prospecting

Meet with your local banker, lawyers, accountants, suppliers, consultants, savings and loan officers, real estate and mortgage brokers, major contractors, congressmen, state and local politicians, and community leaders. Learn about their financial policies and local trends in construction and the economy. Acquaint them with your firm and its services. After all such meetings, follow up periodically by mail, phone, and personal visits. Put them on your promotional mailing list.

Internally, alert the staff to their importance in the business development scheme of things. They all have contacts and relationships that can supplement yours. Create an incentive program which recognizes staff input to the program, whether through bonuses, profit sharing, promotion, added vacation time—something tangible.

Prospect Reference Sources and Lists

1. Studies and surveys by organizations such as Dun & Bradstreet for:
• Prospect identification (and qualification);
• List of corporate contacts.

Lead time for results in a business developement program is about nine months.

2. City, county, state, and regional industrial development councils and authorities, including the Department of Commerce funding program.

3. Past and lost clients

4. *Federal Telephone Directory* published by
    Consolidated Directories, Inc.
    1133 15th St., NW
    Washington, DC 20005

This contains 80 offices and agencies of the federal government.

Intelligence Gathering

Alert the staff to their importance in the business development scheme of things.

The intelligence gathering process begins as soon as a lead is discovered. The initial project qualification call is the first step, with the decision whether to go after the job still to be made. Six basic points should be determined:

1. Identity and nature of the prospective client. If corporate, an immediate effort should be made to get a copy of an annual report.

2. What is the program?
   • Is it a real job? Are planning and construction funds in hand?
   • If not, how much and at what stages will funding have to be obtained? (Sources: bank loan, bond issue, etc.)
   • What is the budget? How was it established? How firm is it? How sound is it?
   • Client's motivation to build?
   • Who will develop program requirements (in-house, the A/E to be hired, other professionals)?
   • If the program is already developed, how flexible is it?

3. Where is the site? If no site, will the consultant be involved in its selection?

The intelligence gathering process begins as soon as a lead is discovered.

4. What is the selection process?
   • How many firms to be considered?
   • Initial screening process to be based on written proposals, interviews, both, or no contact before final selection?
   • Who does the screening?
   • Who makes the final selection?

5. What is the selection timetable?

6. What is the project design timetable?

Know the Competition

A key to staying ahead in any field is knowing what the competition is doing. It is important to involve everyone in the office in keeping an eye on your competitors. The professional and trade magazines tell of new projects won, completed work, personnel changes. Speeches, reports, brochures by competitors can provide information as can clients and potential clients. All such information should be fed to the business development staff who can filter it and disseminate it.

Initial Submission

When the process turns up a suitable project, an expression of your interest and qualifications must go to the prospective client. Preparation of the material is of critical importance. The AIA suggests that several general considerations operate at this stage:

1. Firms with previous experience in designing the type of project planned will be given priority attention.

2. If all firms respond to a given question with the same answer, the question becomes meaningless in the selection process, no matter how correct.

3. Standard brochures will not receive the same degree of attention as specially prepared material, everything else being equal (which it seldom is).

4. The elaborateness of a submission is seldom important. On the other hand, graphic quality tells much about a firm and can be very important.

5. Complete the submission in the briefest possible way.

6. It is important to convey the firm's genuine interest in doing the project but without servility.

7. The covering letter is possibly the most important document in the submittal and it should be a "selling" letter, keeping in mind the point about brevity.

A key to staying ahead in any field is knowing what the competition is doing.

Prospecting for Work by Telephone

Fred A. Stitt

Hundreds of A/E firms use the telephone as their primary marketing tool. Telephone prospecting has served some of them very well; others have fared poorly.

One common failing in telephone solicitation: offices quit too soon. Those who maintain successful marketing programs say they experience time lags of from four to nine months or more, before their programs start to pay off. That's a long time, especially when cash is running low, and most firms immediately slow down on the calls as soon as new work develops.

Architects are especially prone to resist cold calls. They often feel inept, telephone shy, and even guilty about seeking work from strangers. An architect may get psyched up to initiate a program, but doubts creep in and drain energy away. Lots of excuses often come up to turn attention to other, more "pressing" business.

How do firms that successfully use telephoning actually fare? Some get up to ten or more paying projects out of every hundred cold-call contacts. Some only nab one or two out of a hundred tries, but still consider the effort worthwhile. It's not unusual for A/Es to pick up as much as 50 percent of their new work through cold-call data gathering and self-initiated sales contact.

It's not unusual for A/Es to pick up as much as 50 percent of their new work through cold-call data gathering and sales contact.

The calls to prospects are one part of a lengthy process. A good call leads to a face-to-face meeting with the prospective client. After a meeting, there's "reminder" contact. After awhile, there may be formal preliminary screening for an upcoming project. Then there may be a detailed review of qualifications and an invitation for a proposal. There are pitfalls at every step, but each step is possible only because of the preceding one. Confirmed telephone addicts say all the steps are important, but they can never come about at all without that first phone call.

The Call List

Who do you call? There are differences of opinion on this. Some offices say they call "everyone there is." Some focus only on prospective clients who are reportedly considering a definite project. There's no reason not to do both. A good call list would include all major corporations in the design firm's market area; all city, state, and regional government agencies; local representatives of federal agencies; transit authorities; nonprofit institutions; banks and savings and loan companies; unions;

public utilities; and all locally active contractors, developers, and mortgage brokers.

How do you locate those prospects? Any number of directories are available at libraries, such as the *Thomas' Register*, Dun & Bradstreet, or other lists of corporate officers. Some firms use mailing list companies as name sources, trade association membership rosters, subscription lists of highly specialized trade publications, etc. News clippings are a good source of prospects, but you have to respond instantly when a story appears. Other design firms are watching for such news items. So the A/E firm that collects clippings for a week before getting around to call about them has a self-made handicap.

Some A/Es ask their consultants to help find leads of prospective clients. It's only fair. If a consultant wants work, s/he should help the prime design firms find the jobs. Others with a vested interest in helping design firms are the banker, accountant, investment and tax advisors, law firm, insurance broker, office landlord, stockbroker, etc. They may all know of some prospects, and the A/E only has to ask.

When calling a large company, start with its public relations department to identify who in the firm is responsible for dealing with A/Es and construction planning. With other organizations, call the chief's office and tell the secretary you don't want to bother the boss, but you need to reach whoever is in charge of facilities management or new planning and construction. The secretary or receptionist will usually give you the name and extension number or at least direct you to someone who has the information with no question whatsoever.

What To Say
What do you say to a stranger when calling cold? Mainly you just want to know if there's any construction planning in the pipeline somewhere and, in any case, to whom you should send your brochure. It takes practice to come across well on the phone—not too aggressive, not too timid. Some A/Es have tape-recorded their conversations, listened carefully to their lifeless hemming, hawing, and throat clearing, and improved 100 percent overnight.

Telephone prospectors strike gold by consciously seeking information at every stage of a call. A call may proceed through an operator, receptionists, secretaries, lower-echelon employees, or even the "wrong" person when a call is improperly transferred. Any of these people may have valuable data, and most of them will go out of their way to help a caller. Keep asking: "Who do you think might know more about that?" "Who else is being considered for the work?" "Where could I find out more about that plan?" Avoid crossing the boundary line of snooping, of course, but there's nothing offensive about plain up-front data gathering. The tips and leads that can develop from this process are sometimes a bonanza.

Information is drawn out by using what marketing expert Gerre Jones calls open-ended questions. Gerre has been teaching these and related techniques for years. Here's the essence of what he has to say on the

Some A/Es have tape-recorded their conversations and improved 100 percent overnight.

subject of handling telephone marketing and cold calls:

• Some words tend to close down and stop a line of inquiry instead of keeping it open and in motion. These stopper words include: "are," "did," "will," "can," and "could." Such direct words in requests or offers give the other party the opportunity to say "no" and cut you off from continuing the contact you're trying to establish.

• Words that tend to keep questions and answers flowing and maintain contact in conversation are: "who," "what," "where," "when," "why," and "how."

For example, instead of saying, "May I send a letter of interest and a brochure?" you ask: "Where should I send...?" Or, even more useful: "Would Friday or Monday be the best day to drop off our letter of interest? What time is best for you, morning or afternoon?"

• Write down everything you learn when calling around for information within an organization. Then you can use each call as a sort of personal referral for the next one: "Mr. Sanborn at the Real Estate Department and Doug Down at Facilities Planning suggested that I contact you."

• Use names and other information picked up along the way to convey knowledgeability of the organization's affairs. This helps you avoid sounding like an outsider. The key to success is to write down every name, date, address, and phone number that comes up during conversations.

Explore Every Lead

Gerre Jones demonstrates the importance of exploring every possible lead. For example, if a corporate construction manager says they already have a design firm that does all their work, you should get the name of that firm. It's very common that such firms need other design professionals for joint ventures or consulting in the locale of construction. A particular project may be sewed up, but you should establish whether this project is part of a multiphase, ongoing construction program. A company or government agency may say they have absolutely no work. But they may be waiting for a government contract or grant that will suddenly unleash all kinds of expansion. A company's real estate department may say they're selling off their facilities instead of expanding them. But, at the same time, the maintenance department of that company may be planning a million dollars worth of renovation for their offices and plant. Sometimes this kind of information is volunteered freely; sometimes it isn't, and it's up to you to dig it out.

Telephone prospecting can be tiring and frustrating. It's hard to complete more than twenty calls in a day. Prospects are out or sick, calls get cut off, people call back at the wrong times, etc. It can be a stressful process, and frequent breaks are necessary to stay fresh.

A principal or associate usually initiates a phone prospecting program. But once you work out the routine, it pays to hire someone, even at a secretarial level, to handle most of the calling and record keeping. Some small offices have hired outside secretarial services to do this work on a part-time contract basis.

Former clients are always the likeliest source of future work.

Cold-Call Blitzing

Gerre Jones

During slow times for marketing (and marketers) several firms have turned to concentrated cold calling to find and qualify many leads in a relatively short time. The *A/E Marketing Journal* for May 1983 reported on a ninety-day sales effort by Murray Jones Murray, Inc., of Tulsa. Seven volunteer callers made a total of 438 contacts over a three-month period, uncovering forty-seven live leads.

We heard recently from a marketing director in the Northeast who had just completed a one-week cold-call blitz, using twenty volunteers (about a quarter of the total office staff) to make the telephone contacts. The several hundred calls made by the group turned up enough leads to keep the marketing staff busy for "several months." This marketing director says they plan to repeat the blitz technique.

Preparing for a Cold-Call Blitz

One of the secrets in a successful lead-search blitz of this type is advance preparation and research. Lead sources and possibilities (news stories, lead tip sheets, past and present clients, and the like) will turn up many more leads than can (or should) be called. Selectively narrow the list down to the most likely ones—based on their location, probable project types, past contacts (if any), and the likelihood of the projects going ahead (how well financed and dependable is the prospect?).

Several years ago, as a demonstration of how much information can be turned up by classic cold calling, I agreed to spend up to three hours making cold calls to public works directors in Massachusetts. (The time limit was based on personal experience; I can't handle more than three hours of cold-call-induced stresses.) The client type and the area to be worked were selected by the engineering firm I was consulting with.

I knew very little about the geography of Massachusetts—even less about county names or locations of county seats. An observer furnished the name of a county in central Massachusetts and the exercise got under way.

Starting from Scratch

My first call was to the county clerk of county X. She gave me the name of their director of public works and some personal information about him—how long he'd been in his job; where he came from; approximate age; marital status; and a few other items of potential help in bridging the (often) awkward early moments of a cold call.

I then called the public works director (we'll call him Bob Brown here), told him I needed to know what sort of projects the county had coming up in the next twenty-four to forty-eight months so I could see how my firm could be of assistance. Bob was helpful, of course, and passed on information about several small and one or two larger county projects. As I recall, they included a road-paving job, a bridge replacement job, and a maintenance building for county vehicles.

When it appeared that we had county X's program pretty well in hand I asked Bob what the county to the north of X county had in the way of upcoming projects. That part of the call went like this:

Jones: "This is just terrible, Bob. I can't remember the name of the county just north of you."

Brown: "Oh, that's Y county."

Jones: "Of course. And your counterpart in the DPW there is—I can't believe this, Bob, what is his name?"

Brown: "Sam Smith."

Jones: "Of course—now what projects does Sam have planned up in Y county?"

Get Help by Asking for It

To the best of his ability Bob Brown filled me in on Y county's and Sam Smith's plans. As we wound up our conversation I told Brown I would be calling Smith; did he have any message for Smith? As it turned out, Brown did—something about seeing Sam at Kiwanis next Tuesday.

I then called Sam Smith, told him I'd just been talking with Bob Brown, passed along Brown's greetings and the message, and, pointing out that Brown had been helpful about Y county's projects, I needed to be sure I had a complete list so we could see how my firm could be of assistance.

Brown to Smith to Downs

We reviewed Smith's list, picking up a few items Brown didn't know about. When we seemed to have worked through county Y's program for the next several years, I asked Sam what the county west of Y county had coming up. That part of the conversation went like this:

Jones: "Sam, you won't believe this; I can't find the name of the county west of you in my notes..."

Smith: "That'd be Z county."

Jones: "Of course. And the public works director over there is— looks like I need your help again, Sam. I can't come up with his name."

Smith: "You mean Dick Downs."

Jones: "Of course! Now, what projects..."

The procedure should be clear by now. During the three hours of cold calls most of the counties in central Massachusetts were contacted and some forty projects were unearthed, with total estimated construction costs of more than $20 million.

That's all that happened. The projects had only been identified; we had none of them when the calls were completed. But enough leads were turned up and qualified to keep a medium-sized engineering firm busy marketing for three or four months.

By the time the exercise was winding up, incidentally, I was passing along messages from public works directors in western Massachusetts to those in the eastern part of the state, and beginning to feel like a town crier with an expanded territory. In addition to the project leads—the real purpose of the cold-call blitz—I had made a number of new friends in the process and learned a lot about the life of a county public works director. And I had become an expert on Massachusetts geography west of Boston.

Relax, Have Fun, Make Friends, Get Information

Some readers may fault the line of questioning I used with the county officials as misleading, or of no real purpose—even a form of "showboating" because I had an audience.

As I tried to make clear in *How to Market Professional Design Services* (2d ed.), in a true cold call you should make a friend, not a sale; get information, not a project.

The process described above certainly is not the only way to make successful cold calls, but it is the method I'm comfortable with—and one I know works within my style and comfort level. Some marketers and principals tend to be very formal and structured in their lead-finding telephone contacts. I have no quarrel with that approach, if it achieves the objectives of a cold call.

I believe a not-taking-oneself-too-seriously cold-call approach results in the necessary lead information—and at the same time, allows the cold caller to successfully sustain the process over a longer period of time. (Three hours straight is still my upper limit.)

Joint Ventures: Happy Marriage or Sudden Death

Margaret Spaulding

Some firms have developed a national practice in one or more market segments primarily through JV relationships.

Joint ventures can pave the way to new markets and to work in new geographic areas. They can also be costly, disappointing failures. What makes the difference?

According to Tom Page, director of marketing for The Ehrenkrantz Group, success in joint venturing has a lot to do with your whole approach. "We don't go into a JV relationship because we think we need help; we do it because we think the other firm will strengthen our already excellent position. This approach avoids a potentially quarrelsome relationship between the two firms."

Jody Taylor, director of health facilities planning for HOK, says the major criterion for a successful JV team lies in "doing very thorough research on the client's needs, as the client perceives them. For example, if the client is concerned about how he's cared for during design or construction, a local firm to attend to details, backed up by a large out-of-town firm with special expertise, may make the most sense to the client."

Taylor estimates that about 70 percent of our work is in joint ventures and about 50-60 percent of these are with engineers. "We want our JV partners to be as directly responsible for the project as we are. If their name is on the door, we get the principal involved and there's no backing away from responsibility."

According to Scott Braley, head of the general architectural group for Heery & Heery, another key to success is "having the luxury of pursuing projects in a joint venture only when there's a specific marketing reason to do so, as opposed to a technical reason." Because Heery is a comprehensive A/E firm, "technically we don't need any help," Braley says. They sometimes joint venture, he admits, in order to eliminate a key firm from the competition, on the theory "it's better to get part of the pie than none of it."

Some firms have developed a national practice in one or more market segments primarily through JV relationships. Falick Klein architects in Houston, for example, has work in fifteen states by association or joint ventures with local firms, according to Nadine Barna, the firm's director of marketing. "Falick Klein doesn't go in to establish a foothold in the community, but the local association helps us, and our health care experience helps the local firm."

How do you find the right firm with which to form the relationship? The Ehrenkrantz Group goes into a new area, when they know a project will be coming on line, to check out all the firms which would be logical partners. Size of firms is important, Tom Page says. "If the other firm is too large you can become the tail of the dog, even though you brought the prospect to them."

At Heery & Heery, "We seldom go to a firm without doing research first. We can't offer to join them unless we're pretty sure the match will work," Braley says. To research potential partners in a new geographic area, Braley might call a local banker, indicating he may open an account and start doing work in the region. He asks what other architects the banker knows and what kind of work they are doing. "We always ask the client, too, who have they worked with in the past and who they think is a good firm."

Some years back, David Dibner, FAIA, author of *Joint Ventures for Architects and Engineers*, said that to have a successful joint venture "you have to get along and find a way to match large egos." Most important, he added, firms have to find a way of doing so before the commission is awarded.

First, what do you look for in that other firm? And based on what you find, should you create a formal joint venture or merely an association? What's the difference?

In a 1976 *AIA Journal* article, George Rockrise, head of the twenty-five-person San Francisco architectural firm, ROMA, was quoted as saying "mutual respect between professional people joined together for professional reasons rather than political reasons is vital to a successful association."

In the same article, authors C.A. Carlson and Wallie Scott, Jr., of CRS define a joint venture as an agreement between two or more firms to render architecture or engineering services for a single specific project. It "essentially requires that the firms involved pool the costs and divide the profits in proportion to the manpower, time, or money each invested."

They distinguish the JV from an association, which "...allows two or more firms to work under the contractual umbrella of one firm while each participant remains independently responsible for its own facilities, professional performance, legal status, expenses, profits, and losses without affecting others in the association."

The joint venture, they say, resembles a partnership legally and financially. It may resemble one emotionally as well, when the JV assumes an independent identity, with space, staff, and other resources of its own. And there are drawbacks.

Falick Klein, for example, prefers associations over joint ventures, in part because "it avoids the paper work of setting up a formal, legal JV," according to Barna. But clients often prefer the joint venture so that they knowwho is liable. When you have an association, Barna adds, "each firm can point a finger at the other if something goes wrong."

To help keep things from going wrong, many firms establish ground rules before or during the marketing effort. The Gruzen Partnership uses a printed "Preliminary Agreement" which identifies the firms, what the joint venture will be called, who will be prime, who will direct the efforts of the respective firms, and what services will be provided by whom. It also sets out how fees will be established and how marketing expenses will be allocated.

Use of the form helps iron out an issue described by Al Hoover, Palo Alto (CA) architect: "Many national firms want to maintain control of design, even though the local firm is design-oriented." Often, he said, local firms will avoid associations for this reason. (Tom Page tells of a situation where, at the job interview, one JV firm representative stood up and said, "We'll design your project this way...," and the other JV principal jumped to his feet and said, "Oh no we won't; we'll design it like this...." They didn't get the job.)

Other issues to resolve as early in the marketing effort as possible include, where the work will be done. Why? Are we really creating a third firm, vertically oriented, for this project? Can we commit our loyalties to this new venture? Will it have a life of its own? Clear lines of organization and responsibility will help make the JV appeal to the client as well as to the team members.

Ask also, How do we allocate credit for the work if we get the job? Who gets to publish it? Does the JV span more than one job? If one firm hears about another prospect while we are pursuing or doing this one, are they obligated to share the lead? Will we pool our resources and share both profits and losses equally? What should the split be and what is it based upon?

Heery & Heery uses a form to keep track of proposal and presentation costs, both labor and expenses. Most firms, Heery among them, divide "hard" costs (nonlabor) equally with each firm absorbing its own labor expenses. One way to address the issue, Braley says, is to say to the other firm, "Let's assume we don't get the job. How would we handle the costs?" He adds, "Smile a lot when you ask that."

Joint venture etiquette includes: (during marketing) keep your partner informed of all your moves to obtain the job; establish trust; don't play games; don't drop in on your partner unannounced; and (throughout the effort) don't be greedy.

Try to avoid the pig and chicken situation. A pig and a chicken working for a farmer agreed one day to strike out on their own. The chicken proposed that they open a restaurant specializing in ham and eggs. The pig said, "Great, you supply the eggs and, uh, wait a minute. You're going to make a contribution, and I'm making a total commitment." "Well," said the chicken, "in a joint venture, somebody has to die."

Profit from Joint Ventures

As we have said in the past, the best "joint venture" is really a prime-associate relationship. That is because an equal partnership (which is what a legal joint venture is) is fraught with management problems such as who is in charge and how do we obtain liability insurance.

But if you must enter into a joint venture, effective management is the key to making money, according to several firms who are successful at it. If you have had bad luck in the past or would like more profit from your next joint venture, follow these specific tips:

1. Avoid joint ventures with firms who have your capability. Firms with similar capability tend unconsciously to duplicate hours and certain tasks, thus reducing profitability. If your firm is known for design but not for production efficiency, joint venture with firms weak in design but good at producing documents. Then, discipline yourself to do no production.

2. Avoid cost reimbursement contracts with joint venture partners. Instead, establish lump sum fees for portions of the work and divide responsibility accordingly. If one of the partners goes over budget, it doesn't impact the other.

3. Minimize or eliminate joint venture overhead. Have each partner maintain individual liability insurance and assign the responsibility for bookkeeping to one of the firms instead of having the joint venture bank account pay for any expenses. This applies especially to legal or accounting advice.

4. Name one of the partners to be managing joint venture partner responsible for all financial transactions such as billing, collecting, and disbursing funds. And require only one signature on joint venture checks to avoid "check signing" meetings. The managing partner should also be the prime contact with the client.

5. Define very specifically how changes in scope will be handled and how compensation will be made. Most firms we spoke with suggested a straight hourly amount be billed to the client without joint venture markup by each firm. Thus, whoever does the work gets the total benefits from it. The billing rates for changes should be outlined in advance for the benefit of the client.

6. Meet monthly with your joint venture partner to discuss all aspects of the project, including schedule and budget. Firms who have had problems with joint ventures all cited poor communication as a major factor in their disputes.

7. When splitting fee amounts with your partner prior to starting

*Professional
Services
Management
Journal*

If your firm is known for design but not for production efficiency, joint venture with firms weak in design but good at producing documents.

the work, always leave a minimum of 10 percent in the JV account as a contingency. Many firms have found that 15-20 percent contingency is even better.

8. Invest all surplus JV funds in an interest bearing account or money market fund with daily recall capability.

9. Only pay a JV partner's invoices to the joint venture after receipt of payment from the client for the specific identifiable amounts. This avoids disputes and allows the joint venture to keep funds they have invested.

10. Try to contract with the client on a lump sum basis so that scope definition becomes mandatory and fee amounts are set. Avoid percentage of construction cost fee arrangements which can lead to major disputes between the partners over who caused construction costs to go up or down.

Finally, pick your partner carefully by checking past joint venture references. A JV can be a shotgun wedding or it can be a marvelous success, and your ability to pick a congenial partner before going after a project may be the difference.

The Diagnostic Approach to Client Interviews

Fred A. Stitt

What do you do with a prospect when you get one? How do you best set yourself up for sustained further contact? How do you get on the inside track on upcoming projects? We have excellent advice from consultant and educator Dr. Stuart Rose on the subject:

• Diagnosis is the secret of it all. Doctors use diagnosis to take command and zero in on their clients' needs. Lawyers, dentists, even insurance sales people, start with diagnosis. They don't start with statements of their qualifications to do the job; that's taken for granted. Instead they initiate a fact-finding process. In the fact-finding process, the professional takes the client in hand and leads him or her step-by-step toward a tailor-made proposal for action.

• Traditionally, A/Es do most of the talking in their first direct contacts: "We do this and we've done that." The diagnostic method reverses that self-centered approach. You start off by asking questions and spend most of the time listening to answers. First you call the client prospect to ask for a meeting to obtain data about his or her needs. You're interviewing the prospect rather than being interviewed. You're asking for data, not giving it. You're finding out what can be done for the client, not selling yourself.

• What about those questions prospects have about your experience and qualifications? Most of them should be briefly answered before the interview, on the telephone or in a letter of inquiry. Remember, you'll be controlling the interviewing. The more you listen, the more you'll be in charge. When they do, they're not in charge. With this system, you take charge by doing only 20 percent of the talking.

• Use a list of client-oriented questions to guide your interview. The list should deal with client concerns rather than the technical details of the potential project. Whose project is being considered? Who else is involved in it? Who's the ultimate decision maker? What's the context, the background of the project? Where's funding coming from? How does this person feel about the project? Later come the more technical inquiries about design preferences and budget.

• Take notes. Write down only key words and phrases. Too much note taking frustrates the prospect. But if you don't take notes, the diagnostic process will seem meaningless. Although note taking may impose some pauses in the interview, in general people like to see that what they say is important enough to be written down.

• Pause and periodically summarize key points. By doing so, you let

A/Es do most of the talking in their first direct contacts. Reverse that self-centered approach.

the prospect know you really are listening. You also allow the prospect to modify or elaborate on previous statements. This is the point where users of the diagnostic interview technique most often fall down. It's also the point where some of the most significant job facts are likely to emerge if you allow them to. If people have a "second chance" to clarify a point, they'll often experience some tension because they've actually held back some data the first time around. When their words are restated, they'll likely open up far more as they try to clarify or revise what they said before.

• Close the diagnostic interview with the first phase of your next level of contact. Say you'll send a letter summarizing the interview. Also say you'll review the data with your associates and/or consultants and prepare a proposal. The proposal will be a practical list of recommendations for action. Don't get into specifics about the project on the spot. Just say the data deserves careful analysis and you'll check back with further questions and possible recommendations. That leads to the preliminary proposal, which leads to a comprehensive proposal, which, all going properly, leads to getting the job. If and when the client requests complete formal proposals, screening interviews, or presentations, you'll gain the final payoff of the diagnostic interview process. You'll have far more data to work with—data that count in prospect decision making—than your competing colleagues.

Use a list of client oriented questions to guide your interview.

The Forgotten Person at Presentations: The Client

Fred A. Stitt

A lack of responsiveness to the client's feelings is the most common mistake made by design professionals in presentations. With clients reporting as many as one hundred submissions for a major commission, this intense competition can result in a firm's being short-listed with four or more equally qualified firms. In this case, the project is won or lost in the presentation.

Invariably, the firm selected is the one that best demonstrates knowledge of the project and empathy with the client. The winner understands the client's expectations, needs, and biases.

Clients report a desire that design professionals reduce the time spent on self-glorification and increase the time spent addressing the client's specific concerns.

Dr. John M. Turner of Santa Fe Community College in Gainesville, Florida, expressed the following thoughts on the subject, "The economic life-blood of an architectural firm flows from commissions and contracts with clients. Very often, the contracts are awarded as the result of an interview with a prospective client on a competitive basis with other architectural firms."

"These interviews (considering only the time elapsed during the actual interview) generally consume very little time, perhaps a half-hour to an hour. Thus, when one considers the importance of the relatively brief interview to an architectural firm, it is surprising that in many instances little apparent planning or preparation goes into the presentation.

"Do not be dismayed if you are given only 15-20 minutes to describe your firm and its accomplishments. If you feel you cannot adequately describe your firm in that length of time, chances are you are dwelling on things of great importance and interest to you, rather than to the interviewing group."

Know the Project

Dr. Turner goes on to say, "In preparing for an interview find out as much as you possibly can about the proposed project....Adjust your presentation to the group being addressed. The same approach may not work for faculty groups as for trustees, or for a group of attorneys, engineers, or other architects. To this end, determine beforehand, if possible, the composition of the interview group.

Judith Martin, staff writer for the *Washington Post*, echoes those same sentiments regarding her experiences as a member of an

The winner understands the client's expectations, needs, and biases.

architectural selection committee for a school. "Then we got an architect who offered us a skylight, just like the Astrodome had. You remember the story. The Astrodome has a huge skylight and grass growing below, but then nobody could see the ball because of the light, so it was painted over, and the grass died and that, children, is how the world got Astroturf. We loved the idea of having a skylight like that. He told us we could black it out during games, and when the room was used as a theater, we could also black it out. That got us down to three architects....Next we got a team who showed us two slide shows simultaneously, one for each eye, plus a machine which provided guitar music from the rear. They showed us lovely pictures. There was a meadow with flowers moving in the breeze, a lake bobbing with yachts and skiers climbing a craggy mountain trail. We were impressed. Anybody who can design a mountain like that, I thought, can design my old gymnasium any day. But they went too far. They slipped in a slide of man stepping on the moon, and I knew that they did not design that moon. I recognized the slide. You can buy it at the gift shop of the Air and Space Museum.

"However, the sixth architect was the one we picked....He told us about costs and flooring and bleacher seating, and about how it was going to take longer than we had thought and might cost more, too, and wasn't going to look like much, considering our requirements and space. We were delighted, because we believed every word he said."

Real concerns of real clients. And what causes these problems? Lack of understanding on the part of the design professional as to what the client is really interested in.

The Solution: Homework

The solution, of course, is thorough homework prior to the presentation. As Dr. Turner suggests, know more about the project itself than the client does. The site should always be visited, plans of the property obtained wherever possible. Aerial photographs are useful where available. Check on zoning; investigate location of utilities. Determine any potential problems with the site. I do not advocate the development and use of conceptual designs during presentations, but if the size of the project warrants the expense, the preparation of a topographic model of the site can be an effective tool with which to describe design considerations and constraints attributable to the site itself. Simple Polaroid color photographs of the site can be quite effective for use in a small, informal presentation. More often than not there will be selection committee members who have not seen the site.

Whenever possible, identify all members of a selection committee. And don't let titles mislead you. I remember a presentation to a hospital board in which I had done my homework with the "Chairman of the A/E Selection Committee" but later discovered to my dismay at the presentation that a large man with a loud voice was making all the decisions. I had not even bothered to contact him. Needless to say we came in a close second on that one. The point is, contact all members of a selection committee. Talk to them. Do not, however, spend your time selling your firm to

They went too far; they did not design the moon.

them, but rather probe for their feelings. Determine, as best you can, what each of them is looking for in their architect or engineer. And then design your presentation so that it meets all of their expectations.

Often the situation arises where no matter how much homework you've done, or how free with information a client is regarding the selection committee, you may still find one or two strangers sitting across the table from you. What then? When this happens you simply must, before getting into your written agenda (which you should have for all presentations), engage the new faces in conversation to get some information regarding their role in the process and their concerns. This can be done very naturally while introductions are going around and it accomplishes two things. First, it gives you vital information which could necessitate a shift in emphasis of your presentation, and second, it raises the comfort level of the committee member who was probably brought in at the last minute, feels somewht out of place, and has a rather negative set about the whole proceeding.

A Key Client Concern

One of the key concerns of clients today is the project management structure that the design firm proposes. "How is he going to accomplish my job on schedule and within my budget?" There are always options available to the professional for successful management of any project and it is mandatory that enough homework is done prior to the presentation to determine which of these options suits the client best. Such questions to be addressed include: Is a joint venture appropriate? Is geographical location of branch offices or consultants a factor? What level of principal involvement is desired by the client? Is participation of minority consultants or associates important? Are speciaized consulting disciplines a plus?

In summary, do your homework. Meet your client's expectations and you will find, with an ever increasing degree of regularity, that he is meeting yours by awarding you more commissions.

Presentations Are a Preview

Frank H. Smith III, A.I.A.

Professionals seldom utilize the talents they have to design effective presentations.

However you structure a client interview, whatever the message you wish to impart, one fact should always be remembered—the presentation will be, to the client, a simulation of what it would be like for him to work with you on what may well be the most important project of his life. It will be a sample of things to come.

Many design professionals fail to realize this and spend far too much presentation time talking about themselves and far too little time demonstrating to the client their understanding of the project and how they will accomplish it. And very few design professionals are sensitive to the fact that how they perform in the interview has a direct correlation in the client's mind as to how they will perform on the job. A clear understanding of this fact is one of the keys to successful, winning presentations.

What the Client Is Looking for

What are the factors a client is looking for in a designer once his basic experience and credentials have been demonstrated by means of the original written qualifications statement?

These factors include: demonstrated managerial/organizational skills, careful attention to budget and schedules, creativity, thoroughness, enthusiasm, empathy for the client's needs, specificity, responsiveness, to name a few. And these factors are the ones that a design professional must demonstrate in the interview.

It has been my experience that these professionals seldom utilize the talents they have to design effective presentations. The creativity they demonstrate in their projects is rarely applied to their presentations. The net result is that the majority of their presentations maintain a mediocre sameness.

The design professional, who takes each client interview as a design challenge and applies the same creativity he would to an actual commission, will have a great advantage over his cometitors. Prior to the interview he will discover as much as he possibly can about the client's project and his basic likes and dislikes, analogous to the programming stage of the project. He will plan his presentation to be fresh, creative, and responsive to the client (a schematic design concept, if you will).

He will select an interview team composed of the key individuals who will actually be assigned to the project. He will not parade two or more principals of the firm by the client. This will not demonstrate "keen personal interest of all the principals of the firm" even to the least sophisticated client, but will rather show a firm with entirely too much overhead.

Creative Presentation = Creative Designer

A well-organized, forceful, dynamic, creative presentation immediately tells the client, "This firm and these people will demonstrate these same qualities on the job if I select them." A project manager, who gives a crisp presentation utilizing his support people in an effective manner, and obviously communicates well with his team, shows that this will be the kind of performance the client can expect of him on the job.

I have heard the comment, "Oh, you marketing people are all quick on your feet, but we project managers don't have to be good public speakers."

My response is that there is no such thing as a top-flight project manager who isn't comfortable in front of a group. I base this on my belief that the typical marketing presentation requires far less skill than the difficult task facing a project manager when he has to explain a $50,000 change order to an irate building committee!

The true simulating aspects of presentations were vividly brought home to me recently during a workshop in which a very articulate presenter was enthusiastically describing his firm's dedication to precise schedule control.

He was following all the rules of good presentations. However, he was making this point at the thirteen-minute mark of a ten-minute interview, and the message received loud and clear was that if this firm was awarded the commission they would very likely miss their documentation schedule deadlines by a similar 30 percent.

Appropriate Presentation Costs

A design professional's sensitivity to cost control will also exhibit itself to the client based on the elaborateness of his presentation. A presentation that is obviously more costly than the size of the project would indicate, "This firm is certainly not cost conscious." A "dog and pony show," which might be ideal for a certain project, might be totally inappropriate for another. But the presentation should put across the point that the firm produces a quality product consistent with the size and complexity of the proposed project.

The simulation aspects of a presentation need, however, to go beyond the demonstration of "how we'll work together" for they must do it in a manner that shows a sensitivity to the client's goals and philosophy and style. A careful evaluation of each client must be made; for it to be effective, each presentation will have unique characteristics.

Just the type of client will suggest different approaches. For example, a federal agency would normally demand a much more cut-and-dried technical approach as its selection committee will be composed of architects and engineers, who have heard hundreds of presentations. The interview before a school board composed of lay people would usually require more emphasis on the process of design in nontechnical language. Or, as

For it to be effective, each presentation will have unique characteristics.

in the case of a presentation I recently made to a motion picture company, a more flamboyant approach was indicated.

So when you've made the short list and are asked to make a presentation, remember that you and your competition most probably have already been adjudged competent by the client and you are now being given the opportunity to demonstrate how you will solve the client's problems.

Do your homework. Know your client and remember that how you conduct yourself in the interview will be a simulation to the client of how it would be to work with you on their project.

Presentations: A Client's Viewpoint

W ebster's *New Collegiate Dictionary* defines *presentation* "a descriptive or persuasive account (as by a salesman of his product)." This best describes the perspective from which most sophisticated corporate clients view any presentation: a sales tool whose primary goal is to create a profit for the presenter, either directly or indirectly. How persuasive the presentation is depends on these factors: focus, graphic format, and understanding of the presentation process.

The general reason for hiring an outside professional is to provide resources not available in-house to the client. The selection criteria are somewhat akin to those for hiring an employee. The best measure of what you can do for me is what you did for someone else. The client has many driving forces behind him and the project. The successful presenter must focus on those driving forces and relate them to his firm's qualifications. Like the lens of a camera, the presentation requires many elements to focus correctly.

The client's needs are of paramount importance. A presentation is a sales tool, not an exercise in professional narcissism. If the client has identified his needs, problems, and concerns, address them directly. Demonstrate how you have the skills and resources available to address each of those concerns, and how your firm's qualifications relate to the client and the client's concerns.

The Request for Proposal

If you are lucky enough to get a formal request for proposal (RFP), respond in the same order as the RFP is written. Most clients have worked hard preparing that RFP and are usually in a state of consternation during the selection process. You need not make their lives difficult by forcing them to wade through your stock proposal format to find information they need to select your firm. The client's RFP structure usually indicates what the client considers important. Just like the process for hiring new employees, the first cut through the pile of proposals is to eliminate. Your first objective is to make the short list, not to make the administrative life of the client difficult.

In most large organizations the person or committee requesting the proposals will make a recommendation to their management as to which firms should be invited to give a formal presentation. The recommendation will probably be in writing and usually will contain the RFP and all the proposals from those firms recommended for the short

B. A. Whitson

A presentation is a sales tool, not an exercise in professional narcissism.

list. Additionally, this recommendation will supply to management the foundation for their questions during your presentation.

The content of the presentation should provide continuity, linking your proposal to your presentation through certain clearly stated key ideas that the client has requested.

Jargon, Buzz Words, and Double-Talk

You have heard it before, and now you will hear it again, "No jargon!" Jargon is your everyday language. Your trade talk is jargon to the client, in the same way that his everyday language is jargon to you. The unfortunate thing is, nobody is going to admit to not understanding the jargon being used.

Ask your banker to lunch and have him or her read one of your proposals and the text of a presentation. If there are any questions, you have not communicated effectively. Avoid buzz words. Find another way to express that point. Use the language to its fullest.

Caveat: when asked the time, don't fall into the double-talk trap of answering with the theory of time.

The Bottom-Line Approach

Don't be afraid of testimonials, examples, and plain old-fashioned hard dollars to make your point. After all, to some clients you are just another vendor in their daily business life. The "bottom-line perspective" deals with tangibles first, then with the intangibles.

Your most important marketing assets are happy clients and projects you have completed for them that were under budget and on time.

Presentation Quality

The actual presentation is usually the only tangible quality standard on which the client has to compare your firm to others. The nature of the short list presupposes that all firms on that list are equally qualified to do the project.

Quality does not mean more elaborate and expensive, but consistent style of lettering, constant format, no out-of-focus or upside-down slides, etc.

The presentation should be a smooth-flowing production—no burned out bulbs, tripping in the snake pit of wires, or a scene of mass confusion during the setup. The old saw about how you get to Carnegie Hall—practice, practice, practice—also holds true for presentations.

Recording on videotape the rehearsal of your entire presentation from setup to finale, can be quite revealing.

Consistent and Appropriate

Verify the objectives of the client and his objectives for this project. Research the client's self-image and the image others have of the client. If the project is a data processing facility, do not show the new hospital project you just completed. However, you may show the hospital's emergency power system, the uninterruptable power system, the computer room and its Halon system. The objective is to relate consistently to the client and his project.

A presentation that is appropriate to the high-roller speculative developer is not going to win a banker, unless the banker considers himself to be a high-roller wheeler-dealer. Research and consideration of the client's cultural, educational, and past business experiences, and the integration of that research into the presentation will complete the rapport-building process. With all of the technical factors being equal, the close is made or lost based on the degree of rapport established.

The presentations that are remembered and make the best impression are those that:
- are oriented to the needs and concerns of the client;
- make the client's administrative life easy;
- follow the K.I.S.S. rule;
- have no jargon, buzz words, and double-talk;
- maximize your skills as a public speaker;
- use the best graphic techniques available;
- are appropriate to the client's objectives and self-image.

Writing the Brochure Program

David Travers

[*Earlier sections of the book from which the following was excerpted,* Preparing Design Office Brochures: A Handbook, *discuss the function of the office brochure and self-analysis process an office should go through to establish its need for one. Ed.*]

One of those who was involved in the self-analysis and discovery sessions, someone who knows what the firm is all about, should write the first draft of a program for the brochure. Not the design program but the criteria which will guide the selection of the brochure content and its design. It's not time yet to start designing. Haste now will cost you money, time, extra work, and almost guarantee dissatisfaction with the result. The more care taken now, the more hard decisions made now, and the more definitive the program, the more easily and efficiently will flow the design and production of the brochure. And the more certain you can be that it will perform for you as planned. Appalling cost overruns, delays, and unhappiness with the end product seem to be the rule. Of all the possible contributing causes, including inexperience with publication and printing techniques, it is because of lack of thought and care at this stage that most problems are built into the brochure project. You wouldn't begin designing for a client until you were fully aware of his needs and resources. In this project you are the client, so do yourself the same courtesy. An uncertain program makes for an uncertain design and an unhappy result.

Appalling cost overruns, delays, and unhappiness with the end product seem to be the rule.

Describing the Office

The program should describe how the office develops its business and what the role of the brochure is to be—to respond to inquiries, to generate inquiries, or a combination—and how flexible and adaptable it should be. For example, if you are a growing firm, you will want to be able to modify your brochure annually, or biennially at most, to include new projects, new clients, new information. This should be called out in your program.

Describe in the program the scope of your services and those that are the most profitable to the firm. List the kinds of projects the firm has done, the number of projects done in each category, and again those that have been most profitable. An analysis of this kind can bring surprising things to light.

It would save time if at this point in your planning you set someone in the office to work compiling a complete list of projects undertaken by the firm with a capsule description of each, containing a statement of the design problem, its solution, the size and cost of the project, the name of the client, and the nature of the firm's involvement in the project.

Decide whether yours is a "Design Office," a "Volume Office," or a "Line of Strength Office." If the latter, what are your lines of strength (in addition, of course, to design skill)? What are the strengths each principal and key staff member contributes to the capabilities of the firm? Who are your clients? That is, who are your readers going to be? If your brochure is going to be effective, it is essential to know who your audience or audiences are. What you say and show should be what the prospective clients want to know and see. Not because servility is the keynote of your brochure, but because at this point your interests coincide: you want to impress the prospect favorably and, although skeptical, he wants you to impress him favorably. He's looking for a good consultant and he wants to learn from your brochure why you should be considered for the commission, why you stand out from the others seeking the job. The content of the brochure, then, should state and substantiate those qualities which constitute the strengths of the office—from the viewpoint of the prospects you are trying to influence.

Know the Reader

The program should set this forth so that whoever writes the text, selects projects to be shown, and chooses the photographs can do so with a complete understanding of what it is the office is trying to communicate and to whom. Experience, reliability, stability, efficiency, service to the client, all of these in addition to design quality are important to the prospective client. The order and degree of that importance, however, depends on the needs and predilections of the prospect.

For example, a consulting engineer, who is usually hired by the architect not the owner, will want architects to know that he is sensitive to architectural design and the architect's intentions, that he understands his role is to support the architect's solutions and to help bring the job in on time and budget. A professional advisory committee to a public agency is looking for a different balance between design quality and the other factors than is a speculative builder. Similarly, a land sales subdivider is looking for different qualities in his planner than is a socially conscious new town developer. Establishing the kinds of prospects that will be reading your brochure will tell you what to emphasize, what the tone and direction of the brochure should be.

A land sales subdivider is looking for different qualities in his planner than is a socially conscious new town developer.

Most professionals want to broaden their market areas and must direct a brochure to more than one sort of client. This can be a problem. Even within a single building category, the owners' needs can differ wildly. The corporate client planning a headquarters office building isn't interested in an architect's successes with speculative office buildings, nor is the investment builder vice versa. That the brochure is called upon to persuade different kinds of readers with frequently conflicting needs and interests is one of the major design difficulties. If the conflicts are not too violent, they can be reconciled in a permanently bound brochure, but only if you clearly understand those differences. Spell them out in the program.

There are three more elements necessary to the program: a budget, time schedule, and selection of the project director.

The Budget

To this point in the brochure planning process, costs will all have been in time spent in exploratory meetings, drafting the program, reviewing the draft, and rewriting the program. The time has, of course, all been properly charged to whatever indirect labor account the firm has for administration or general promotion and not buried in some hapless client's job. Now, if the decision is to go ahead with a brochure, it is time to draw up a budget for its design, preparation, and printing.

The design professions often look upon client budgets as a threat to quality and a burden upon creativity. The tighter the budget, the more inimical it is. Cost control is treated with the same hostility. The young designer who lives by this rule as an employee will come to suffer by it as an employer.

This attitude toward client budgets often causes offices to avoid imposing their own internal ones. Don't make that mistake. The incidence of brochures costing more than twice as much as preliminary estimates is so high as to suggest that the problem is endemic. A budget must be fixed and controls imposed.

Give the Brochure a Job Number

What frequently happens is that enthusiasm grows as the brochure begins to take shape. Everyone now gets involved. Decisions already made about theme and content are challenged. Ideas which should have been generated in the planning phase now emerge. Good ones are incorporated, requiring changes which are justifiable in the interest of a better brochure, but which can be and usually are expensive and time-consuming. As a result, much already done may be thrown out or have to be redone. Planning and programing will help to some extent: that is, by drawing the ideas out of everyone early, by asking for them in the program draft stage, by getting people to think, and by continuing to encourage ideas in the planning and schematic design phase. And then cutting them off. This will help. But still without a budget and controls you are rudderless. Give the brochure a job number and run it through the office as you would a client project.

The question of how much to spend on a brochure should be answered in terms of the overall promotional budget. Establishing that budget is beyond the scope of this work, though there is need for a thorough airing of the subject. The rule of thumb used by many offices is: "When times are good, spend; when they are bad, don't spend." This is perhaps better than no budget planning at all, but it does nothing to reduce a firm's subjugation to external circumstances. It's like crossing the Pacific on a raft with nothing but a sea anchor to offset adverse wind and tide.

Larger offices have added a sail to the raft by setting promotional budgets as a percentage of billings (something between 4 and 9 percent, depending upon what is included as promotional expense), but this is still primitive. Corporate planners in business and industry long ago discovered that tying marketing costs to sales volume rather than to profits on sales is (to try another metaphor) like flying a kite without a string.

Give the brochure a job number and run it through the office as you would a client project.

Average Brochure Costs

A brochure functions as part of a promotional program. What proportion of the promotional budget should be allocated to the brochure depends upon importance of the brochure to that program. The average brochure printing cost of the offices contacted was about 12 percent of their promotional budgets (among those few design firms having promotional budgets). Although very few had any idea of their in-house costs, the expense of preparing the brochure for printing probably approached twice that figure. This is much too much. If you follow the suggestions in this book, you will avoid many of the problems which push costs up. I recommend a budget of 10 percent of your promotional budget for design and preparation and another 10 percent for printing. Since the usual printing of a design office brochure constitutes at least a two-year supply, that represents a total of 20 percent of the budget spent in one year but averaged over two or more years—up to a maximum of $30,000. No firm, no matter how large and profitable, should spend more than that on a single brochure. Given the limited role of the office brochure, it just does not make good business sense.

These figures apply only to brochures printed in black and white with at most a second color on the cover. Scandalous four-color costs are railed at elsewhere in the book. Also not included in the recommended budget is photography, which is so infinitely variable in cost that it would be useless or, worse, misleading to estimate it here.

For those offices without a promotional budget, which means those derelict and irresponsible offices not having a promotional program, the approximate dollar translation of the percentage figures goes something like this:

Fee Volume	Brochure Budget
$ 150,000 (3- to 4-man office)	$ 1,800 (sufficient for a 6-page folder)
700,000 (15- to 18-man office)	8,000
1,200,000 (25- to 30-man office)	15,000
3,000,000 and up	30,000

I urge you again not only to budget but to adhere to it. At the very least, keep records of staff time spent on all aspects of the brochure done in-house. There will always be another brochure, and if you choose to be complaisant about the budget this time, you'll go in with your eyes open wider next time.

The Schedule

If an office does it own brochure—designs it, writes the text, and prepares the camera-ready art—it is going to take longer than expected.

Much longer. Even if the brochure is planned and programed and there are no delays due to changes of mind and heart, a brochure can take up to twice as long as projected. Not in the number of hours actually worked on the brochure—although these are likely to swell enormously too—but in the length of time over which those hours are worked. The reasons are quite simply stated:

1. When an office has client work to do, the brochure tends to get shelved. At best, vital decisions needed from the principals are not made and work goes slowly. At worst, everyone is busy and no work at all is done on the brochure.

2. When work drops off, so does available manpower and money. Staff is reduced and the principals are—or should be—out scouting for commissions.

The first is, of course, the happier of the two situations, but it also causes longer delays than the second. The reason is that when things are slow, given their aversion to marketing, the principals will often choose to work on the brochure more and on getting jobs less. Also, they will humanely put staff to work on the brochure rather than lay off, so the brochure continues to move ahead. This is particularly true if it has reached the enthusiasm stage.

Below is a flow-chart for the preparation and printing of an office brochure based upon my experience and an average of the experience of the many offices contacted in my research. The numbers running horizontally are units of time, which vary with the size of the office. For example, the unit is one week for the small firm of up to fifteen people. For the office having 100 or more employees, the unit represents one month. The longer time is not only because the larger firm will have a larger brochure, but even more because the larger the firm the greater the chances of divergent opinions strongly held. Decisions are bound to be harder to come by. Moreover, unless the graphics department head or consultant is tough and shrewd, he will be pushed and pulled in opposite directions by principals unable to keep their hands off the brochure.

If an office does its own brochure it is going to take longer than expected. Much longer.

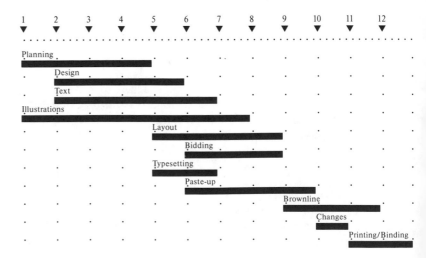

That the large office is likely to have been through the brochure process before seems to avail nothing. Experience doesn't seem to help here. This is probably because with each new brochure an office wants something entirely new and different. Only the amount of work and bungling remains unchanged. An example: one large A/E firm with an eighty-year history and many previous brochures under its belt threw in the towel after spending nine months trying to design a new one in-house. The effort miscarried and the job was turned over to an outside graphics firm.

Who's in Charge?

The person in charge of the brochure program should be someone of the highest, unquestioned authority in the firm. That is, a principal.

• For some reason, employees give a higher priority to projects that a partner is running.

• Putting a brochure together is one of those so-called "unproductive" labors, and it's an article of faith among employees and principals alike that such is to be done only in the absence of paying, client work. For an employee to break this commandment, he must be authorized, even ordered to do so. This requires someone in charge of the brochure who is in a position to make such an authorization stick all the way up the organizational ladder.

• Just as important, it is much more likely that the brochure will truly reflect the character and personality of the firm if a partner is directing the project. He is one of those who have given the office its special capabilities and qualities; he probably knows his partners best and what each contributes to the firm; and he is best able to get the cooperation of his partners, elicit their ideas, and reject those that are woolly.

This is a powerful array of reasons for putting a partner, a strong partner, in charge. I've yet to hear a persuasive argument on the other side.

The person in charge of the brochure program should be someone of the highest, unquestioned authority in the firm.

Video as a Sales Tool

Russell Faure-Brac

Video can be a powerful marketing tool when used in an interview for A/E services. Our firm, EIP Associates of San Francisco, has recently been hired to work on several projects after we gave a video presentation at the interview. We have also lost some jobs using video. This article is an account of how we have incorporated video presentations into our marketing program and it offers some insights gained as a result. While I'm not a video expert, I've had firsthand experience breaking into its use and finding out what video can and cannot accomplish.

Why I Became Interested in Video

EIP Associates is a forty-person multidisciplinary planning firm with a strong background in the preparation of environmental documents such as EIRs and EISs. We are diversifying the range of services we offer and, as a result, we are encountering competition in new market areas. To be successful we must find ways to market more effectively than the competition.

I first heard about the use of video in marketing when a friend at Parsons Brinckerhoff Quade & Douglas described how his firm had won a new transit job after showing a videotape at the short-list interview. I had also heard of video in marketing through the SMPS Awards Program. Then a consultant friend bought a video recorder and began using it in his business. Somehow it just seemed like a good idea.

Once I decided to explore the use of video, I wasn't sure how to begin.

Cracking the Ice

Once I decided to explore the use of video, I wasn't sure how to begin. EIP rarely even uses slides in interview presentations. New technology at EIP consisted of several recently acquired personal computers which we were learning to incorporate into our business. So I started small, bought a video recorder for home use, and taught myself how to operate a VCR. Then I rented Frank Stasiowski's tape, "The Use of Video for A&E Firms." I took notes and learned that:

• Because of television conditioning, clients have high standards and expect to be entertained.

• You have to develop a treatment, prepare a script, and create a story board.

• You must use ¾-inch tape; ½-inch is not acceptable.

• Professional outside help is a necessity and a video consultant should be selected through competitive bidding.

• It costs between $6,000 and $10,000 to do a ten- to twenty-minute video if you're going to do it right.

While the tape was very educational, this information was discouraging. I didn't know what treatments or storyboards were and I couldn't afford $6,000-$10,000 per video, so I proceeded to ignore every one of these basic principles. We bought a home-style ½-inch video system for the firm (the camera, monitor, and portable recorder cost about $2,500) and used it as a training tool to tape interview rehearsals.

A convenient opportunity then presented itself. An existing client asked us to submit a sole-source proposal to develop an instructional videotape on building roof maintenance for the client's use. Using in-house staff and equipment, we put together a video version of our proposal, which we submitted along with the written proposal. It was a totally amateurish effort. Yet, despite the dubious quality of our video, we were hired. We later found out that our client contact liked the video because:

• It gave him flexibility in showing the proposal to his superiors at a time that was convenient to them.

• The material was short and to the point. It got the message across while by-passing the wasted time that occurs in an interview (introductions, preliminaries, etc.).

• It kept the process clean. There was no direct contact between the consultants and the decision makers, and our client, a federal agency, was grateful to be able to avoid any appearance of impropriety.

Turning the Corner

Despite our success with this sole-source proposal, proposal leaders at EIP were still reluctant to use video in competitive interview situations. Whenever we received an RFP that involved short listing, I enthusiastically suggested, "Let's prepare a video for the interview." There were always good reasons why it wouldn't work: we didn't have enough time; it wasn't appropriate for the client, etc. I realized that if it was going to happen, I had to take the initiative.

The opportunity came about through coincidental circumstances. Margaret Spaulding of Management Design introduced me to Nick Despota, a professional video producer (the kind that use ¾-inch tape). At the time we were preparing to give a presentation on our fishery study capabilities to a prospective client. EIP was also conducting a major investigation on a hydroelectric project that would soon require public workshops. I saw a way to effectively combine all these factors. Why not hire Nick to prepare a video illustrating the field techniques we were using on the hydroelectric project, show the video at the public workshops, and use the video in our presentation to the prospective client.

The main constraint was that we had seven calendar days in which to do the video. Ignoring any thought of treatments, script, and storyboard, I prepared a list of twenty interesting questions and told Nick to go to the project site, interview various people, and get the results on video. Two days later he returned; we reviewed many reels of random footage and

I didn't know what treatments or storyboards were and I couldn't afford $6,000-$10,000 per video. Obviously I hadn't followed all the rules on how to properly prepare a video, but it worked.

then pieced material together to form a story. He was then to prepare a draft dub for my final review, but we got behind schedule and I had to use Nick's draft tape. Fortunately, it was an excellent product. I was impressed to see what a professional quality video tape looked like.

Obviously I hadn't followed all the rules on how to properly prepare a video, but it worked. The entire job was completed for under $3,000 and the video was well-received by the prospective client, who has since invited us to propose on new work.

As many of our staff had never been to the site of the hydroelectric project, I showed the video at a subsequent staff meeting. The staff were stunned by the dramatic impact of the tape. At the next marketing meeting, as we were deciding to propose on a job that involved an interview, someone exclaimed, "Let's do a video!" I figured we have finally turned the corner on the idea of using video in interviews.

Use of Video in Winning a Job

The first competitive job where video played a major role in our winning was a road-widening project in a city near San Francisco. We filmed our project manager driving down the road as he pointed out intersection problems, trees that would need to be removed, and other land-use conflicts. When our team entered the interview room carrying video equipment, the client was turned off: it was too big-city, too slick. However, after seeing the video, the interview panel was so impressed that we were immediately hired for the job, with the requirement that we prepare a video of our study results to present at public hearings on the project. We did and we have now completed our first environmental impact report in video form.

Why Use Video?

• It is extremely dramatic and engaging, incorporating action, color, and sound—lots of sensual appeal.

• It can enhance credibility by showing an actual event instead of relying on first- or third-person descriptions.

• It's novel; panel members are not yet used to seeing video routinely used in interviews.

• At the same time, people are becoming more accustomed to video. Twenty percent of American households now own a VCR, and by 1990 those figures are expected to jump to 60 percent.

• You have great control over the cost. For simple, straightforward situations, a video can be produced on ½-inch tape using in-house resources and equipment; or a professional can be hired for a day or two to prepare a very effective film; or a major production effort can be undertaken.

• If the project site is at a remote location, you can film it and, in effect, bring the site into the interview room.

When Not to Use Video

• When it would be too slick for the client or would represent overkill.

• When there is not enough time to do it right.

• When the video is used to take the place of a strong presentation by the proposal team members, rather than to supplement their presentation.

• When it is done merely for its own sake. There must be a logical reason for using the video.

• When the quality of the video is superior to the quality of those presenting it.

• When glitches must be avoided, which is always. A video foul-up in an interview is worse than a slide being upside down in the tray.

Summary

Video is a very effective, versatile, and flexible marketing tool. Its use can raise your marketing effectiveness in relation to the competition. The biggest hurdle in using video is the first step. Don't worry so much about how to produce a perfect video. Your main objective is to win the job, not receive an SMPS award. If one person in your firm will make the personal commitment to using video, then it can happen.

The Video Production Process

Nick Despota

Most design professionals recognize the potential value of video as a component of their marketing efforts, and as a documentary or research tool. Yet, for most, it remains only a potential. Their hesitation is justified, their caution understandable: "Can I control the results, the content, and the cost?"

The intent of the outline presented here, a video production primer, is to give the reader more confidence in approaching this medium. This outline provides an overview of the terrain covered in most professional productions, representing a generalized map. Not all productions follow exactly the same course, but here is a typical itinerary.

Preproduction

You have met with two or three different producers, viewed samples of their work, discussed your project and objectives with them, and have chosen one with whom you feel comfortable. Now he or she works with you through these preproduction steps:

• Define program objectives. What should the tape accomplish?

• Consider your audience. Who are they? What are their attitudes and expectations? What is the physical context for viewing, and to what extent can you control it?

• Determine your production budget. This outline implies the basic budget elements. Costs include professional fees, equipment rental, facility rentals (editing suite and, if one is required, a studio), tape stock and supplies, transportation, and expenses. Typical costs range from $500 to $1,000 per minute of finished program. The less expensive program isn't necessarily less professional, it is just more simple.

A production schedule should be developed before production begins and a contract can link production "milestones" to a payment schedule. It is usual for a producer to require one-third to one-half of the total anticipated price to be paid up front, in order to defray production costs.

• Develop the treatment, storyboard, script, or "shot sheet." These are all approaches to the basic communication that occurs between you and the producer. What do you want to demonstrate, and how? Who says what, and where?

• Set up your production schedule. Communication adapts to circumstance: if need be, preproduction can be condensed down to a

Most design professionals recognize the potential value of video as a component of their marketing efforts.

thirty-minute conversation, and tape shot in the morning can, with great effect, be displayed in the afternoon (TV news). Conveying a more complex message, however, is a design process that takes time. Not surprisingly, most people underestimate how much time.

• Site visits may be justified. Unforeseen features of a location, either interior or exterior, can cause costly delays in a production schedule. Consider such things as vehicular access, terrain, power supply, lighting conditions, acoustic features, etc.

Production

"Production" in this context refers exclusively to the business of getting your material on tape in a raw, unedited form. It does not include the editing of selected segments into a finished product, which is postproduction.

In addition to the crews that operate the equipment, you may also work with a director. The director's job is to coordinate the action in front of the camera with the requirements of those working behind it: determining the beginnings and endings of individual shots, or "takes," their sequences, camera angles, and so forth. In smaller productions, the roles of producer, camera operator, and director may all be managed by one or two persons.

The most common production technique for projects such as those we are considering here—documentary or promotional programs with budgets in the $3,000-10,000 range—is referred to as ENG (electronic news gathering) style production.

The heart of ENG production is a lightweight, battery-powered camera designed to be either hand-held or tripod mounted. The camera's output, the video signal, is recorded on a portable videotape recorder, typically in ¾-inch-tape format. The introduction of a new recording technology, known as "component video," is starting to displace the high-end ¾-inch production format. Component systems such as Betacam and Recam produce images that surpass ¾-inch recordings for resolution and clarity.

Minimum practical crew size, using either ¾-inch or component format, is two: a camera operator and a sound technician/tape operator. A video monitor is used to check the recording during and after shooting. The production equipment package is complemented by portable lighting gear, a fluid head tripod, and a variety of microphones. The cost of this type of production, including equipment and crew, ranges from $500 to $1,000 per day for ¾-inch-format recording and from $900 to $1,200 per day for component formats.

Multicamera production enables simultaneously recording different perspectives on the same subject or action. Crew sizes increase to include not only additional camera operators but often a lighting director, a technical director, and an audio technician. A two-camera shoot, including the necessary personnel and equipment, can range from $1,500 to $2,000 per day. Multicamera production is much less mobile than ENG style.

Postproduction

You have gathered all the major elements that will be present in your finished program: location footage, interviews and statements, slides and graphics transferred to videotape. Now they must be woven together.

No one with whom I have worked through this process for the first time has failed to remark on the quality of magic inherent in the synthesis called videotape editing. It can be a lot of fun. If preproduction and production have left major gaps, it can also be a lot of headaches. A standard joke in the video industry goes: "Don't worry. We'll fix it in post." Don't count on it.

The need to quickly locate and accurately designate any segment of video source material dominates the editing technique. For this reason a time code and an edit list are usually used in professional productions. The time code is an electronic signal that has been recorded on the original tapes, providing an "address" for every moment of tape. The address format is "Hours:Minutes:Seconds:Frames." (There are thirty frames to the second.) Copies of the original tapes are made, often in VHS format for economy and convenience, which display the time code numbers superimposed in a small window over the picture; hence, these work tapes are often called "window dubs." The client, the producer, or both together review these dubs and select the "in-points" and "out-points" for each video and audio segment, listing them in the desired sequence. This is the edit decision list, or EDL.

During this stage, a voice-over narration can be written in order to give emphasis, create transitions, or provide information not present in the original videotape. If a narration was written before shooting began, which is often the case, now may be the time to revise it in order to conform more closely to the actual video that was recorded. The narration is now recorded.

The work tapes are used to make a rough edit, assembled on an inexpensive VHS or ¾-inch editing system. Such systems rent for $100 to $200 per day. The EDL is followed; but as the material is actually put together, if the need for changes from the initial list becomes evident (and it does), then other possibilities can be tried out and incorporated. For this reason, it is usually valuable for you to be present during the rough edit.

The purpose of the rough edit is to provide the opportunity for review and revision. People who were not present when the initial editorial decisions were being made yet have a controlling interest in the program's ultimate form can suggest changes. Since the rough edit was made from the window dubs, the time code numbers still appear on every shot. Revisions, therefore, are easily notated and the source material can, if necessary, be quickly located. Also now, with a good approximation of the program's overall form, judgments can be made about title graphics, special effects, and music.

The final edit is made from the original tapes, which do not carry the visible time code display. The time code is nevertheless still present as an electronic signal on the tape, thus enabling an operator to rapidly assemble the final program from the revised edit list. Rates for editing systems, including operators, range from $75 to $400 per hour. This broad range reflects differences in the capacities of various systems: the quality of electronic typography, the ability to produce dissolves or wipes from one image to another, or to produce special effects that involve geometric manipulation of the image, and whether the edit will be made on ¾-inch, 1-inch, or component format. Such choices determine which facility is appropriate for your project.

The videotape onto which the program has been edited is referred to as the "edited master." It must be protected. Rather than subject it to the physical wear of repeated playbacks, or to the possibility of loss, common practice is to use the master only to make duplicates, or "dubs," for use and distribution. These dubs, of course, can be made in whatever format is most convenient: ¾-inch, VHS, or Beta are the most common.

Bear in mind that with videotape editing, the original tapes are never cut or otherwise altered, as is the case in film editing. Therefore, it is useful to secure ownership of your tape originals, as well as the time-coded work tapes. Just as with your slide library, these tapes become valuable sources to which you can turn for use in future productions.

Advertising as Information

Fred A. Stitt

A/Es are treating advertising as an extension of professional services. Ads are used to convey useful data or otherwise serve a larger function than self-promotion.

The usual informational advertising theme is, "Here's what design firms actually do." Information ads have been placed with good response in airline magazines, regional and city magazines (particularly those with a large business/professional readership), and trade magazines serving administrators of schools, banks, public utilities, hospitals, and other development groups. Chamber of commerce magazines are very highly rated for locally directed advertising.

Mailers and newsletters are the dominant mode of advertising: A/E, small office, large office, monthly, quarterly—all shapes and sizes. A few outstanding ones clearly headline client concerns, problems, and opportunities while giving specific usable data on the headlined topics. Newsletters often provide news of rehab grants, solar financing, tax legislation, finance, environmentalism, and design and construction innovations.

Mailers and newsletters are the dominant mode of advertising.

Many newsletters are half-hearted efforts, a form of hometown news and self-congratulations presented with uneven graphic quality. The effective ones are so effective that they're clearly worth the substantial professional investment they receive.

Innovative Approaches

Other outstanding and innovative advertising approaches A/Es have taken:

• A design office buys space in its city theatrical programs. The intent is to reach a large portion of the city's highest level executive and professional population. The $190/month ads present a positive image of the firm in a context that shows support of worthy cultural events.

• An engineering firm chips in on local Public Broadcasting Service presentations of "Washington Week in Review." The goal: name recognition among education/influential members of the community. That is provided by the announcement: "This presentation is made possible by a grant from...." That message, at the opening and closing of the broadcasts, cost the firm only $1,800 for the year, about $35 per program. This firm later connected itself with local PBS broadcasts of the popular economics series, "Free to Choose."

• A small architect/interiors firm discovers an unmet need: a new apparel trade mart is opening, but there is no single source for the design of exhibition space. The architect sends a mailer to 300 prospective exhibitors offering design-build services. The mailer cost is shared with a selected contractor who will execute the designs. The result: twelve responses, five contracts, and a spin-off lead on an additional New York project. (Everyone familiar with direct mail advertising warns not to expect that high a return except in extraordinary circumstances.)

"Just follow the rules," says one marketing consultant. Many firms don't and won't, and will waste budgets accordingly. Here are some of the most important guides:

• Prepare advertising as part of a larger integrated marketing and management plan. Piecemeal efforts get piecemeal results.

• Define your audience very clearly, and go after a specific response. The response should be inquiries, requests for more information—something that leads to further sustainable contact. But be selective. One phone book display ad on design services pulled in a very large response—mainly from the wrong people.

• Set limits and goals, budget an ad program, and proceed through a testing period. If you get a certain percentage response from a test ad, all things being equal, you'll get the same response when advertising to a larger number of the same audience. Once results become predictable, it's possible to control inquiry response rates to whatever level you desire.

• The best possible advertising is not an ad, but articles in magazines and newspapers. Articles can be placed by learning and following the editorial rules. See the article on "How To Publish Your Work" in the Public Relations section for more information. Once an article is placed, order lots of offprints (reprints of the article) and turn them into a mailer or new additions to the office brochure.

• Always address prospects' interests and needs. (Sales wisdom says that clients are looking for someone who will save them time and money, take over project responsibility, and make them famous in the process. So show how you will do that.)

Paid Advertising by Smaller Firms

Some A/Es who accept the inevitability of advertising still resent the idea. "We have no need for it." "Just another expense and a nuisance." So say the heads of two major design firms. Their areas of client contact are well established. They don't believe they will reach any more clients through advertising than they already reach by other means.

Some younger, smaller offices see it differently. They say the larger architectural firms need to reach a relatively small number of corporations and agencies. Smaller offices have to reach out to a much larger number of potential clients in order to find work. They feel hampered by costly traditional methods of personalized client search and inquiry.

A partnership in Berkeley tested a small ad in a community newspaper. The ad drew several inquiries daily over a couple of weeks' time. The firm has also bought ad space in a skiing magazine to attract vacation

Prepare advertising as part of a larger integrated marketing and management plan.

Ads by themselves don't sell. It's the follow-up that counts.

home clients. In addition it distributed flyers to local merchants on store design and remodeling services, which brought in some renovation work. Final results: some new work—not a lot but enough to survive through a troublesome recession.

Another small-office architect has placed small photo ads in a weekly newspaper over a period of months. These have brought in several modest owner-builder consultantships and design contracts. Nothing sensational, but this architect says he's remained busy while others like him have not.

A/Es who favor advertising argue that it's a data service. They say ads are especially helpful for people who could profit from highly specialized design services. Many people don't know such services exist. Most people, including business people, still don't know what A/Es do, how they do it, what value it has, or how to go about contacting an A/E to find out. Widespread advertising would help to close this information gap.

Ads by themselves don't sell. It's the follow-up that counts. Ads attract inquiries about types and range of services, fees, the A/E's experience, etc. These questions are appropriately answered in small brochure pamphlets. The ad invites people to ask for the pamphlet, which answers questions and tells how to arrange for preliminary consultation with the design firm.

The foremost rule in advertising is to emphasize the client's needs. Advertising pros like Rosser Reeves of Ted Bates & Co. say the most common error is overemphasis of the advertiser's virtues. These should be mentioned, but they must be specific, not general, and presented in the context of their value to the buyer. Always think, "What does this do for the buyer?"

Readers of an advertisement usually remember only one main point. If the purpose of an ad is to encourage readers to send for more information, then that is the point to make. Generalities and unsubstantiated claims don't go over. Straightforward, factual statements about the advantages of the service tend to bring the best response.

Pros and Cons of Paid Advertising

An AIA officer tells us advertising will increase costs without any increase in benefits. There's only so much work out there, he argues. Why spend more just to get the same slice of the pie?

An opposing argument says advertising will create more jobs and keep everyone busier. A small-office architect (not AIA) says he did well during a crunch only because of his classified advertising in local newspapers. He says his ads encouraged people to start projects they wouldn't have thought about otherwise.

Another argument points to the fact that most construction is nonarchitect designed. More of this market might go to the architects if the advantages were aggressively advertised.

Does advertising add to the cost of services? It has to, according to its opponents. But statistical evidence, one way or the other, has been scarce until recently. Consumer groups have gathered figures and publicized them in the press and in courtrooms. They find the quality of advertised services are no worse than unadvertised ones, but costs/prices are substantially lower. One explanation for this seeming paradox: incentives for experimentation and efficiency are virtually nil in markets where advertising has been restricted or prohibited.

Would new or smaller firms be crowded out by large offices with huge advertising budgets? Just the opposite, according to studies by economist Phillip J. Nelson of the State University of New York. He finds "monopoly" power is kept down by unfettered advertising in the general business world. This could be the case in the A/E realm, since smaller firms currently have the most trouble getting their messages out to prospective clients.

Though many firms are interested, there's been no headlong rush into massive advertising. One architect suggests advertising would be useful occasionally to smooth out the highs and lows in work flow. Depending on one's financing resources, the best time to build at lower cost is when other people aren't building. Advertising could make people aware of that.

How to Choose and Work with an Ad Agency

Gerre Jones

There are perhaps 300 different services offered by advertising agencies.

"We learned a lot about selling techniques by becoming a client," says Jo Ann Stone, CM Associates, Inc., Houston.

"Advertising agencies are a lot like us...the people that we interviewed are selling their services, too. We narrowed our selection down to two agencies—either one could have taken the account. They were both talented and their fees were comparable. We chose the agency that we felt most comfortable with," Ms. Stone said.

There are seven basic steps in making a thorough search and an accurate choice of the right ad agency. If you already retain public relations counsel who offer advertising services, by all means give them a chance at the account if they have performed well for you.

1. Decide what is needed from an advertising agency. There are perhaps 300 different services offered by advertising agencies. They range from analyzing your company's capabilities to speech writing. Within this assemblage there are five relationships you can establish with an agency:

• prepare and place advertising only;

• prepare and place ads and produce other sales promotion material as needed;

• serve as marketing counsel and advise on marketing planning, research, and execution, and produce the ads;

• become a full marketing partner, sharing responsibility for the total marketing effort of your firm;

• provide marketing leadership by initiating the planning, coordinating research, and directing the execution of your firm's total marketing program.

2. Set down the criteria for the ideal agency. Basically, an advertising agency should have proved it has the ability to create potentially effective advertising and is selective in placing it where prospects are most likely to be reached efficiently.

To promote services as complex as those offered by a design or a design-related firm, the agency should know the difference between marketing and selling. (Marketing is trying to find out what preferences clients have and then looking for profitable ways to satisfy them.) The agency should also be able to define the difference between selling a product and marketing professional services. Most advertising is product oriented and based on a wholly different intellectual construct. (An excellent discussion of this topic is in Aubrey Wilson's *The Marketing of Professional Services*, McGraw-Hill Book Co., Ltd., London, 1972.)

You might also ask a prospective agency for its definition of "promotion." A general description is: letting people know what you are doing and how well you are doing it, communicated to people who should know about it.

In addition to technical skills, you should feel comfortable with the agency, as Jo Ann Stone pointed out, and this is purely subjective. You could compare your capabilities for original thought, professional philosophies, and commitment to the quality of the product with theirs.

3. Find out what a good agency expects from its clients. One agency head said his firm has thirteen specific criteria for the ideal client; when they have gone to work for clients who failed to meet most of them, the relationship invariably failed. Advertising literature in your local library can supply you with a workable list. Or you can develop your own list by defining your ideal client. Include such requirements as integrity, fairness, respect, loyalty, top-management support, appreciation, and constructive criticism.

4. Make a preliminary selection of prospective agencies. Apply your highly developed sense of visual literacy to the advertising output. From all the ads that regularly bombard you in newspapers, magazines, on television and radio, select the ones that appeal to you. Find out from the media who the placing agencies are. Contact five or so by letter, giving your criteria for the ideal agency and a list of basic questions. These are much like the questions prospective clients pose to you:
- brief history;
- size in income (not billings);
- number of employees;
- names of key people and brief biographies;
- services provided;
- the firm's standards;
- how the agency wants to be paid—commissions, fees, or some combination of the two;
- client roster (including those lost in the last few years).

Is the agency too big to serve you properly?

5. Screen the preliminary choices and develop a short list. An opening query could be, "What do you see as the task of advertising?" Answer (or reasonable facsimile), "To find fresh, imaginative ways of imparting meaningful information on behalf of the seller to the public on its own terms."

Some other problems: Why are you interested in our account? What specific capabilities and facilities do you offer? What are your strengths? How would you organize to work on our account? How would you describe your agency's work?

6. Choose one. Keep three things in mind when making the final selection. 1) Size. Is the agency too big to serve you properly? However glamorous its name, an agency will give a client only as much attention as its value calls for. On the other hand, a small agency should not spread itself too thin by taking on your account; an account should get the atten-

tion it needs on an ongoing basis, not just at the beginning of the relationship. 2) Perception of your needs. Remember that you are buying the agency's ability to question you. 3) Personal and organization chemistry. Decide which agency presented the best potential program for your firm, by people you are likely to be able to live with.

    7. Become an enlightened and involved client.

How to Develop an Ad Campaign

Now that you've put advertising into your marketing program, here's how they mesh: marketing is finding out where the dollars are and advertising is getting to where the dollars are in as direct a manner as possible, at the lowest cost per thousand.

In advertising a professional service, remember that its most valuable payoff is in letting you know where potential jobs are, giving you leads that you may not have garnered from other sources.

Product advertising moves goods. Service advertising identifies potential buyers of the service. And, on occasion, it may sell the services directly. More often it is a vehicle for potential buyers to find out more about what they may be contracting for—and with design and design-related services, the expenditures could be considerable. Advertising supplements whatever prospect identification programs you already utilize. When advertising starts bringing in requests for information, put your follow-up program into action.

How much should you spend on advertising? Define what market or markets you are going to pursue, the media you plan to use to reach them, and the costs involved in creating the right campaign. You can add the total dollar figure to the marketing budget or reallocate promotional funds. Modify the advertising expenditure if the total is not financially feasible. Or you can say to the agency, "I have $10,000 to work with. Come up with the optimum size message in the strongest publications, with attention-attracting layouts that can be produced reasonably." (Note: most of our references in this article will be to the print media.)

You and your agency should fully understand what you are selling in a campaign. If you are large enough you could have several campaigns running concurrently. This is the case at Bechtel, which runs corporate image ads and specific market ads for its divisions. Heery Associates advertises its construction management services in general business and specific market publications. CM Associates, which began advertising this year, is in a specific market program.

The better you are able to tell the agency what you want the campaign to do, the better it will be.

A good campaign should be interesting, vital, imaginative, and honest. The better you are able to tell the agency what you want the campaign to do, the better it will be. Frank Lloyd Wright's comment, "The best designs are for the best clients," applies to advertising, too.

Appeal generally to basic human emotions and to your markets specifically. Keep in mind who they are; why they do what they do; what they believe and what they don't; what they can and can't be taught.

How to Evaluate Ads

A fine book directed to newcomers to the advertising client role is *How to Advertise*, by Kenneth Roman and Jane Maas, St. Martin's Press, New York, 1976. It's a brief (156 pages), well-written guide to becoming a knowledgeable advertising client.

The admaker is charged with building bridges between what the advertising wants to say and the potential buyer wants to see. You and your agency decide on the approach.

In product advertising, the promotional approach gives the product its personality. In advertising a professional service, the ads reflect what already exists—the business personality of your firm. Capture readers' attention quickly, give them one thought to remember, and let them know how to contact you!

Here are a few figures on ad appeal:

- The attention value of an ad is approximately twice as important as the actual convincing power of the text itself.
- For every person who reads the copy, four will read just the headline.
- About 5 percent of the audience you paid to reach will take the time to read what you wrote.
- An average of one-half of the body copy will be read by those who take the time to get past the headline.
- You have 2.5 seconds to flag down the reader of a newspaper or magazine page.
- Your ad has the best chance for recall if it can tell its story in 100 words or less, and be comprehended in fifteen seconds or less.

Market researchers have all kinds of sophisticated measuring models for gauging response to product ads. Professional service ads have been rare, and are less quantifiable at this time. Be confident that there is a market out there that your advertising will make an impression on. If your ads do not bring in some live leads, restructure the campaign and try another approach. Don't give up the first time around.

Case Studies

1. CM Associates, Inc. Director of communications is Jo Ann Stone. Advertising agency is Ketchum, MacLeod & Grove. Based on their growth rate, CM Associates decided to advertise to generate more leads. The education market was singled out as the target market and two publications were selected: *American School and University* and the *American School Board Journal*. Initial budget for space and preparation was $25,000.

Client and agency decided on a long copy approach. Said Ms. Stone, "We are selling a big ticket item—$100,000 and up in fees. We felt that we wanted to tell our readers something about construction management, and that we were the ones to handle it. It's our belief that the person who is a genuine lead will take the time to read our message."

CM's campaign began in May, running six times in each publication over an eight-month period. Response to the ads via reader service

About 5 percent of the audience you paid to reach will take the time to read what you wrote.

If your ads do not bring in some live leads, try another approach. Don't give up the first time around.

cards has been good, although to date no direct inquiries have been attributed to the ad.

A similar format, two-page ad is running in the *Houston Business Journal* in a staggered schedule through February. The first two exposures brought four responses, and two of them had real and sizeable projects.

Ms. Stone feels that CM Associates has seen the result of advertising in terms of response, and will expand its advertising efforts.

2. Heery Associates, Inc. Agency is James Moore. Heery Associates ran a full-page ad in the January/February 1977 *Harvard Business Review*. The same ad has also run in *Forbes*. Smaller space ads are appearing in these publications, as well as in *American School and University*, *Hospitals*, and *American City and County*.

The firm has been advertising for several years; the current annual ad budget is about $100,000.

"There are a great many people who do not know what construction management is," said Mr. Moore. "From the media we can get them interested in learning more about it, and then find out about specific projects they might have. We've had pretty impressive responses to our ads. We tried the heavy copy approach but were not as successful with it. There is much to be said for both approaches, however."

3. Bechtel. T. W. Wright is Bechtel's advertising manager; McCann-Erikson is the agency. Bechtel has been running corporate image-building ads for the past ten years. The current "Bechtel builds..." campaign is appearing in *Newsweek* and *U.S. News & World Report*.

"Our corporate campaign shows areas in which the company has capabilities," Mr. Wright commented. "We have eight operating divisions, and we run ads for the particular markets according to the division's business development needs."

Contracts and Negotiation

4

Selecting the Right Contract

Barry B. LePatner

Wittingly or unwittingly, the law of contracts weaves itself into the fabric of an architect's daily activities. Even before commencement of any design services, the owner quite likely has executed contracts for the purchase of the property to be developed, the building loan, and tenants.

One would, therefore, believe that the architect would have little difficulty in requesting the client to execute a contract for the design services on the same project. Yet, the opposite is precisely the case.

Having secured the commission, perhaps with only a letter of agreement, all too many architects and engineers are ready to launch into their work without securing the benefit and protection that come from a comprehensive set of documents that spells out the rights and obligations of each party. It should matter not that the owner is an old, valued client, that the project is small, or that the final scope of the work is narrowly circumscribed.

The Meaning of a Contract
What is the real meaning of a contract? My well-worn copy of Webster's *New World Dictionary* defines a contract as 'an agreement between two or more people to do something; compact; covenant; an agreement, usually written, enforceable by law'.

There is a substantial body of law that surrounds the making, breaking, and enforcement of a contract. As a statement of general application it might be observed that in the eyes of the law a contract is given special status. If clear and unambiguous, it is treated with sacred regard.

It should be some source of comfort to know that the realm of the law of contracts is based primarily on common sense. More precisely, the law looks to the intentions of the parties at the time of the making of the agreement. As such, a written agreement contemplating all anticipated contingencies is far more preferable in terms of resolving disputes than a vague, poorly drafted agreement.

Three Early Steps
There are three early steps to securing a good contract. The first step requires the architect to become familiar with the scope of the project. This requires knowledge as to details of the owner's needs, the extent to which standard or unique design/construction techniques may be

With only a letter of agreement, too many architects and engineers are ready to launch into their work.

needed, and the budgetary range that will define what may or can be done.

Knowledgeable architects will spare no effort to develop this information.

According to Alan Schwartzman, a partner in Davis, Brody & Associates: "The farther we go in defining the scope of our service, the more precise we can be in getting the right contract." Identification of these elements is a critical step and one often overlooked in the rush to proceed.

(For valuable reference tools, see *Compensation Guidelines for Architectural and Engineering Services* and *A/E Supplement to Compensation Guidelines*, 1978, published by the AIA. These publications, surprisingly little known, offer several analysis forms which can be used in the precontract stage.)

Ask if your firm can capably perform the work that will be required.

The second stage requires the designer to gain an intimate knowledge of the client. Researching the owner's background, financial capability, reputation in the business world, and experience with architects and engineers can aid immeasurably in gaining the insight necessary to secure a properly drafted contract.

Just as the owner has reviewed a design firm's resume and past experience, so should you familiarize yourself with the party retaining your firm's services. Where any doubt exists, a credit check is a wise investment and could help to avoid prospective problems.

Finally, after gaining a good understanding of the project and your client's needs, it is equally important to ask if your firm can capably perform the work that will be required. Is the in-house capability present or will outside consultants be needed? Is there adequate time to devote to an intensive design schedule or will there be conflicts with existing business? Does this project coincide with the firm's future business goals or is it being taken on merely to keep the staff busy?

The Most Important Decision

The selection of the contract will be the single most important business decision during the job. From this decision will flow all related financial issues, governance of the work itself, and the means of resolving disputes which may arise out of the performance of the parties. It is at this point, at the latest, that competent legal advice should be sought. Memorializing an agreement on substantial construction and fee dollars should not be done in a vacuum.

To your client, the decision to go forward with you as the architect on this project manifests the client's commitment. To the architect, it is the opportunity to make an initial impression that his or her business acumen will be committed to representing the owner's interests as well.

And let there be no mistaking how that early impression can be best made: by submitting a well-drafted contract for professional services that protects the business interest of both parties.

It is well to remember that owners do little in their business lives without consulting their lawyers; contractors follow the same rule. If you as an architect believe you are more skilled in the business and legal nuances of the construction industry than the owner and his or her advisory team, you are playing dangerously with your future.

Review the Contract

A review of the contract is also important. Increasing numbers of design firms are making contract review part of their standard business procedure. On this point, Schwartzman says, "Not only should you have your attorney review each contract, but at the same time, you are wise to have your professional liability insurer review it to ensure that any claims arising under the contract will be insurable." Seeking both legal and insurance counsel at any early stage in negotiations enables Davis, Brody to have significant input into contract formation. Says Schwartzman: "Some clients take issue with certain revisions we have made to the standard AIA agreement, and ask us, 'If it's good enough for the AIA, why isn't it good enough for you?'

"We are able to explain the reasons for each change that was made. In general, the client is receptive to this approach. If he is not, or if he proposes revisions, we will ask our carrier for guidance on how far we can go and still have an insurable provision."

To highlight the fact that successful firms insist on a contract, Eason Leonard, a partner in I. M. Pei & Partners, states: "We may begin work on a project pursuant to a letter agreement. But this will only cover design concept services, and carry with it the understanding that a detailed contract for the balance of the project is to follow."

The use of standard AIA/NSPE forms, though widely employed, should be carefully scrutinized. It is important to recognize that these forms have been designed to cover the broad base of situations that may arise during most standard projects. Recent decisions in state and federal courts may substantially affect provisions in the standard agreements, warranting ongoing review of their applicability to a given project.

Responsibilities Must Be Clear

Do not become responsible for things you cannot control. Of course, the services of the architect will also be affected by decisions of the client, the coordinated efforts of the construction team, and decisions of the construction manager, if one has been retained by the client. Leonard is quick to note: "The architect's cost and profits will be affected substantially by the procedures decided on by the client to complete the project. Do we go out to bid with a complete set of drawings? Will a construction manager be used to get an early start on construction? We can only be responsible for those things in our contract which we control, and our contracts must be very clear for this reasoon."

Certain provisions of the agreement must be viewed as critical to protecting the rights of the architect. In addition to the scope and payment provisions, these include (1) additional services, (2) scope of reimbursable expense items, (3) ownership and use of documents, (4) termination requisites, and (5) equitable adjustment of compensation in the event of project suspension for more than an agreed-upon period of time.

Recognizing the importance of the contract in defining and pro-

Recent decisions in state and federal courts may substantially affect provisions in the standard agreements.

tecting the rights of the architect is, as shown above, an important step in the development of a successful practice. Learning how to integrate an agreement into overall operation of a well-run practice will provide innumerable benefits in both the short and the long run.

Profitable Contract Terms

Frank A. Stasiowski

W ith the economic climate continually uncertain, the emphasis on solid contract terms in your design contract is increasingly vital to your firm's financial success. Most clients are demanding more work for less in fees, and firms that do not reexamine the specific terms of a contract often find themselves without enough fee to break even let alone make a small profit. When negotiating your next contract, first remember to negotiate scope, not price, because the scope of the work should control the price.

Next, break down your price into many small pieces which relate to specific scope items so that you can eliminate a portion of the work if a prospective client thinks your price is high, and more importantly so that it will become difficult for a client to argue with any small piece of the work when negotiating. Finally, attempt to insert as many of the following ten terms into every contract so that your final fee price will be less significant than without them.

1. Get partial or full payment of fees before starting.

Bad economic times mean that everyone is tightening belts. Therefore, now is the best time to start asking for money up front. Your client may not like the change but will have more understanding now, because everyone else is doing the same thing. Also, if you get money up front, deposit it and don't credit it to the client until the last invoice, allowing you to avoid a bad debt, and also to earn maximum interest on the deposit.

2. Have the client pay unusual reimbursable costs.

In addition to normal reimbursables, ask for reimbursement for items such as liability insurance premiums, computer time, messenger service, outside project accounting, etc. With government clients this term may reduce your overhead, making your contract price more attractive. With private sector clients, this term can dramatically increase profits.

3. Include a streamlined form of billing and payment.

Have the client agree to a simple monthly payment schedule tied to the scope and schedule of work, eliminating-time consuming breakdowns of hours and expenses all throughout the project as well as pages of backup which cost you and the client many accounting hours to verify. Then sit down at the end of the project, audit it, and make appropriate adjustments in amounts paid and owed.

4. Have the client's staff do some of the work.

When negotiating your next contract first remember to negotiate scope not price.

Even though this term may appear obvious, consider specific applications which usually aren't included. For instance, instead of delivering prints to your client using your messenger, specify that the client's messengers will pick up and deliver all correspondence and prints. If this term were in all of your contracts, you might even eliminate one messenger from your staff.

5. Shorten the client's schedule and then work overtime.

In general, shorter schedules produce more profitable projects by reducing excess perfection. Also by working overtime for private sector clients, you may be able to charge clients at your normal billing rate without incurring additional salary or overhead costs.

6. Shorten the billing/payment cycle.

To improve your cash flow, ask your client to pay you weekly in smaller amounts, again tied to a predetermined schedule of payments. Shortening the cycle reduces your borrowing, thus saving you interest expense, and also tells you sooner whether or not you have a potential "bad debt" for a client.

7. Agree to a split savings on under-bid construction amounts.

This term requires an independent estimator, but could save your project's profitability. If you agree to a design fee lower than your original fee estimate without a corresponding scope reduction, you should also seek not to share in losses if the project comes in over bid because you have taken your lumps already by accepting a lower than normal fee.

8. Agree to guaranteed interest for late payments.

Discuss interest with your client and be certain that the word "guaranteed" is included in this term. If the client won't pay interest, use this discussion to negotiate for an advance payment as a form of interest.

9. Insert a limit of liability clause.

Be certain to limit liability to your net fees on the project and not gross fees.

This term can save you a considerable amount on professional liability insurance premiums. Be certain to limit liability to your net fees on the project and not gross fees.

10. Insert a provision which measures scope changes precisely.

For instance, it can be written that the client will sign a record copy of the drawings at specified calendar dates in the schedule, indicating that decisions made as of that date are known to the client. Do not tie the signature to completion of a phase since the definition of phase completion may be impossible to decide.

Few of the above terms standing alone will produce significant improvements in project profitability, but by adopting the attitude that as many of these terms as possible should be inserted into every contract, you could make even more profit on every project during recessionary times.

Another term now used by many consultants is to have the owner make fee payments directly to the consultant instead of through another prime design professional. Firms using this term tell us that it eliminates the long-standing problem of one design professional holding the funds of another to collect interest. Also, all design contracts should contain a date after which all monetary provisions of the contract are subject to renegotiation at the option of the design professional, allowing you to increase fees if the project is shelved for any reason whatsoever.

Finally, since many of your projects are done based on letter agreements or without a contract at all, we recommend that you incorporate these terms plus any additional terms you have into a one-page typeset, preprinted sheet which you attach to all letter agreements.

Remember that from the design contract comes all profit and all problems. Write your contracts to avoid as many problems as you can and to include specific terms designed to increase profitability.

How to Negotiate

Fred A. Stitt

Negotiating: a mixed world of dirty tricks, imaginative trades, and psychological discipline. A/Es have to hold their own against pros who know all the tricks and are trained to the hilt in the latest methods.

Most A/Es resent having to haggle fees or other conditions. "It's unprofessional." And for many, it's just plain unpleasant. But hard bargaining is a way of life for contractors, business people, and representatives of government client agencies or regulatory agencies. Like it or not, A/Es have to learn the rules or stay on the sidelines and limit their career growth.

Many aids are available: texts, seminars, case study courses. We've compiled key points from the latest material being offered.

The Main Tricks and Ploys

In the tricks department, some common ploys to guard against:

• Sharp negotiators take ownership of meetings. Small advantages are taken to build psychological leverage: holding a meeting on home turf, taking the chair at the head of the conference table, providing the agenda, leading the discussion. A subtle aggressor who's actually in a weaker negotiating position can give a convincing show of being on top and take the initiative away from an unwary adversary.

• Agents soften up the opposition before real negotiation begins. The agent of a bargainer can gain concessions while shrugging off the authority to grant any. The principal negotiator gains leverage, and gains data on the other side's position/arguments, while giving nothing in return. The data lets him or her prepare effective counter-arguments before negotiations formally begin.

• Passing out the rope, an old ploy of lawyers. An opponent is pressed into misstating a fact or making a simple error. If caught and embarrassed about showing ignorance or incompetence, the participant may be pressured into evasions to cover up. Pressure is exerted by the opponent who uses a chilly, superior tone of voice, and a strong distrusting glance. Once caught in error plus evasion or caught lying to cover up an error, the victim loses face along with credibility, and is set up to be more easily milked of concessions. (The emphatic lesson here: always admit errors immediately, avoid making excuses, and move on.)

• "Misunderstanding" to gain free concessions. A negotiator pretends to misunderstand a point and rephrases the other side's position to make it more favorable to his or her own. An opponent may let this pass by. (Participants are sometimes shaky over their ability to explain themselves clearly and will surrender a point just to dodge the issue.)

• Deliberate misunderstanding has other uses. The "misunderstood" party may try to restate a position, but in that process takes the risk of softening his or her stand or dropping a point during the restatement. A related device: a negotiator may not respond at all to a statement or argument, implying by silence that it's irrelevant or too ridiculous to take seriously. Or a negotiator may flatly deny objective facts. These tactics are designed to psych the opponent out of hanging onto good factual data or valid argument. If the ploy is caught in time, the evading negotiator has to back down on this irrational tactic and will claim s/he misunderstood the argument or didn't hear the facts correctly.

• The "screaming fit" can unnerve an opponent, and prod a quick concession. A sudden emotional outburst may send the opponent rushing to soothe bad feelings. The other party is fooled into thinking the point(s) in question must mean a great deal more to the upset counterpart than to self, and that the loud complainer has been pushed to the limit, endangering the entire negotiation unless s/he backs down. It's just a device. Adult people don't have screaming fits because they are uncontrollably upset. They do it to get control over people and they do it because it works remarkably well.

• Yelling, swearing, and insults may be used to goad real anger in an opponent. An angry opponent is more likely to make rash statements or errors and lose the thread of a reasoned argument. A further reason for this gambit: an emotionally upset opponent temporarily loses analytical capacities, and becomes more susceptible to suggestion and emotional appeals.

• The "Mutt and Jeff" team play on aroused emotions. A negotiating team may feature a "hardball player" who presses unrealistic demands. When an opponent's resentment is aroused, the "soft" team member steps in as an "ally"—a mediator with a compromise. A compromise is proposed to ease the tension—all staged and designed to favor the Mutt and Jeff team.

The sharpest negotiators ask for kickers even after a settlement is wrapped up.

• An offer to split the difference can salvage a bad position. The opponent has a valid claim—as in a cost dispute—but the negotiator stalls and won't concede the point. The stubborn negotiator finally relieves the opponent's frustration by offering to split the difference or meet him halfway. The opponent justifies taking some loss as a legitimate compromise, a small price for instant settlement. In reality, the "compromise" is strictly one-sided and a total giveaway.

• Last-minute kickers are asked, and often granted. When major points are settled, a negotiator offers to close the deal if some "minor" additional concessions are thrown in. The sharpest negotiators ask for kickers even after a settlement is wrapped up. This tactic exploits the relaxed state participants fall into when they think bargaining is over at last.

Strategies for Successful Negotiations

Tricks, games, and ploys are a small part of the professional negotiators' arsenal. Preparation and operating procedures for straight give-and-take get the most attention. Here are some points consistently emphasized in negotiator training sessions:

• Gather personal and financial background on participants. Credit checks, knowledge of actual vs. assumed decision-making authority, observations from others who have dealt with participants, the more the better. It can be assumed that the other side will do the same.

• Prepare a bracket. A bracket includes the highest and lowest realistic ranges of what may be asked and expected from negotiation. Participants sometimes enter a meeting without defining limits. They later cause delay and confusion by trying to decide on limits in the heat of a negotiating session.

• Plan a scenario, a list of the likeliest points to be raised, and possible trade-offs in concessions. No meeting will follow all the specifics of a plan or scenario, but prior awareness of the widest range of possible trades helps to speed up the process.

• Prenegotiate as many points as possible. Prior contact provides background data and guidance to the other side's needs and negotiating methods.

• Do some psychological rehearsal. Professional negotiators emphasize that you should resist feeling panic if the other side threatens to walk out. Prepare to hold back and play a waiting game if the other party presses for an unrealistic bargain. Plan to withhold remarks and delay decision making when you feel stress.

Operating Tactics

Here are some common operating procedures used by professional mediators and negotiators:

• The sequence of negotiation moves from simplest, most easily agreed upon points, to the more complex. The idea is to establish a good pace and pattern of agreement and compromise.If a point isn't quickly resolved, shelve it temporarily. (Solutions to small disagreements often pop up later and resolve themselves in the course of dealing with other issues.)

• Keep precise notes (or tape recordings) of concessions, the sequence of agreements, and the reasons given for agreements. Confusion and disputes arise after an agreement if a participant forgets a concession and can't recall any reason for having made it.(Contracts are sometimes modified—later concessions replace earlier ones—but both the original and the contradictory modifications may accidentally be kept in the final agreement.)

• Practiced negotiators tune into nonverbal cues from other participants. Body gestures and other physical mannerisms usually telegraph a person's mood and responses to circumstances. If body language is saying "yes" while the person is saying "no," the perceptive negotiator acts accordingly.

Dealing with Client Demands

How do A/Es deal with client demands for concessions on fees and services? Most fade out in hard bargaining. But we find many A/Es have learned techniques to protect their self-interest and still satisfy wary clients. We've also uncovered helpful advice from professional salespeople who handle tough demands as part of their day-to-day routine.

Most demands are variations on a theme: "We've only got so much budgeted for this, can't go a cent higher." "It's not me, but I've got to give the partner (or wife or committee or board) some signal that you're willing to meet us halfway." "I'm speculating, the bank's speculating, other design firms speculate. Why can't you?"

One discovery: demands are commonly misinterpreted as a sign that the prospective client is wriggling off the hook. This isn't necessarily so. Just the opposite. Corporate sales representatives say that demands or hard-nosed questioning are usually expressions of interest and a desire to buy. It's when they stop talking that you have to worry. The questioning and bargaining prospect is saying: "I'm interested. Now sell me."

One question often lurking in the back of a prospective client's mind: is the design firm holding back a better deal? This is most common among the single-building clients rather than experienced multibuilding clients. Most business negotiations start with a first offer. Then other options are trotted out later to crack resistance or provide a kicker or sweetener to close a deal. Many clients expect this and are disconcerted if it doesn't happen.

The A/E may not play the game according to the client's expectations and may have made the best offer right off the bat. Now s/he faces real loss by having to throw in a further concession to hook the resistant client. The failure to bargain when bargaining is expected is a common source of confusion and resentment on both sides.

Farsighted negotiators work out varied concessions in advance—mainly optional trade-offs that can be mutually advantageous. A client's concern over fee, for example, is sometimes answered by an agreement to defer payments with an appropriate added interest charge.

Preparation especially pays off in high-pressure situations, such as when the client corners the A/E with a demand for a split-second decision. It also pays off when the client is a nibbler, one who holds back demands until the last minute before finalizing an agreement.

Clients often sweeten demands with promises. "If you will give us a break on this job, you will be at the top of the list for the rest of our work." Or, "There will be plenty of publicity for you on this, worth more than any fee." The A/E who gives in on expectation of such reward is trading a tangible value for an intangible promise. It sounds as if something is being offered, but when you look closely, the offered concessions are not enforceable unless listed and spelled out in a contract.

One architect looks for unspoken questions that may underlie a client's nagging demands. He notes that clients are reluctant to raise certain questions or concerns overtly but they're there and they're interfering with direct negotiation.

> The questioning and bargaining prospect is saying: "I'm interested. Now sell me."

245   *CONTRACTS AND NEGOTIATION*

The architect borrows psychotherapists' techniques for drawing people out through "active listening." That is by answering statements and demands with feedback instead of argument. Here's a sample:

Client: "Can't you do better than that (regarding the scope of services and fee structure)?"

Architect (feeding the statement and it's apparent accompanying emotion back to the client): "You have some doubts."

Client: "I'm awfully strapped. It seems like a lot of money."

Architect (resisting the temptation to argue): "It seems like too much?"

Client: "I don't think a larger operation would have to charge this high."

Architect (still in control and resisting the urge to argue): "You think you might be able to get a better deal from a larger firm."

Client, now getting to the real concern on his mind: "At least I'd feel more confident about the work getting done on time. They'd have more people on it."

The architect doesn't debate or question in the above exchange—that would short-circuit the fact-finding process. He only feeds back the client's statements one by one through a series of modifications until the underlying problem emerges. If the fee had been the issue, the client could have reaffirmed that position clearly. Instead, the feedback allowed him to bring out more basic worries based on his misconceptions of differences in service capability between larger and smaller offices.

How to Win Arguments

Fred A. Stitt

How do you win arguments? There are ways of getting your arguments across that are both fair and extraordinarily effective. They're based on one winning rule in persuasion: always prepare the other person to listen. Without such preparation you won't get a hearing. When you're talking, the other person will be spending his or her energy thinking up more comebacks. The trick is to stimulate another's readiness to listen and to grasp the ideas you want to convey. Once you've provoked a receptive state of mind, you will get some agreement or at least some move toward compromise. Here's how.

Listen First
• Take the initiative. To get the other person to listen, you listen first. That means withholding objections and arguments and only listening and feeding back as necessary to confirm and clarify what you think you hear. When you can sum up another's views to his or her satisfaction, you've practically won the case.

• Find grounds of agreement with the other's needs and concerns. Share concern over their economic well-being, over the success of the project, over common "enemies" and problems. And share interests and values outside the controversy of the moment. The preparation is a matter of establishing rapport, a sense of being on the same side. The purpose is to avoid being labeled as an enemy by the other side. You can have an honest disagreement but once the other party views you as a true enemy, the disagreement will be viewed as an outgrowth of your selfishness, irresponsibility, craziness, and other unpleasant things.

• Enhance rapport and receptivity to your views with straightforward compliments. Others tend to give credence to your judgment when you compliment them. If you want the most intense interest and attention paid to your words, introduce them and surround them with some flattery.

• Don't press your views on others when their danger signs are up. Expressions of impatience and distraction mean receptivity is down. You will only regain receptivity by linking what you say to the other person's interests. Another danger signal: a flat, contrary assertion in a definite tone of voice. Another: silence combined with physical expressions of doubt or withdrawal such as folded arms, distancing posture, hunched shoulders, and visible facial tension. When contrary assertions are

If you want the most intense interest and attention paid to your words, surround them with some flattery.

repeatedly expressed in a stressed and impatient tone of voice, you can be sure the barriers are rigidly in place. Call for a break or a major change of subject to change the emotional atmosphere.

• Be ready to move fast when the positive signals appear. One of the clearest signals is questioning on the listener's part. (This means genuine inquiries—not belligerent challenges with question marks tacked onto them.) Another very promising sign: expressions of reflection and self-doubt.

• When receptivity is up, question rather than argue any opposing positions. Asking nonthreatening questions leads the listener to question his or her own judgments.

• Don't get upset when a listener suddenly seems to steal your ideas. It's natural for those resisting a point to avoid listening to it consciously. They hear it subconsciously, and often make enough connections during the argument to suddenly comeup with that point as if it were their very own idea. That's exactly what you want so don't spoil it by insisting that this is what you've been saying all along. That will just lead to more resistance and another argument.

Two final time-savers in argument, selling, and persuasion:

• Never argue somebody's "consideration" or "reservation." People need to say their concerns out loud just to get them mentally out of the way. It's part of getting a mental grasp of the total situation. Stating an opposing view isn't arguing for it, it's just a normal housecleaning process required for people to feel they have considered all aspects of the subject being discussed. If you argue a stated consideration or reservation, that just forces the other party to defend it.

• Never assume that the other party is greedy, evil, arbitrary, irresponsible, or crazy—no matter what they say. Maybe they are, but that's the rarest circumstance. Such assumptions lead to emotionally thoughtless actions that slow down the proceedings and interfere with your conscious control over the negotiating sequence.

The Kicker

Kickers are valued as a means of closing negotiations. Here's some potent advice on the subject from a PR consultant:

"After getting the client to want your services, you have to give him a good excuse to act on that desire. No sensible person acts only on his favorable impression and desire. They form the groundwork, but he needs some definite reason to justify his action. This is why good real estate salesmen and lawyers save up a 'kicker' to swing a favorable decision after making their case.

"The kicker can take many forms, but I especially favor two. First is the offer of the no-risk feasibility study; the architect (or engineer) can offer this service 'at cost' and, assuming the project is feasible, this is the surest lead into a job. Second, when a client wants a building but is undecided in his choice of architect, it is almost certain (all other things being equal) that he will select the person who is most emphatic about wanting the job. The client's rationale is that this person will work harder

After getting the client to want your services, you have to give him a good excuse to act on that desire.

for him. This rationale has proven correct in my experience; generally it is the people who work hardest and are most effective in promoting themselves who also work hardest and are most effective in all their professional activities."

Some A/Es are always ready to provoke client action by offering the smallest increments of service as a minikicker just to get some action going on the job. Services comprising a feasibility study are subdivided, for example, into smaller job units requiring less client commitment. Units of service include parking/zoning study, site review, market profile, regional construction cost survey, photo survey and measurement of existing conditions, preliminary programming or checklisting of project requirements. These small introductory tasks get the job moving along while the client makes up his or her mind on larger aspects of a professional relationship. The client gets some low-cost services and the opportunity to observe the A/E's capabilities without risk or further obligation.

How to Negotiate Long-Term Client Contracts

Fred A. Stitt

A business rule of thumb says 80 percent of your work volume will come from 20 percent of your clients. It's a remarkably accurate rule, and it has important implications for the growth of your practice.

One implication is that a large amount of your marketing effort should go toward keeping old clients and to creating long-term relationships with new ones. This is a turnaround from the usual situation; offices commonly take their steady clients for granted. And, when going after new clients, they focus on a specific job instead of focusing on securing a long-term relationship.

The long-term relationship (called an "account relationship" in business language) helps everyone. Profit margins go up on repeat work for a familiar client. For the client, it means consistent and reliable service. Developers and corporate clients say they prefer to stick with one good design firm. But they're rarely approached on that basis. More importantly, A/Es often fail to market ongoing services after a job is completed.

Account relationships have another value—they grow larger. According to IBM, the average business account will grow eight-fold in a six-year period. Well-nurtured small accounts can become impressively large assets for a practice in just a few years.

Profit margins go up on repeat work for a familiar client.

The Account Contract

One way to keep clients is the account contract. This type of contract, very common in the business world, cements a long-term relationship. Most A/Es meet prospects who definitely would like to have design services at some future date. But time passes, and people lose touch. When a job finally comes up, it goes to whatever qualified firm happens to be on the scene at the right time. Such work can be secured ahead of time, in advance of client need, by means of the account contract.

The account contract sets the stage for future transactions. It stipulates a retainer or a fee schedule for interim consultations and a contract duration. During the life of the contract, the A/E will be on call to assist with feasibility studies, site selection, meetings with planning agencies, and other tasks relevant to any future project. Then, as a project shapes up, the A/E has already established the design service relationship and is well positioned as the strongest possible contender for the total package.

Here's how the marketing director for a well-known design firm goes about rounding up new, long-term contracts.

1. He approaches recommended loan officers, contractors, real estate people, accountants, insurance brokers, and other finance executives in his region. They are sources of client contact, but not necessarily client prospects themselves.

2. He explains that his firm is looking for long-term relationships only with the most solid and reputable business people in the area and asks for referrals. This is selective, of course. He's not looking for single-building clients. He's seeking companies likely to do a substantial amount of building over the long haul.

3. When recommendations are given, the marketing director asks if the referral sources will provide an introduction. Often they will. If favorably impressed with the design firm's intentions, the referral sources know they will be doing prospects a favor which will reflect well back on them. Also, if new work grows out of an introduction, they may share in financial benefits related to the transaction.

4. The third-party introduction to prospects, since it's made by people of superior reputation, counts well in the A/E's favor. (Some referral sources, if strongly and favorably impressed, go to bat for the design firm and become continuing sources of new leads and recommendations.)

The key selling point is service, not buildings. The A/E with an account relationship will discourage a client from building if it's not in the client's best interest to build; recommend remodeling an older structure rather than starting from scratch; even recommend purchase of a metal prefab building if such would best meet the client's needs. The promise of this level of client-oriented service is very appealing to prospects.

There are two helpful books on establishing account relationships. These are business books that do not deal directly with A/E marketing, but contain principles and examples readily adaptable by the profession. Ask your book dealer to order *Industrial Marketing: Cases & Concepts*, by E. Raymond Corey (NJ: Prentice-Hall, Inc., 1976, $19.95); and *Sales Program Management: Formulation and Implementation*, by Benson P. Shapiro (NY: McGraw-Hill, 1977, $18.95).

The Long-term Maintenance Contract

When clients turn off to new construction, they're increasingly open to maintenance contracts. Clients need ongoing inspection and consultation services for virtually any recently completed building project.

To initiate this service, the A/E offers monthly, quarterly, or semi-annual inspections. In addition, standby consultation or design services can be provided on an hourly or fixed annual retainer fee basis.

Maintenance inspections are designed to spot unexpected problems and opportunities in building use. A/Es can recommend profitable changes in plan or building utilization to meet postconstruction changes in client circumstances. If the client decides to add equipment, such as air-conditioning units on the roof, the A/E's advice prevents costly errors. A/Es also provide new legally or economically mandated audits of safety, energy use, and handicapped access.

The surest route to future work: sustained relationships with past clients. To ensure sustained relationships, use maintenance agreements along with "living documents." Some clients require more drawing after construction than before. Some buildings are subject to continuous alterations: new office spaces, subdivisions of tenant spaces, changes in laboratory facilities, and related changes in electrical and mechanical systems.

Living documents expedite design and drawing of all the changes that occur in the life of a structure. With overlay drafting and screened shadow prints, it's comparatively easy to separate existing work from new construction and keep an ongoing record of such work in pristine condition for the client. Similarly, by using systems drafting paste-up techniques instead of pencil-drafted drawings, originals can be reprographically exploited for building maintenance manuals, publicity graphics, rental brochures, etc. Updates in graphics to match alterations are easy too. Relatively few design firms currently market these added postconstruction services, although clients prize them highly.

The surest route to future work: sustained relationships with past clients.

Negotiating Tips

O. C. Tirella

Words like "but," "however," and "nevertheless" are erasure words. When a speaker uses an erasure word, the thoughts preceding it should automatically be forgotten by the listener, because the speaker's main point will come after the erasure word.

Erasure words can be effectively used during contract negotiations by both the consultant and client. As the consultant, you can make a negative comment to a client that will be received in a more favorable light. For example, a client indicates during negotiations that a project should be handled in a certain way. The consultant disagrees with the client. If the consultant responds, "That's impossible," it is probable that the client will become angry and negotiations will come to a standstill.

On the other hand, if the consultant responds, "That's a great idea, but did you ever think about the handling the project this way?" the client's reaction is more likely to be positive. Comment before the counteroffer; the client will be more receptive to the consultant's alternatives. By using erasure words during the negotiation process, the consultant is more likely to be successful in persuading the client to see his/her viewpoint.

But a client can also use erasure words during negotiations to throw a consultant off guard. For example, the client states, "Your overhead rate is acceptable and your labor effort is according to our budget, but your total price is too high." If the consultant relaxed upon hearing the "good news" about the overhead rate and labor effort, he/she would be unprepared to respond to the real intent behind the message.

Listen very carefully to every word your client says during negotiations! A conscious effort on your part to recognize erasure words can assist you during the negotiation process. You, as the negotiator, will be better prepared to respond to your client's demands.

Does Your Client Emit NVC?

NVC stands for nonverbal communications, the messages a person transmits without words. Knowing what certain NVC mean can be very beneficial to a consultant during negotiations. By reading the client's body language, a consultant has the extra advantage of determining what the client really has on his/her mind without a word being spoken.

Observing NVC is becoming a common practice during negotiations. As a matter of fact, Japanese negotiating teams even go to the extreme of assigning one team member the task of studying their opponents' NVC.

NVC is done through gestures, postures, facial expressions, sounds, and sometimes silences. Some common attitudes communicated nonverbally are openness, unbuttoned coat; defensiveness, arms crossed on chest; evaluation, stroking chin; suspicion, not looking at you; readiness, sitting on edge of chair; cooperation, tilted head; confidence, steepling (with hands); territorial dominance, feet on desk; self-control, clenched hands; nervousness, clearing throat; frustration, tsk sound; boredom, doodling; acceptance, touching gesture; and expectancy, rubbing palms; unchanging attitudes, legs wrapped around chair.

At your next negotiation meeting, observe your client's body language. Notice the team's expressions. Are their eyes wide open, lips tightly closed, corners of their eyebrows down, and nostrils flared? If so, you are probably dealing with a hostile negotiating team. Watch for simple gestures; sometimes what initially seems to be a nondescript movement could have a major impact on the outcome of your negotiations. For example, you've just made a counteroffer to your client. The client stands up and begins slowly walking back and forth across the room stroking his chin. This simple gesture is an indicator that the client is evaluating your offer. Therefore, the best thing you could do at this time is to keep your mouth shut! The last thing you want to do now is to interrupt his thought process and evaluation.

Being able to read NVC can help break a deadlock. Several years ago, I participated in a negotiation that reached an impasse because both parties would not compromise on a major issue. The issue was belabored for most of the morning and the atmosphere became extremely tense and hostile. I was sitting directly across from the client's chief negotiator, a gentleman who would not budge an inch from his position. I decided to conveniently drop my pen on the floor so I could read his NVC under the table. Sure enough—his feet were locked around the chair legs, indicating to me that his brain was locked in his position. As the impasse continued, I thought about how to break the lock. Luckily there was a blackboard in the room. I got up and wrote my firm's position on the blackboard. In turn, I asked the chief negotiator to do the same. By getting the chief negotiator to physically move, the "lock" was broken. An hour later, our differences were resolved to the satisfaction of both parties.

Erasure words and NVC are only two of the many negotiating techniques and strategies that the consultant needs to be aware of in today's competitive world. As our clients become more sophisticated in negotiating, we consultants need to be aware that negotiating is an art, not a game.

An excellent book on NVC is *How to Read a Person Like a Book*, by Calero Nierenberg, Hawthorne Books, 1971.

Sometimes what initally seems to be a nondescript movement could have a major impact on negotiations.

Accent on Negotiations

Michael R. Hough

Principals in planning and design firms are, as a general rule, very poor negotiators. It must be our professional upbringing that prevents us from standing up for our rights in fee discussion with clients.

Because of this inability to negotiate competently, many firms go into negotiations at under 10 percent profit, leave the bargaining table somewhere less than 8 percent, and finally end up with 4 percent (or less) after the project is completed.

On the other hand, a number of firms consistently end up with at least 15 percent profit on all their projects (both government and private). To illustrate how this is done, let's take the example of Jones Associates.

The basic attitude of Jones Associates is different. Instead of acting surprised and grateful for the chance to do the project, Jones Associates conveys the impression the client is the lucky one because he will gain many tangible and valuable benefits from having selected Jones.

And this is not just public relations hogwash. Jones is outstanding at what he does. For example, the firm can point to an exclusive in-house energy analysis computer program that saved nine clients 13.3 percent on their fuel bills during 1985. Also, there is Jones' strong project management organization and procedures which have in six of the past seven projects resulted in zero time and budget overruns.

Because of this perception of Jones as an invaluable member of the team, the client is much less likely to nickle and dime the firm during the negotiations.

Other Techniques

Other techniques used by Jones to negotiate more effectively include:

1. Never leave the initial client meeting without saying something about the fee. From the beginning, the client knows that Jones is both a business and a professional firm.

2. Always know the scope of the project backward and forward before sitting at the negotiation table.

3. Also know project costs such as labor rates, overhead, and other direct costs but resist showing the client too much detail.

4. Finally, take the project lump sum whenever the scope is well defined enough. And do not let the client decide this.

Naturally, the firm must manage each project well to be sure it makes money at the end, but this is easier if the negotiation process has

A number of firms consistently end up with at least 15 percent profit on all their projects.

gone well.

Is Jones an idealized example? Yes, in many ways. But it is an example that more of us should emulate.

Collecting Fees

5

Creating an Effective Collection System

Telephone contact is your most direct and convenient means of expediting your payments. Someone has to be assigned to routine phone contact. It can be anyone in the firm who enjoys this type of work and has a friendly and professional telephone manner. At least one principal, or the business manager of the firm, has to watch over the general process and be available to handle special cases.

Here are questions and answers on handling telephone contacts.

Question: How do you start contact? Whom do you call?

Answer: On small jobs, it will be the client. Beyond that it may be a secretary/bookkeeper. As client organizations get larger, it becomes less obvious who is really in charge of handling the money. The best time to identify the person in charge is before submitting the first bill. Call to ask who you should talk to about submitting statements. Then ask for and write down the following information:

- Who should you send the statements to?
- Who actually completes the payment process after approval?
- How many copies of the statement should be sent?
- What's the deadline for submittal to get in on any regular payment period? (Many firms pay the bills that are received before a certain date in that month and those that arrive a day later will wait for a month.)
- How much and what kind of documentation is needed?
- If receipts for expenses are required, do they need copies or originals?
- Can a special payment period be established for you, such as mid-month, to allow you both to stagger and spread out the bookkeeping and paperwork?

The point of this initial questioning is to get a verbal tour through the bill processing procedures. Having this data will put your office well ahead of others who are competing for payments. They're the ones who will send statements to the wrong person at the wrong time in the wrong format with the wrong documentation. Sometimes payments get stuck in limbo for sixty days or more while statements are put aside for special action, then sent back to the creditor for clarification, then revised at the creditor's office, rereviewed by the client, and so on. There are times when a client badly needs a valid excuse for delaying a payment. Faulty bills are a godsend on such occasions.

Some business managers will visit a client's office to get together with the person who will handle their bills. They get a firsthand look at the

Fred A. Stitt

As client organizations get larger, it becomes less obvious who is really in charge of handling the money.

There are times when a client badly needs a valid excuse for delaying a payment. Faulty bills are a godsend on such occasions.

steps of processing. Some go out of their way to make friends and find hints of that individual's personal interests. They look for common interests and they pursue some friendly conversation accordingly. That kind of contact helps to set up an atmosphere for future contacts that can remain cordial no matter how difficult the payment situation may become. The point of all this is that there are always times when a client doesn't have the funds to pay all creditors. Some get paid and some don't and the decisions are usually left up to your contact person. If that person likes you and appreciates the way you've dealt with him or her, you'll get the treatment you want.

All the gathered data must be recorded in a consistent format on "tickler" sheets. Later, when accounts have to be discussed, these forms will tell you whom to talk to, when you last spoke with them, what the status of payments is, reasons why payments are late, etc. When calling about an overdue payment, the caller always notes the date or dates of the next step or action, and the tickler card is filed accordingly.

Question: After initial contact isn't it better to call again before an account is overdue?

Answer: Yes. Especially when you're dealing with large sums. It's even better to call just before sending the bill. Say the statement is on its way and you want to be sure it's done according to their requirements. Ask them to please let you know immediately if it's not. If you're dealing directly with the client, chances are he or she will volunteer a commitment on immediate payment or give you warning if there might be a delay for some reason. In lieu of a prebilling call, a friendly call after mailing a statement to ask only if a bill has been received and if it's in order is part of systematic collection management.

Question: What's the most effective thing to say when you call about an overdue account?

Answer: Your call is not to threaten, cajole, or embarrass—its sole purpose is to gather the following information:

• Has the statement of account been received?
• Has the bill been or is it being processed?
• Is there any question or problem about the statement—about its content, format, or its documentation?
• Has payment been authorized and/or sent?
• If not, when may payment be expected?

Normally, you'll get answers to all the questions at once, as soon as you ask if the bill has been received.

More on What to Do or Say
If the bill hasr.'t been received, then say you'll send a duplicate immediately and will call in a couple of days to verify that it is in order.

If the statement is being processed or reviewed, ask for a call if there is any question about it. Then say you'll call on a specified date if you don't hear from them. Then call back as promised to check on it.

If there's a question or problem, of course, deal accordingly.

If payment has been authorized or sent, say thanks and wait for a few days. You can say you'll call back if it doesn't come in for any reason and name a date. Your action depends on whether you perceive the need for more general pressure on the other party.

If there's a "check right on the desk," and the sum is substantial, say thanks, and if practical, send somebody over to pick it up.

If there's some question as to when the payment may be sent, just ask for an approximate guess as to when. Get a date for when to call back if the payment isn't received.

Question: That information all seems one way. Shouldn't you convey some information about your needs too?

Answer: Absolutely. The standard message you may wish to convey is that you have a cash flow problem. You need money to meet your payroll or to pay your consultants. The person or firm that clearly states they need payment, and need it most urgently, normally gets the priority treatment.

Question: What if you have to go after the client, not just a bookkeeper, and the client hides out and won't return your calls?

Answer: Leave explicit messages that you're willing to renegotiate any necessary changes in the account. Calls about accounts are embarrassing, and most clients will prefer to return calls than have others in the office get wind of such problems. And, since you're being nice, the client can't dismiss you to the secretary as someone to put off because you're "harassing" them.

If there's a "check right on the desk," say thanks and send somebody over to pick it up.

Don't Threaten to Sue

Use the trick top sales people have used since 1900: make friends early on with the client's secretary. Establish a first name relationship. Find out about family and hobbies. Invest a few minutes to joke on a friendly basis. Secretaries and receptionists are not commonly treated as human beings, and your attention will be rewarded with genuine help in getting your messages through to the secretary's boss.

When your call is important, and creditor calls always are, ask for that note to be added to the message slip. Calls marked "Important" or "Very Important" almost always get a higher response rate.

Question: When things get bad, can't you shake some money loose by threatening to sue?

Answer: Never bluff with the threat of legal action. It forewarns the real deadbeats to shield assets or lets them know you're just a bluff. It is usually damaging to the relationship and it closes off further action by the sincere client who is truly trying to work out of a bad situation. When you are ready for legal action, go to it directly without emotion and without warning.

Other ways to handle the serious situations (ninety days and more overdue):

Say, with utmost regret, that office policy requires that you notify your attorney. That's not a threat to sue, it's just a notice of a further step.

Use an attorney for collection purposes who is connected with a credit bureau. The statement that you'll have to pass an account on to an

Never bluff with the threat of legal action.

attorney carries much more punch if it also implies a threat to a credit rating.

Preventing Overdue Accounts to Begin with

Some clients are deadbeats. And there are those who are not deliberately out to cheat, but when a project falls through, they keep the A/E's bills for services in the bottom of the drawer.

There are the clients who split up their partnerships, skip town, go bankrupt, or pass away with bills unpaid. All part of the normal risks of professional life. But normal problems are compounded by a tight national money situation.

Risk of client delay or default on payments is rising. Everyone needs more capital—about 15 percent more every year—just to stay on an even keel. Meanwhile, banks trim their loan accounts, especially with developers. Corporations scramble for high-cost money to pay off previous loans. The credit crisis grows within other money markets as stock values fall and investors fail to meet legal margin requirements. Overshadowing it all is the prospect of a major federal deficit that may require 25 percent to 50 percent or more of the new money supply to service government debt.

Some design firms find a hedge in commercial credit insurance. It's a protection most often used by manufacturers and wholesalers, but it's fully adaptable to the special needs of service companies and professionals. The credit insurance company OKs the credit worthiness of a prospective client and insures the account at a cost less than 1 percent of the amount covered. The deductible is also usually less than 1 percent of the sales volume covered by the policy.

A credit insurer can also handle delayed payments. Slow payments are more costly than sometimes realized. Besides the inflation factor, there's the interest paid by the A/E on loans that might otherwise be paid off. There's loss on uncollected fees that might be invested and making a high return. An extended delay in payment may add up to a two-figure percentage loss that wipes out any potential profit on a job.

For further data: Check with your insurance agent, or write for a complete literature packet from Executive Office, American Credit Indemnity Co. of New York, 300 St. Paul Place, Baltimore, MD 21202. (301) 332-3000.

The Credit Card Option

Small A/E firms can have as much trouble collecting a couple of hundred dollars as larger offices have getting large fees. The problem is equally acute and worrisome at either end of the spectrum.

For convenience all the way around, you can let your small job or one-time consultation clients pay their fees with bank credit cards. It's convenient and fully professional. Doctors and hospitals do it. And the American Bar Association has cleared credit card payment for their membership.

You pay 3 percent or so service or "discount" charge. The fee buys quick cash from the charge card company and reduces collection ex-

Risk of client delay or default on payments is rising.

Let your small job or one-time consultation clients pay their fees with bank credit cards.

penses. Chargeable maximums vary from a few hundred dollars to a few thousand, depending on the client's credit situation. For information on how to set up your own charge card system, contact your local bank handling Visa or Master Card. Your banker will advise you on the financial statement you have to submit, and any other application requirements.

There's Always Barter

Tight money means more opportunity for trades with clients. Design firms can propose exchange of services where appropriate, free or discount rental in a new building, part ownership of a new project, or a percentage bonus in return for allowing deferred payment of fee by the client. Agreement on a fee "bonus" is easier to obtain early in negotiation than later, when it takes on the onus of a penalty.

There are hundreds, possibly thousands of "barter clubs" and brokers in communities all over the nation. Barter arrangements have existed for years between A/Es, doctors, dentists, lawyers, landlords, and contractors who bank credits for goods or services provided to one another and collect in like kind.

Of course cash needs come first to pay one's own outstanding bills. But when there's no cash, creditors may be able to settle with you by straight-on trades. Such transactions are supposedly taxable, as cash would be, but most people don't comprehend the logic of a tax on a one-on-one trade of a good or service. Also, if you trade professional services for a down payment on some major investment, such as real estate, you're assuming a nontaxable debt rather than a taxable fee.

Cash shortage or no, trades can be a better long-term deal. A structural engineer in New York, for example, took fees for a minor job in the form of part ownership of an Italian restaurant. Many other A/Es have equity in housing, shopping centers, hotels, and office buildings on the same basis and find that over a period of time such equity is many times more valuable than plain cash payments.

One negotiating stance to press for when trading services for project equity: trade for a solid percentage of ownership, not just for an amount equal to your normal design service fees. There's always a risk element in any investment of either funds or services, and that risk has to be compensated for by the possibility of a considerably larger long-range return than just a normal fee. As long as the prime developer can keep using others' resources to press a project to completion, s/he will consider any equity share request very seriously.

Final caveat: when you go in as part owner, make sure your attorney handles the contract and keeps your risks minimal in case the project fails and the prime developer disappears with lots of unpaid bills for work and supplies. This happened with a large hotel project in a southern city, and the remaining architect partners discovered much of the materials, furnishings, and equipment billed to the project had been diverted in shipment and resold elsewhere. So the partly completed building was not an asset, it was an over-liened hulk of debt. This process of sticking partners with immense debt and virtually no assets to pay them with is standard operating procedure on mobster-linked projects.

Investigating a Client and Getting Credit Ratings

We find that A/Es still rarely use helpful, long-established information services to get credit ratings. Information is valuable in the following kinds of situations: the developer has a promising project, but needs some delays in fee payment to help carry the job; the contractor puts in a low bid and promises much cooperation, but there's a question about experience and reliability; a new job applicant looks like a red-hot prospect for handling a new project, but another applicant has shown up from out of state who looks even better. In all these cases, some extra data is needed to help nail down a choice.

Confidential credit reports provide the missing data links. A report on the developer, for example, might show a spotless record—strong evidence that it would pay to help him through a tight period. The contractor with the low bid might be seriously overextended—sending out low bids in a desperate effort to hold the company together. The out-of-state job applicant may have drinking and domestic problems, be well liked by former employees—but be a risky choice to manage any long-term projects.

Relevant personal and financial data on those you're considering doing business with are available from any part of the country through offices of the Equifax, Inc., or TRW Data Systems. Costs are moderate in terms of avoiding some major headaches. General personnel reports, for example, are available in the $20 to $70 range, and they are often far more revealing than resumes and letters of reference. (They can also be in error, so any major detrimental piece of information should be checked with other sources.) Contact local offices of Equifax or TRW for brochures and price lists, or call national offices for information: Equifax, Atlanta, (404) 325-5500; TRW, Los Angeles, (213) 445-9861.

The best-known source of business credit information, of course, is Dun & Bradstreet, 99 Church St., New York, NY 10007, (212) 285-7000. Call or write for literature and price lists of their data services.

While most A/Es know about the D&B services, not so many are aware of Dun & Bradstreet's Building and Construction Division credit services. It's a means of checking out prospective contractors and subs. Contact the local branch office of D&B or the New York main office cited above.

Other Credit Checks

Besides D&B and similar credit data services and ratings, consider these options:

• Ask the client's banker. It's not commonly known, but banks will give you whatever information they feel you have a right to know about their depositors. They won't give privileged financial information, of course. But if you describe your relationship with the client and indicate your desire to have a broader view before entering a long-term relationship, most bank officers will be glad to cooperate. They'll respond to questions regarding growth of the client's account, length of the client/

One financial consultant suggests that you have clients fill out credit application forms.

bank relationship, any general impressions about the client's financial reliability and acumen, etc.

• Subscribe to a clipping service. If you're dealing with client companies of major substance, keep tabs on their financial status through the business press. Clipping services will scan any journals or newspapers you specify for stories about the companies, their officers, projects, leading competitors, etc. You can locate local clipping services in the yellow pages in any large city. National services are listed in directories such as Bowker's or *Literary Marketplace*, available at virtually any library.

• Ask any major companies the client deals with for a credit recommendation. A couple of calls to materials suppliers for a development company, for example, let one architect know that his prospective client no longer had any credit rating whatsoever.

• The business partner for a medium size A/E firm says he always digs up information about clients that will be of use later if he has to attach bank accounts or go to other extremes to collect fees. He gets the data early on when there are no problems on the horizon. The data includes:

1. The client's bank(s).

2. Home addresses and phone numbers as well as business.

3. The spouse's name and business address and phone. (Spouses are often a source of attachable assets.)

4. Plus the same data regarding the client's business partners, or partners involved to any degree—active or silent—in the project.

• One financial consultant suggests that you have clients fill out credit application forms. That will give you most of the above data, as well as help in establishing credit worthiness. This is a major departure from common A/E practice and we don't yet have a reading on the effectiveness or practicality of the idea.

How to Collect Overdue Fees

Fred A. Stitt

Fees for design services go overdue and unpaid mainly for the following reasons:

1. No principal in the firm is expressly responsible for overseeing methodical and businesslike fee collection.

2. If someone is responsible, s/he treats the task as secondary and tends to put other work ahead of collecting receivables.

3. The person in charge of fee collection does not have a specific structure and system for the process. S/he sends out statements in routine fashion and doesn't worry about collecting until payments are overdue. Overdue in these times often ultimately means never paid.

A few design firms have remarkably good cashflow records because of well thought out and well practiced, step-by-step accounts receivable procedures. Most such systems start with friendly contact with the person in charge of disbursements at clients' offices; stringent adherence to the clients' requirements in submitting statements; and sustained telephone contact regarding details of the account.

Rules of the Game

Put someone in charge of implementing the policies and steps enumerated in this checklist: a bookkeeper, secretary, associate, partner, or even a drafter who's low on work. The person you select must be methodical about paperwork, personable as well as businesslike in manner, and enthusiastic about "scoring" with payments.

A guiding rule from professional collection managers everywhere: always assume the best of motivation and behavior from any overdue client while rigorously planning for the worst. Everyone gets into trouble from time to time—even fully honest, responsible, and profitable companies. The more respect you show, the sooner you'll receive your payments.

Delayed payments are not always due to a shortage of cash. Often they're a signal that the client isn't overjoyed about the services but just isn't saying so out loud. The person in your organization who may know this—the project manager—may be the last one to want you to know about the problem.

Payments are sometimes delayed because someone in the client's organization has reason to think that lateness is OK with you. Case in point: a client's representative apologizes over lunch about a delayed phase payment. The design firm representative, to appear reasonable about it,

Always assume the best of motivation and behavior from any overdue client while rigorously planning for the worst.

says, "Oh, that's no problem, we know you're good for it." That statement gets circulated at the client's office, and your notices henceforth go to the bottom of the monthly pile.

Slow Invoicing Means Slow Payment

Payments are most often late because the statements are late. Slow invoicing is the clearest signal that you aren't too concerned about receiving prompt payments. Or, often enough, the statements are incomplete, or incorrectly done, or directed to the wrong person, etc. When some extra work has to be done with your statement, it will sit until everything else is processed.

Always call when a payment is overdue. Always get a new agreement as to when the next payment will be made. Especially call again and renegotiate a payment date if the first agreement falls through. Call back to say "thanks" when you receive the payment and your bank clears it. This degree of sustained friendly contact puts you well ahead of competing creditors.

When a client is seriously delinquent, the next step is to negotiate a new payment schedule—limited partial payments on specific dates. The A/E must insist on at least some partial payment in return for continued service. This is a preferred option over cutting off work entirely or fruitlessly continuing to work for free. This approach will give the strongest possible clue as to the likely long-term outcome of the situation. Most often the client who can't handle even small partial payments is in such hot water that no one is likely to provide additional needed financing. Perceiving this, other creditors will start pressing legal action. So that's the clue. Failure to agree to make even partial interim payments means real trouble in most cases.

Somewhere along the way the matter may have to be passed on to an office principal. A direct call or personal letter from chief to chief often untangles longstanding problems immediately.

If the client fails to live up to a partial payment promise, it's time for a principal to say you'll have to refer the matter to your attorney. You're not threatening to sue, you're just passing the collection function on to someone else. It pays to make clear that this is the last thing you want to do, that you'll hold off another few days if it will help, but otherwise your attorney, company policy, and/or another partner insist that you must take this step.

Streamlining Fee Collection

Get as much advance payment as possible. Write it in the contract, negotiate for it, give incentives in terms of prioritizing the client's work, perhaps offer a slight discount on the fee—whatever it takes to get up-front money. Ask for 20 percent of the fee and settle for whatever you can get. Ten percent is very desirable. Do not credit the advance payment to an early phase of work; hold it to cover late payments or defaults. With an advance payment, you can continue work during a reasonable period of delayed payment without serious risk.

One device for helping reassure the client about advance payment

Slow invoicing is the clearest signal that you aren't too concerned about receiving prompt payments.

Failure to agree to make even partial interim payments means real trouble in most cases.

is a bond that guarantees a refund of the advance in case the design firm defaults. You'll pay a fee of 1 percent or so for the amount—cheap insurance and less than the interest you'll earn on the retained amount.

Many firms now stipulate an interest penalty on overdue accounts. The only problem is that most clients ignore the penalty when they pay late. Also, contract law usually requires that you offer some reward to balance any penalty provisions. Some firms say they've had better luck offering a 1 percent to 1.5 percent payment reduction for accelerated payment. Some companies go for such discounts as a matter of policy, and many government agencies are required by law to take such options when offered. Clients usually judge a discount offer for accelerated payment and an interest penalty for lateness as a fair combination.

As policy, see to it that all preliminary work in billing is completed as early as possible. Documentation, clarification calls to the client, and miscellaneous paperwork should all be done before, not during, the invoicing process. Many firms don't start the process until mailing time, like habitual latecomers who don't start getting ready until the time they're supposed to leave. They're the ones whose bills arrive a "little late." And a little late often means a month or more delay in payments if current cash runs out.

The Timecard Bottleneck

A longstanding bottleneck in preparing statements promptly is a slow timecard collection system. When timecards are only turned in weekly or bimonthly, staff members and associates sit around making up plausible looking approximations of how they spent their time. Sometimes those who have considerable chargeable time may not be available to turn in cards when they're due. So the data are delayed on one hand and incomplete or inaccurate on the other. It's a serious hindrance to the whole accounting and billing process. Many offices now collect timecards twice daily, rather than daily, weekly, or bimonthly—once at noon, and once at the end of each day. That helps maximize accuracy, since memories are fresh and it's hard to fake distribution of time in such small increments and on such short notice. It helps the bookkeeper maintain all accounts right up to the minute prior to each billing period.

Mail or deliver statements the fastest way possible. As noted above, a single day's delay in invoicing can easily mean a month's delay in payment. And that month may see other bad news. Don't, for example, allow outgoing invoices to sit in an "Out" box all day. Use Express Mail where available, or Federal Express for overnight package delivery nationally. When time is truly of the essence and large sums are involved, it's smart to hand-deliver the statement to the key person involved and to review the statement on the spot for any questions or problems.

Many A/Es pick up their checks in person. Some fly across the state or across the country when necessary, and when large sums are involved. Personal pickup, instead of waiting for the mail, can do wonders for cash flow. (One architect who has done this successfully for years once traveled a thousand miles and returned home with an unsigned check.

A longstanding bottleneck in preparing statements promptly is a slow timecard collection system.

Read the check and make sure signature(s) are complete.)

Never let a payment check sit on the desk. It may be a good check in the morning and a bad one by noon.

Simplify billing. It isn't always necessary to do a complete breakdown of time and costs (unless they're compiled automatically on computer). Specify that you'll just submit a summary statement of a preset monthly rate that will approximate what a monthly itemized statement would be. Then pick up the loose ends by means of an audit at the end of the project.

If the client has to have an audit before OK'ing final payment, you may face a long, money-losing delay. Keep that final payment statement small. Get in the bulk of what's due you at least a month before the final submittal.

A small office architect makes the completion of each phase of a job a cause for a small celebration. He sends a gift, such as a small rendering of the building, a book, or other item that pertains to some personal hobby or interest of the client. The gift along with a personal note accompanies each billing. It's hard for clients not to respond to such touches.

Some firms use the "Mutt and Jeff" approach popular with the police. One partner plays the hard-nosed caller, another acts like an understanding pal. People never enjoy calls from someone who's developed a practiced hard and demanding manner in his calls. They will go to great lengths to avoid them. The "soft" partner exploits this to the hilt by getting promises of payment, saying things like: "I'm relieved. You know how old Sam is," or, "I hope you can give me something I can use to placate old Sam or we're both in for it."

There's no law that says you have to bill monthly. There are advantages to having statements sent at odd times when your bookkeeper, as well as the client's, is less rushed. Also, any payment system that runs faster than a monthly billing is that much easier on the cash flow. Billing periods can be any time you agree on: every three weeks, every two weeks, even weekly.

To measure the success of your fee collection system, divide your average receivables by your average sales. Use that ratio as a baseline for past and future measurements. The lower the number, the better you're doing.

There's no law that says you have to bill monthly.

Getting Government to Pay

Lowell V. Getz

Everyone who has had a government agency for a client knows the frustration of having to wait for bureaucratic procedures to get paid. Following are tips that might help speed your next payment from the government.

1. Modify government purchase orders to include payment terms. The standard purchase order is primarily used to purchase goods rather than services. If it is signed without modification, you may have to wait until completion of the work before any payment is made. Type on the printed form the requirement for advance payments or progress payments (whatever is negotiated) so there is no misunderstanding about the terms.

2. If your standard payment terms with private clients state that you receive half the contract amount in advance, and the other half during the project, make this known to public agencies. In some cases, particularly on smaller contracts of short duration, you might be able to convince a public agency to comply with terms which you use for all other clients, since they must get this treatment from you by law.

3. Believe it or not, certain agencies fund projects with quarterly advance payments. The reasoning is justified because interest expense on short-term bank loans is still a disallowed item in overhead. A carefully worked out budget for the entire project on a monthly basis must be prepared and an estimate of subcontractors' work included so that funds are appropriated to pay them as required.

4. Government letters of credit are not letters of credit in the standard commercial sense, but rather a procedure for getting immediate progress payments. If the agency agrees, it can set up a letter of credit in your name that allows you to draw against it up to the contract limit as the work progresses. Requests for disbursement are sent to your nearest Treasury disbursing office and the money is forwarded directly into your bank account. Your bank then sends you a credit advice when payment is received.

5. If you cannot negotiate any advance payments, at least insist on monthly progress payments as the work progresses. Do not get tied to payments based on stages of completion or approvals of portions of the work which can hurt your cash flow.

6. Discounts for prompt payment are not widely used by design firms because of the thin margins on government work, but if they are offered to private clients, the same terms must be offered to the government as well. Regulations require that a government agency take all

Believe it or not, certain agencies fund projects with quarterly advance payments.

discounts offered. This can be an effective way to speed up collections, since bills with even a .25 percent discount must be paid within the discount period by the agency.

7. Certain public agencies allow an interest clause on late payments to be included in the contract if you ask for it. Often the agency is limited by law as to the maximum rate of interest it can pay on late payments; however, any interest rate is better than nothing and it is a strong inducement for prompt payment.

8. The first and the last invoice are the most difficult to collect because they are exceptions to standard routines. Submit your first invoice quickly. If you begin a government project toward the end of a month and have not accumulated many charges by month end, submit an invoice anyway to get the payment routines started. Special forms, procedures, and supporting details should also be clarified at the time the first invoice is prepared.

9. The accountant in your office should know someone in the government disbursing office in order to follow up on the status of your invoice. It may be necessary to visit the government disbursing office and physically walk through the various approval processes.

10. Negotiate the contract so that all retainages are withheld from the last few payments to you rather than throughout the contract. Also, define clearly when the retainage will be released so that it is not withheld for inordinate delays over which you have no control. For example, if a retainage cannot be released until a final audit on the project is complete, there could be a delay for six months to a year.

Bills with even a one-quarter percent discount must be paid with the discount period by the agency.

Getting Paid

*Professional
Services
Management
Journal*

Clients know that A/E firms are patsies when it comes to being paid and they take advantage of this. Principals use several excuses for not being more aggrressive: "It is unprofessional to dun clients" (it is unprofessional not to manage the firm competently); "we really do not need the money now" (later it may be impossible to collect); "all our clients are government agencies" (don't you think toilet paper suppliers get paid on time?).

Especially today you should be pushing to get paid. Even if you do not need the cash to cover operating expenses, any excess funds from an aggressive collection effort could be earning you 10 percent. Here are some suggestions:

1. Seventy-five percent of all firms we surveyed are charging interest on overdue accounts. Here is what one large architectural firm recently wrote its clients: "Due to unprecedented increases in bank interest rates in recent months, we are obligated to increase interest chargeable on invoices outstanding more than thirty days to 1.5 percent per month. Further, we must insist on collection of these amounts."

2. Consider the possibility of giving a discount (say 2 percent) for payment within ten days. We understand that government clients are obligated to take this discount.

3. Prepare a preprinted and typeset one-page boilerplate attachment to all contracts (even one-page letters) which would include legal-type statements on the following:

- overdue accounts are subject to interest charges;
- work will stop whenever payment is overdue more than forty-five/sixty/seventy-five days (pick one);
- project presentations or plan submissions will not be made unless payment is up-to-date;
- invoices will be submitted in the firm's format.

A successful collection effort is consistent and persistent. Be the squeaky wheel that gets the grease (paid) by following these steps:

1. At fifteen days, have the project manager call his counterpart to see if the invoice was received and if there are any problems (but do not press for payment).

2. At thirty days, send a statement or second notice adding on the interest charge.

3. At forty-five days, stop work on the project (if the contract so

states) and/or have your financial type call the client's financial type.

4. At sixty days, have your lawyer send one of their intimidating letters (this can be stored in the lawyer's word processing equipment).

5. At seventy-five days, take appropriate legal action.

Note that this automatic procedure can be modified for a specific client, but only for a good reason approved by the principal.

By following this squeaky wheel process, you will still have some clients who will not pay anyway—but your average day's receivable will drop substantially. Note that national average for this is about seventy-two days; you should be considerably less than this.

6

Staffing and Good Business Sense

Barry B. LePatner

Among the most significant stories in the business world in recent years has been the impact of the book *In Search of Excellence*, by Thomas J. Peters and Robert H. Waterman, Jr. Their book, subtitled "Lessons from America's Best-Run Companies," has been a bestseller for over a year. Its impact on the way successful businesses can be built and maintained will last much longer.

Though how-to books and books on business management are churned out on a daily basis, Peters and Waterman have struck a deeply responsive chord in the message they communicate as to why some businesses succeed at levels far beyond their competitors. And because the lessons they cite are so basic and applicable to businesses of all sizes, they are worth discussing as signposts for design professionals. For the next decade will undoubtedly test the abilities of design firms to effectively manage their business practices, as well as adapt to changing technologies and the need for creating new markets for their services. Successful architectural and engineering firms will see intensified competition, the onset of universal computerization, greater reliance on other technological advances, the increasing need for specialized areas of expertise, the dissolution or merger of prominent firms with lesser-known but more profitable ones, and more spending to develop and market services.

Peters and Waterman tell of their study of America's excellent companies and the common traits that distinguish them. In essence, they found that such companies were "brilliant on the basics [and] worked hard to keep things simple in a complex world. They persisted. They insisted on top quality. They fawned on their customers. They listened to their employees and treated them like adults."

It is important to recognize the truth in the elements described above. For, if there is one common theme running through the chapters of this book—a theme essential to the effective management of a design firm—it is that successful firms will treat others, clients and employees alike, as they wish others to treat them.

Quality, Reliability, Service

Inner direction and insistence on excellence are, of course, important elements of a successful venture. But too many hard-driven, inner-directed men and women founder on the rocks of their own obsessions. Rather, Peters and Waterman cite the need to add quality, reliability, and service to a firm's sense of dedication. Commitment to a

People in important management positions should be selected for their ability to engender enthusiasm among their associates.

client's goals, in conjunction with quality, almost always ensures profitability.

Take the philosophies of several major companies cited in "Success." In reading them, try to see the application of the basic tenets they convey and their applicability to your design firm.

• Growth is not our principal goal. Our goal is to be a quality organization and do a quality job, which means that we will be proud of our work and our products for years to come. As we achieve quality, growth comes as a result. *Digital Corporation*

• If you don't shoot for 100 percent, you are tolerating mistakes. You'll get what you ask for. *American Express*

• The organization should have objectives and leadership which generate enthusiasm at all levels. People in important management positions should not only be enthusiastic themselves, they should be selected for their ability to engender enthusiasm among their associates. *Hewlett Packard*

In seeking a philosophy, each firm should search its roster of talents and strengths to decide what the firm stands for as a whole. Professional pride is a tremendous motivator. It can be used in numerous ways to achieve common goals for a design firm and its clientele.

A Loyal Staff Is Integral to Building Quality

Yet, all too often, the most disregarded asset of an architectural, engineering, or interior design firm is the talent itself. Consider this: the loss of a single trained professional employee with the concomitant need to replace him or her can, for a time, cost almost twice the salary of the lost employee—even if the new employee earns the same.

Those who study their successful competitors will observe that the better managed firms do not have a high turnover. Each year we read of widespread layoffs by design firms at year's end followed by new hirings in the following months on an as-needed basis. There is a terrible cost— both emotional and financial—that a firm must pay for such cavalier treatment. For one, how much loyalty and extra effort can a promising designer give to a firm with such a policy? Employees who are led to see themselves as "throw-away" talent can hardly be expected to do their best.

Also, any management that cannot accurately assess its manpower needs is not doing all it can to ensure the protection of the quality people who undoubtedly will be thrown out with the dirty bath water. Time after time, I have been told by the principals of a newly formed firm of their sincere intention not to allow such employee uncertainty to permeate their business operations. It is this type of empathy which will do much to foster a greater sense of commitment and loyalty in design firms in the years ahead.

Employee Recognition

The principals of every firm would do well to encourage and reward the next generation of talent in their firms. Such approbation is needed by each of us as a means of recognizing our efforts to do a good

Those who study their successful competitors will observe that the better managed firms do not have a high turnover.

job. In many ways, those who lead, lead best by example. They are the father figures by whose actions we judge ourselves and measure our growth in the pursuit of our careers. The universality of this human sentiment, applicable to both principals and staff alike, was best expressed some years ago by essayist and critic John Leonard when, referring to the need for that pat on the back, he wrote: "You can't get too much approval. The secret we keep from our children until it's too late is that we seek their approval as much as they seek ours. We will say that they are brilliant if they will admit we are grand."

Leadership is another important element that every successful firm will require. Each of the successful businesses pointed out by Peters and Waterman had a strong figure at the helm. "Associated with almost every company was a strong leader who seemed to have had a lot to do with making the company excellent in the first place." But leadership is more than that. Good leaders nurture and develop talent. They promote those who best exemplify the traits which strengthen the philosophy of the firm. Well-run firms foster winners; and winners who are rewarded in a firm encourage others to emulate their success.

The principals of every firm would do well to encourage and reward the next generation of talent in their firms.

Design professionals who read *In Search of Excellence* will be impressed by the emphasis the authors place on rewarding those who are innovative within a firm, who know how both to identify a problem and to resolve it on a cost-effective basis. Such individuals look at problems as a challenge and do not pass them on to others or shrug them off as impossible to solve. Recognizing and rewarding such individuals will assure the sound management of a design firm five years from now.

But between reading an excellent book on successful management and achieving one's own success lies commitment as well as steadfast discipline. Most design firms will never achieve the level of prominence cited in any book on management. But most design firms can achieve some degree of success toward improving their business basics. In order to do that, it will be necessary to build on the talents that exist in your firm so that financial stability can allow those talents to flourish.

The source of strength for your firm's future lies with the people who produce the work.

Basic Steps Will Set You on the Right Path

• Remember, first and always, you are in a service business that rewards dedication to your client's needs.

• The source of strength for your firm's future lies with the people who produce the work. They must always be treated as valuable resources.

• Innovation and creativity, at every level, should be encouraged, not stifled.

• Stick to the basics of what you are good at—entering fields with which you are unfamiliar will cause problems.

• Keep the format for managing your firm as simple as possible.

The most successfully managed (and financially secure) design professionals that my firm represents carry out defined programs which incorporate most, if not all, of these goals. And size is not an issue in discussing quality of management. Many small- and medium-size firms can easily establish definable plans to improve service to clients, encourage employee participation, and create a warm, working environment that entices talented people to develop to their fullest capabilities.

There will be no easy road to developing a sound financial future in combination with a reputation for design excellence. For some, marginal profitability will not only be possible, but in some cases, acceptable. The clarion call is to those who seek a better way. But, if recent history is any example of this new trend in design firm management, more and more firms will be devoting themselves to their own search for excellence.

Keeping Key People

Nora Lea Reefe

An interesting phenomenon is accompanying the resurgence of business in professional design firms. Many firms are losing key long-term employees with ten to fifteen years' (or more) experience. One explanation for the increased turnover is, of course, that firms are actively recruiting experienced people to produce the jobs which marketing departments are adding to backlogs. However, what is motivating people to leave firms where they have invested most of their professional life?

Perhaps the most common explanation for making such a job change is increased compensation. However, compensation complaints often occur only when there are other unsatisfactory aspects of a job. Interviews with numerous architects and engineers reveal that they really leave jobs because:

1. They feel unappreciated by the firm.
2. They don't believe they are growing or developing technically or professionally.
3. They want more responsibility or participation in decision-making.
4. They don't know where they stand in the organization.
5. They cannot see where they are going in the firm.
6. They have personal conflicts with other people in the firm.
7. They lack the authority to carry out assigned responsibilities.
8. The firm places demands on them which are unsuitable for their personalities or which interfere with nonwork-related goals or priorities.

If, in fact, these are the real causes of increased turnover, they are also clues to more effective management of people in design firms. They indicate the kinds of things which A/E firms need to do to attract, retain, and motivate people who will be productive team players. They indicate that effective human resource managment depends upon:

• frequent and regular expressions of appreciation for efforts expended as well as results;

• a performance appraisal and interview process which focuses on strengths, provides feedback on job performance and position within the firm, includes appropriate measurement criteria and adequate training for interviewers and appraisers, and is conducted in a timely and consistent manner throughout the firm;

• a professional development program which is tied to an observable career path and an appropriate salary administration plan, includes the

Proper people management produces not only a stable work force, but also a more productive one.

provision of appropriate rewards for individual achievements, is related to long-term goals for the firm as well as for individuals, and includes appropriate funding for continuing education and involvement in professional societies;

• active involvement of people in major decisions affecting their career development or their work life;

• job assignments which are compatible with personalities, behavior styles, and personal goals;

• constant communication about activities going on in the firm and the marketplace;

• adequate communication on office policies and procedures which are consistently applied to all employees.

Proper people management produces not only a stable work force, but also a more productive one that is willing to make sacrifices of personal time when the work load is heavy. With the increased pressure of new business which the current and future economies promise, design firms need to adopt more appropriate human resource management practices. They need to consider investing in a professionally trained human resources director who can help them develop and implement responsive programs designed to attract and retain competent, productive people. It is, after all, the collective skills of a group of people that leads clients to hire an A/E firm. Only through proper management of those people can their skills be used to manage projects in such a way as to satisfy client needs and produce profits for the firm.

Many of the popular management books today focus on the changing needs and desires of people in the workplace. *In Search of Excellence* by Peters and Waterman is a prime example of a book whose major focus is on responding to and taking care of people. A/E firms which have recognized the value of responsive human resources management are more successful in keeping key employees. These firms manage people instead of projects. They pay more than lip service to the idea that people are in fact the real asset of any design firm, and they do this by making real commitments of time and money to human resources management. They place a real value on "people skills" and assist managers to acquire them. They incorporate effective people management into the goals set for project managers, and they ensure that all employees receive regular performance feedback and career path assistance.

To meet the challenges created by a more competitive market for experienced personnel, A/E firms should evaluate current management practices in light of the reasons why key people change jobs after a number of years with one firm. If your evaluation reveals shortcomings in any area, turnover among key people may occur during the coming months. Keeping good, experienced people in whom a firm has invested much time and money is one of the most significant challenges facing firms for the remainder of this decade.

Successful firms manage people instead of projects.

Human Resource Function

Paul G. Dombroski

You are the president of a well-established, growing professional services firm. The firm has grown approximately 15 percent a year for the past five years and you have just passed the 100-employee landmark. You find that your time as well as that of other key managers has been redirected from projects and clients to internal problems. You are having problems recruiting qualified people. Some of the employees feel alienated because "we're getting too big." One of your best project designers is upset because the last hired person is making more money. Your engineers are starting to complain about the lack of a profit sharing or pension program, and you've received a call from the Equal Employment Opportunity Commission with a complaint filed against one of your managers for not hiring a minority applicant.

The example might seem exaggerated but it makes a basic point: your firm is experiencing growing pains which, when unchecked, have a tendency to decrease the managerial efficiency of a firm. The dollar impact on the bottom line caused by these problems is staggering, especially in the area of employee turnover costs.

Turnover Costs

Let's examine one case: a growing design firm lost one of its better engineers to a competitor. The employee told management that he would be receiving more money at the new firm. In addition, the employee felt that his current boss was insensitive to his problems and gave very little help in developing his talents. What did it cost the firm?

Productivity loss. The position went unfilled for two months. The firm lost the employee's profit contribution.

Overtime costs. It forced management to work others in the department overtime in order to meet client schedules. Some employees were not happy working extensive overtime, thus lowering morale.

Replacement cost. The firm spent $2,000 running ads in newspapers and trade journals with little response. Finally, it was forced to use a search firm and had to pay a fee of $10,500 (30 percent of the first year's salary).

Additional training cost. Supervisory time used in orienting the new employee to the firm, its projects, and its clients was substantial.

Relocation expenses. The employee was from out of the area and studies show that the average cost per relocation in 1979 was $16,000. A

> The dollar impact on the bottom line caused by these problems is staggering.

number of firms have had to pay mortgage interest rate differentials which can drive the cost up to $20,000 or more. In this case, it cost the firm somewhere between $30,000 and $35,000 to replace one engineer.

That's money right off the bottom line. If you multiply that figure by the number of professional people your firm loses each year, the financial impact is huge.

If we go back to the original reason the engineer left the firm, we find several key factors that could have been resolved by asking a few questions about the firm's policies and programs:

1. Better money. Is your compensation program competitive?

2. Better benefits. Again, are you competitive?

3. Poor relationship with supervisor. Do your managers need training in interpersonal relations skills?

4. Talents not being developed. Do you have a career path planning program?

Affirmative Action

Another key area that deserves mention is government compliance. How many firms that solicit government work have a formal affirmative action program? What positive steps is the firm undertaking to recruit minority applicants? If you are going after governmental work, you should be prepared to answer those and other questions. The items mentioned are just a part of the total spectrum of areas that need to be examined.

It is no longer a question of whether the human resources function is necessary but how it is managed. Should every firm establish a human resources function? Yes. And if a firm is experiencing any of the problems touched on here and is large enough (say one hundred employees or more), it should consider acquiring in-house capability. Smaller firms could perhaps better utilize the services of a consultant in handling these problems.

If your firm's policies and procedures are up-to-date and competitive within the industry and your managerial people properly trained to handle those under them, any problems you are encountering in this area will diminish and overall profitability increase.

It is no longer a question of whether the human resources function is necessary but how it is managed.

Personnel Manager

*Professional
Services
Management
Journal*

Accoording to personnel consultant Jill Henderson of Boston, there are nine functions for the personnel manager in a design firm today. Many large firms have hired personnel directors to perform all duties necessary within the personnel function; however, smaller firms continue to divide the activities among a variety of professionals. Is each of these nine tasks being performed in your firm?

1. Staff forecasting/planning. Manpower planning, attrition rate, and employee turnover are functions which must be measured by someone in the firm.

2. The recruitment, selection, and placement process. Someone in the firm must maintain legal applications, employment contracts, interview records, and personnel policies so that new and existing employees are managed effectively. Additionally, someone must become aware of the legal impact of discrimination and know how to deal with it.

3. Performance appraisal. The process of performance appraisal must be managed in today's design firm so that everyone receives an appraisal and records are adequately retained.

4. Professional development. Because training can become an issue in a discrimination suit today, it is imperative that a firm maintain a professional development program which trains employees at every level in the firm.

5. Labor relations. Although most design firms do not have labor unions, the issues which create labor unions in the first place must still be managed in today's large- and medium-size firms.

6. Compensation. There is an important function in every firm for maintaining job descriptions and a salary administration system which is fair and compensates all personnel according to industry standards and corporate goals.

7. Incentive programs. Someone must manage bonuses, profit sharing, ownership, and other aspects of a firm's incentive programs.

8. Benefits. Are your benefits up-to-date? Could you lose employees because someone is simply not keeping track of how your benefits compare in the industry and in the marketplace?

9. Personnel policies. Don't reinvent the wheel. Write them down. There should be policies on snow storms, pets at work, lunch hours, smoking/nonsmoking, and a raft of other personnel issues that never seem to be clear enough.

PSMJ observes that more firms are now hiring human resources or

Someone must become aware of the legal impact of discrimination and know how to deal with it

personnel directors to fill all of the above functions. This position is generally created when a firm reaches about seventy-five people.

Salary Administration

J. Douglas Dietrich

A firm's ability to make meaningful external comparisons with the market to ensure proper competitiveness is a major financial management responsibility. A key step is to apply meaningful, comparable, and current external salary survey data to various benchmark positions relative to the firm's comparable positions.

Once survey data is selected, you can relate each position in your firm to what you are paying as compared with what the marketplace is paying people in comparable positions. It is from this comparison that you are able to knowledgeably assess your pay practice position and establish your own pay policy and structure.

Basic Pay Policies

The three basic pay policies to consider place the firm as a follower, a middle-of-the-roader, or a leader in compensation; and management must establish a philosophy as to where they want their pay practice to be in order to achieve the best results for the firm. Too often companies have established their pay policies by a telephone call to a friendly competitor asking him what he is paying; by what the newspaper ads are saying; or by what applicants coming for jobs are asking.

Since people are the major capital investment of a professional service firm, establishing an intelligent pay policy is one of the most important tools management has to control the dollars within the firm. Once the company's pay policy has been established from an objective comparison of meaningful information, you can then proceed toward establishing your own salary ranges with a degree of confidence that these ranges will properly aid you in distributing your salary dollars wisely and competitively.

One of the most misunderstood and misconstrued parts of any salary program is the salary range. It simply has a bad image as the little black box that confines an individual's opportunity to grow. (We can't pay you this because it's above the range.) I have rarely found a properly derived salary range to inhibit an individual's growth; if anything, it is a means of applying pressure on management to find ways to more fully utilize his capabilities.

Salary ranges should be reviewed regularly for upgrading (or downgrading) based on the marketplace. The proper use of this tool is the cornerstone of every sound salary administration plan.

One of the most misunderstood and misconstrued parts of any salary program is the salary range.

Pay for Performance

Since I advocate the concept of pay for performance in rewarding employees, the salary range should have a minimum and a maximum within which varying levels of performance can be rewarded. If an individual is a high performer, management should be willing to pay him a top salary for that level of performance. If an individual is a subaverage performer, he should not be getting the level of income for top performance. A salary range guides management in equitably distributing its dollars across these various performance levels.

I personally do not advocate a separate cost-of-living adjustment, since this can very easily be worked into the salary increase guideline used for adjusting compensation. I would much rather see a firm give its salary increase dollars in the form of performance recognition rather than "giving it away" through a cost-of-living adjustment where no recognition is accorded the company for having given this money.

Performance Evaluation

The last but not least element of every sound salary program is an effective performance appraisal system. It is due to the poor job done in performance appraisal that many programs break down. Performance evaluation is one of the most difficult management functions. Whatever format you might decide upon for performance evaluation, be careful that it measures concrete job achievements on a rational and objective basis.

More important than the actual format is the method management uses to communicate this performance evaluation to its employees. In all cases an evaluation interview should occur at least annually where the employee and his supervisor discuss the results of the performance evaluation. Too many employees are left in the dark about their own performance achievement level, unless they make some critical error, and then they never stop hearing about it.

The performance evaluation interview is a vital management tool in effectively communicating to employees their level of performance as assessed by their managers. This interview should consist of a review by the manager of the level of achievement of the employee in fulfilling his responsibilities and, just as important, suggestions by his manager on ways to improve his specific performance level and professional growth.

Loaded Questions Help to Hire the Right People

Thomas M. Rohan

"**I**f we were to call your immediate past employer or your immediate past supervisor, what would he tell us about you?"

That question from the employment interviewer is designed to create shock waves and elicit revealing responses from a job candidate.

"Do you think you should be able to criticize management?" is another loaded question.

"How do you react to rumors on the job?" also poses a tricky test for the prospective employee.

By using a series of such carefully phrased questions, a company can improve its chances of selecting the best candidate for a job, managerial or otherwise. With many companies now in a hiring mood, the methodology is particularly significant.

Interview Technique

The questions and approach have been developed by an unusual Philadelphia legal firm specializing in labor law and industrial relations. Pechner, Dorfman, Wolffe, Rounick & Cabot has spent more than ten years in refining its system, whose users include about fifteen of America's one hundred largest corporations.

"Management today looks almost solely at a person's skills, not his attitude or value system. And, in interviewing, there is an awful lot of rambling and shooting from the hip," says partner Stephen J. Cabot. "Obviously the candidate must have the skills, but his attitude is virtually just as important. These tailored questions used in carefully structured interviews are intended to be a tie breaker where skills are about equal."

There's no quick, all-purpose list of questions. The questions are developed by the law firm for each company, depending upon the top executives' views on the type of employee desired. The answers are then scored by the number of "desirable" and "undesirable" character or attitude traits noted by the interviewer; these depend upon the particular job, company culture, and other factors.

The questions and interpretations are developed by industrial relations specialists within Pechner, Dorfman who have advanced degrees in psychology and extensive organizational development experience.

The more commonly sought positive traits include a sense of achievement, a desire for success and recognition, goal and teamwork orientation, and pride in one's work.

The candidate must have the skills, but his attitude is just as important.

Among the characteristics typically considered undesirable are a rigid mental approach and a know-it-all attitude. Companies also wish to weed out chronic complainers, people who will do only one job at a time, nonteam workers, those who don't believe in management authority, and those who don't believe in a day's work for a day's pay.

"Pregnant Pause."

The questions don't address these subjects directly. Rather, they subtly prompt replies or such indications as abnormal nervousness and rebelliousness on the negative side, or creativity and independence on the positive side.

Now, a closer look at some of those tricky questions:

About the question as to what a past employer would say of the job candidate, Mr. Cabot observes: "The applicant doesn't know if we'll make the call or not. There is usually what I call a pregnant pause. Usually the 'rotten-apple' type applicant will pause a long time and not know what to way—which can be very indicative.

"A common response is, 'Well, I suppose that he may tell you that I was a reasonably good employee. But I must caution you that that person and I had a personality conflict.'

"That response with the pregnant pause and the cautionary words and hedging are a far more accurate [indicator] than any job check. I'm not suggesting that companies ought not to check references. But they are not a panacea."

The reason for asking how one would react to rumors on the job is to find out whether the employee would be willing to listen to communications from management and be compatible with management's wishes.

Half of the people interviewed—based on a ten-year data bank of responses kept by Pechner, Dorfman—say they don't pay any attention to rumors. This indicates a general negativism, an unwillingness to be candid or honest, and a lack of sufficient interest.

The ideal answer, Mr. Cabot says, is along this line: "Generally, I don't pay attention to rumors on the job. However, if I hear something that concerns me, I want to check it out with my boss."

Confidence?

In asking whether an employee should be able to criticize management, the intent is to determine whether the prospect has respect for authority and whether he or she has enough self-confidence to criticize or question management.

About 65 percent of those queried will answer "no," but the ideal response is something like: "I don't expect to criticize management on everything it does, but there are times when management is in error and there are certain procedures that ought to be followed to let management know what went wrong."

In one case, Mr. Cabot's firm was asked to interview final candidates for the job of financial vice president of a major corporation. When the question about criticizing management was put to the leading candi-

Determine whether he or she has enough self-confidence to criticize or question management.

date, he replied that he envisioned the job as simply handling finances—and that he had no intention of going to the chief executive officer and informing him where he erred.

When the CEO heard this, he decided to hire another candidate.

Another stratagem used by the Cabot group is to develop an idealistic, four-paragraph employee-policy statement for the hiring company and hand it to applicants. The interviewer then observes, or asks for, their reaction to the statement, which stresses that there is a need for mutual trust between company and employee, that pay and benefits are competitive, and that both employee and the company can grow together.

About 10 percent to 15 percent of the applicants will simply take the statement and lay it down without reading it or asking about it, indicating apathy and indifference, Mr. Cabot explains. Around 20 percent to 25 percent will read it, chuckle, and hand it back; this also is considered negative because it illustrates an inability to express their real feelings.

Another 20 percent will read it and—after a long pregnant pause—will overreact, saying something like: "This is the greatest company in the world. I've dreamed of working for a company like this. You've got to hire me." This person definitely should not be hired, Mr. Cabot says, since the response shows he's simply not being candid and cannot be trusted on other questions, either.

Another 20 percent will read it and respond more honestly—for example: "I don't have any trouble with that; it sounds good." This is considered a positive answer.

Same Questions

This technique is obviously not an exact science, but Mr. Cabot believes that most of the subjectivity is removed by having all interviewers ask the same questions concerning a specific job. They're basically the same for management, production, and clerical employees and for both men and women.

Thirty days after hiring a candidate, a carefully structured attitude survey is taken. This measures job satisfaction. Should major differences show (from what was expected from the interview), the questions are modified and the system fine-tuned.

Although this whole screening approach is basically designed to find more productive, cooperative employees, the results also can be interpreted to classify prospective employees into those prone, and those not prone, to unionize.

At one new plant where management wanted to avoid unions, Mr. Cabot's firm was called in to help with the hiring interviews. Based on productivity levels at its existing unionized plant, the parent company had estimated that more than two hundred workers would be required.

But the new plant, says Mr. Cabot, met its output goals with just one hundred workers, selected on the basis of these special questions. The effectiveness of the interview system is credited with a major assist in avoiding work rules and job classifications, and the poor labor practices that develop in older plants.

"I've dreamed of working for a company like this. You've got to hire me." This person definitely should not be hired.

The Ideal Employee

Here is a range of typical characteristics from which a profile of wanted and unwanted employee candidates is developed by Pechner, Dorfman in consultation with the hiring company. Depending upon the job, the company culture, and other factors, some traits can be desirable or not.

The personnel interviewer asks job candidates ten or fifteen carefully structured questions and marks the traits indicated by their replies. From this a score for desirable and undesirable traits is developed to help judge candidates against the ideal profile. (The most commonly desired traits are italicized.)

Desirable—*Achievement-oriented, success-oriented, recognition-oriented, goal-oriented, teamwork-oriented, pride,* accomplishment-oriented, willing to compromise, less critical/vindictive, less need for sympathy, fewer emotional needs, requires less attention, less restless, perseverance, resolute, creative, independent, religious background, flexible, involved, obliging, accommodating, open-minded, empathetic, good family background, strong work ethic, a leader.

Undesirable—Desire to be led, aggressive, critical, vindictive, restless, uncertain, uninterested, low productivity, happy-go-lucky, rebellious, antiestablishment, injury-prone, cause-oriented, poor work history, under eighteen without work history, bull-headed, needs emotional support, no tenacity, poor family background, poor community environment, single, single parents, financial problems, vocal, divorced, staunch, stubborn, hardheaded.

Reprinted with permission from *Industry Week*, January 21, 1985.

Cost-Effective Hiring

Charles M. McReynolds

Hiring a clerical or lower level professional staff member can be an expensive process, but it doesn't have to be. The major expenses are the cost of an employment agency and the time required to interview those who apply for the position. Many firms don't use employment agencies at all and have found ways to speed up the interviewing process. Here's how:

An employment agency will charge between 50 and 100 percent of the first month's salary of the person selected. Based upon the salary of the person you wish to hire, calculate how much your fee to the agency will be. This amount becomes the kitty you have through doing it yourself. Use a small part of the kitty to place an ad in the local paper. Describe the position you are trying to fill, and note the qualifications that are required. Give a name and a telephone number for interested persons to call on Monday for an interview (ads are usually placed in the Sunday classified section).

The person whose name appears in the ad must personally answer all of the calls that come in on Monday. On the telephone, it will become the task of that person to determine whether the person calling has the skills, the personality, and the other important aspects which warrant granting an interview. No more than four interviews should be granted. That means you have to make notes concerning all of the people who call in, and then invite in for an interview those four who sound best suited.

Preliminary Screening

Questions that are usually asked over the telephone which help establish the caller's qualifications include:

1. Have you ever held a position like this one before? If so, where? When? Why did you leave?
2. What other jobs have you had?
3. What are your salary requirements? How much did you make on your last job? What do you expect to make within a year?
4. I need a person who is at work, on time, every day. Are you dependable? How much time did you miss on your last job?
5. Do you have your own transportation? How will your get here?

By preparing a list of these questions beforehand, and making fifteen or twenty copies of them, you are ready for the phone calls. Don't bother writing down what the answer to each question was, just write down *yes* or *no* if the answer is acceptable or not. What you are trying to do

An employment agency will charge between 50 and 100 percent of the first month's salary.

is eliminate, over the telephone, those candidates who are not acceptable, and boil all the callers down to a group of four.

After answering all of these questions, the callers will properly feel entitled to some kind of response. There are three possible responses:

1. To the person who for any reason is not to be interviewed. "I'm sorry, but your experience (or salary requirements or lack of transportation or whatever the reason) doesn't seem to fit as well as that of some others I've talked to. However, if you'll give me your name and telephone number, if I'm not able to make my selection from among those others, I may call you to talk some more."

2. To the person who sounds acceptable. "You sound exactly like the kind of person I'm looking for. However, I've already scheduled interviews for all day tomorrow. If you'll give me your name and telephone number, if I'm not able to select a person tomorrow, I'll call you and invite you for an interview on Wednesday."

3. To the person who sounds perfect. "You sound perfect. What's your name and telephone number? Can you be here for an interview at 8:00 a.m. Wednesday?"

Write down the name and telephone number of each person who calls on a separate copy of the questionnaire pages you prepared. You are fortunate if you are able to select four perfects. Chances are there will be some acceptables among your group of four finalists. Postponing the interviews until Wednesday allows you time to talk to everybody who is going to respond to the ad, and to rank the acceptables. Invite those for interviews who seem to most closely match your requirements.

Try to take no longer than ten minutes per phone call. Avoid talking about your company or the job. If a perfect needs to be sold, then do whatever it takes to be sure he or she comes in for the interview. Be polite but firm with the others, saying, "We'll talk about the job and the company when we meet; I'm sorry I don't have time to do it now."

Schedule the four best candidates for 8:00, 9:00, 10:00, and 11:00 a.m. on Wednesday. Make up your mind Wednesday at lunch which one was best. Call that person that afternoon and have him or her return for a second interview on Thursday. Following the second interview, if the applicant still seems to be a good candidate, check references, and if they are acceptable call the prospect Thursday evening and offer the job to start Monday morning.

The advantages to this process are the following:

• You have saved the expense of the agency (although you have incurred a lesser expense for an ad).

• By using the telephone effectively, you avoided inviting unacceptable people in for a time-consuming interview and granted interviews only to those you knew to be acceptable.

• By scheduling the interviews all to take place in one morning you controlled the interview process, and the decision you made concerning whom to offer the job to was an easier decision to make than if the interviews had been spread out over a period of time.

By using the telephone effectively, you avoided inviting unacceptable people in for a time-consuming interview.

Hiring and Firing

Fred A. Stitt

In the hunt for talent, some offices score and some don't. Our ongoing review of quality offices reveals unusual, almost fanatical selectivity in hiring employees. Their attitudes and methods work well for them and may provide tips for others who want to upgrade hiring practices and office quality.

Some employers say they have the answer. They suggest that efficient management and improved production systems mean little if employee quality is not tops. If employees are the best, jobs seem to run themselves and come out fine, no matter what methods are used. They say it costs less to find people who are twice as good than to invest in new methods to double the production of mediocre employees. (There's another side to this: top employees are often systems conscious and active in implementing reforms and improvements in equipment and techniques.)

Superior employees bring extra benefits to the office. The most capable turn out several times the work of other equally experienced staff. Their faster pace is contagious. Supervisors and other employees are prodded to more intense effort to equalize work flow. Secondary benefits include reductions in staff, overhead, office confusion, and downtime. Another point repeatedly emphasized: high-quality employees upgrade the office in good times and often mean the difference in survival during problem times.

In seeking quality, hiring procedures differ. Most bosses say they're limited in choice by circumstances; they can't afford to interview until they're ready to hire. Applicants are rarely the best. Time pressures prevent careful screening.

Quality offices never stop looking. An open house policy is common: visitors and job applicants are always welcome whether the office is hiring or not. A file is maintained on the best prospects. When the time to hire approaches, the prospects are called. Some are ready to come to work even if currently employed elsewhere. The hottest prospects are sometimes secured months in advance of actual hiring by the promise of work on particularly interesting projects.

Evaluating Job Applicants

Who's really the best? The question bothers many as sharp-appearing applicants turn out to be office drones. Screening is rarely

If employees are the best, jobs seem to run themselves and come out fine.

thorough. Quality offices show they've learned from the techniques of professional personnel managers. Here's how they handle it:

• First, and considered most important: careful review of former employers' recommendations. This requires persevering phone calls. Ex-employers tend to be generous and hesitate to hurt the applicant's chances of getting a new job. Honest evaluations can be drawn out with specific questions about the applicant's previous duties, quality, speed, self-sufficiency, reliability, rate of advancement, and evidence of personality problems. Questions on the applicant's greatest strengths followed with an invitation for an opinion on weaknesses often allows the ex-employer to open up and give a complete picture.

• College transcripts offer vital data on younger applicants. These are seldom requested by architects, but they provide one of the best available measures of office potential. Transcripts are easy to forge, so they should be obtained directly from the school's records offices.

• Testing is increasingly used to rate technical employees. Good-looking work samples often fail to reveal the applicant's actual construction knowledge and may lead to overrating capacities for self-directed drafting. Some offices use short technical tests based on specific office needs; some test informally by inviting comments on elements of a set of the office's working drawings. Generally, those well grounded in construction stand out markedly from applicants with limited knowledge. But questions have to be asked.

• Credit checks are considered a sound practice, particularly when filling a high-level job slot. Strength in personal financial management is so often reflected in good job behavior that some personnel managers give it nearly top priority in ranking job applicants.

Relevant personal and financial data are available from any part of the country through offices of the Retail Credit Co. or TRW Data Systems. Costs are not low, but can be considered moderate in terms of avoiding some major headaches. General personnel reports, for example, are available in the $20 to $50 range from Retail Credit. Contact the local offices for brochures and latest price lists.

Numerical Evaluation

Guesswork in evaluating job applicants is reduced somewhat further by use of a numerical evaluation system. A numerical system means the office has set standards for what is wanted in an employee and has given relative numerical weight to these standards. It's especially handy for making final tie-breaking choices among competing job candidates.

The process is clarified by breaking it down into three prime areas of evaluation: (1) the applicant's handling of the application and interview process, (2) job qualifications, (3) evidence of personal responsibility and reliability.

The applicant's conduct during the interview furnishes the basis for preliminary screening. Extremely poor performance means other factors won't be considered. The application may be discarded on the basis of unannounced no-show for the appointment or extreme lateness. Inade-

Guesswork is reduced by use of a numerical evaluation system.

quate or no portfolio, lack of references, lack of documentation in the resume, hedging on questions—any of these are grounds for crossing the name off the list of candidates. If the applicant passes the preliminary screening, the simplest rating scale of performance is: 1 for fair or average, 2 for good, 3 for very good, 4 for excellent.

Rating of work samples and experience is equally simple but generally divided into two parts. The parts are: job qualifications and references. Your overall impression of the work samples is recorded in the 1, 2, 3, 4 fashion described above. Quality and authenticity of recommendations by previous employer(s) or school are also number rated. A negative rating of unacceptable or very poor for either part disqualifies the candidate. Below average is rated as -1 or -2. Good work with poor recommendations, or good recommendations with poor work are contradictory and indicate possible fraud.

Judgment of personal responsibility and reliability is the final step in screening. As one guide, here's a list of subfactors and numerical values, based on those used by lending agencies in judging loan applicants: 1 point if married, 1 point for one to three children, 1 point for car ownership, 1 point for two years' or more tenancy at the same address, 2 points for home ownership, 1 point for over two years' stay with a previous employer. Comparing these points for otherwise equally rated job applicants may provide the factor needed for a decision. General observation shows that those who assume and handle the largest number of personal obligations are also most likely to give the most reliable job performance.

Evaluating Employee Performance

A formal evaluation system reduces errors from snap judgments or prejudices for or against individual employees. It works best when several people (principals, managers, job captains, other trusted employees) participate. Users of systems recommend monthly scorings for new employees, quarterly for tenured.

Performance scoring helps keep superior employees. An objective rating procedure permits faster, surer response to good performance. And when raises must be denied, the chart provides a fair standard for an employee's self-evaluation and points up areas for improvement required for advancement in the office.

Low motivation and low output are not always easily detected. Cover-ups are easy. An employee may be shuffled through a variety of assignments under different supervisors. Ultimately, no one is sure of the employee's actual overall performance.

Low motivation and low output are not always easily detected.

Losses from problem employees are cut by offices that use a systematic employee performance evaluation system. An evaluation system summarizes observations of employee performance and rapidly locates employees who are mismatched with their jobs.

Evaluation charts ease the discomfort of firing employees. Comparisons of scores and salaries show averages or office norms for workers in various job categories. An employee working somewhat below the norm can compare his or her total score with others. If later evaluation shows no improvement and an employee is to be dismissed, the reasons for firing are a matter of record. Employees working well below the norm who are to be dismissed are shown comparative scores. Many elect to resign under such circumstances, rather than be fired.

Here's an outline of the evaluation system used by several well-managed firms:

• The individual employee's file includes a chart for numerically rating such qualities as speed, reliability, technical knowledge, accuracy of drawing, quality of drawing, initiative, inventiveness, cooperation, leadership potential, plus other factors of concern to the office.

• Numerical rating for each factor may be 3 for excellent, 2 for superior, 1 for average, -1 for below average.

• If some factors are considered more important than others, each factor is given a numerical weight. Weight—or importance of a factor being rated—may be 3 for very important, 2 for important, or 1 for desirable. If an office considers drawing accuracy very important, that factor has a weight of 3. If the employee is evaluated superior in drawing accuracy, s/he gets a rating of 2. The weight (3) is multiplied by the rating (2) for a final score of 6.

• An employee's overall performance score is the total of all weight-times-rating scores of various factors shown on the chart. The final total is compared with those of other employees.

Unproductive Personnel

Almost every office has people who act as detours or cul-de-sacs to the work flow. They take work in and they put work out with little noticeable benefit to the office or to the jobs at hand.

A New York architectural firm was recently jolted when the boss discovered three top-echelon people whose positions added virtually nothing to the work flow. Lower level employees knew about the problem but didn't feel it was safe to say so. An outside management consultant had to deliver the news.

We've never seen an office with six or more people where the problem didn't exist to a serious degree. Some examples:

• A senior designer was always first to latch onto new projects. He made numerous flowcharts and bubble diagrams which were turned over to project architects, who then did the preliminaries. The project architects never consulted the charts and diagrams. Each thought the others must use them, but, individually, none found them usable in the process of actual project design.

• An office manager was officially responsible for intraoffice coordination and allocation of personnel from project to project. Over a period of time, the office's principals took over these functions. The office manager became an intermediary, carrying messages from principals to employees and, beyond that, performing no actual work. Following Parkinson's Law, the manager remained fully busy long after his job became obsolete and useless to the office.

• Job captains have frequently been assigned to run projects only to

Most architects have noticed that a "key" employee's prolonged absence had no negative effect on production

find an associate or principal repeating most of the same work.

• Many times, during clean-up after a large project, architects find drawers stuffed with design studies or detail studies that clearly contributed nothing to the jobs they were charged to. Also common: most architects have noticed at one time or another that a "key" employee's or associate's prolonged absence from the office had no negative effect whatsoever on overall production.

Finding the cul-de-sacs isn't hard—it just takes a little nosing around. The difficulty lies in acknowledging the problem and doing something about it. It may mean unloading an old friend or a faithful employee with many years' seniority. No one has an easy solution for this one. It's easier to look the other way or invent elaborate projects to justify keeping someone on the payroll.

The problem may be in the job role. A change in role may bring a person back into the mainstream of office productivity. When that isn't possible, most firms opt for generous severance settlements as the most painless way out.

Costs have to be looked at head on. Most offices are squeezed between rising costs and declining income. It's easy to argue that someone is a "good person" and has done a lot for the firm, but the question remains: does that justify an expense of $15,000 to $30,000 a year for unnecessary work? Our observations indicate the problem is nearly universal—worth careful scrutiny by any firm.

Firing or Laying Off Personnel

When firing someone "for cause," it is imperative these days that evidence of wrongdoing be conclusive. Rarely does an employee do something overtly and willfully that justifies on-the-spot dismissal. More often it's an accumulation of problems: slow work performance, excessive absenteeism, failure to carry through instructions. These occur sporadically, but they add up until one day someone gets fed up and fires the person. Such firing can be challenged if there is no written record of infractions and warnings. The best procedure—always—is to record each problem situation in a memo and deliver a copy to the employee as a warning to shape up. The office manual can include a stipulation that three warning memos within a year will be grounds for dismissal.

Research by *Personnel* magazine shows production increases and absenteeism decreases when employees are given generous notice before time for a layoff. This goes against the very common view that layoffs should come like a bolt from the blue. The *Personnel* survey showed that most people scheduled for layoff work harder to merit a good recommendation and that other workers step up their pace to avoid being laid off themselves.

Some architectural firms avoid or reduce the number of layoffs by renting their better people to other offices during slack periods. This saves the cost of severance and later recruitment expense when work picks up again. Several large offices in the same cities have standardized their office manuals and drafting standards to facilitate trades, rental, and bor-

When firing someone "for cause," it is imperative that evidence of wrongdoing be conclusive.

rowing of employees.

Moonlighting

Should design offices prohibit employee moonlighting? Many now do on the advice of attorneys and liability insurers. The risk isn't that employers will ultimately be held liable for the independent acts of moonlighters. It's that time and money can be lost from being in range of a nuisance shotgun lawsuit. If an employee is sued, the client's attorney will likely say: "Sue everyone who might be involved or who might be able to pay. Just in case." That means the moonlighter's boss.

Some offices state the prohibition of moonlighting in the office manual or periodically in a memo. Some require employees to sign and return a memo on the subject.

The prohibition won't stop some employees from moonlighting. They'll do it no matter what rules you set. But the memo will help keep employers off the hook if lawsuits arise. Note: some offices get into trouble by failing specifically to forbid employees from using the office telephone number, drafting facilities, and conference rooms for private dealings. That could easily lead a moonlighter's client to think the employee was acting as an agent for the office and that the office is responsible for any problems. Judges and juries are likely to agree.

Should design offices prohibit employee moonlighting?

The Four-Day Week
and Flextime

Fred A. Stitt

Most offices went to a four-day work week several years ago but retreated back to the standard schedule when problems emerged. Since then some offices have found ways to cut out or reduce the problems and have attained a very satisfactory four-day system.

The main problem has been the long workdays. They're tiring, and in major cities employees were missing out on commute transportation.

Making It Work

Here's an outline of one solution that involved some give and take between an office and its employees but has whittled the workday to a reasonable length and still provides the popular three-day weekends:

The starting point was a forty-hour work week. Workdays were 8 a.m. to 5 p.m. with a one-hour lunch and two fifteen-minute coffee breaks. The first trade-off was the coffee breaks, which were eliminated in favor of coffee any time at the board (already standard in many offices). This provided an extra half-hour per day.

The lunch hour was reduced to thirty minutes. Again, this isn't unusual in many offices, although an extra thirty minutes is often added on paydays to allow formal group lunches and check cashing time. With breaks eliminated and lunch hour shortened, one hour has been added to each workday without changing the basic 8 a.m. to 5 p.m. schedule.

The 8 a.m. to 5 p.m. schedule was modified and changed to run from 7:45 to 5:15. This added still another thirty minutes each day without creating any serious commuting problems.

At this point, one and one-half hours have been added to the workday. Four days of this means an extra six hours, almost enough to allow the fifth day off each week.

Eight paid holidays were eliminated. They are considered part of the normal three-day weekends. If a holiday falls on Monday, the work week goes from Tuesday to Friday. If the holiday is on Wednesday, the work week is Monday, Tuesday, Thursday, Friday. Eight paid holidays total sixty-four paid hours per employee per year, or an average of slightly over one hour per week in a fifty-week year.

The vacation week accumulated time was refigured on the basis of calendar weeks rather than five-day weeks. This freed another one to two days' added work time per tenured employee. And finally, the previous ten days' paid sick time per year was reduced to six days. The five to six days added another forty hours to the work year and completed the adjustment

> **The vacation week was refigured on the basis of calendar weeks rather than 5-day weeks.**

needed to get forty hours' work in four workdays with minimum dislocations.

One selling point in negotiating this change with the employees was that the travel time to work and back, averaging one and a half hours a day per employee, for the day off was eliminated—a free-time gain of an average of seventy-five hours per year.

The restructuring of the forty-hour work week just described has to take a different form in some cases. Some firms already run at forty hours with no formal coffee breaks and only a one-half-hour lunchtime. Some operate on thirty-five- or thirty-seven-hour weeks. Many firms don't care for a nine-and-a-half-hour workday and would prefer to squeeze it down to nine, or even eight and a half hours, if possible.

Adjustments have been made to suit these varying circumstances. One firm that wanted four eight-and-a-half-hour days suspended wage increases for a year to make up for the added cost to the office. The office had planned on about a 10 percent across-the-board increase, and this 10 percent equaled four hours per week per employee. This was apparently agreeable to the employees, who gained short days and long weekends, and the office considers their changeover quite successful.

Architectural offices that have made successful changeovers report the following economies: overhead is reduced because paid holidays are eliminated; absenteeism and tardiness decline dramatically; overtime payment on rush work is eliminated; and employees tend to pump out the routine work more energetically.

The best textbook on the subject is *4 Days 40 Hours*, edited by Riva Poor. A paperback edition is available for $1.95 plus $.25 handling cost from The New American Library, Inc., P.O. Box 999, Bergenfield, NJ 07821.

Absenteeism and tardiness decline...and employees tend to pump out the routine work more energetically.

The Flextime Alternative

Flextime is here—and here to stay—according to a special report in *Harvard Business Review*. Flextime has numerous variations. In its purest form, it permits employees to set their entire work schedules, including total hours.

Employee problems? Most are tossed out with the old forty-hour, nine-to-five setup. There's no more hassling and haggling over lateness or absenteeism. Supervisory personnel can find other things to worry about. The one hundred employees of Germany's Hengstler Gleitzeit Co., for example, all have keys to the factory and are allowed to come and go and do as they please. The result: a 400 percent increase in production over a three-year period.

Getting Maximum Value from Employees' Time

Fred A. Stitt

Paid time off for sickness creates a built-in absenteeism problem. Employees try to use up sick time that is "coming to them." The allowable absenteeism increases the management burden of job control and coordination of work assignments.

A reward system alleviates this problem in some offices. An extra day's pay is promised as an annual bonus at vacation time for each allowable sick day not used. If the office grants five days of paid sick time, an employee can pick up five days of extra pay.

A "double-time" pay bonus for not using sick time seems generous but it costs no more. For example, if one week's pay is allocated as payable sick time for a $300/week employee, and he or she takes full sick time off, the cost is $300 for zero day's work. If the employee takes no sick time off, the cost is $600 for five days' work. The resulting cost of total work time and paid sick time is the same as in the standard system. Besides rewarding diligence instead of absenteeism, the office gains in continuity of production.

A few firms bolster reward systems by sending "office news" notices home to the spouse. If an employee feels like sleeping in, his or her spouse—aware of an extra day's pay going down the drain—may persuade the employee to resist the temptation.

Boosting Loyalty and Enthusiasm

An endless challenge: how can you boost office loyalty and job enthusiasm at the most reasonable cost? Here's how some do it:

• Many offices benefit from periodic open house parties. An open house brings spouses, family, and friends together to see the office's work and staff members' job roles. Such gatherings improve family interest, understanding, and support for what the employees do at work.

• Small gifts along with promotions and bonuses have an impact all out of proportion to their cost. Bonus money gets spent on bills, but employees almost always keep office gifts on display as objects of pride. A gift says: "You're important." And that, in turn, makes the office important to the employee.

• Another morale aid: a gift to the spouse. Some bosses mark a promotion or raise by sending flowers or other appropriate token to the employee's spouse. This is explicit recognition of the mate's role in helping the employee stay on top of the work. A mate's support, or lack of

How can you boost office loyalty and job enthusiasm at the most reasonable cost?

it, is often crucial to job performance.

• Offices are more open about letting employees do some work at home. Some types of computer work, report writing, research, etc., are much more efficiently done at home away from office interruptions. Managers and bosses often spend a half-day or more at home on their most important paperwork. "It has many of the nice qualities of the four-day week," says one architect, "but you still keep on working."

• Early work is often the best work, so a few offices offer incentives for employees to come in as early as possible. Incentives vary depending on employee needs. Some get reduced total work hours and can take Friday afternoons off. Some are paid for commute costs. Everyone gains from the added productivity during relatively interruption-free work time; early employees miss the normal rush-hour delays; and for many, early work hours match their normal daily energy cycle.

Employee Productivity

Fred A. Stitt

Most employees in most kinds of work spend somewhere between 55 and 75 percent of the average workday actually working. That estimate remains consistent over the years and is confirmed by management consultants from coast to coast. The reasons cited are predictable: lack of motivation, lack of rewards, job boredom, lack of drive, the daily afternoon slump, interruptions, etc.

A/E employees give the same self-appraisals in terms of hours of real work and the reasons for the slowdowns. Designers and drafting staff members we talk to say they can only really push themselves five to six hours a day.

Even the most highly motivated workers— self-employed professionals—throw away about 25 percent of their work hours, according to research by the Booze Allen Hamilton consultants.

One management consultant uncovers a provocative explanation for a large chunk of employee inaction. O. Mark Marcussen reports on studies that show an average of 3.6 hours of wasted work time daily. He noted that 1.2 hours are lost for varied personal reasons and unavoidable circumstances. The remaining 2.4 hours are wasted because of supervisory inefficiency.

First-level supervisors usually only have a vague idea of the time spans required to finish tasks, according to Marcussen. That in itself generates 35 percent of the time waste. Unclear assignments, incomplete instructions, and unstated deadlines and checkpoints cause another 25 percent of time loss, says Marcussen. Overstaffing, understaffing, and down-times add 15 percent more to lost production. The remaining time losses come from gaps in general discipline: lateness, extended breaks, personal calls, errands on the job, etc.

First-level supervisors have a crucial role as front-line managers, but they usually have no formal management or supervisory training. They've come up from the ranks and usually operate on a common sense, seat-of-the-pants basis that leads to crisis management. They sort priorities and give out assignments and deadlines according to day-to-day urgency or lack of it, rather than according to long-range planning.

An ingenious test has been devised that illuminates the consequences of common managerial habits.

Measuring Manager Productivity

In the past it's been difficult to measure a manager's productivity.

In the past it's been difficult to measure a manager's productivity.

For one thing, while managers might like the idea of measuring employees' time and production, they haven't wanted that kind of scrutiny applied to themselves. Further, managers' work is hard to measure in simple quantitative terms of so many drawings per month. Thus, managers can ride along for quite awhile before it becomes clear whether they do their jobs well or not. And if they manage to keep switching from project to project in midstream, it never becomes clear.

The new test sets up a simulated work situation that condenses the features of a workday, or week, or even a whole project. It's designed as a self-training process and it works like this:

The manager is put to work in a hypothetical situation: new desk, new office, new job. He or she is taking over the job of a suddenly departed personnel manager. The in box is brimming full. There's a tough day's work ahead under complex circumstances: new situation, unfamiliar surroundings and procedures, ambiguities and blank spots in the information available, and an unknown system of measuring performance. (Like real life in many offices.)

Besides a lack of clarity in the work situation, there's more work in the in box than can possibly be finished on time. (Also like real life.)

The great lesson in all this is prioritization and planning. The short-sighted managers plow head-on into the in box and grind away from top to near-bottom. They find an emergency situation and sometimes spend hours trying to resolve it. Later they find another document that resolves the emergency automatically. Also, toward the bottom of the pile they find the most important tasks of the day waiting to be started. They've been tricked just as in real life.

Superior managers seem to take it easy at first. They sort through the pile of work. They consolidate related tasks. They screen all tasks according to urgency and importance. The sorting process eliminates the contradictory, redundant, and obsolete tasks that appear early in the pile.

Some managers start off well, get all their work neatly organized, and then quit being productive. They get intrigued by work that appears intensely interesting but which is really trivial, or they take on tasks that should properly be delegated to others.

Sorting is just half the initial work organization process. Once work is sorted, superior managers list the tasks they should do and give themselves a time budget for the day. They focus on the most important work, schedule it first, and allow those items that should be done, but can't be, to fall off at the end.

The final prescription then for improving that 55 to 75 percent of actual work time on the part of employees: start at the top. When management is in shape, the rest of the team won't be able to fall far behind.

Superior managers screen all tasks according to urgency and importance.

Supervisory Management: Communications

Fred A. Stitt

Many A/Es still don't know how to deal with their employees. Here are the main trouble spots:

• Secrecy. Employees tell us it's like pulling teeth to get the information they need to do their jobs. Technical data, new design decisions, budgets, future job prospects for the office—all are kept as big mysteries. The worst offenders: insecure middle managers who lock up office data as their private property.

• Disorganized management. A draftsman says: "We spend lots of hours faking it with busy work because the job captains don't plan ahead on assignments." A project architect: "The partners keep making the same policy decisions over and over, and nothing happens. Nobody does anything about them."

• One-way/top-down communication. A junior staffer points at nearby drafting stations and says: "Those drawings won't be done on time. They're such a mess, the bids will come in way over budget. Everybody knows who made the problem, but there's no way you can tell the bosses."

Open up Communications

There's one overriding solution for all the problems. A project architect of many years' experience sums it up: "This is the only office I've been in that has a long-range plan. They named goals and objectives. To implement the plan, they've had to define a clear management structure and open up communication channels throughout the firm. Compared to working in other offices, this is like working in the sunshine."

A multitude of good ideas grows out of long-range planning. They deal with employee needs as well as furthering the interests of the office. Here's a sampling from several unusually well-managed firms:

• A "project status" board shows everyone in the office what's happening with the work flow. This is usually a large bar graph calendar board that lists all current and upcoming projects and shows their progress from week to week. Some firms keep the board in a major conference room and use it to brief new clients on how their jobs will be scheduled relative to other projects (many clients properly worry about being sidetracked relative to other jobs). Architects Seracuse Lawler in Denver keep their status board near the coffee area, where it provides a continuous stimulus for discussion by employees.

Project status boards are a shot in the arm for employees.

Project status boards are a shot in the arm for employees. Staff members are always eager to know upcoming work prospects and to see how their current projects are doing relative to others. Management usually underrates the importance of that data to the staff and misses out on an important morale and coordination booster.

• Another communication tool: the Friday "wine tasting" or social hour. Usually held monthly, these start as a briefing on office progress and prospects, then become open-ended for after hours socializing. Some firms ask team leaders to display project drawings as openers; others go straight to socializing. The main value is in cross-fertilization of ideas and communication between departments, staff, and management. Important data often flow to management in the less inhibiting social setting.

• A buddy system at the progressive Dallas firm of Jarvis-Putty-Jarvis cracks through the mystery and alienation most employees face in a new office. Principals are asked to alternate in a big brother role with each newly hired staffer. They take the newcomer to lunch the first day, orient him or her to the firm, and are on call after that to deal with questions or problems. Additional lunches are scheduled to assure personal contact and exchange of information. JPJ president Bill Smith reports that the principals benefit from and enjoy the contact as much as new staff members do.

• An easy way to dredge out hidden problems is used quarterly by a smooth-running, midwestern engineering firm. The office circulates file cards and asks employees to jot down any ideas they have on how the office might improve its services to the clients. This is a way of asking for complaints and problems without saying so. Employees feel safer in expressing problems in the "how can we help the client" format. The more promising ideas are circulated back to staff members for comment and evaluation. Authors of winning ideas are taken to lunch, and, barring unforeseen glitches, the best suggestions are put to work.

Here are the main items employees say they want when an office asks for suggestions or complaints: (1) information on salary scales; (2) standards used to evaluate performance and allocate raises and/or bonuses; (3) job budgets.

Old-line management is very stingy with that kind of information. Salaries are often inequitable and unrelated to performance; advancement is often due to subjective evaluations and politics rather than productivity; and job budgets are kept secret to prevent demands for bonuses and profit sharing. Those are common motivations of secrecy-oriented management, and that's exactly how the employees perceive the situation.

Open communication follows from long-term office planning. When principals clearly see where they want to go and how to get there, they're not reluctant to bring employees along with them. As one partner told us recently: "It's the employees who will make us good and profitable. So why not give them what they need to do it?"

The Office Manual

W e once read a lengthy office manual paragraph that began: "In accordance with current standard professional and business custom...." The point of this one hundred-word essay was: "Standard work week: 40 hours."

Many manuals are so wordy and obscure that whenever an employee has a question on policy, s/he's likely to ignore the manual and go directly to the front office. Those who do read the manuals find remarks such as: "You are expected to be neat and clean at all times." "Please be courteous enough to refrain from unnecessary conversation in the drafting room." These are not well-accepted forms of direction for employees in general, and to the mature professionals in the office they are grossly offensive.

Use an outline format to convey office policies most clearly and concisely. The following show generally accepted policies written in abbreviated form. Common alternate practices are described in brackets.

Office Schedule

Daily: 8:30-5:30 (for commuting problems, see office manager or principal).

Lunch: 12:30-1:30.

Coffee: 10:00 a.m. and 3:00 p.m.—15 minutes each. [Many offices provide no specific coffee break time, but ask that work proceed at the board whenever the employee is having coffee.]

Pay Period

Span: [Usually weekly, biweekly, or 1st and 15th of each month.]

Pay time: Friday noon. [Many offices allow an extra 15 or 30 minutes at payday lunch time for check cashing.]

Timecards: Due by noon Thursday before payday. Estimate job times for remainder of the week; make corrections on next pay period timecard if estimate is mistaken. [Many offices include a sample of the timecard to show how to record data. Time is usually rounded off to the half-hour.]

Time Off

Paid holidays: New Year's Day, Memorial Day, Independence Day, Labor Day, Thanksgiving, and Christmas; one-half day on Christmas Eve and New Year's Eve. [Washington's Birthday and Veteran's Days are often

Fred A. Stitt

Use an outline format to convey office policies most clearly and concisely.

included. Many offices allow an extra paid day when a major holiday occurs on Thursday or Tuesday. Some will trade the extra day off for work on Saturday of the previous week. One-half day on Good Friday for Catholics, and on Jewish holidays are commonly allowed. Some offices permit voluntary work on holidays (under supervision) for double-time pay or double-time vacation credit.]

Paid sick time: 10 days per year. Notify office before 9:00 a.m. each day of sickness. Notify supervisor if you need to leave the office early. [Often not provided until after three-six months' seniority.]

Make-up of unpaid sick time: permitted in some individual cases; see office manager. [A wise, unstated policy of many offices is to permit make-up time only when supervision is available.]

Leave of absence: up to two weeks per year, job schedules permitting. See job captain and office manager or principal. If more time is required, see principal. Six months or more may be allowed in special circumstances, but employee must send payments to office to maintain insurance benefits.

Vacations: five workdays in first year, after six months' seniority. Ten workdays per year after one year's seniority. See job captain and office manager for scheduling.

Jury and military duty: difference between salary and pay for jury and part-time military service after six months' seniority.

Election day: up to two paid hours, morning or afternoon.

Architectural registration exam: all exam time paid after six months' seniority.

Slack times: employees are encouraged to take time off (without pay) when work load is exceptionally light.

Restrictions: job captain and office manager must be notified in advance of anticipated absences, or payment may not be authorized.

Call it a handbook instead of a manual.

Overtime

Pay: time-and-a-half of regular salary, computed hourly. [Many offices allow voluntary overtime at straight hourly pay or in trade for later time off—usually on a select basis and when supervision is available. Supervisors who don't receive overtime pay are usually compensated with equivalent time off.]

Restrictions: no overtime pay for work done without authorization. Authorization granted only by job captain or principal. Authorization will include a specific limit of overtime hours.

Severance Pay

Layoff: one week's salary plus accumulated vacation, sick time, and bonus, after six months' seniority. [One or two weeks' notice commonly provided when possible. Some time off without pay allowed for job hunting.]

Firing: accumulated vacation and sick time. Firing for unsatisfactory performance or actions detrimental to the office will be preceded by verbal and written warning. Actions that require more than one warning per quarter or more than two warnings in a year will be grounds for dismissal. [Many offices provide a week's notice for firing, but notice and prior warnings are not customary in instances of extreme irresponsibility.]

Employee's voluntary severance: accumulated vacation and sick time. Please provide two weeks' notice, if possible. [Some offices pay a one or two weeks' salary severance bonus on a select basis.]

Tenure
Probation: first four-six weeks of employment.

Intermediate status: first six months of employment.

Regular status: benefits such as paid sick time, etc., as noted elsewhere, apply after six months of employment.

Senior employment or associateship: negotiated on an individual basis. May be considered after three years of regular status employment.

Employee status review: [Although methods of determining raises and promotions vary widely, quarterly reviews for hourly wage increases of $.25 to $.50 per hour are fairly standard.]

Bonus
[Bonus policies vary, often from year to year in the same office. Bonus payment is usually made during the week before the Christmas holiday. Some offices add payment for accumulated, unused vacation and sick time.]

Benefits and Office Contributions
Deductions: [Social Security, withholding, workmen's compensation, and other deductions coded on the paycheck may be defined here. Some offices make it a point to say that an employee is allowed to increase deductions for dependents in his withholding if he wishes to assure income tax refunds.]

Hospitalization, group life insurance, United Fund: [Usually explained in accompanying brochures and application forms.]

Profit sharing, mutual fund investment: [Usually explained in separate, detailed prospectus.]

Payment by office of professional society dues, book purchases, and subscriptions to journals.

Some Advice from the Employees
Several offices, in planning or redesigning their manuals, solicited and received some helpful advice from the people for whom the manuals were written. Suggestions included:

Call it a handbook instead of a manual. A manual is thought of as an office rule book to be read only once. As such, an office would need only one copy for occasional reference. A handbook denotes a professional tool worthy of constant use and improvement.

Don't "update" the manual with disciplinarian memos. Memos about excessive tardiness or abuse of telephone privileges are often misdirected to the entire staff rather than to the specific offenders. Responsi-

When principal, manager or job captain make occasional verbal "exceptions," the manual is soon generally ignored.

sible employees have expressed strong resentment of this policy; they point out that it makes no friends for the manual and its contents.

Emphasize design values in the manual format and in the select office drafting standards. Working drawing standards of keying symbols, schedules, title blocks, and detail sheet format can be simple and readable, but elegant. The use of ugly standards will be strongly resisted by conscientious employees—especially since they must think about the drawings they'll be showing when looking for the next job.

Encourage participation in the manual's growth. Provide some specific, formal system by which employees can present proposals for improving and updating manual content. Use a three-hole-punch, loose-leaf binder for maximum flexibility.

Add copies of technical articles and clippings about the work of the office. One office, responding to this staff suggestion, began leaving stacks of helpful technical literature in the coffee area. All copies were snapped up without prompting. As a spin-off, individuals, on their own initiative, began supplying significant articles on materials, spec writing, etc., to fellow employees.

Don't contradict the manual. All changes should be authorized by principal(s) and distributed as formal amendments. When principal, manager or job captain make occasional verbal "exceptions," all content of the manual is thrown into doubt and soon will be generally ignored.

Don't force the staff to keep reinventing the wheel. When someone has researched some data for his or her job that might apply to future jobs, put it into the manual.

When someone has researched some data that might apply to future jobs, put it into the manual.

Public Relations

Commentary

Design firms are showing increasing interest in public relations/publicity programs to supplement their marketing efforts. The most common objectives of such programs are: (a) broader recognition to support geographic or discipline expansion; (b) support of direct sales through increased recognition and credibility; and (c) flattering the egos of the principals.

All three of these objectives can be valuable supplements to a marketing program. (Yes, even ego gratification can be justified if it is the right type and it increases the self-confidence of principals in selling situations.) However, in moving to achieve these PR objectives, many design firms have been frustrated trying to locate PR professionals or agencies that will do the job on what appears to be a realistic cost/benefit basis.

There are to date only a small handful of PR agencies with specific expertise serving the design community, and there are as yet too few in-house staff PR professionals to be cloning any sizable cadre of experienced people for other firms to hire.

In the broader PR world, there are a large number of qualified firms and practitioners willing to talk to design firms, but their background in business and institutional work rarely prepares them to respond directly to what a design firm may need. Instead they propose comprehensive communication analyses and image surveys to develop the basis for a PR program and the design firm client feels the approach is too vague to justify the investment.

This is a natural reaction on both sides: inexperienced (in the design professions) PR practitioners need you to pay them to understand your business; yet at the bottom line most design firms can't get enough real value from PR publicity to justify such a front-end investment.

Learn about PR

If you want to initiate a PR program, it is far better in practice to learn enough about what PR can do for you on your own, decide exactly what you want, and then ask PR firms or practitioners to respond to that specific need. You will thereby be better able to assess the value of what you are offered, and the PR person/service will have clear direction where to apply its skills.

Design firms that have been through all this generally agree that the scope of PR/publicity services worth paying for fall into the following

Weld Coxe

Decide exactly what you want, and then ask PR firms or practitioners to respond to that specific need.

categories:

1. Placement of articles, chiefly in trade press, about the firm's work. To do so, a PR service must research and write background papers on the subjects or projects, assemble illustrations, contact different publications, and endeavor to get a commitment from an editor to publish an article.

There will be some value to the direct exposure the firm may receive from readers of the publication, but by far the greatest benefit will come from having reprints of the article for use in the firm's direct mail program and as sales tools to accompany proposals.

Placement of three to six such articles per year generally represents a sufficient PR output for the typical design firm. The average PR cost per placement can be evaluated against the value of the reprints generated. (But don't try to buy single placements. An annual retainer with the objective of yielding a set number of placements is the only way a PR firm—or employee on salary—can properly serve you.)

2. Client-oriented PR support: a publicity effort that collaborates with your clients' PR departments by providing fact sheets and assisting with project announcements, ground breakings, public awareness programs, employee orientation, leasing, etc., can pay very large dividends in assuring that the design firm receives due recognition whenever the client communicates about the project.

3. Special services: PR professionals can do many special tasks ranging from developing the firm newsletter, arranging public appearances for the principals and writing their speeches, ghostwriting books, helping with preparation of brochures and sales tools, etc. These services can consume a lot of the PR effort and budget and it is important to budget their relative value in balance with the rest of the publicity effort. In general, these special services work out best only if accomplished as part of a retainer or full-time staff PR relationship.

An annual retainer with the objective of yielding a set number of placements is the only way a PR firm can properly serve you.

Planning the PR Program

Public relations in a design office is a support activity in furtherance of the firm's business and professional goals. It should be as carefully planned as any other activity of the office. PR is a means not an end, and its most important purpose is to help the firm's marketing effort—the indisputable premise being that a client cannot commission you if he doesn't know you exist.

A public relations program should contain the following elements:
1. A statement of PR policy.
2. A statement of PR objectives to help achieve the corporate, professional, and marketing objectives of the firm.
3. PR tasks, procedures, and priorities for achieving those objectives:
   • publicity tasks;
   • support materials development tasks;
   • marketing support tasks;
   • employee relations tasks.
4. PR budget and controls.

Crucial to an effective PR program, a precondition for success, is the development by management of its corporate, professional, and marketing goals and objectives. These are the source from which all activities of the firm, including PR, must flow. (See "Where is the Office Going?" and other articles in the first section of this book for help in establishing these.)

To proceed further, then, we will need here to assume some goals and objectives.

Corporate and Professional Goals

1. Achieve controlled growth over the next five years to n-person office.
2. Double present billings to $_____ a year.
3. Achieve annual pretax profits of 10 percent. (See "Myths and Truths about Compensation" in the Financial section.)
4. Do interesting, challenging, prestigious work while being able to refuse the opposite kinds.
5. Attract and hold the best possible professional talent.
6. Provide and be recognized for design vigor and excellence, technical innovation and proficiency, in our field.

David Travers

PR is a means not an end, and its most important purpose is to help the firm's marketing effort.

Marketing Objectives

1. Increase billings by 15 percent a year (derived from Corporate Goal 1).
2. Increase:
   - (educational, wastewater, or whatever) facilities planning and design work by _____ percent.
   - public work in (project type and/or geographical area) by _____ percent.
   - et cetera

Since the corporate and marketing goals and objectives are necessarily suggested rather than definitively set, so must be the public relations program that is outlined below.

PR Policy

All public relations efforts and activities are to spring from and to help further the company's goals and objectives. There is to be no aimless publicity or publicity whose sole purpose is the piling up of column inches. Every communication should be scrutinized to make certain it is accurate and that there is no unwitting or careless inconsistency with the firm's purpose. Not just its planning and design but everything that emanates from the office should bespeak honesty and excellence.

PR Objectives

1. Help to create a favorable firm reputation and image.
2. Attract sales inquiries.
3. Reinforce client loyalty.
4. Attract superior employees.
5. Provide sales materials.

All public relations efforts and activities are to spring from and to help further the company's goals and objectives.

PR Tasks

1. Publicity

Here there should be a list of suggested articles, news stories, and other publicity items. They should be grouped by categories corresponding to the kinds of projects the firm has most experience in and wants to do more of. The target media for the publicity should correspond to the firm's present and prospective client areas. Thus, the publicity will be directed at supporting (1) what the firm should be trying to sell and (2) to whom it should be trying to sell it. (See "Improving PR Performance" for a detailed hypothetical case of publicity tasking.)

The accompanying communications chart outlines audience groups and various objectives and actions related to them.

2. Materials Organization and Development

There is usually urgent need for action in these areas: no system exists for the preparation, storage, or retrieval of the raw materials necessary for an effective promotion program.

PR files and library. (See also, "What to Do—Order from Chaos" in the Marketing section.)

- Print files. (Black and white and color prints.) All existing prints

Communications Group	Objective	Management Action	P.R. Action	Channel	Message
Clients	Loyalty, goodwill, respect more sales.	Produce good service, product.	Publicize good work. Cooperate with client P.R. Mail reprints and other information. Evaluate.	Newspapers, professional journals, business press, direct mail, personal contact.	Good design, experience, proficiency, innovation, efficiency.
Prospective Clients	Sales.	Market program, P.R. program, articles, speeches.	Publicize work, encourage management action. Evaluate.	Newspapers, professional journals, business press, direct mail, personal contact, slide presentations, conferences.	Good design, experience, proficiency, innovation, efficiency.
Profession	Respect, recognition, recruiting.	Good planning and design, participation in professional activities.	Publicize good work and new "evolving" firm image; encourage management action. Evaluate.	Foreign and U.S. professional magazines, mass media, conventions.	Exciting work, good design, innovation.
Employees	Loyalty, high morale, efficiency, productivity.	Provide satisfying work, promote pride in firm and self-respect, "fun." Good internal communication.	Publicize good work and management changes. Encourage good internal communication up and down. Evaluate.	Professional magazines, mass media. Company publication, bulletin boards, slide presentations, project reviews, management-staff meetings.	Exciting place to work. Legacy being passed along to new generation. News about people and firm direction.
General Public	Goodwill, support, respect.	Work in public interest, support community projects, do good work.	Encourage management action; publicize.	Mass media.	Professional excellence; social responsibility.
Mass and Business Media	Respect, confidence in statements and work.	Responsive to inquiries, low b.s. to truth ratio.	Cultivate eds and writers. Be of help. Write and speak the truth.	Personal contact.	Experience, excellence. Firm is doing things readers are interested in.
Professional Media	Respect, confidence, recognition.	Produce good planning and design. Meet and cultivate eds and writers.	Encourage management action. Follow up. Be of help. Be accurate.	Personal contact; publication in respected foreign professional magazines.	Exciting work and people. Design and technical excellence.

and proof sheets should be brought together into an alphabetical central photo file.

• Slide files. Original slides should be collected into plastic-sleeve notebooks in alphabetical order. These originals should never leave the PR library except to be duplicated. A small selection of representative of the best slides of key projects (those most useful for marketing) should be collected into separate notebooks. Four or five slides of each project should be sufficient. A duplicate set of the above select sets should be made. These will be the slides which go out of the office for presentations. All slides should be identified as suggested in "What to Do—Order from Chaos." All slides are to be signed for when removed from PR. If there is concern that dupe slides do not have the quality or effectiveness of originals, the office should start having multiple originals shot by its photographers.

• Project information files. Each major old and new project should have full factual and design descriptions.

3. Collaboration with Client PR

It is a frequent and disturbing occurrence for a design firm to read an account of one of its projects in the press without mention of its role. This usually happens when it is the client who originates the story. To avoid this, PR should establish close, friendly, and cooperative relations with its counterpart in the client's organization at the outset of a project and maintain them during the life of the job.

4. Associations and Conferences

PR should compile a list of associations whose memberships are congruent with the firm's business and professional objectives. The time and place of annual conventions should be noted in a "pop-up" file so that an offer of a speaker or other participation can be made by the firm before the program is closed. (A valuable reference here is the *Encyclopedia of Associations*, Gale Publishing Co., Detroit.)

5. Marketing Support Tasks

Coordination of boilerplate production.

• Project description sheets. Key projects should be documented in standardized, single-sheet format containing a brief factual outline or description and an illustration or two.

• Biographies. Standardized biographies should be prepared for people frequently proposed for key project roles. Several variations can be prepared for the more versatile people.

• General statements about the firm. There should be several, relatively brief (200 words) introductory statements, each emphasizing a different aspect of the firm's experience.

Assist in the preparation of:

• Proposals.

• Brochures. See "Writing the Brochure Program" for these tasks.

• Permanent (but continually updated) slide presentations.

• Other sales materials.

6. Employee Relations Tasks

The director of public relations should initiate and be involved in employee-management communications matters, including:

• Editorial supervision of the employee newsletter.

• Preparation of the office policy and procedures handbook.

• Bulletin boards.

• Assisting and encouraging management to maintain effective, open channels of communication upward, downward, and horizontally.

PR Budget and Controls

1. Budget. The following guidelines for the PR budget are based upon three factors:

• It is generally accepted that on the average design firms spend about 6 percent of gross billings for promotion, i.e., marketing and public relations.

• How this figure is divided between the two depends on the nature and intensity of a firm's marketing activities. That is, what the balance is between direct (selling) and indirect (PR) promotional activities. For the sake of simplicity, we will assume an even balance.

• It seems to be the rule that the percentage of gross billings (the 6 percent average) is applied to the previous year's billings. It makes more sense to base marketing expenditures on what they are supposed to produce. Thus, the total promotional here should be based on Corporate Goal 1, a 15 percent increase over last year's billings.

Assuming for the moment a firm of 100 people with billings last

It is a frequent occurrence for a firm to see one of its projects in the press without mention of its role.

The director of public relations should initiate employee-management communications matters year of $4 million gives us a $4.6 million projection for this year. Six percent for total promotion is $276,000 and half of that for PR is $138,000. The PR budget might look something like this:

PR Budget

Expense	Description		Monthly Average
Salaries	Department head: $2500/month Secretary/assistant: $1500/month		4,000
Travel	Two 3-day trips to NYC to see mag editors:	$3000	
	Attendance at national professional society convention (two people):	$2000	
	Attendance at state convention:	$ 500	
	Other:	$3000	700
Entertainment			300
Photography			2,000
Printing	Reprints, materials, newsletters		500
Special Projects	Principal and staff direct labor; outside PR consultants for special efforts		3,000
Contingency	15 percent for special opportunities in PR or marketing.		1,500
		Total	$11,500

2. Budget Controls. PR should be given a job number and all PR expenses charged to that number. Accounting should assign subaccount numbers to the categories of expense outlined in the hypothetical budget so as to produce a monthly readout like the following:

PR should be given a "job" number and all PR expenses charged to that number.

PR Expenses For (Month)

	This Month	Monthly Average	Budgeted
Salaries			
Travel			
Entertainment			
Photography			
Printing			
Special Projects			
Contingency			

PR Director

Qualifications. To perform the public relations tasks, the staff person in charge of PR must be skilled, energetic, and experienced in his or her craft. He should have eight to ten years' experience in PR, advertising, journalism, or some combination of these. Three of those years should have been in the construction industry, the closer to architecture and design the better so that he is familiar with the local and national media in design and construction. He should have a reputation for integrity in dealing with the media.

He must be a productive writer, good at assembling facts and careful in setting them down. There must be no tampering with the truth; while he should be judicious in what facts he gives, those given must be truthful in detail and in the overall picture they present.

He should be assertive enough to build himself into the firm's communications channels, including attendance at management meetings. He has to know what is going on and why to be effective. He must be well organized and a good administrator—no matter how tiny his department. He will have many tasks going simultaneously and will be coordinating and directing activities which involve the professional staff and management.

He must have a positive attitude toward budgets and cost control.

Responsibility. The director of public relations should answer only to the president, though he must be responsive to the director of marketing and others.

Authority. His authority, derived from the president and made explicit, should include the power to

• call on designers and graphics staff for help in developing material for publicity purposes;

• require project managers to provide him with written project descriptions;

• approve labor and other charges against the PR budget;

• refuse requests from anyone for withdrawal of original slides or other irreplaceable material in his charge.

Inquiries. All media inquiries are to be directed to the PR director unless the inquirer asks for a senior staff person by name. Any staff person so contacted should advise the PR director of the nature and purpose of the contact.

A PR director has to know what is going on and why to be effective.

How to Improve PR Performance

P erhaps because they consider PR an unseemly pursuit for a professional to engage in and look upon it without relish as something which does unpleasant things to overhead and takes time, money, and energy away from important work, many offices treat PR with inadvertence. They will hire a PR person or consultant under a vague directive to get favorable publicity. Then, uncertain how to measure his effectiveness, they add up the column inches at the end of the year to see how he has done.

This is extravagantly inefficient. If an office is going to go to the considerable expense of trying to communicate with its various publics—community, professional, clients, employees—the undertaking should be as carefully planned as any other area of its operation. Purposes should be clearly stated, roles and responsibilities assigned, strategies outlined, tasks and priorities set, and an evaluation-review procedure established.

Without the direction afforded by a clear and specific program, the usual PR man is lost. Frequently he ends up doing semi-skilled promotional-clerical work at a salary of $25,000-$30,000, maintaining bulletin boards, planning the office picnic and Christmas party, turning out news releases about new contracts and staff promotions, acting as custodian of whatever passes for PR files and materials, and serving as another pair of hands in the preparation of RFPs.

Recently I prepared a program which departed from this traditional and unsatisfactory approach to PR. It is quite simple in concept, consisting of assigning point values to the various tasks which made up the PR program and setting target figures based on reasonable performance expectations. The simplicity of the idea is, of course, deceptive because it requires that PR objectives, tasks, priorities, and so forth be developed. Only then can points be allotted to the tasks.

Planning PR

As an example of how it works, let's say we are a sixty-man engineering office in Dallas. We have a lot of experience in industrial work throughout the Southwest, including a number of oil and gas refineries. After a recent successful association with a small architectural office, we have decided to expand into architecture by buying the associated office and making its principal a principal in the combined firm. He is an architect born and raised in Latin America but professionally educated and trained in the U.S.

David Travers

PR should be as carefully planned as any other area of the operation.

Our business goal is to double annual billings over the next five years to $5 million and to continue to do what we consider exciting and challenging work, while maintaining our comfortable level of profits and high quality of work. Realizing that growth in the present slow-growth economy will require aggressive marketing, the firm has prepared a business development program aimed at increasing our industrial and refinery work by (1) solidifying our position in the Southwest and (2) expanding geographically into Latin America, using our strength and experience in industrial development and the background of our new design principal.

Publicity tasks were developed as part of a total PR program in support of the marketing objectives. The firm's current and recently completed work was surveyed and projects selected which were felt to have publicity potential that would aid the marketing effort. An example or so should be enough to illustrate the principle.

The first project is a small, 25,000-barrels-a-day refinery for a processor of foreign oil, most of it imported from Venezuela. The design and engineering included innovations which reduced costs substantially, primarily by means of a simplified construction system which allowed use of unskilled and semiskilled labor. The firm believes that the project should be of interest to potential clients in the U.S. and also in Latin American countries such as Venezuela, which has both oil and unskilled labor in large quantities.

Magazines were researched in *Standard Rate & Data Business Publications* and *Bacon's Publicity Checker* to find those most likely to be interested in articles about the project and whose readership included prospective clients and others the firm wanted to reach. Points were assigned to the publications based upon the size and quality of their circulation.

The editorial emphasis, or "slant," of the articles would be (1) the new design and engineering features which resulted in lower cost and ease of construction, and (2) in the case of foreign magazines, the application of the project to Latin America. Publications to be courted:

1. *Petroleum Today*. Largest coverage of the market with a circulation of 110,000 . . . . 20 points
2. *Oil and Gas Journal*. Circulation 50,000 . . . . 10 points*
3. *Hydrocarbon Processing*. Circulation 36,000, fewer than *O&GJ*, but more focused . . . . 10 points
4. *Petroleo Internacional*. Circulation 5,800—small but important for expansion into Latin America . . . . 20 points
5. *Exposicion Industrial Internacional*. Circulation 5,000; almost as important as *Petroleo Internacional* because even though it isn't strictly oil processing in content it is published and circulated in Venezuela where the oil is. . . . . 15 points
6. *National Development/Modern Government*. Spanish language edition 28,000; larger circulation than the above but less focussed . . . . 10 points*
7. *Dallas Morning News*. The firm is located in Dallas . . . . . . 5 points*
8. *Houston Chronicle*. The project is in the Houston area . . . . 5 points*

Magazines were researched to find those whose readership included prospective clients.

Because the U.S. magazines are in competition, it is unlikely that more than one would publish an article on the project, so only the 20 points for *Petroleum Today* are included in the total possible points

Total possible 75 points

Recognizing that given the limited resources of the firm and its PR staff the total of the allotted points is not an attainable goal, the principal in charge of marketing and promotion and the PR director got together on a reasonable target indicated by the asterisks in the point column. That is, 10 points for one of the U.S. journals, 10 points for *National Development/ Modern Government*, which is published here and interested in promoting U.S. industry abroad, and 10 points for the two newspapers.

Target 30 points

Example Two

A second project, done with the now merged architectural firm, is a manufacturing/administration/R&D complex for a large Texas industrial company. The program was a complicated one, calling for a building capable of overall expansion to double the first phase construction but with each of the divisions of the company growing at differing rates and percentages, some of them unknown and unpredictable. The client and the firm are happy with the project—the client because it works, the firm because of the quality of the design by its new design principal.

Slant here is (1) a large project for an important client; (2) exceptional design quality; and (3) a building designed for change, i.e., to accept predetermined growth in some of its functions but undetermined change in others dictated by as yet unknown technological advances.
Publications:

1. *Industry Week*. Circulation 176,000 . . . . 20 points
2. or *Factory*. Circulation 100,000 . . . . 15 points
3. or *Plant Engineering*. Circulation 85,000 . . . . 15 points
4. or *Industrial Construction*. Circulation 52,000 . . . . 10 points*
5. *Texas Industry*. Circulation 7,000 . . . . 5 points*
6. *Progressive Architecture* or *Architectural Record* . . . . . . 20 points*
7. *DOMUS*. Italy, international circulation . . . . 20 points
8. A + U. Japan, international circulation . . . . 10 points
9. *L'Architecture d'Aujourd'hui*. France, international . . . . 10 points
10. *Dallas Morning News* . . . . 2 points*
11. *Houston Chronicle* . . . . 3 points*

The high level of points in the first three architectural magazines reflects their importance to company objectives other than marketing—improved design image, higher employee morale, improved recruiting. Points for the newspapers are less here because Dallas and Houston are not centers of manufacturing where they are the centers of the oil industry and publicity for the industrial complex probably won't be as beneficial.

Total possible 90 points
Target (*) 40 points

Readership the Critical Factor

The scale of points used in the examples is an arbitrary one and could just as easily have been one to 100 as one to 20. An office can select its own scale, keeping in mind that it is not the numbers themselves that are important but what they imply. It's not the inches of type that are critical but what that type says and who reads it.

In the first example, for instance, *Petroleum Today* is given twice as many points as the *Oil and Gas Journal* because its readership is twice as large and thus presumably twice as important. On the other hand, in the second example, *DOMUS* is given as many points as *Progressive Architecture* and *Architectural Record* even though it is much smaller than either of the U.S. magazines because it is far greater in prestige value. An office which has one of its projects presented in *DOMUS* will find itself standing taller in the profession and able to recruit better people. Hearts will be much lighter and heads higher in its drafting room.

One more word on the subject of the scale. It goes out the window if a firm finds itself written about favorably in one of the mass circulation magazines—*Time*, *Newsweek*, etc. The benefits to the destiny of so fortunate a firm are almost incalculable.

Other PR Tasks

It must be remembered that publicity is only one area of public relations, albeit the most visible one, and I suggest that all important PR tasks be quantified in a like manner, client relations, employee relations, professional relations. To ensure that there is a proper balance of PR activities, separate target figures should be assigned to those categories and to any other promotional tasks that an office may decide upon, such as the creation of brochures and other marketing tools, stocking and organizing a photographic library of the firm's work, etc.

The assigning of points is likely to be quite subjective and should be done in collaboration with the PR director. He must feel that what he is being asked to do is not only possible but reasonable.

The advantages to this quantified approach to PR are many. First, it requires a firm to plan and prepare a PR program—in itself a revolutionary advance. Second, it allows management to evaluate performance on a measurable, objective basis (not forgetting, however, that the points have been arrived at by something less than pure objectivity). Third, since the points allotted are scaled to the relative importance of the various tasks assigned to him, the PR man knows not only what is expected of him but priorities are quickly grasped. And finally, for those firms into management by exception, the numerical values make deviations from the targeted objectives easy to detect.

It must be remembered that publicity is only one area of public relations, albeit the most visible one.

How to Publish Your Work

Fred A. Stitt

Some editors say they are starved for material; others say they are swamped. Over a span of weeks, the situation may reverse. Some journals maintain consistent editorial requirements for years; others are likely to change staffs and policies overnight. Because of the variables and uncertainties of the publishing world, some conventions have been devised to smooth things out for everyone.

One such device is the query. The query is an outline of material that can be provided to an editor. If the editor finds the material interesting, he or she will write back and ask for specifics. The primary advantage of the query is that it permits you to check out all potentially interested publications simultaneously, instead of wasting time sending finished material in sequence to one editor after another, which is often done by A/E firms who are unaware of the query method.

Where do you send inquiries? You can locate the name and title of regional or department editors on or near the contents page in U.S. journals. Otherwise, a good source of names, addresses, and editorial requirements is *Bacon's Publicity Checker* or the *Literary Marketplace*, available in most public libraries.

If you are proposing to write an article, the query should outline the subject, direction, and the main points. An interested editor will respond with a list of the ideas that should be emphasized for his readers and other suggestions, including submittal specifications. Some editors require certain margin widths, line spacing, and numbers of copies of the manuscript; others couldn't care less about such details. It is customary to double-space the lines. Again, the query helps to get such information to the author before s/he wastes time completing an unacceptable manuscript.

The query permits you to check out all potentially interested publications simultaneously.

Magazine Requirements

If you are submitting a building project, the magazine's staff will most likely write the text from information submitted. In this case the query should include a photo of a plan drawing and a couple of photographs which explain the project. These should be the work of a professional photographer to give yourself the best chance of acceptance. They should be 8-by-10, black-and-white glossies if the magazine prints only in black and white. Slides are acceptable for those printing in color but the editors will probably ask for black and white also if interested in the project. So have your photographer shoot in color and black and white. He should shoot multiples of the 35mm slides so that you don't have to send dupes or your only originals.

The photos should be labeled with the firm name and the project title but, so as not to damage the prints, either use a separate sheet of paper taped to the back of the print or write on the back with a soft felt pen or grease pencil. Slides can be labeled (clearly) on the mountings.

A brief description of the project—the program, your solution, construction data, and credits—should be provided.

A form used by offices that have their work published regularly follows this outline:
- Name of prime design firm(s)
- Description of project requirements and problems and how the design meets them (e.g., extremely low budget, tight urban site, historical area, quick construction, new construction system, etc.)
- Client.
- Project address.
- Structural and mechanical systems used.
- Square footages, number of floors with square footage breakdown (number of beds for a hospital, rooms for a hotel).
- Total construction cost.
- Date of completion (actual or estimated).
- Consultants' names.
- Designer, project manager, other key personnel.

Consult the magazines you are submitting to for whatever other information is regularly included in their presentations. Some A/Es add such data as site area; cost of site work; parking areas, decks, terraces; dimensions of the structure; occupancy of building; cost of building per occupant; building efficiency; breakdown of costs of land, construction, utilities, furnishings, equipment, decorating, and landscaping; names of main subcontractors. Some editors consider such information essential. Others find it extraneous.

The Magazine's Response
An editor's response to a query may consist of acknowledgement of receipt and word that the project will be used as is for a brief news feature. S/he may ask for more photographs, graphics, and information, or announce that an associate editor or photographer will contact you to gather such material. The editors will try to return promptly any rejected or unused material if you provide a stamped, self-addressed envelope with your submittal. But remember when sending anything irreplaceable that a lot of submissions go through their hands never to be seen again.

Editors have provided suggestions for improving chances of publication. Some valuable points:
- Although you can send queries to a number of editors at once, many editors expect exclusive rights to feature article material. Once you receive an acceptance, consider the project the property of that journal for the time being. This rule applies only to competing journals. Identical material for a new bank, for example, could be submitted and published in a

Remodel projects require "before" as well as "after" photos.

regional real estate publication, a national banking magazine, and an architectural journal simultaneously without offending any of the editors.

• Query photographs need not be of the highest quality but those submitted for publication must be well done (read "professionally done") and preferably strong in contrasts.

• Plans and sections should be black ink or tape. Photostats of pencil drawings are generally too weak to reproduce.

• Editors often receive photographs of remodel projects that would be publishable, except the designer failed to get any "before" pictures. These are mandatory. Construction progress shots are often appreciated.

• Contributing editors, free-lance photographers, and writers who contribute to magazines of interest to you may live in your area. If so, it pays to get in touch with them to learn firsthand of the special interests, needs, and requirements of the publications they work with.

What is publishable? Some editors declare that virtually anything is publishable, at least as a news item, simply because it exists. Beyond this, the criterion stressed repeatedly is the existence of some degree of innovation or problem solving of interest to that segment of the population served by the journal in question.

Structures do not have to be new to be publishable. A design that has shown itself to be a lasting, proven solution to client problems or needs is always of interest. Examples would be a school that adapted well to major changes in learning systems, or a housing project that maintains exceptional occupancy rates over time.

Some high-quality publications are produced solely to advertise certain building products. Some of them will not consider any material not submitted by or through their sales representatives. If a particular project is making good use of a product or construction material, it pays to ask the representative about possible use of the project in the manufacturer's promotional literature.

How to Start a Newsletter

Gerre Jones

One newsletter publisher suggests that the two most basic ingredients of a successful newsletter are gossip and an appeal to greed, adding that the information conveyed must be "useful, fast, and without frills."

He was talking about commercial newsletters, of course—the weekly or monthly publications such as *Professional Marketing Report* that are written, produced, and sold in hopes of profit.

Not a New Format

Newsletters, with their unique journalistic format, began in the sixteenth century to serve commercial, social, and political interests. After a relatively long period of disuse, they came back from obscurity early in this century, primarily to fill in gaps left by business publications and newspapers.

Variations on the newsletter format include mininewspapers (tabloid size or smaller), magazines, special booklets, and updates to a general capabilities brochure on a fairly regular basis.

If you have been considering a newsletter for your firm, this article may help you to make the necessary decisions.

What a Newsletter Can Do

One advantage of a newsletter is its relatively low cost, compared to other types of publications. We'll get into detail on costs a little further on. As a marketing tool, a newsletter is particularly well suited to specialized communication; the rifle, rather than a shotgun, approach.

A newsletter can

• keep open a direct line of communication between a design firm and its clients and prospects. It also serves as a public relations device—showing your concern for and interest in individual clients.

• interpret and analyze important forces at work in the design profession and the construction field, alerting readers to significant developments now and in the future.

• guide reader decisions on what to do, how to do it, when to do it—based on sound, current advice from authorities in the field.

• soft sell. Newsletter experts say that once reader rapport is established, items about a service or a product produce a solid response. But a newsletter should never hard sell or even sell directly—otherwise it becomes an obvious piece of self-serving promotion.

As a marketing tool, a newsletter is particularly well suited to specialized communication.

Starting Up

In the book *How to Produce Professional Design Brochures*, in the chapter on "Supplemental Publications," we pointed out that starting a newsletter closely parallels the customary early steps in designing and producing a new office brochure. Some thought should be given to the publics a firm wants to reach and what the objectives of the newsletter are.

Likely audiences, or publics, to zero in on include:
- past and present clients;
- lost clients;
- prospective clients;
- financial community;
- media;
- staff;
- libraries of nearby professional schools;
- suppliers;
- consultants.

The objectives are usually a little tougher to define. They might include:
- to explain new services offered by your firm;
- to reflect staff changes and added capabilities;
- to aid internal staff morale;
- to serve as a continuing contact (bridge) between your firm and its clients and prospects;
- to reflect your firm's experience and competence through the use of case histories, letters from client, and other means.

The first five audience groups are made up of people who, for the most part, are already bombarded by media messages almost every waking moment. So anything new to be added to their reading load must be good—well above average—to get their attention.

Newsletter Survey

Earlier this year the McArdle Printing Company made a survey of several hundred newsletters published in the Washington, DC, area. Some of the survey results are pertinent to our subject.

Of the 448 newsletter editors or publishers reporting, 86.8 percent used the standard 8½-by-11-inch format. Quantities ranged from a low of 50 copies to a high of 265,000 circulation.

Slightly more than 40 percent of the newsletters gave four as the usual number of pages. Only a fourth of the respondents said that each issue always had the same number of pages—the need usually dictated the number of pages.

Frequency of publication figures looked like this:

weekly	11.7 percent
biweekly	6.5 percent
twice monthly	2.3 percent
monthly	44.1 percent
bimonthly	12.4 percent
other	23.0 percent

Anything new to be added to their reading load must be good to get their attention.

(Some of those reported under "other" are quarterlies, but a surprising number, according to McArdle, are produced on an irregular basis.)

Seven our of ten newsletters covered in the survey are typewritten; about a third are set by photo composition (as is *Professional Marketing Report*), and the remaining 3.5 percent are printed from metal type. Over a fourth of the newsletters are printed in-house.

Color, Paper, Mailing

One color is used by 62 percent; two colors are preferred by 35 percent; and the small remainder use more than two colors. Three out of five newsletter publishers prefer white to colored stock and the same proportion mail the newsletter in an envelope, in contrast to sending it as a self-mailer (no envelope).

Content

Before going much further on this subject, we should mention that the ideal situation is to have two newsletters; a purely internal one for executives, staff members, and their families—and an external newsletter for the other publics we listed above.

Some larger firms do have such twin newsletter publishing ventures, but it is not a practical approach for very small- to medium-size firms. So keep the content of your newsletter as client-oriented and unparochial as possible; otherwise it may be an early casualty to an overload of staff marriages, new babies, photographs of the principals, and bowling league scores.

Of potential interest to outsiders (particularly to lost, past, present, and prospective clients) are items about staff promotions, project case histories, new work, and honors won by principals and staff. Occasional service articles about new trends in design and construction, or a different (money saving) approach to a specific project type, usually get good readership.

Use plenty of photographs, drawings, diagrams, and charts.

Use plenty of photographs, drawings, diagrams, and charts. Such visuals, along with short, active headlines, allow busy executives to grasp the main thoughts more quickly—and help them decide whether or not to take time to read into the text.

For an idea of what others think is important in a newsletter, get copies of some published by other design and construction firms.

Layout and Format Considerations

Referring to the newsletter survey cited earlier, the majority of the respondents put out a monthly four-page newsletter, typewritten or in simulated typewriter type, in one color of ink on white paper.

Two or three columns in a vertical 8½-by-11-inch format are preferred over a single column. There is a long-standing debate as to the optimum width of a line of type for the best legibility. One rule of thumb calls for a line width 1.5 times the point size of the type used; that is, a fifteen-pica width for a ten-point type; eighteen picas for twelve-point type, etc.

Another rule limits the width to the equivalent of 1.5 alphabets of the type used. *Professional Marketing Report* uses a ten-point type (a point is .013837 inch, or approximately ½₂ of an inch), in a twenty-pica column width (a pica is twelve points or .166 inch).

Still another column width rule of thumb suggests ten to twelve words as the maximum in one line for eye comfort, legibility, and comprehension.

Unfortunately, relatively little recent research has been done in this field. One study sometimes quoted was written by M. A. Tinker and D. G. Patterson for the June 1929 *Journal of Applied Psychology*. Almost fifty years ago they determined the optimum line (column) width for ten-point type to be eighty millimeters, or about nineteen picas.

There is no point in getting caught up in such esoteric debates. Use two columns to an 8½-by-11-inch page and set the column width between eighteen and twenty picas, or between three and four inches. Use at least ten-point type, with two points of spacing between lines. Remember that most of your readers will not be nineteen-year-olds with unimpaired twenty-twenty vision.

Format Variations

There is nothing magic about the 8½-by-11-inch vertical format for a newsletter. The Boston Museum of Science *Newsletter* uses the same 11-by-17-inch sheet as for an 8½-by-11, four-page format, but three-folds the paper into six 5¾-by-11-inch pages. A final fold for mailing makes it into a 5¾-inch square. Each page has two fourteen-pica-wide columns, with ragged right margins.

This paragraph is set ragged right for illustration. The normal set for *Professional Marketing Report* is justified both sides or flush right and left—which means that each line of type is spaced out to exactly twenty picas wide, as in most books and newspapers. Tests have shown that most people are not aware of whether the right margin of something they have just read was ragged or justified. Text can also be set ragged left (difficult to read) or in a centered or midline format (each line symmetrically arranged, as in book title pages and some poetry).

Frequency of Publication

Our recommendation is to begin a new newsletter on a quarterly publication basis. Even four pages can get to be difficult to fill with interesting material when the editor is on a part-time basis. Some newsletters use a number instead of a date, avoiding any tie-in with the calendar. (One firm began its newsletter as number 100 to give it an instant publishing history. Luckily no one ever asked for back copies of numbers 1-99.)

Since there is no consideration given by the receiver for the kind of newsletter under discussion, you are not legally bound to maintain any regularity in its publication. There is a certain amount of credibility and reader loyalty to be gained from a regular publication schedule, however—on a monthly or quarterly basis.

The Procedure

Once the news and illustrations for an issue are in hand, the routine steps in publishing a newsletter are:

1. Prepare a dummy (usually a rough dummy).
2. Have type set—or type it on a typewriter.
3. Have photographs made into halftone prints—called Velox prints. Get other artwork reduced to the proper size.
4. Paste all of the elements (type, photos, illustrations) up in their proper position on "mechanical"—illustration boards or heavy paper sheets—ready for the printer.
5. The printer makes paper or metal plates from your "camera-ready" art and runs the job.

Here we are considering only the offset printing process for a newsletter, since that is undoubtedly the way it will be printed.

One other procedural matter is the method of getting the newsletter produced. Some firms opt to have an outside consultant take full responsibility for the job. Others manage to find the right people in-house. Still others use a combination of consultant and in-house staff. If yours is to be a quarterly publication it should not require more than a couple of days a month of some staff member's time.

Perhaps the best initial arrangement is to have a consultant work with the in-house person, doing the layout, editing, preparing mechanicals, and dogging the printer's heels. After the experience of preparing a few issues, the staffer should be able to do most of these things. Since everyone needs an editor, use the consultant or someone competent from your staff to do a final read of all copy before it goes to the printer.

Costs

The expense of a newsletter normally comes out of a firm's marketing budget.

The expense of a newsletter normally comes out of a firm's marketing budget. If the publication is produced entirely in-house, all costs should be identified and charged back to the proper budget item.

If the newsletter is to be photo typeset, with justified (even) right and left column margins, the type will cost around $2 per column inch, or $40 to $50 a page to set. Paper and printing costs for 400 copies will add another $400 to $500.

Mailing the newsletter at first-class postage rates costs 22 cents per piece. If you mail to at least 200 persons you may want to check out third-class bulk-mail costs. Third class requires a special annual $50 permit, the filling out of forms for each mailing, ZIP coding the pieces in order, and delivery of the newsletters to the post office. Cost of third-class bulk mail is 12.5 cents for up to 3.33 ounces, or a theoretical annual saving of $406 if you mail 400 copies each month. The $406 saving will probably be eaten up in internal costs for the handling described above. The average eight-page newsletter will weigh one ounce or less, so the extra weight allowance in third class is not that important.

Totaling up the above costs for typesetting, printing, and postage for a four-page, 400-circulation newsletter gives us a range of $754-$788 for one issue, depending on whether the newsletter goes first or third class—or a unit cost of from $1.90 to $1.97. None of these calculations include time of the inside staff to write, lay out, and mail the newsletter, of course, or the cost of a consultant.

Project Management 8

Project Management: The Third Discipline

Project Management:
The Third Discipline

For the sake of argument let us assume that, once the client has signed the contract, the practice of architecture within an office may be divided into three disciplines. The first discipline is design (including programming and interiors), the second is production (covering all operations to develop the total contract documents), and discipline number three is project management. Office administration (supporting staff, accounting, maintenance, supplies, etc.) is not included as a specifically architectural discipline because it applies to professional offices of all types.

In both large and small architectural offices, the disciplines of design and production are conventionally defined as two distinct departments, comprising personnel with different talents and interests. But project management is still undergoing development in a separate discipline and struggling for equal status with design and production. Of course, there have always been project managers in fact if not necessarily in name, because buildings had to get built. But the definition of title and exact responsibilities to be discharged came much later than those for design and production. Even now, when one mentions the design and production departments a clear picture comes to view, but not so with the project management group—because the latter varies so much in its organization within different offices.

Project Management a Full-time Job

Originally, a project manager might have been a designer or production person simultaneously responsible for managing projects on a catch-as-catch-can basis. In many cases, the person given the dual assignment was hard put to do justice to both roles. In order to relieve design and production personnel of such chores, project management slowly developed into a full-time job involving tremendous responsibilities.

Unfortunately, the project manager became something of a second-class citizen in the office, especially in the very beginning, owing to the "elitism" of designers, which was sometimes tacitly, if not overtly, encouraged by principals in the office. Frequently, the very designers who looked down on the project manager's role were the most dependent on it, and even with a fine set of contract documents could never have got their designs built without the project manager. With time, even the die-hards began to acknowledge the project manager's value, and project managers

Paul W. T. Pippin, AIA

The very designers who looked down on the project manager's role were the most dependent on it.

themselves began to come forward and make their presence felt.

The mission of a project manager can be seen as having three goals:

1. To assist the office in producing the best possible architecture.
2. To help keep the office out of trouble.
3. To make a profit on every job.

In order to realize the above goals, the project manager must first be well trained architecturally and have extensive experience in either design or production. (It is my personal experience that a design background offers more versatile experience for a project manager.) Second, he must organize his daily work and orient the staff assigned to the project so that he reviews all operations and contacts on the job coming into the office, as well as leaving it. The latter procedure is of prime importance and it has tremendous appeal to clients. It also prevents unilateral action by project staff that could not only short-circuit communications and create serious problems within the office but erode the client's confidence as well.

Project Manager Responsibilities

It is only with the assumption of overall control of a project by a single manager that work can move forcefully in a definite policy direction toward a successful conclusion. This can be achieved if the project manager carries out the following responsibilities:

• Prepares the owner-architect contract for the partners' approval.

• Reviews the owner's contract with the general contractor or construction manager if requested to do so by the owner.

• Prepares contracts with consultants for the partners' approval.

• Prepares a master schedule outlining critical deadlines for the architects and consultants during design, production, and construction.

• Prepares the in-house operating budget.

• Schedules regular meetings to coordinate the activities of design and production as they relate to all parties involved. These meetings ought to include weekly in-house coordination meetings with representatives of the owner, architect, consultants, and general contractor or construction manager.

• Attends all major presentations and follows their preparation to make sure they are on schedule.

• Reviews all minutes of meetings before they are distributed.

• Reviews all job progress reports.

• Receives all correspondence on the project directly, routes all communications, and initiates and signs all correspondence.

• Prepares owner's and consultant's billing schedules for the duration of the project.

• Reviews all requisitions, bulletins, change orders, and certificates of payment for approval.

• Permits no extra services or overtime without the owner's approval.

• Reviews and approves all invoices before they are issued.

• Carries out all conditions of the contract.

It is important that all project managers in an office be charged with the same responsibilities and perform them in compliance with policies and procedures set down by the office. There is nothing more confusing and frustrating for an employee, or for a client, than to work with different project managers who operate according to totally different methods. The only way to standardize operating procedures is to have a project management department headed by a general partner. Standard project management operating procedures do not demand hard-and-fast rules, but rather procedures that are applied judiciously in working on different types of buildings with different clients, different in-house staffs, different contractors, or different construction managers. The fact that there is usually no project management department per se in most offices does not preclude the urgent need for such a department. It must also be remembered that there is a subtle difference between managing a project and the operations known as "office practice." Project management means just what it says—the management of a project—not running the office.

How does an office establish the procedures for a project management department? The first step is the development of a manual, prepared by a capable project manager within the firm. This manual would include input from all experienced staff and the official approval of senior members. A series of meetings should then be held to review the material with the project managers as a group and, once this orientation period is over, the project managers should meet monthly to keep the manual realistic and up-to-date. If the office does not have an experienced project manager capable of developing such a manual, a consultant may be invited to conduct seminars, or a selected group might be sent to courses given outside the office.

Even if an office has an organized group of project managers, regardless of how well they have been trained, there is little hope for a truly successful operation unless the principals in the office are equally well informed on their policies and procedures and fully support their implementation. Too often the principals in a large office are too busy, "too important," or too quick to minimize the value of project management to attend orientation sessions or even find out what the process is all about. This is perhaps the greatest problem a project manager has to contend with in his own firm.

Charrettes are a disruptive problem in any office. Diligent project management can greatly reduce the occurrence of expensive and exhausting crash effort by carefully monitoring the project daily, holding weekly in-house meetings with project staff to check that assignments are on schedule, and arranging for assistance exactly when it is needed instead of a day or two before the deadline. Charrettes are frequently brought about by partners who are too busy to follow the job carefully until it has progressed for some time and then attempt to make last-minutes changes that put the project way behind schedule. A strong project manager can overcome this practice in the early stages by having the senior designer assemble all material developed to date for thorough review by a partner.

The only way to standardize operating procedures is to have a project management department headed by a general partner.

Project Managers Are Indispensable

Project managers are indispensable for the successful administration and coordination of team efforts, especially as architects engage more and more consultants for specialized fields of work. The fast-track approach, which involves a series of deadlines to issue bid packages during the actual development of the project, also requires constant supervision and scheduling by the project manager to meet the demanding timetable of the general contractor or construction manager. Punctuality is especially important, now that inflation makes conventional bidding almost prohibitive.

An able project manager can increase the profit of the firm beyond anyone's imagination without sacrificing the quality of architecture or understaffing the project. These goals are accomplished by monthly monitoring of budgets, selective staffing appropriate to each project, assignment of personnel only as required, careful control of expense accounts and nonreimbursable costs, billing clients for extra services not covered in the base fees, and, when possible, investment of accumulated fees in short-term MMCs or Treasury bills until the fees are needed. This last option is especially feasible when the project manager stipulates that if invoices are not paid within the specified deadline a late-payment charge is required.

A growing number of architectural schools are recognizing the importance of project management by offering courses in the subject. The fact that students voluntarily and enthusiastically enroll in such courses, which are usually available only as electives, indicates that they are aware that there is more to architecture than just design. In the future, these courses should be required, not just elected. At any stage of an architectural career, project management procedures are basic to the development of good judgment and decision making according to the particular characteristics of a project.

It can be shown over and over again—in small offices as well as large—that satisfied clients, trouble-free projects, and increased profits can all be realized by a well-structured project management system. The size of the office has absolutely nothing to do with the policies and procedures. The only difference is that in a small office you may be doing the actual work yourself while in a large office you may be directing others to do it. The organization of a project management department in your own office is worth a try. There is nothing to lose and everything to gain.

> **An able project manager can increase the profit of the firm beyond anyone's imagination.**

Project Management:
Planning

Design offices are rushing to new systems and tripping on an old problem. The problem is people: staff and management who cannot or will not plan their work in terms of the final desired product.

How is it possible? A/Es are specifically trained as planners. How could they possibly fail to think ahead while planning their own work? Apparently it's easy. Every month prior to giving a workshop I receive questionnaires from attendees describing their worst problems in the office. The universal complaint comes in many forms: "Drafters don't think ahead." "Designers don't think ahead." "Management doesn't think ahead."

Part of the problem is school. School projects are pieces mistaken for the whole. Architecture students spend months on general design projects and virtually no time on the overall design management, production, and construction process. Thus, to this day, designers create final plans, elevations, etc., that cannot be directly reused by the production department. They have never thought, or been taught, to do anything else. Architects still give to consultants plans that have to be redrawn from scratch. Working drawing drafters produce documents that are overdrawn in obvious trivia and lacking vital construction data needed by contractors. A/E offices still routinely redecide and redraw almost identical design and construction elements month after month in job after job.

A costly mistake for many A/Es these days: counting on systems graphics and computerization to solve the problems. Advanced systems won't work without first solving the preplanning problem. Computer graphics, multicolor offset working drawing printing, overlay and composite drafting—all do wonders, but only for those who know the secret.

The secret: create a clear, complete image or model of the final graphic product and then work backwards to plan out the entire production and design drawing process.

A production plan includes:

• Miniature sketch mock-ups of the sets of design and working drawings. Simple schematics on gridded 8½-by-11-inch sheets are fine.

• Transparency sketch mock-ups showing how base and overlay sheets work together both in drafting and reprographics.

• Checklists and diagrams showing how data on varied drawing sheets relate to one another.

Fred A. Stitt

Drafters produce documents that are overdrawn in obvious trivia.

• Notes and flags to show what portions of the final drawings are paste-ups, photos, standard notes or details, and computer plots.

It's always obvious how a set of construction documents should have been done after they're completed. The redundancies, conflicts, lapses in use of systems, underdrawing, and overdrawing, are fairly obvious by that time. They can be made obvious before they become part of a job by doing the process in miniature.

All this becomes crucial when working with CADD. The potential for chaotic documents is multiplied drastically by the computer. The potential for waste, for loss of documents, for excruciating slowdowns and backtracking—all become multiplied and magnified.

One cautionary note: project mock-ups should be designed and drawn by project managers. If designers and drafters do it, they'll tend to overdraw what's nonessential and underdraw what's important— as they do with the full-sized documents.

The potential for chaotic documents is multiplied drastically by the computer.

Project Management:
Unnecessary Work

Fred A. Stitt

It could be that most of the work time spent in A/E offices is redundant and unnecessary.

Years ago we discovered that 30 percent to 40 percent of design development drawing and working drawing drafting was unnecessary. Now we find a similar picture in office and project management. It appears that much of the problem solving, research, decision making, communications, and similar office processes can be radically changed and virtually eliminated through automation.

Take one example, architectural project research. Be prepared for a shock if you objectively analyze the research that's done on interior spaces during typical architectural projects. The subjects of research, the steps, and the final conclusions are all essentially repeats of what's been done before on all similar projects, no matter who does the design.

The repetition makes sense. There are obvious common requirements or limits when doing offices, restrooms, elevator foyers, etc. What doesn't make sense is that every day of the week thousands of design professionals spend thousands of hours doing thousands of projects, and they're all coming up with the same inevitable conclusions and decisions about the same kinds of rooms.

The conclusions aren't in question. The question is why should all these people keep redoing the same work to get the same results time and again? People research the following decisions for each type of room: floor, wall, and ceiling finishes; fire requirements; acoustical requirements; required lighting, power, and communications; door types, door frame, and hardware; plumbing; fixtures and equipment; HVAC requirements; etc. Economics, codes, tradition, or common sense will dictate either identical decisions or limited ranges of possible decisions in virtually all cases.

Why not maintain office manuals in which all the normal requirements are listed for each room type?

Design Attribute Standards

If the preferred or mandatory choices for finishes, etc., were provided in an office room attributes schedule, most or all that project-by-project research time could be eliminated. The few firms that have established room attributes schedules as part of their office standards have reduced their project design research and decision time by possibly as much as 90 percent as an officewide average.

Design and building attribute standards are found mainly in specialized firms for obvious reasons. Firms that do mostly office spaces, medical buildings, or hotels, for example, create in-house design decision manuals almost automatically in the course of doing their projects. But every office can benefit from the idea whether its building types vary widely or not.

Even if a design firm does dozens of different building types a year, the room types involved won't vary that much. Executive conference rooms, parking garages, and janitor's closets are much the same whether they be in airports, office buildings, hospitals, or hotels. Why not then maintain office manuals in which all the normal requirements or common choices of everything from bases to door key systems are listed for each room type? That way you consolidate reference data that are typically spread out among dozens of different sources.

The commonality of room-type attributes is just one example of redundancy in building design processes, and it illustrates a general principle: the value of creating an office design data base for all aspects of design and documentation. Standard details, standard notation and keynotes, master specifications, standard form letters for proposals, are all well-established time and money savers because they block staff members from repeating the same work time after time in all those areas.

Another special application is management by checklist. Most of the steps in doing a project proposal, planning a presentation, doing a feasibility study or a code search, programming a building, doing working drawings, writing specifications, measuring existing conditions, making field observations, and on and on, can and should be checklisted. That, in effect, automates the process. The decisions as to what steps to take, the best sequence of steps, delegatable tasks, etc., don't have to be rethought on every new job.

How to Create Data Bases

How do A/Es go about creating data base resources such as room attribute schedules and operational checklists?

The documentation starts in the process of doing normal day-to-day project work. That's the painless way to establish a standard detail library, for example. Details have to be drawn anyway, so why not prepare them in such a way that master copies of all new details can be filed and retrieved later for reference and/or direct reuse? That means drawing them on 8½-by-11 sheets with detail file numbers, leaving off project-specific data, and setting up an efficient reference, retrieval, copying, and paste-up system.

The idea of creating a data base in the process of doing routine project work can be applied to creating a room attributes schedule. The research has to be done anyway, room by room, project by project, so just start collecting such information in reusable form. Create a data sheet that lists room attributes and, as such sheets are filled in for each job, they'll form the bases for a later master set of attributes schedules. An added benefit: when information is gathered and documented for potential reuse, staff members tend to give the work some extra care and attention.

Similarly, supervisors can be asked to note their steps of planning,

Systematization and automation mean gathering the best information and procedures, hanging onto them, and improving them with each reuse.

instructions to subordinates, and various steps of action as they go through their project. Such data should be systematically listed as part of job diaries anyway. Usually the steps are listed as they come up, but are not categorized. If you add categories and subcategories of action to your job diaries, such as code search, presentation preparation, etc., after a while most of the normal steps and substeps of project work will be noted on the list. Later that information can be compiled into an officewide project management checklist to guide project planning, instruct staff, assign work, check completed work, and document the project design/production process.

If the time and money aspect weren't enough, creating data base resources is integral to the quality control programs now being initiated by A/E firms everywhere. Systematization and automation mean gathering the best information and procedures, hanging onto them, and improving them with each reuse. Three main benefits result:

1. Original cost of work is cut nearly in half with each reuse of data, graphics, or checklists.

2. Quality and value of the data base is enhanced each time through feedback and refinement.

3. Staff members don't have to wonder what to do and be slowed down because of inadequate data and support.

Project Management:
Preventing Changes

Fred A. Stitt

How can you prevent those excessive last-minute design changes? That's a persistent question we get from A/Es everywhere. Midstream revisions are costly, demoralizing to staff, and they throw schedules to the winds.

Here are some good answers:

• West Coast solar home designer Doug Hayes programs all design decisions in advance. He leaves little opportunity for oversights and last-minute flashes. His central tool is an extensive "dream list" created during a client interview. He covers everything a client might possibly be concerned with—from ceiling heights to finishes to furnishings—before he draws a line. All items are systematically rechecked through design development. By the time production drawings are under way, virtually everything has been decided and confirmed. Late changes are few and incidental.

• Another, much larger Midwest firm also does a systematic, itemized, room-by-room walk-through with clients. Jerry Quebe of Hansen Lind Meyer says: "The system catches those potential later embarrassments, such as finding out there's a filing cabinet in front of a light switch." When HLM completes detailed room layouts, it has the client formally approve them. This checklist approach and systematic programing mean the documents are basically ready to build from at the close of design development. That lets HLM gain direct reuse of design documents as production drawings. Working drawings are off to a flying start, with 20 percent of the work already completed and little chance of later, major changes of mind by the client.

• California designer Lee Ward has a special device that inhibits clients from making arbitrary late changes: a Pert diagram with time and costs recorded as originally estimated for design and production. A copy of the diagram is part of the design service contract. When a client requests revisions after design approval, s/he has to review the Pert diagram with the designer and participate in changing the time and cost budget. This makes the time and cost consequences of design revisions completely clear to the client.

• Sophisticated systems drafting offices say they've beat the design revision problem at both ends. At the front end, composite assembly and overlay techniques make it possible to explore all reasonable design options in minimal time. Instead of drawing and redrawing variations and options, drawing components are physically moved around on paste-up

Midstream revisions are costly, demoralizing to staff, and they throw schedules to the winds.

sheets; completed design studies are printed as reproducibles; and pieces are moved around some more to test other options. Design possibilities have been exhaustively studied by the time the project moves into production drawings. That reduces the chances of later changes. At the other end, if late changes are required, they amount to picking up paste-up pieces and replacing them or changing their locations. That's faster and easier than the usual erasing and redrafting process.

Care during Design

Familiarity breeds blind spots during building design process. Some common results:

• Much time is spent refining surface details that end up out of viewing range when the building is completed. Conversely, some elements given passing design attention (such as penthouses, bulkheads) turn out to be prominent visual features.

• Some carefully proportioned buildings seem strangely distorted, diminished, or out of place when seen in context of overall surroundings. Distant background structures often have an impact not considered by the designer.

• Buildings change character and may look garish from nighttime interior illumination, an effect that wasn't considered in drawings or study models.

Architects Keep Learning

Architects keep learning, find fresh viewpoints that catch trouble spots before they are built in. Some examples:

• An old trick: viewing plans, elevations, and perspectives in a mirror or in reverse prints. If the design isn't symmetrical, the reverse views give a whole new look. Difference is sometimes startling; points for improvement become instantly obvious.

• Elevations and perspectives are sometimes printed on negative paper to bring out previously unseen qualities. For example, when rendered drawings have darkened fenestration in the original, a negative print will show approximate nighttime appearance.

• Details of trim, railings, fenestration, etc., sometimes change relative scale dramatically and reveal problems when blown up to full size. Some offices draw up details, textures, material patterns, on wall-sized sheets for careful study and refinement. Others use opaque optical projectors as a more economical means of achieving near full-size approximations from small sketches.

• Some top design firms put building designs on the site photographically. Method is simple: photographic color slides are taken of the site and later "back projected" onto a matte acetate or translucent polyethylene screen at the office. Study models (or mock-ups of elevations) are placed in front of the rear projection screen and viewed at pedestrian eye level. The setup of model and projected site images is photographed in turn. This permits easy comparison of variations in positioning, proportioning, and color relative to actual site conditions.

Study and presentation models often mislead designers.

• Study and presentation models often mislead designers because of the habit of seeing them at bird's eye level. Details are elusive, even when viewing at simulated ground level. Ten inches is about as close as the eye can get to a small model without distortion. Extra large models are one answer and are used plentifully by a few offices. But this is expensive. A larger number of designers gets inside and up close to small models by using the Modelscope. This is a miniature periscope that brings the observer's vision down to model ground level with model-sized perspective.

The Project Organization

Professional Services Management Journal

In the past year more and more professional services firms have decided to strengthen their project management organization. These firms have realized that the project manager (PM) is the single most important individual in the firm.

The firm does not exist to pay salaries and bonuses to the boss and other top brass. Nor to allow the marketing people to wine and dine potential clients. Nor to permit the financial types to count beans. Nor to give the computer jocks something to program.

The firm exists for only one reason: to solve client problems. And this is done by successfully completing projects. Without this nothing else happens.

Competent project management is vital to the successful completion of the project. Successful completion means: technically solving the problem and thereby enhancing the reputation of the firm (while keeping liability premiums down); satisfying the client and thereby generating repeat business; and finally, making a profit and thereby ensuring the continued existence of the firm.

For this reason, we believe that the professional services firm should be organized around the project and those who complete projects. Yet too often the firm revolves around the boss, or the very complex financial controls, or the rainbow-chasing sales people.

The purpose of this article is to suggest ways to be more project oriented in your firm.

The Project Organization

The centroid of the firm should be the PM who has total responsibility and authority for each project. Everyone in the firm—from president to office boy—exists to support this individual.

The PM has day-to-day control of the project and anyone who works on it. In many cases the actual technical work is directed by a discipline or department head, but the PM approves the department's fee budget and time schedule.

This PM is a competent, experienced professional who is on his way to but has not yet reached the level of senior management. It would not be unusual for the PM to be paid $40,000 per year.

There are a number of advantages to having this strong project manager organization. First, the fact that one individual has complete charge means that key tasks do not fall through the cracks. When more

Everyone in the firm—from president to office boy—exists to support the project manager.

than one individual has responsibility for a project, in reality no one has.

The project manager frees partners and principals for more important tasks, such as making high-level contact with present and potential clients and directing the overall management of the firm. This type of organization can also be a marketing advantage since more and more clients (particularly the federal government) are choosing engineers based on who will really be the project manager. Few clients are naive enough to believe the principal in charge will do more than oversee the project in a general way.

Implementation

Some firms have not organized around the project for a number of reasons. First, they do not have (or feel they do not have) qualified project managers. Most planning and design professionals are not trained in management and therefore are reluctant to leave their familiar technical skills to move into a management position.

Another obstacle is the present organizational structure of the firm, which often prevents the project manager from exerting the necessary authority required to do the job right. Typically, there are a number of discipline or functional departments (such as architectural design, mechanical engineering, soils, and production) where all project work is done. The department heads sometimes will oppose the project manager, feeling they would be cut out if all work is done by the project team under the project manager's direction.

Finally, adopting an entirely new form of organization is a traumatic move. Since most people avoid change even when it will help them, most firms choose to keep the status quo. To develop strong project managers, the firm must start by hiring qualified young professionals who have the potential ability to manage.

Give the project manager more control over the people working on his project

After hiring these potential managers, the firm must pay them well and maintain an atmosphere that will retain this high caliber of professional. For example, employees should be rewarded and promoted solely on their performance and not on how long they have been with the firm.

The firm must have an organized program to develop managerial skills in present and potential project managers. The best training is on the job, where young professionals are gradually exposed to all facets of the strong project manager's job.

Installing the project organization should be done gradually, one step at a time. Firms that try to do it all at once usually fail because the change is too cataclysmic.

The first step is to designate a project manager for each project. This individual should be drawn from the discipline with the most to do with the project, e.g., a sanitary engineer for a treatment plant, and he should be recognized for his management ability.

This individual should be given more and more responsibility for the project. For example, he should get involved in the actual selling of the project, he should be the primary contact with the client, and he should receive regular information on the progress of this project. Eventually, he should be pulled out of his discipline department and put into a project manager group. This will give him visibility and allow him to deal with other departments on an equal basis.

The next step is to give the project manager more control over the people working on his project. Unfortunately, this conflicts with the department heads who are responsible for directing the people working on their portion of the project.

A way to use the project manager in combination with the department organization is the matrix form of organization. Under this system, projects are the reponsibility of project managers who report to a vice president for operations. The technical work is done by professionals who report to a department head.

One drawback to this system is that the technical professional on the project has two masters: the project manager and, for example, the chief of hospital design. Also, there is a fuzzy line separating the responsibilities of the project manager and the department head.

These problems can be overcome if everyone understands the true contribution that each makes to the firm. The project manager's true role is successfully completing the project on time and within a budget while satisfying the client and exerting day-to-day control of the project staff.

The department head's true contribution, on the other hand, is to maintain the firm's excellent reputation for doing quality work. Thus, he is responsible for quality control for his function or discipline, firmwide training in his specialty, and assignment and utilization of his professional staff.

Project Management Training

David Travers

Involve those who are to participate in an improvement program as deeply as is practicable in the planning of it.

No matter how sincere a firm is in its efforts to help and encourage its architects and engineers to improve their professional performance, it is the people themselves who must do it. Development is self-development, and employees at whatever level must willingly accept what is being offered to them for it to be beneficial. I have found that the best way to achieve this acceptance is to involve those who are to participate in an improvement program as deeply as is practicable in the planning of it. This gives the participants a proprietary interest in the program and its success.

I believe this approach to be doubly appropriate for professionals learning about the business aspects of their professions. Architects and engineers are still having difficulty accommodating to the idea that their professions are businesses, too—and highly competitive ones at that. While they may accept operational efficiency in a building as a necessary end product of design, they do not always embrace its application to the design process itself, often considering it an interference, a stultifying constraint, even a threat. Thus, wittingly or not, they may resist it.

Training Objectives

My experience has been that when embarking on any effort to improve the administrative performance of an architect or engineer, best results are achieved if care is taken to assure the professional that the purpose is not just to improve the bottom line on projects or even to open the way for his advancement in the firm. There must be an appeal to his professional as well as personal self-interest. That is, he must feel that learning to manage his projects and people better will make him a better architect or engineer.

The course outline and a clear statement of its objectives should be worked up by top management in collaboration with those who are to participate in the program. In addition to engendering the proprietary interest of the latter, it is vital to get their input to avoid any impression that the program is being imposed unilaterally from above. That top management is taking the initiative is good; that it is impressing its will, no matter how laudable the intent, is not so good.

The program should be tailored to the needs of architectural and engineering project managers generally and to your people specifically. To this end, it should not only be planned in-house, it should be presented by your principals, supplemented by the firm's banker, lawyer, accountant, and clients. The reason for this is that one of the biggest managerial problems in any business is said to be difficulty of inter-managerial communications. A company course attended and taught by a firm's managers and by managers of other businesses which work closely with the firm will help to evolve a common language and mutual understanding which will enable all to work more effectively and productively together.

Course Content

The content of the course should be carefully structured in accordance with the above general observations and caveats and within the limits of what your personnel are ready for and able and willing to absorb. The three major problem areas encountered by project managers in the administration of their projects are (1) project financial control, (2) good client relations, and (3) effective leadership. Most of the particular and individual problems your people may be encountering will fall under one of these three and they should be fully covered in the course.

One important exception would be interference from above and other gripes about top management; you should be prepared for the subject to come up. If one of your project managers has the balls to suggest that it be included formally in the schedule, do so; otherwise let it arise during the series naturally.

Project Financial Control

Good financial control and performance on a project are a matter of attitude and understanding. Assuming your project managers have the responsibility and have been given the authority necessary to bring a project in on time and budget, failure to do so is either attributable to negligence, lack of knowledge, or a combination of these. The content of the course should be directed at instructing managers not just in the "hows" of project financial control, but in the "whys." For best results, the course should probably follow your firm's method with only as much general theory as is necessary to illuminate the principles underlying your system.

Emphasis: avoiding unpleasant surprises through careful project planning, estimating, budgeting, monitoring, accurate reporting, and strict contract administration.

Instructors: principals in the firm drawing on staff specialists as needed.

Time: six hours in two or three sessions.

Client Relations

Most of the client relation problems which arise are due to lack of clear communication between client and consultant, which in turn is due to lack of common understanding and to differences in client- consultant vocabularies and goals. It falls to the A/E firm to take the initiative in breaking down the communication barrier. This again is the reason for involving clients, bankers, lawyers, and accountants in the program. They can provide project managers with a solid and valuable understanding of the problems of development on the client's side of the fence—the true

Good financial control and performance on a project are a matter of attitude and understanding.

costs of building, where the money comes from, and what it is expected to buy. If your architects and engineers can join in a discussion of the cost of a project in relation to equity capital requirements, discounted cash flow, etc., instead of reacting with uncomprehending stares, they will have taken a quantum leap in the client's opinion and confidence.

Emphasis: understanding the goals and problems of the client. The course should cover basic economic theory and practice, including short- and long-range financing, simple interest, return on investment, discounted cash flow, rudiments of the stock market, problems of banker lending on different types of construction, tax implications of building, legal implications, redevelopment and the redeveloper's problems.

Instructors: firm principal moderating all sessions with presentations from your accountants, banker, lawyers, and representative private and public clients.

Time: twelve hours in six meetings.

Leadership

Leadership is subject which fills libraries. I believe, as with client relations, good managerial relations are a matter of mutuality of understanding and clarity of communication. They are also, as with project financial control, a matter of attitude. The program should improve the manager's ability to hear what is being said to him by his subordinates and—just as important—what is unsaid.

Emphasis: listening and hearing; knowing what you want from a subordinate before asking for it; making certain you know what is wanted of you.

Instructor: the most able leader in top management; if your leadership is weak, go outside for someone to moderate.

Time: two hours, one session; follow-up will probably be indicated.

Getting Back on Track

Frank A. Stasiowski

Every firm has projects that get behind schedule or run over budget. Figuring out why is important for preventing similar occurrences next time, but doesn't help current projects. Since no amount of prevention can completely eliminate schedule or budget problems, your firm should develop its own alternative techniques for getting back on track, which every project manager should completely understand.

Based on input obtained from project managers faced with overruns, we have assembled the following suggestions for projects in trouble now.

For Projects behind Schedule

Work overtime. Everyone works overtime, and usually overtime is the first technique used to get back on schedule; but be careful not to consider overtime as a cure-all. One study by a large engineering firm determined that nine hours per day is the most efficient workday and that a firm receives only 10 percent productivity from the tenth hour and beyond. If you work overtime, use Saturday and Sunday instead of working until midnight for better productivity.

Change work assignments. The causes of schedule problems may include the inappropriate assignment of tasks to people. Not only may staff be in over their heads, but they may not be receiving adequate instruction on specific tasks. Reassigning individuals can provide new blood with fresh drive to take over the problem of getting back on track.

Temporary help. Each firm should maintain a list of permanent temporary help which includes retired employees, former staff who could work a second shift, and students. Having a permanent list assures that each temp hired will know your firm, and be immediately productive when hired.

Use principals. Putting principals to work on the boards can take advantage of available expertise which generally charges time to your project anyway. Also, an experienced professional may accomplish in one hour what an inexperienced technician does in five.

Reassess contingencies. If your schedule has unrealistic contingencies built in because you have assigned a 10 percent contingency factor to each task, you may actually be on schedule but not know it. Examine your schedule progress task by task to measure past and future requirements.

Involve the client. Instead of immediately asking for an extension,

Putting principals to work "on the boards" can take advantage of available expertise.

suggest five or ten ways in which the client could help you to achieve the target date including the use of client staff to perform certain tasks.

Reorganize drawings. Conduct a planning meeting with consultants, drafting help, a representative from your blueprint company, and your word processing operator to talk about how to produce the required construction documents using less sheets and less information on each sheet (especially elaborate details). Also, seek to implement more reprographic techniques such as photocopying details or entire sections of a drawing. Eliminate hand lettering notes where possible.

Eliminate excess perfection. Most design decisions are 95 percent perfect the first time around, and we then spend whatever time is left making them 2 percent better. Closely examine your project to stop further research into alternatives, and get on with document production.

Do performance specifications. Instead of completely writing the specification, require contractors to submit material specifications for your approval. Be certain before using this technique that you determine your firm's professional liability status, and your contract with the owner.

Ask the client for an extension. This is last on our list. Clients don't like firms that can't perform on time, especially if financing is contingent upon your performance. Therefore, our rule is to quickly attempt all of the above, and if unsuccessful, directly confront the client with your request.

For Budget Overruns

Examine the figures. Before making any changes, be sure that you are really over budget. Check all charges of time and expense to your project. Ask your financial manager for a current assessment of your overhead charges to be certain that all charging to your project is exactly what was planned when it was budgeted.

Use higher paid staff. Instead of just putting lower paid people on a project, consider the efficiency of whoever you charge. Some more expensive people are more efficient than less expensive technicians.

Shorten the project schedule and work overtime. Since overtime hours generally do not carry the same overhead factor as regularly charged hours, they are more profitable to the firm (varies depending on how you calculate your overhead rate). Also shorter schedules require more succinct decisions which can't be revoked.

Renegotiate subcontracts. If the total budget is behind, perhaps aspects of the problem were caused by other consultants. If so, you may have complete justification for contract renegotiation. Also, if certain tasks will not be needed which were part of the original scope of a sub-consultant's contract, eliminating them may save a project budget gone astray.

Get paid for changes in scope. If your budget is running over because you have performed scope changes without identifying them and charging for them, immediately build a piece-by-piece case for getting paid for each change. Don't wait until a project is finished to collect for changes, and always account for changes using separate project subnumbers or other forms of identification.

Use temporary help. The firm can save the payment of some fringe

Most design decisions are 95 percent perfect the first time.

benefits by using temporary help. At current figures of 35 percent of direct labor, a considerable budget savings could be derived *if* the temporary help is immediately productive on a project.

Be a squeaky wheel. If your project is overbudget, don't hide it. By informing everyone in the firm that you are in trouble, people (like principals) who might otherwise charge a random hour to your project will think twice. Even if this activity saves you one hour per month on your budget, it may be the difference between profit and loss.

Ask for a budget or fee increase. If circumstances have changed, don't be afraid to go back and ask for more. Even if a client says no, you have at least informed the client that you are closely watching changes which could prohibit the client from calling with nickel and dime changes henceforth. Also, you just might get what you ask for if it's legitimate.

Finally, it is important to realize that schedule and budget are completely independent of one another, and that a project may be ahead of schedule, and behind budget, or vice versa. An independent assessment of budget and schedule performance is critical to project success and client satisfaction. Therefore, use these eighteen tips as a starting point from which to build your firm's policies when projects are off track.

An independent assessment of budget and schedule performance is critical to project success.

Production Management

Production Management

Concerned about office productivity? IBM and other corporate giants have people who spend their working lifetimes studying the subject, and they've learned some vital lessons that apply to all of us.

Try these observations from Clair F. Vough, who spent ten years enhancing IBM employee productivity.

"The most crucial single thing that motivates people to greater productivity is a three-letter word—PAY.

"Our greatest productivity gains have been achieved not by doing more work, but by eliminating unnecessary work. Our productivity has been increased far more by good use of minds than by speedup of hands."

Vough established measuring and monitoring systems at IBM to gauge productivity improvements and insure that people were directly rewarded for their innovation and productivity. They were especially rewarded for reducing or eliminating their jobs. That's where productivity enhancement systems usually break down. What employee would want to be increasingly productive without direct reward or to be so innovative as to innovate himself out of a job?

Vough lays it out: "By setting our sights on higher productivity, we are asking people to turn out more goods in less time. If possible, we'd like last year's forty hours of production to be turned out next year in thirty hours. Better still, we'd like every producer to think up ways of eliminating his work altogether—and we've had people gladly and ingeniously do just that....But there's only one way we can ask people to strive toward that goal. They must be absolutely assured that by eliminating their work they are not eliminating themselves—or anyone else. They must know, without doubt, that elimination of work will bring not a penalty but a reward."

Work Simplification

The first step was to bring every worker and supervisor through a course in work simplification. The training in job innovation and improvement taught employees to follow these four steps, as enumerated by Vough:

1. Record all details of your job. Use diagrams and flow charts to show the movement, the progressive steps and processes of your work. For many, this step leads directly to instant improvement.

2. Pick a problem in doing your job that you'd like to solve. Examples: bottlenecks, wasted motions, poor sequence of operations,

Fred A. Stitt

Our greatest productivity gains have been achieved by eliminating unnecessary work

inadequate reference data, inconvenient work station.

3. Question the problem situation with an open mind. Write lists of questions and lists of possible answers about every detail of the problem situation. In recording each detail, ask what, where, when, who, how—and above all, why.

4. Develop an improvement. You may achieve an improvement by simplifying the steps, combining the steps, changing the sequence of the steps, or best of all, eliminating the steps altogether.

To implement the four steps, employees draw their work functions as flow charts. These charts show what precedes each task and what follows it. Many office tasks, while brief in themselves, require many steps of preparation. More than the task itself, often it's the preparation that has timesaving potential. And sometimes it's the follow-up auxiliary work that has opportunity for streamlining.

Since employees are given responsibility for their own productions, they have to take on managerial-level problem solving. To prepare them, the IBM system includes training in creative problem-solving techniques such as brainstorming. For training exercises, officewide problems are brought up for employee consideration, such as this one as expressed by Vough:

"Each piece of paper creates work, often spawning dozens of other pieces of paper. For example, what happens as a consequence of an order to buy a certain material? It may lead to freight bills, inspection reports, test records, an invoice from the vendor, an account payable, an approval to pay, and a check to the vendor. Is all that paperwork really necessary to keep a business going? What needs really must be served, and how can they be served with the fewest pieces of paper and in the least time?"

Many firms have pursued such inquiries, incidentally, to discover that procedures and job roles people had followed for years served no useful purpose.

Japanese Management

Vough's methods correspond to the spectacularly successful techniques of modern Japanese management. It's still not well known, but so-called "Japanese management" was invented by an American, Dr. W. Edwards Deming. Deming introduced his productivity and quality control systems to Japan when he served with the occupation administration under General MacArthur. The war-devastated Japanese business community first adopted the Deming System as a desperate experiment. It succeeded beyond anyone's wildest expectations and is now being exported to the United States.

The Deming System is based on the radical premise that the employees know more about doing their jobs than the bosses do. A corollary is that the best way to improve production and quality is through constant measurement and statistical analysis. In the Deming System dominant in Japan today, the employees are responsible for most of the statistical analysis, task planning and assignments, and production problem solving information is needed and how to get it. If there is disagreement,

Japanese supervisors don't tell workers how to do their jobs, they ask them.

the differences are resolved by gathering more data and/or further analysis, not by argument.

Japanese employees have the option of joining "quality circles." These are groups of from five to twenty-five workers who meet regularly to discuss methods for improving production and services. In some companies, even laborers and janitors have circles. As in the IBM system, people never lose their jobs for eliminating inefficient work; instead they're rewarded with new jobs and bonuses.

Japanese supervisors don't tell workers how to do their jobs, they ask them. And they ask what management can do to help. Meetings between staff and management are devoted to factual analysis of problems, not to exchanges of opinion. If there isn't enough factual information for participants to reach agreement on important actions, then the participants identify what information is needed and how to get it. If there is disagreement, the differences are resolved by gathering more data and/or further analysis, not by argument.

Westerners have mistaken the Japanese approach to disagreement as a face-saving oriental consensus system. It's actually a method of objectifying and clarifying problem situations. If there's disagreement, it's a signal that all the facts aren't in yet. In non-Deming style management, a manager with power over others can force opinions through regardless of factual merit.

U.S. firms that are now coming under Japanese management report sharp reductions in work backlogs, dramatically improved quality control, and employee-generated time- and money-saving innovations applied to all work functions. American management is seeing the light and getting up-to-date with the source—the American who many Japanese believe saved their nation—Dr. W. Edwards Deming.

Simple Remedies

You don't have to await radical changes such as the Deming System to help employees improve productivity. A Lou Harris survey in the late 1970s found that 74 percent of white-collar employees are hamstrung by easily correctable working conditions.

The most common and troublesome barriers to getting work done, according to employees surveyed:
- Inadequate instructions for work assignments.
- Poor lighting.
- Inadequate conversational privacy.
- Inadequate work surface space and storage.
- Poor access to other areas and departments.
- Lack of convenient access to tools, equipment, and materials.

These simple items hamstring workers at every turn. They start tasks with tight deadlines and then discover management is playing hide-and-seek with vital information and tools. They make errors and redo work because of bad communication, lighting, or improper work tools. The pace of work is stop-and-go, with little chance to get up momentum because of inadequate work space and too many distractions and interrup-

Bosses who seek to change the work place get on the wrong track. They consult everyone but the workers.

tions from others.

If typical work places are that bad, why doesn't management change them? Mainly because of the dominant problem: communication. In the Harris survey, 63 percent of the executives thought employee satisfaction had improved over the previous five years. Seventy percent of the employees said otherwise.

Even bosses who seek to change the work place get on the wrong track. They consult everyone but the workers and decide that remodeling and refurbishing will enhance working conditions. The employees disagree once again. They say they don't mind amenities, but what they need most are the items listed in the survey: adequate work space, some privacy, and easy access to the people, good tools, and proper materials necessary to do their job.

For more on how to improve productivity on all levels, read:

• *In Search of Excellence*, by Thomas J. Peters and Robert H. Waterman, Jr. Published by Harper and Row, 1982, hardback $19.95. Subtitled "Lessons from America's Best Run Companies," this book is loaded with managerial insights of value to any design professional who wants to run a first-rate office.

• *Productivity: A Practical Program for Improving Efficiency*, by Clair F. Vough and Bernard Asuell. Published by the American Management Association (AMACOM) in 1979 for $15.95. The book is hard to get now but may be in your city business branch library or it can be ordered through bookstore book-finding services.

• *On the Deming System: Quality Circles, Changing Images of People at Work*, by William L. Mohr and Harriet Mohr. Addison Wesley publisher, 1983, $27.25.

• *Putting Quality Circles to Work, A Practical Strategy for Boosting Productivity and Profits*, by Ralph Barra. McGraw-Hill, 1983, $19.95.

Overlay Drafting, Nice and Easy

Fred A. Stitt

Everyone has done overlay drafting whether they know it or not. Any time you have laid paper over an existing drawing, either for tracing or to pursue a design process, you have done overlay. Contemporary pin register overlay drafting just elaborates on that process, formalizes it, and at the same time generates some remarkable graphic and coordination benefits.

The benefits include:

1. The opportunity to test out more solutions to plan and design problems and to show more options in presentation drawings, without spending extra time on the process.

2. A big reduction in repetitive drafting even for small building projects.

3. Much improved consistency between drawings produced by architects and those done by consulting engineers.

4. The chance to use special printing techniques that sharply differentiate and clarify different kinds of information on the drawings. For example, you can print the walls of your floor plan as a subdued, "screened" background-dotted image while the feature data of that drawing appears in contrasting bold solid line. Or, you can unmistakably differentiate two or more kinds of data by printing drawings in different color inks with offset printing.

That's an important array of potential benefits. But they don't come without some problems. You may have heard about, or experienced, some of the overlay drafting problems: confusing numbers and combinations of base and overlay sheets, complex and costly reproduction processes, resistance by consulting engineers and their staffs. Without dealing with these issues in detail right now, let's just say that all these problems had specific causes and they've all been taken care of.

Essential Components

The essential components of the overlay drafting process are the base sheet and the overlay sheet. The base sheet is a print, on polyester film, of repetitive data. For example, a floor plan, used as background for a number of different engineering drawings, is repetitive. Instead of having different drafters redraw the plan as part of their work, the plan is turned into base sheets by making multiple copies onto clear sepia line "slick" films. Drafters get ready-made copies instead of having to redraw them.

The plan is turned into base sheets by making multiple copies onto clear sepia line "slick" films.

The overlay sheet is an original drawing. The base sheet laid on the drafting board is a copy, acting as what we call a "constant" of reference data. The overlay will contain the unique, or variable information, such as electrical, plumbing, and HVAC systems.

Both base and overlay sheets have to remain consistently stable in size relative to one another. To assure stability, we use polyester (Mylar) for both the printed base sheets and the drafting overlays. Polyester will not stretch or shrink as tracing or print paper does.

Since the image drawn on the overlay sheet has to remain stable relative to the base sheet, both sheets have to be kept in precise registration with each other during drafting and printing. For that we use prepunched holes across the top of each sheet and pin bars that match the punched holes. The pin bar keeps base and overlay in registration in a very direct physical way, independent of visual alignment and registration.

The one-on-one base sheet and overlay sheet relationship is fairly straightforward. So where's the complexity people complain about? Mainly in the job planning and printing processes. Although you only deal with one base sheet copy and one original overlay in the drafting process, you may have to combine three, four, or more different sheets when making a single print. For example, a final print of electrical work may involve the floor plan, a separate "format sheet" with title block and border, the reflected ceiling plan as an intermediate overlay sheet, and an electric power drawing as the final overlay in the print sandwich. Multiply that multisheet complexity in printing by several dozen or several hundred times and you can see the potential for mix-ups, time lags, lost sheet, and high repro costs.

We're now going to review several uses and phases of overlay work, from the simple to the complex. We will lay out the fundamental steps of overlay, one by one, and in the process name the major "dos and don'ts".

The First Step: Overlay in Design Drawings

The key to efficient overlay drafting management is the concept of "stop points." For example, if you're doing rendered presentation drawings of plans and elevations, you stop work on the drawings before doing any rendering. Stop work and then proceed with overlays for all the rendered titles, shades, shadows, furniture, etc. That way, when you later proceed with the project, you can reuse the uncluttered original base sheet directly in working drawings.

The question always arises: why not just make copies of the plans and elevations as backgrounds, and then do your renderings directly on those? In some cases that will work fine. But often there will be some changes in the original work, or a need to show options and variations. When you make changes, you will have to revise both the rendered drawings and the original—double the work. If you show options and variations, you will have to make even more changes on even more drawings every time there's a change in the original concept. When using the base-overlay system, you reduce the total number of hand-drawn changes that have to be made in any revision situation. Revisions are made once, on an original base, and further copies are made through printing processes instead of hand drawing. That eliminates the errors and discontinuities that are likely to creep in when people copy by hand.

The Next Step: Stop Points for Consultants' Base Sheets

After design development and presentation drawings are completed, architectural floor plans are firmed up for use by consultants. That means the floor plans are completed only up to a limited point, where they contain only information of common use by both architect and engineers. That means the plans do not yet have strictly architectural notation, door symbols, window symbols, finish schedule symbols, interior dimensions, etc. All that architectural data is reserved for the architectural overlays.

Plans are brought to a partial state of completion without the strictly architectural data and then copies for use as base sheets by consultants and architectural drafters. This top point of completion excludes data not important to the engineers and includes data that is. For example, the plans show door swings because that's important to electrical consultants for coordinating their light switches. But they don't include door schedule reference symbols because that information is not needed by the consultant.

The floor plans will include restroom fixtures, drinking fountains, hose bibbs, slop sinks, floor drains, fire hose cabinets, plumbing chases and access, structural elements, etc., for the plumbing consultants' drafters. Reflected ceiling plans will show sprinkler heads when set by the architect for design reasons.

For the mechanical engineers, plans will include shafts, equipment to be vented, door swings, mechanical equipment, mechanical equipment bases and curbs (built-in and not part of the mechanical contract), changes in floor and ceiling levels, and structural elements. Reflected ceiling plans will show changes in ceiling levels and outlines of mechanical fixtures and equipment.

The key to efficient overlay drafting management is the concept of "stop points."

Besides door swings, plans for electrical consultants will show locations of electric closets and panels, shafts and chases for electric and communications wiring risers, electrically powered equipment (such as clocks, automatic doors, fans, etc.), special light fixtures (such as for fire exits), concealed lighting, fixtures, switches, and outlets that are specifically located by the architect for design or planning reasons. Reflected ceiling plans show fixtures, access panels, hanging electric fixtures and equipment, etc.

Structural work is a special case. All the other engineering disciplines require the same basic data as that listed above, but the structural work precedes and underlies most of the other items. So at first structural drafters get very rudimentary base sheet data: mainly basic building dimensions, foundation outline, and structural grid. Base and overlay coordination comes into play a little later as architect and structural engineer coordinate locations and sizes of slab openings and depressions, raised floors, curbs, stairs, elevator shafts, drains, etc.

Beyond the Stop Points: Base and Overlay Coordination

Just as the consultants' drafting staffs receive copies of the original floor plan brought up to the stopping points just described, so do the architectural drafting staff. They continue adding the unique architectural data on their overlays: finish schedule keys, door and window schedule keys, detail and section bubbles, interior and exterior dimensions, fire walls, material indications, cabinets, built-in furniture, wall-mounted panels, shelves, etc.

The question often arises as to whether room names should be on the base sheet or on an intermediate overlay. The argument for the overlay separation is that room names might overlap and conflict with consultants' drafting. In general, we favor including room names on the base sheets. It is "constant" data of use to consultants, and since all base data will be screened and subdued in final printing, it won't matter if there are overlaps. Hard line data by the consultants will stand out clearly even if drawn or lettered over base sheet notes or titles. For that reason it's not a major problem if architectural drafters add more information than is strictly needed for the engineers' base sheet stop points. It's very desirable to hold to the stop points, of course, but you do have some hedge factor because of screening if someone goes a little too far in original base sheet drafting.

Inevitably, as working drawings proceed, there will be revisions in the architectural plans that affect the work of the consultants. Most changes will be minor and won't require a new submittal of revised base sheets. Information about changes is sent to all drafters via memo and marked check prints, or by prints of revised portions of the plan to be used as slip sheets under the base sheets. The revised area of building is slipped beneath base sheets, and if that affects the drafter's work, he or she can make the necessary changes. If it doesn't affect the work, then nothing more needs to be done.

After a while enough changes may accumulate to make it necessary to send out new base sheets to everyone. At this point it's mandatory that all currently used base sheets be returned, logged in as returned, and destroyed. If there's no record and control of base sheets, it's inevitable that drafters will accidentally use a rescinded one and be working over obsolete information. Although the coding and tracking of base and overlay sheets are management functions, everyone on a project should be responsible for guarding against such hazards as obsolete base sheets.

If there's no record and control of base sheets, it's inevitable that drafters will accidentally use a rescinded one.

Systems Drafting and Graphics

"I feel like we've been drawing on stone slabs with berry juice." That was one architect's response to a recent systems drafting workshop. It's an understandable response. Some firms have advanced so much in just the past couple of years that traditional offices seem a generation behind by comparison. Even newcomers to systems technology report startling results as they try new methods. Here are some examples described by participants in my lectures and at the University of Wisconsin extension's annual conferences on drawing production:

• A Phoenix architectural and engineering firm budgeted 2,400 drafting hours on a county government building project and finished in 1,300 hours. That was its first all-out systems job—using keynoting, typewritten notes, and composite and overlay drafting.

• A Connecticut architect scheduled 1,600 hours to produce a nursing home, but wrapped it up in 900 hours. The systems approach used: mainly paste-up and overlay, using an in-house vacuum frame.

• A two-person firm in Ohio estimated three months' production time on a housing project and finished in less than six weeks. The firm used a systems approach centering on paste-up, using a vacuum frame. Concerning a similar project that followed, the architect said, "It was so easy, I almost felt embarrassed to accept the fee."

What's the magic behind these spectacular improvements? It's all wrapped up in one concept: reusability. Most of what we create is reusable in one way or another. And most of what we do is, in one way or another, a repeat of what we've done before.

Take drafting as an example. All drafting is repeat drafting. All drafting is the recreation of information that already exists. Every note, every title, every north arrow, every door swing, every line has been drawn before and will be drawn again by thousands of designers and drafters. The problem has been one of how to store and retrieve all that original data if it is reusable, instead of re-creating it from scratch.

Now we have solutions to that problem. Effective solutions. Low-cost solutions. Much more so even than when I first wrote the book *Systems Drafting*.

The Necessity for Change

Let's look at the situation on another level. Look in on a typical drafting room and you're likely to see the following kinds of events:

1. A building designer has just gotten the go-ahead from the client to

Fred A. Stitt

A Phoenix architectural and engineering firm budgeted 2,400 drafting hours and finished in 1,300 hours.

proceed and pass a project on to working drawings. So the designer hands over design development drawings showing the site plan, floor plans, elevations, and a couple of cross sections. The production team will now take those plans, elevations, etc., and, no matter how accurate the originals are, redraw them from scratch. Why? Because the originals are covered top to bottom with rendering entourage: furniture, oversized titles, shades, shadows, textures, and all the other images used for presentation drawings. Those drawings could have been reused directly in working drawings, but they weren't made with that in mind, and so they can't be. They have to be redrawn.

In contrast, many offices now routinely begin their working drawings as a continuation of design development drawings. They don't start over, and, thus, when they begin production, they're already automatically 20 percent finished. That's a big head start that can mean the difference between success and failure on a job.

2. During the development of detail drawings and schedules, it becomes obvious that the sheets haven't been well planned. Information has to be moved, a detail moved over, a schedule inserted, other details erased.

Instead of picking up a detail drawing that has to be moved and moving it, the drafter has to make a print, erase the original, and then trace and redraw the detail in its new location. The same is true with the schedules to be moved. They were redrawn from other samples to begin with. Now they're erased. Then they're redrawn in new places on the drawing sheets. It's absolute madness.

3. And it goes on. A designer is a little rushed and doesn't check the latest zoning restrictions, so the building drawn on the site plan has to be moved over five feet. Instead of picking up the building and moving it, which would be the sensible way of making the change, the designer erases it and redraws it in the new position. And later, because of the need to widen a service driveway, it will be erased and redrawn again.

4. The redrawing disease is spread onward from architect to engineer. The architects may have created perfectly good plans and sections for the engineers. But the engineers' drafting staffs receive prints which they have to copy. They redraw the building from scratch and, likely as not, misdraw it in the process.

The engineers' drafting staffs have to redraw the building from scratch and, likely as not, misdraw it in the process.

Those were the kinds of things that confronted me when I first entered the drafting room twenty years ago. And they're still more common than not. The nation is changing to systems, but most design firms subject their staffs to exactly that same level of plodding, tedious, erase-and-redraw process. And if anyone wonders why design professionals, architects in particular, are so poorly paid, you can begin to glimpse the answer.

It was this kind of experience and observation that drove me into research and education. It was clear that the profession I loved was in trouble and dearly needed some help.

It All Adds Up

Bosses of architecture and engineering firms have argued: "Sure you can save a few minutes here or there, but it's a whole lot of trouble to do it. And what difference does it make anyway?"

I had that very statement thrown at me by a semiretired architect-engineer. He runs a part-time practice in Berkeley—pretty much a one-man show, as it always has been throughout his working life.

I was visiting and poking through his files at random while he was working on some wall sections. I noticed that the sections he was doing now were identical to others in previous drawings. So I showed these drawings to him and said, "You've been drawing the same wall sections for years. Why don't you set up a standards system so you can just reuse them directly?"

No one appreciates unsolicited advice, and he was no exception. He exploded: "Just can it, Stitt. I know all about your bloody systems. I know I could save a few minutes on these jobs, but what the hell difference does it make?"

I didn't quite know how to answer at the moment because of the magnitude of the real answer. The truth is that those who go to the fuss required to start "saving a few minutes" start to salvage 5 percent, then 10 percent, then up to 30 and 40 percent of time and cost over traditional drafting. I don't make up these numbers, it's the constant story I get everywhere from people who have gone the whole route. It shows there's always been that much fat in the traditional pencil-pushing process.

So "what difference" a few minutes makes in this case is that we have a fellow who has been pushing a pencil for thirty years. Ten years of that time could have been spent doing a third more work to augment income, or traveling, or pursuing self-improvement, leisure, or what have you. Ten years! That's the difference "a few minutes" can make over the years.

And, in truth, a large part of the impressive long-term time and money savings of systematic procedures is bound up in what may seem to be trivial little time-savers. Shaving a few seconds here and there on a drafting operation or design drawing won't seem like much. But if that operation is repeated many times, day in and day out, by a drafting room full of people, the total time involved is significant after all.

Slightly over 17 hours per drawing were required for a recent $6.5 million multi-school project.

Examples of Time and Cost Saving

Here are some more specific cases, all publicly stated by architects and engineers at various systems workshops and lectures:

• A housing architect tells of completing fifty-four drawings for a sixty-unit project in three and one-half weeks with two staff members. Another reports doing permit drawings for 1,800 units—five towers—in ten days with seven people. Reuse of design drawings, translucent paste-up techniques, overlay drawings, and in-house vacuum frame contact printers are credited for the extraordinary work flow.

• It took an average of 10.8 work hours per drawing for a custom condominium project, according to Ronald Fash of Rapp Fash Sundin, Inc., of Galveston, Texas. The 24-by-36-inch drawings would take from thirty to forty hours using traditional methods, according to Mr. Fash.

• Slightly over seventeen hours per drawing were required for a recent $6.5 million multischool project, according to Michael Goodwin of Tempe, Arizona. Architectural drawings were completed by one project architect and a drafting assistant. The main time-savers included intensive production planning, typewriting and keynoting of all notation, plus applique drafting and photo composite paste-up and overlay drafting.

• Forty-five architectural drawings for a medical facility were finished in 900 work hours—less than twenty hours per sheet—at the office of Ronald T. Aday, Inc., in Pasadena, California. The firm estimated that normal drafting time without using systems would have been typically thirty-five to forty hours per sheet.

• "Around 38 percent savings" was the estimate by Ed Powers of Gresham, Smith and Partners in Nashville. Besides extensive use of composite and overlay drafting, they've created a comprehensive detail file. With the file they can produce composite detail sheets in about twenty hours for institutional buildings for which detail sheets used to require 100 hours.

• A 1978 General Services Administration cost comparison study suggests even greater savings. A value management study of alternative methods of producing drawings for a $2.5-million alterations and restoration job concluded that traditional drafting and materials would cost $34,320, paste-up drafting would cost $15,190, and overlay drafting would cost $13,226. (The third figure includes $2,754 in materials and repro costs as opposed to $120 in materials and printing costs for the traditional method.)

Some firms tell us they've made no major reductions in project time. But they do much more work within traditional time frames— more design, more refinements, more detail studies, etc. Many firms now achieve both—more work and faster delivery. The owner of one medium-sized firm, using paste-up and overlay techniques, can now produce four complete 24-by-30-inch presentation drawings in three hours. He says the graphic techniques, plus tight financial management, have more than tripled their annual profit margin.

These are all signs of a new production revolution. And it's not just in drafting. There have been major changes lately in every aspect of the design professions. It's a whole new game in marketing, financial management, quality control, corporate organization, and real estate development, to name a few.

New techniques require new data. That means education. Education for designers, drafters, and managers at all levels. So architects and engineers are heading "back to school" in droves. Their schools aren't like the old ones: they include resort retreats, hotels, and drafting "laboratories." The classes range from high-priced professional seminars to informal, brown bag, lunchtime "professional development" courses for office staff and management. Many architectural and engineering firms hire professional educators and turn their studios into classrooms for day-long training sessions and "motivators" on everything from project management to creative problem solving.

Teaching materials are as varied as the topics: packaged slide

He says the graphic techniques, plus tight financial management, have more than tripled their annual profit margin.

shows, tape cassettes for both office use and "learning while driving" correspondence courses. And coming up of course: videotapes and disks and computerized programmed teaching. More on how all this works will be presented in the next article.

Educating Yourself and Staff Members in Systems

Why bother with systems is an oft-pondered question by architects and engineers. Many professionals view the implementation of systems as too bothersome to allot time for training personnel in the use of new techniques or they feel that changing methods would disrupt office production and morale. Others view systems as being too expensive, requiring a large outlay of dollars for new equipment and materials.

There is an element of fact in all the above reasons for not implementing systems. Introducing systems and training of personnel does require time, can be disruptive to present office procedures and will require an expenditure of dollars for new materials and equipment. However, the transition can be smooth and profitable to the firm that makes a full commitment to changing present methods and carefully plans each step for implementing the system.

The transition can be smooth and profitable to the firm that makes a full commitment.

Fully 75 percent of the A/E firms nationwide and approximately 40 percent of those in Canada have had some exposure through seminars, workshops, or books and manuals on the subject of overlay drafting. Other firms have experienced exposure to techniques such as cut and paste and photodrafting. But according to a survey conducted by the Photo Products Division of E. I. DuPont de Nemours Corporation of Wilmington, Delaware, only about 12 percent of all A/E firms are actually using systems officewide; others are using it only on select projects.

The Payoff

Systems is paying off for offices which are using it extensively. Professionals have found that costs and errors have been reduced and many have discovered an added bonus—systems has provided them with a new marketing tool....Systems is being used by progressive firms as a means of securing new clients.

The time saved in the construction documents phase can be given to the design phase.

Another bonus for professionals who are applying systems has been that the transition to computer-aided drafting and design was simplified. Firms which have not used systems drafting techniques such as overlay, cut and paste, photodrafting and keynoting with standard details, word processing, and other automated systems have found the changeover to interactive graphics time-consuming and, in some cases, a failure. The discipline that is required for personnel to plan and create drawings using systems drafting prepares a firm for CADD.

Architects and engineers who have not progressed to CADD but who are applying systems know that the longer a job is on the boards the smaller the profit. Working drawings must be produced in the shortest time possible to ensure a profitable commission. The time saved in the construction documents phase can be given to the design phase. Systems drafting shortens the time required to produce working drawings to about

30 percent of the total project budget. Gresham, Smith and Partners has revised the standard AIA breakdown of phase billing percentages due to new drafting production techniques employed by the firm which tend to cause more work to be done in schematic and design development phases. The revised breakdown is:

Phase	Standard AIA	Revised
Schematics	15%	20%
Design development	20%	25%
Working drawing/specs	40%	30%
Bidding/negotiation	5%	5%
Construction administration	20%	20%

This revised breakdown of percentages, if implemented, can have a decided impact on cash flow and profitability. Systems drafting allows a firm to do a better job for the client while at the same time improving the firm's financial base. Another bonus for the firm using systems.

To further substantiate the fact that systems does working drawing production time, let's consider a report furnished to top management of Gresham, Smith and Partners which clearly indicates the time required for UNIGRAFS or systems produced drawings versus conventional drafting on past hospital projects. The projects are relatively equal in size, cost, and number of beds. (Cost differences reflect cost of labor and materials, seismic requirements, and inflation for different locations and year built.)

The evidence that systems pay is clearly shown in the above figures. Renovation and addition projects can produce even greater savings because existing drawings readily become part of the new set. (Existing drawing sheets are photographically made into base sheets for new construction.) This is indicated by the difference in time required to produce Chippenham versus North Florida Regional Hospitals.

During the next decade, offices who develop an action plan for implementing systems which produces a stable chemistry of people, procedures, and equipment will increase in size and profitability. Those who do not plan and adopt new methods stand a good chance of not surviving through the decade.

Gresham, Smith and Partners made the commitment to systems drafting in 1975. In that year the firm had less than fifty employees in their main and only office in Nashville, Tennessee. Today the number of employees is 275 in their home office and four other states. There is a parallel between the use of systems, which allows working drawings for hospitals to be drawn and released to contractors in ninety calendar days, and the growth of the firm.

The Key to Quality Control

Details are the focal point in the quality control programs of hundreds of U.S. design firms. There are four main reasons why:

1. "Most construction failures occur in the details—either in design, drawing, or construction," says architect-engineer and building failures expert Ray DiPasquale. He makes the point that while engineering students, for example, learn moment diagrams and how to use shear and load tables, the main danger points are in the joints, the detailed connections. A knowledgeable Cambridge, Massachusetts, engineer quoted in *Engineering News-Record* concurs: "A large percentage of the time, collapses seem to be related to details rather than large structural principles." He adds: "It's the odd detail that you don't do every day that gets you into trouble." This doesn't mean you stop inventing new details. It just means taking care—extra care through a systematic master detail system and a coordinated system of working drawing project management and quality control.

2. Details, when coded by the CSI numbering system, can become an integral link that helps tie together every part of design and construction, including broadscope drawings, notation, schedules, specifications, and project decision-making documentation.

3. A systematic detail management program involves every aspect of systems drafting and graphics: paste-up, overlay, ink, typing, keynotes, computerization, etc. And a detail system provides the perfect lead-in for introducing all such systems in a simple, methodical way that both builds upon itself and pays for itself as you go along.

4. Besides quality control, architects and engineers achieve great time and cost savings from master detail systems. An innovative residential architect, for example, gets 30 to 50 percent of detail reuse from his files. He originally didn't expect any reusability because of the diversity of his practice and the novelty of his designs. He learned, as have many others, that fundamental construction remains constant despite highly divergent design details. Thus, floor drains, roof drains, insulated drywall partitions, roof scuttles, metal ladders, cavity walls, etc., are found in only a very limited variety and are mainly repetitive from building to building. Larger office users of standard or master detail files often report that 80 percent or more of the details on a complex detail sheet may come directly from the master files. That's an immense savings over time. And, it's a savings achieved by improving, not diminishing, design and construction quality.

Fred A. Stitt

It's the odd detail that you don't do everyday that gets you into trouble.

The Essentials of a Detail System

I've spent years researching detail systems and creating the beginnings of what I hope will become a national master detail system, and there's one thing that emerges loud and clear: most working drawing details are repeats. They're copies, to one degree or another, of previous details. Those that aren't copied are researched and redrawn from scratch time and again in office after office. Whether your drafters are copying old details or reinventing them, it's a huge waste of time and money.

I'll elaborate on all the specifics of creating and running a master detail system shortly. First, here's a synopsis of the main components of such a system and how they come together.

First is a reference detail library collected from past jobs, other architectural and engineering firms, and published manuals and catalogs. Details are sorted and filed by category in sort of a custom, in-house version of *Graphic Standards*. The details cover all kinds of construction, especially unusual, one-of-a-kind conditions. They're for help when the one-of-a-kind circumstance comes up again. Importantly, when you go to an integrated master detail system, you get multiple use of every single detail that will ever be drawn in the future. Those that aren't suited to a master or standard system for direct reuse are still at least useful in the reference file.

Second, in addition to reference details, comes a file of generic or prototype details. These may be like our *Guidelines* detail starter sheets that include only major elements that are most repetitive and leave off the minor items most likely to vary from job to job. Ed Powers of Gresham & Smith sends their new generic details to construction-related trade associations for review and comment. That's an outstanding effort to record the very best construction information available and make it an integral part of design documentation.

The third quality control tool: master details. These are more specific details—mostly originated for ongoing projects by elaborating on starter sheets or generic details. They're left partly undone, copied, and the copies later reviewed for inclusion in the master detail file. If they don't quite cut it for the master file, they go to the reference file.

The fourth tool, a job site feedback form, keeps the detail system fully up-to-date. If there's a troublesome detail discovered on a project, project representatives are required to send a brief memo back to whomever is in charge of the quality control-master detail system. The memo names the detail-type file number (which is printed with title and scale with every detail used in drawings). The system manager looks up the detail, and, while identifying the problem, looks at the detail drawing's detail history form. That's a space on the detail format sheet that identified where else and when a detail has been used. The combination of job site feedback form and detail history form uncovers problems, allows quick corrective action on other projects that may be using the detail, and constantly screens and upgrades the entire master file.

Reference details are those you might review for guidance in de-

When you go to an integrated master detail system, you get multiple use of every single detail.

signing for some unfamiliar construction situation. They might be from previous jobs, from other offices, from product manufacturers, or from guide books such as *Graphic Standards* or *Time-Saver Standards*.

Most offices don't keep a formal reference detail file. They may keep useful details from previous work, but the details are usually not filed or indexed in any systematic way. Systems drafting oriented offices use reference details increasingly these days. They're an excellent supplement for any master or standard detail file.

Master details represent standard construction. They show the repetitive conditions and are designed to be used directly—with or without revisions—in working drawings. Master details commonly include site work conditions, door and window details, standard wall construction, and connections of manufactured items such as roof drains and metal ladders. Even small offices sometimes compile and use as many as 5,000 details showing common construction situations.

Besides being a major time- and cost-saver, master details allow you to create and store the very best of construction practice. Offices that maintain well-managed detail files report a noticeable decline in problems at the job sites. And there are definitely fewer problems with the buildings after construction.

Keep in mind the difference between reference details and master details. Reference details are a source of data in creating new original data. Master details are directly reusable drawings of common repeat items of construction.

Even small offices sometimes compile and use as many as 5,000 details showing common construction situations.

Creating the Details

People don't have to be taken off other work to create an office master detail file. You can create a master file by doing all future details in such a format that if they can be used in the master file, it'll be easy to enter them in it.

Details created in this fashion are drawn as usual but in a special format on 8½-by-11 sheets. All details are later reviewed for potential re-usability in future projects. Even if a detail isn't acceptable as a master detail, most likely it can still be useful as part of the reference detail file. Either way you gain additional usage and value from most details long after they've been drawn for their particular project.

If you follow the *Guidelines* format, you'll be creating your future details within an approximate 5¾-inches high by 6-inches wide window on 8½-by-11-format sheets. The format sheets will show how to size and locate the detail title, how to align lettering, etc. When everybody uses the same format, details assembled on carrying sheets will look consistent.

The general rule in creating new details for future projects will be to split the drawing process into two steps:

1. Bring the detail to a point of near completion. "Near completion" means to leave off the material indications, dimensions, and notes that might vary in different circumstances. Some opening sizes or fabrication sizes might be variable, for example, so they're not specified at this step.

The idea is to avoid putting so much information on the detail that it loses its potential reusability.

2. After creating the detail up to a point of potential reuse, make two copies. Proceed to finish up your work for the job at hand on one copy. Add those variable material indications, dimensions, and notes that are necessary to complete the detail. The other copy is to review later for its potential use in the reference or master detail files. The original is filed separately. If a detail is selected for the master file, the separate original provides a backup—insurance against possible loss of the file copy.

The copies will be sepia line diazo polyester reproducibles. If the original is clean, clear, and crisp, the reproducibles should be the same. The reproducible copies should have little or no background haze and no loss of line quality.

Each detail accepted either for the reference detail file or for the master detail file will receive a file number. This number will be integrated with the office's master specification numbering system. File numbers, and a master file number index, provide slots or "address numbers" for all filed details. It makes for the most convenient retrieval and cross-referencing of details after they've been filed away.

Retrieving Details from the Master File

As just described, each filed detail receives a permanent address or file number. The number identifies the detail's construction division relative to specifications. The detail may be numbered according to dominant material or by function. The specification number system determines exactly what numbers to use to identify the major divisions and their subcategories, or the broadscope and narrowscope.

The division numbering is reflected in the actual physical detail file. The file drawers contain hanging Pendaflex-type folders. Each folder is marked with a specification division name and broadscope number. Within each folder are smaller folders that contain the subcategories of details within a particular broad division. For example there might be a large folder identified as Site Work – Division 2. Within that might be individual folders for Curbs, Parking Bumpers, etc. Each of those folders has a CSI-related number. Then the details within a folder each have their single identifying number. Thus a detail might be numbered 02528-4. Following the CSI format, that number would mean "concrete curbs within Division 2 site work." And the number following the hyphen would mean that this detail is the fourth concrete curb detail in the file.

It would be inconvenient to poke through a lengthy index of detail names and numbers to find a detail that you hope might be on file, so you need a convenient cross-reference system. One that shows what details are available and tells how to find them in the file.

The cross-reference or "lookup" system is in the form of a three-ring binder, a detail catalog. The detail catalog is a filing system ancillary to the file number structure of the file folders. Instead of being shown in the catalog in the way they're filed, details are shown in the sequence that people would be most likely to look for them. If you want to check out

You can create a master file by doing details in a format that can be used in the master file.

some window details, instead of looking through separate divisions of steel windows, aluminum windows, and wood windows—all separate specifications sections—you'd look in the general category of the catalog labeled Exterior Walls. Then you'd search for the alphabetical subsections under W for windows. Within that you could look for further subdivisions of window types and materials. When you locate some details in the catalog to try out, note their file numbers and have the masters retrieved and copied for you. Then make up either a detail book or a large, sheet-size paste-up of the masters. Add special data unique to your project to complete the details, finish the paste-up if you're doing paste-up, and proceed with check prints.

Retrieving from the Reference Detail File

If you're working out some new details dealing with data not on file in the master system, check the reference detail file for help. Reference details will be filed according to the same index number system as the master details. To avoid confusion of the reference details with master details, some firms start reference file numbers with a distinctive R.

If the reference detail library is very large, details will be kept in file folders similar to the master file just described. If it's practical, however, it's desirable to keep reference details in a binder—the office's own version of *Graphic Standards*.

Liability and
Quality Control

*Professional
Services
Management
Journal*

V irtually every design firm professes to emphasize quality control above all else. Nothing is spared to make sure the plans and specs are as error free as possible.

In our experience, this is a crock. Most firms do not have any formal quality control procedures. The majority of those that do ignore them a good part of the time. The only project that gets an adequate review is one with a lot of fee left; where there is more than enough time remaining; and when the staff is sitting around on their hands. Which almost never happens.

The consequences of poor quality control are numerous. At the minimum it means a lot of minor problems during construction which eat up valuable staff time and turn the client against the firm. At the worst it means a project that just does not work: the roof collapses; the treatment process cannot meet effluent specs; it is impossible to cool the building.

It is not that firms consciously ignore quality control. It is just that it falls somewhere far down the line on the priority list. The number one priority is get the job; second is get it out the door as soon as possible. Our recommendation is to place quality control before this second priority; the purpose of this article is to show you how to do this.

Some Suggestions

Send a message to everyone that quality control is a vital component of each project and not something being forced on the project team. And it extends from the overall design concept to the simplest details.

An atmosphere of quality should pervade the firm. Everyone should think zero defects and systems should be designed to ensure this. There should be standard procedures and checklists for all project types; progress on projects should be rigidly controlled; simple production systems should be used to minimize the possibility of error; the firm should have a master spec which everyone follows.

Remember that quality control starts back in the conceptual stage where major decisions are made.

Remember that quality control is not just checking the final plans. It starts back in the conceptual stage where major decisions are made. Make sure the basic design concept is right before going into details. Get the firm's experts involved early, via a design review committee or other such formal process.

Many firms designate one individual to be responsible for firm-wide quality control (in small firms this person has several hats). Among this person's responsibilities:

- coordinate the preparation of standard procedures, manuals, checklists, etc.;
- chair the design review committee which reviews all major projects in conceptual, preliminary and final stages;
- oversee the upkeep of the master spec, design details, etc.;
- act as clearinghouse and disseminator for all quality control information such as that received from the professional societies and liability insurer;
- organize a firmwide training program in design procedures and quality control.

When estimating compensation for a project, include the cost of quality control reviews. Also allow sufficient time in the project schedule for these reviews and for incorporating any design modifications. Use quality control as one of your selling points to the client.

Other Suggestions

1. The overall responsibility for quality control on a project lies with the project manager. However, the PM should manage and coordinate the efforts of others such as department heads rather than doing the reviews personally unless the project is small.

2. Have a nonthreatening method for calling in expert help from outside the project team. This encourages using the firm's true experts to solve the problems.

3. Require complete communication between all disciplines—especially when everyone is in-house. It is a common phenomenon that quality improves when outside consultants are used, no doubt because they tend to communicate better.

4. Quality suffers when projects drag out. The best jobs have very tight (but adequate) deadlines because under these conditions technical professionals seem to do it right the first time.

5. Spend scarce project time checking design concepts and details rather than seeking unnecessary design perfection.

6. Have a firm policy to freeze the design after design development or preliminary design. Do allow changes but only after top-level concurrence. This will eliminate the frivolous, unneeded changes and thus speed up final design and eliminate many coordination problems.

7. Always coordinate final plans for all disciplines and check against the specs. The prime is responsible for this and should not assume anyone else is doing it. Nurture people who do this checking well—maybe have them do it on a permanent basis.

8. Constantly emphasize on-the-job and outside training for all technical personnel: job site visits, brown bag discussions at lunch, informal design critiques, technical seminars, and university courses. The seminars given by liability insurers are especially good, but send the project people and not the top brass.

9. Finally, always do a postconstruction evaluation of the project to see which design elements did not work in construction or operation. Then feed this information back to the design staff.

It is a common phenomenon that quality improves when outside consultants are used.

Ownership Transition

10

Ownership Transition

Bowing out Gracefully,
Taking over Diplomatically

Until recently, the average life of the typical architectural practice was thirty-five years—the career span of an architect who became a sole practitioner. But the life expectancy of firms has been steadily increasing as practices have grown, and concerned principals plan for the continued existence of the firm after their retirement or withdrawal. The process a firm must undergo in order to survive the separation from its founders is ownership transition.

Successful management of ownership transition taxes the accumulated wisdom of all parties and their ability to work together in long-range planning based on complex economic and social factors.

Late in 1983, AIA sponsored a round table on this critical topic, and the following is the first of two articles developed from ideas that emerged during the round table discussions.

This article covers planning for ownership transition, approaches to negotiation, and implementing the transfer of control. The following article covers legal considerations and methods of firm valuation.

A firm undergoing a transition in ownership is vulnerable. The vitality of the organization, and perhaps even its survival, is in jeopardy.

The stakes are high because ownership transition strikes at the heart of client service. Clients want uniquely skilled design talent, but within the context of an organization with continuity. The organization must be available to solve problems that might arise during the life of the project. A successfully managed architectural firm is one that produces excellent design consistently.

During a period of ownership transition, the key challenge is to provide clients with continuity, without compromising the goals of the sellers and the buyers.

The nature of a firm's transitional program will depend upon the relationship between the goals of the sellers and those of the buyers. Their goals might not be compatible.

The first step in a rational approach to ownership transition is to evaluate separately the goals of each party, and then to compare them.

Goals of the Owners

The founding owner of a firm is seeking fulfillment of goals like these:

- Maximum financial return on investments in the firm.
- Completion of a sale within the constraints imposed by estate

Contributors:
Douglas Bevis, AIA
Weld Coxe, Hon. AIA
Thomas Eyerman, FAIA
Paul Lurie
Marc Roth

planning and tax considerations.

• Professional fulfillment through the immortalization of the firm as an institution.

• Loyal service to clients and to the concept of professionalism.

• Rewards for loyal associates, regardless of their leadership capabilities.

• Presentation of the reins to those having the will to succeed.

• Maximum benefit to the firm's employees and the continuity of the professional staff, a purely people-oriented approach.

• Retention of the reins of power for as long as possible, while potential successors leave in frustration.

• Termination of the firm, and retirement—a waste of the investment that was required to build the firm.

Goals of the Buyers

• Purchase at minimum cost, particularly with minimum initial cash outlay.

• Development of a purchase agreement with optimum tax advantages.

• Maximum management control of the firm, with financial considerations a secondary goal.

• A career built from an existing base, instead of a firm started from scratch with few clients and no organization.

• The challenge of leadership.

• Acceptance by a core group of professional colleagues, belonging, not leading.

• Fulfillment of personal, philosophical, and professional commitments.

Seeking Resolution: Ground Rules

The goals of sellers and buyers are almost inevitably in conflict. A successful ownership transition program is developed through negotiation, in an atmosphere of fairness that seeks to balance the interest of both parties.

A basic ground rule for negotiation is that both parties are willing to do business. The seller must be sure about wanting to sell, and the buyers must be serious about buying. Otherwise, the discussions will go nowhere. A second basic rule is that the financial transaction cannot be one-sided. The selling price will most likely be a compromise between the owner's assessment of fair market value and the buyer's ability and willingness to pay.

The purchase price per unit or share of ownership is frequently the most volatile issue in purchase negotiations. The human relations factors of emotion and personality are often as important as money in the outcome of negotiations. The sensitivity of the pricing issue is exacerbated by the low disposable personal income and limited capital available to most buyers, who are typically in their thirties and forties. When such buyers believe the price is too high, many vote with their feet and look elsewhere for personal fulfillment.

Sellers, particularly founders, tend to place a higher value on the firm. No matter what valuation formula is endorsed, founders often demand and deserve a special, one-time bonus as recognition and reward for building the firm. But key advice to sellers is not to drive too hard a bargain on the selling price. The firm's highest value is as a going concern. If the sellers drive away buyers by overpricing, the going concern value can erode to a liquidation value.

Firm valuation is complex and will be covered in detail in the next article. For now, it is important to recognize that the primary issues, even in negotiating a purchase price, are the goals of the buyers and sellers. The value of a firm is transitory, at best, due to limited assets, soft markets, and mobile staff.

Beyond basic differences in philosophy or concepts of value, the specific circumstances of different parties can have a radical effect on value.

Consider the case of a major firm with substantial losses in consecutive years, looking for a merger. Its healthy local rival may make a minimum purchase offer or none at all. The healthy firm could just as easily hire away professional staff and pirate clients. But a profitable and aggressive out-of-town firm would pay much more for the same losing firm if the buyer were seeking (1) to enter a new geographic market by buying the client base and the professional staff of a going concern; or (2) to use the losses as tax loss carryforwards to shield its high earnings.

One aspect of transition planning that is frequently overlooked is the essential need for the firm to be highly profitable if the plan is to be comfortably financed.

Due to naturally different motives, buyers and sellers do not always agree on this. The buyers would like to buy the firm as cheaply as possible. They often have an unconscious incentive to limit its financial performance so they will not have to pay so much for it. The sellers want to be well paid if the firm is highly profitable, but are often reluctant to share profits with new buyers who have not yet earned any sizable share of the net.

Buyers and sellers must realize that the only source of financing for internal transition is the firm itself. The price must be earned by the firm, or it will not be paid. These principles often seem self-evident and minor at the outset of transition planning. The rub comes later when the sellers expect (justifiably) to continue to take high salaries while being paid for the value of the firm, while the buyers begin to feel (also justifiably) that their salaries are too low for them to make the additional payments necessary to purchase the firm.

The only way to ensure that the financing provisions will be comfortable to both buyers and sellers is to keep the firm very profitable, so all parties share enough money while the equity is being paid. It is as simple as that. Highly profitable firms just don't have trouble financing ownership transition plans; unprofitable firms do.

Because of the sensitivity of price and financing negotiations, sub-

Key advice to sellers is not to drive too hard a bargain on the selling price.

Buyers and sellers must realize that the only source of financing for internal transition is the firm itself.

jective issues are certain to arise. Each party will wonder whether the other's commitment to the organization will override personal interests. Mutual trust often is difficult to achieve, but it is essential to assure the success of the transition. Both buyers and sellers have a stake in assuring that the firm continues to serve and expand its client base.

The obstacles to trust are rooted in the way many people believe organizations should operate. Information about financial performance, compensation, bonuses, and the like is frequently kept under lock and key, to be doled out in an atmosphere of extreme confidentiality. Decisions on major policies, or even job assignments, are often made behind closed doors and then handed down without any opportunity for comment from those affected. Again and again, responsibility is assigned but authority is withheld.

In organizations where these conditions prevail, transition often begins in an atmosphere that provides no foundation for open trust. Sellers may even hesitate to share the development of the transition plan with buyers. They meet in private with their lawyers, accountants, and consultants to try to tie all the loose ends of the plan together before discussing ownership with those invited to buy. The prospective purchasers in turn take a suspicious view of the offer and hire their own lawyers in the hope of striking a better deal.

When these conditions prevail, it is best for the buyers and sellers to sit down and talk openly about their goals for the firm and the ways they hope to work together—in other words, to get to know each other.

This open sharing of goals and aspirations doesn't happen over dinner, after work, or in three hours on a Saturday morning. It requires a series of meetings—some short, some involving several days at a retreat location—over a period of several months, with time in between to absorb and understand new information, to research alternatives, and to reflect on individual, personal goals.

Planning for ownership transition should begin before the owner reaches 50.

Trust and confidence can only develop simultaneously and in an atmosphere that permits:
- Sharing of information, especially financial data.
- Clear willingness to seek and give input before major decisions are made.
- Confident delegation of authority and responsibility.

When the present and future owners of an organization can operate with mutual trust, the climate for transition is at its best, and the chances for success are greatest.

New Leaders Must Be Trained and Motivated

Key advice for sellers is not to wait too long. Planning for ownership transition should begin before the owner reaches fifty, and the program should be implemented before the owner is fifty-five. After that time, options for the owner and the organization may narrow rapidly. Gradual transition works best.

Without early planning, an abrupt changeover in leadership may be the only option. If no one within the firm has been groomed to take over, the alternative will be sale to an outsider, which usually is not beneficial to existing staff. The firm may stagnate or lose its best people, who may set up competition in the same markets.

Entrepreneurial founding. Successful architects who found their own practices generally do so when they are in their middle to late thirties. During the early entrepreneurial years, they struggle to build a practice while meeting and building relationships with contemporaries who are either also starting out or are just beginning to rise in large organizations. In the entrepreneurial stage, considerable energy is devoted to positioning for the future, and absolute power seems just out of reach.

Arrival. Suddenly, everything falls into place. For architects, this is when they are offered participation in the major decisions in their community or field of specialization as their contemporaries arrive at positions of power and can award commissions to their peers. Work flows in with relatively little effort, and firms grow rapidly.

Maturity. Architectural firms level off at the top when the leaders and the clients begin to grow old together. The firm may have many repeat clients, but fewer new ones. One by one, the loyal older clients are succeeded in their organizations by a new command generation. The newcomers may not retain the established architects. When a firm begins to have trouble retaining the old clients and landing new ones, the end of its reign as command generation is near.

Clearly, new generations of leaders must be motivated when they are young enough to build strong relationships with their entrepreneurial peers. They must be given sufficient power to act as leaders in their own right when their peers arrive.

This is much easier said than done. Many architectural firms spawn their own competition because the leaders, having struggled to get to the top, are so intent on enjoying it that they do not offer attractive opportunities to the best of the generation immediately behind them. Such firms can continue to succeed well into maturity, but when transition finally begins, the younger generation then in control may not have arrived. Such firms may remain at a disadvantage until another generation arrives with its own peers.

There is no simple way to address these timing questions in a transition plan. Firm size is one factor to be considered: small firms may not be able to accommodate two or three overlapping generations of leaders, while larger firms can do so quite successfully. Some firms welcome younger practitioners to key, competitive roles early; others simply cannot function if they must divide control among too many individuals—of whatever age.

The importance of the timing issue is that it must be considered when shaping a transition plan. A firm that begins transition while the founders are still young can nurture several succeeding generations before the founders retire. It will have a very different transition plan from that of a mature organization that has skipped one or two generations of successors.

Owners cannot avoid relinquishing control if they want to assure the continued success of the firm.

Transfer of Control

Power transfer is a critical element in an ownership transfer. It is the relinquishing by the principals of the authority and responsibility for the firm's growth and future. There may be an interim sharing of authority and responsibility, but nevertheless a new generation of principals gradually is assuming the absolute powers of ownership.

Owners cannot avoid relinquishing control if they want to assure the continued success of the firm. Ownership distribution plans that spread ownership widely among employees without providing for the divestiture of at least some control may be helpful morale boosters, but they are not sufficient motivators to ensure retention of, or top performance from, the best successors. Several years ago, financial conglomerates acquired architectural firms by paying founders handsomely. The investors expected good returns, but their success record was poor because key younger people in many of the acquired firms could not be induced to remain and operate the practices for outside owners. They left to practice where they could have more control of their professional futures.

This control instinct is basic to leaders in all enterprises, but it is especially strong among architects. Most good designers place a very high value on the right to make final decisions. As long as the founders of an architectural firm do not share or delegate this last-word authority, their best potential successors will leave the firm in their thirties (the entrepreneurial age) and set up their own shops.

Also, when control is concentrated at the top of an architectural firm, the second line of management usually represents complementary, not duplicated skills. This complementary group may be essential to the continuing performance of the firm, but, as noted above, leaders must be developed by being challenged and motivated in their formative years.

The best motivator for leaders is the opportunity to make some of their own decisions and to accept responsibility for the consequences.

Sellers and buyers must address how much control will be transferred, and when. A 100 percent owner may find that offering a 1 percent interest to a colleague will create, in spirit, a partner who expects to participate in every decision. When the purchasing partner finds this is not to be the case, the result is often the same as if there had been no ownership transition at all.

On the other hand, successful ownership transition does not require relinquishing so much control that the result is anarchy. The degree of control that will motivate buyers often involves only a small proportion of the vast number of decisions needed to run a firm.

Sellers and buyers planning a transition should talk these issues through in advance, and be sure both are comfortable with the control climate envisioned.

In most cases, ultimate control issues cannot be resolved clearly at the outset of a transition plan. Rather, the balance of control shifts gradually over time as the sellers and buyers become more comfortable with each other's roles and performance.

Provisions that can be incorporated in an ownership transition plan to encourage the gradual shift of control:

- Make it clear whether new owners will participate in partnership or board meetings; how often the meetings will be held; what level of decisions will be made at these meetings; and whether issues will be decided by votes based on shares. The specifics of these policies are usually less important than the need for all parties to know that the policies exist.

- Give new owners some additional responsibilities or roles concurrently with their acquisition of a share in ownership. New owners cannot begin to act like successors if they are restricted to totally subordinate roles.

- Whenever possible, give potential successors maximum authority and visibility at the initial stages of transition, and expect their performance in due course to live up to the position, not vice versa. Firm leaders have tried again and again to tell subordinates, "If you start performing like a principal, then we will make you one." This seldom works. It is far easier for younger architects to begin acting like principals if they have the position, the authority, and the visible status on the letterhead.

The founders of a firm are naturally concerned about the risks of delegating too much control before they are sure it will be used properly and effectively. The fear of losing control of what one has created by making a mistake in the choice of successors is a legitimate concern.

The fear of losing control of what one has created by making a mistake in the choice of successors is a legitimate concern.

Five-Year Vesting

The solution is to structure the vesting provisions of an ownership transition plan so that there is a period of several years before a buyer owns full rights to what is granted in the buy-sell agreement. A typical vesting arrangement would give a buyer full principal status and authority at the time transition begins, but could provide a five-year period during which the seller could buy back if the buyer's performance does not meet expectations.

For example, in a matrix organization, the designated successors are often project managers already. They have the responsibility for the in-house organization and management of projects. If the principals decide that this management role should expand, the project managers could be charged with becoming more visible outside the firm, seeking new clients and new projects. Increased responsibility can play a part in the transfer of power, but by itself it is not to be considered the transfer of power. In the example above, the project managers should be given a role in identifying new markets, allowed to set goals for the firm, and to readjust those goals if they are not met.

Since no transition plan is ever perfect, one theory suggests that founders should allow at least two five-year cycles to find their successors. Thus, a founder hoping to retire at sixty-five would begin a transition plan at least by age fifty-five, allowing the option to start again at age sixty if the first selection of successors did not work out. A more liberal interpretation of this theory would suggest that it is time to bring in several new potential owners every five years, regardless of the age of the founders. With either approach, there is wisdom in allowing a five-year

vesting period for new owners. If they achieve the performance anticipated, they should be allowed to carry on as fully vested owners. If they do
not live up to expectations within five years, it is probably best for both
parties to admit the shortfall, and for the firm to try again with a new
group of successors.

The arrangements for investment transfer should be formally established in a legal written agreement between sellers and buyers.

In some cases, principals make arrangements for employees to acquire a noncontrolling interest of up to 50 percent. Since financial control
is retained by the original principals, this does not constitute ownership
transfer.

In an ownership transition situation, investment transfer involves a
change in the level of commitment and risk for both the principals and the
designated successors. The level of commitment generally covers an extended time during which the designated successors are afforded the opportunity to increase their relative investment in the firm. As the level of
relative investment increases, risk to both participants in the transfer increases. For the new principals, a substantial personal financial commitment is frequently involved. For the original principals, the risk involves
gradual loss of control of personal investment.

There is wisdom in allowing a five-year vesting period for new owners.

Image Transfer

The final element in an ownership transition program is image
transfer. The designated successors are given titles that reflect the new
positions in the firm. Actual titles vary. Announcements may be sent to
clients and other business contacts. The new principals may assume increased client contact, demonstrating an increase in ownership authority.
Tangible benefits such as a new office or increased expense accounts may
be in evidence.

Clients must also be involved for several years before ownership
transfer is complete. Their acceptance will be most readily won if the new
owners have become the closer-doers known to them. Social and business
community activities, as well as national client and professional associations, are also sources of important contacts that take years to nurture. In
many cases, these contacts are not transferable, and each generation will
have to make its own way. A clearly defined, staged transition can help
this process.

Ownership transition can be accomplished in just a few years, but
laying the foundation for an effective program may take a decade. The
actual transition is merely tactical; the essence of an ownership transition
program is solid organizational development.

Reprinted from *Architectural Technology,* Fall 1984.

Ownership Transition

*Agreeing on Price, Financing the Deal,
and Making It Legal*

Agreeing on price is almost always the toughest part of business negotiations. Fair valuation is an especially slippery concept when it concerns something as intangible as an architectural practice. Each firm is unique, and, unless stock in the firm is publicly traded, there is generally no basis for price comparison.

The adage, "Everything is worth what the purchaser will pay for it," is the operating principle in firm valuation, but it is always difficult for owners and internal buyers to see things that way, because the firm itself will in the end finance much of the price.

Several things can be done to make the climate surrounding valuation discussions more amenable to quick and workable agreements.

• Establish goals and objectives: the buyers and the sellers should clarify what they each are trying to get out of the negotiations (the goals) and why (the objectives). Goal clarification, covered in more detail in the previous article, can help the parties resolve, or at least be aware of, underlying conflicts before they begin negotiations.

For example, an owner interested primarily in assuring the continued existence and health of the firm will have different criteria for economic valuation than one who is willing to admit his or her primary goal is maximum profit from sale. The former may agree that the price will be what people who are well qualified to run the firm will agree to pay; the latter would probably define the price as the best offer, period.

• Select the team: the lawyers, accountants, management consultants, bankers, insurance advisors, and personnel consultants working on ownership transition arrangements must be selected carefully for their ability to clearly understand the goals and objectives and the criteria upon which the economic valuation will be based.

• Plan the strategy: a plan for the valuation based on the goals and objectives should be developed. The plan will identify the method of valuation chosen and the other factors that will be considered in establishing a fair price.

Why Valuation Is So Difficult

Firms that are not publicly traded are difficult to appraise for many reasons:

• The true earnings of many firms are difficult to establish because earnings are distributed principally through compensation and fringe benefits. This makes analysis of income streams difficult.

Contributors:
Douglas Bevis, AIA
Weld Coxe, Hon. AIA
Thomas Eyerman, FAIA
Paul Lurie
Marc Roth

The true earnings of many firms are difficult to establish.

• Historical data such as annual income flows can be distorted by unusual market circumstances.

• Many firms may not have the liquid assets available to justify values established by analyzing assets and liabilities based on the accrual method of accounting.

• The founding owners often have an emotional commitment to the firm that inflates their estimates of the value of their interests. If they sell to employees, their authority in the firm can allow them to impose their views.

• Transient factors such as a firm's reputation and goodwill are often considered in valuation.

Three Methods of Firm Valuation

Following are three methods, two based on future worth and one on current worth, that will establish some bench marks for valuation of a firm.

Method 1: Earnings Capitalization

The earnings capitalization or earnings ratio method of valuation is based on projections for the future worth of the firm. The average annual earnings for the most recent three- to five-year period are calculated and multiplied by a reasonable price/earnings (P/E) ratio.

The annual earnings of a professional service firm should be readily accessible from the firm's accounting statements. The earnings are the income (after partner or principal salaries) generated by the firm, plus any compensation to principals in excess of their reasonable salaries.

The price/earnings ratio, on the other hand, can be very subjective. It is an estimate of the rate of return on investment in the firm. The price/earnings ratio would be higher for a stable firm than for one with volatile results, and is almost never used for smaller firms. Where firms are listed on a stock exchange, one can see how investors evaluate the firm's P/E ratio.

Method 2: Discounted Net Cash Flow

This method is also based on the future worth of the firm and depends on three assumptions:

• Cash today is worth more than cash one will receive in the future.

• Future cash flows are reasonably predictable.

• The cost of capital and alternative returns on invested capital are similar. In other words, if one can receive 10 percent on invested capital, one must assume the discount rate will be 10 percent.

For a professional services firm to have a reasonably predictable future cash flow is an accomplishment in itself. Some firms with stable work loads are able to project net cash flows for several years. (Net cash flow = incoming cash – outgoing cash.)

Combining Methods 1 and 2

It is obvious that one can combine the discounted cash flow and capitalized earnings methods of evaluation.

$$\text{Capitalized Earnings} = \frac{\text{Average Earnings (actual or projected)}}{\text{Rate of Capitalization}}$$

For a professional services firm to have a reasonably predictable future cash flow is an accomplishment in itself.

Average earnings may be the actual annual earnings over the last three to five years, or it could be the estimated average annual earnings projected by the firm for the next three to five years.

The rate of capitalization is 100 divided by the price/earnings ratio. Thus, a price/earnings ratio of four would also be a capitalization rate of 25 percent.

Method 3: Excess Assets

The least subjective and most conservative method of valuation is excess assets, based on the current worth of the firm. This is calculated by adding all assets of the firm and subtracting all liabilities. The net result should be the book value of the firm.

Although this appears to be an exact and clear-cut method of valuation, it is important to understand that no two accountants will ever yield the same valuation with this method. Careful review of the assets and liabilities is necessary. Particular attention should be brought to accounts receivable and fixed assets—two areas where subjectivity may arise.

The excess assets formula is based on estimates of the value of the firm if it were liquidated, while the discounted cash flow and earnings capitalization formulas treat the firm as an ongoing business concern. An ongoing concern is inherently more valuable than a liquidated firm.

The least subjective and most conservative method of valuation, is excess assets, based on the current worth of the firm.

Other Factors Affecting Value

The three valuation methods above can establish a framework for discussion of the true value of the firm. The following very subjective factors also have an important impact on the true value of the firm:

• Nature of the business (consulting, design, research, A/E, etc.).

• Economic outlook for the firm in the context of the national economy and forecasts for specific markets.

• History of the firm (stable vs. volatile).

• Firm's reputation and expertise (can be ephemeral).

• Major firm projects (some may be particularly desirable or undesirable).

• Key individuals in the firm, their abilities and plans.

Methods of Payment

After the firm value has been discussed, and before price negotiations are concluded, it is important to consider how money or its equivalent will be exchanged.

Two basic principles are important here:

Fixed valuation. The value of the firm should be frozen on the date of ownership transfer. The value may be subject to increases or decreases after that date, by renegotiation, but the bench mark should always be the agreed-upon value on the date of transfer.

Equality of earnings. If the former owners are to remain active in the firm, their current compensation should be arranged for short-term objectives on the premise that "cash motivates." They should be paid on the basis of fees earned for services rendered. If the current compensation of former owners is based on a share in the firm profits, it should be clear that expenses associated with the acquisition or purchase of the firm will not be charged against the former owners' share of the profits.

Incentive Compensation

Ownership transition plans commonly provide for payment to former owners through a base salary plus an incentive compensation. The base salary can be payment toward the principal valuation amount and current activity, while incentive compensation can provide additional payment for current activity.

The size of incentive payments must be based on objective factors. The usual basis is firm profits, excluding expenses associated with the sale of the firm. Some firms use receipts, gross new commissions, and so forth.

To reward sustained growth as preferable to cyclical growth, it is best to base incentive compensation on cumulative results. Firms usually pay a portion of the incentive compensation annually, with deferment of the balance over at least a five-year period.

Transition Team

Attorneys. A firm can save time, expense, and anxiety by consulting an attorney in the early stages of the transition process. Attorneys will be needed to prepare partnership or corporation documents, buy/sell agreements, and stock issuance papers.

It's important to select an attorney with experience with design firms, and specifically with ownership transfer. This experience can allow the attorneys to counsel the firm on the repercussions and long-term consequences of legal decisions.

An attorney for the firm legally represents the firm's position as an independent entity. The buyers and sellers may want to have their separate interests represented by different attorneys.

Accountants. A detailed and complete financial review is important input for financial decisions involved in ownership transition, including establishment of the firm's worth. Accountants also advise on stock valuation, financial reporting, and records.

The financial history provided by an accountant should be adjusted to assure that each year's financial status is evaluated on the same basis. This consistency allows for internal comparisons from year to year, and external comparisons with the performance of other firms.

The transition process may involve a change in the firm's financial approach in the treatment of assets and liabilities. Accountants can help identify alternatives to reduce tax liabilities.

Firm accountants, like attorneys, represent the firm and not the principals or other parties involved in the transaction.

Insurance Advisors. All insurance policies should be reevaluated during an ownership transition. Insurance agents advise on the extent of coverage required, identify weaknesses in the present coverage, and regularly review and update the coverage as the firm grows.

Bankers The establishment of an ongoing relationship with bankers is important to any architectural practice. Ownership transfers often require outside financing, so a strong and secure line of credit can be especially helpful during ownership transitions. A banker can determine the amount of loan required and the time frame for payback. Bank representatives may be included in meetings where major financial decisions are discussed.

Management Consultants. Management consultants are sometimes called upon in ownership transitions to analyze the existing firm structure and suggest workable alternatives. They can also advise on valuation and options for managing the transfer of power. Consultants can play an important role by providing an objective and unbiased perspective on the issues. It is best to use a consultant with experience in dealing with ownership transfer and knowledge of architectural practices. Consultants who specialize in human dynamics can identify conflicts that might occur or may already be occurring among the parties, and help resolve them. They can also be a link among the lawyers, accountants, and other members of the team.

Personnel Consultants. Personnel consultants are sometimes brought in when the principals have not found suitable successors and want to accomplish an ownership transfer quickly. Personnel consultants have the expertise and resources to search for appropriate candidates.

Employee Stock Ownership Plans (ESOPs)

ESOPs are stock bonus or profit-sharing plans that invest their assets primarily in the firm's securities and afford tax savings to plan participants. ESOPs can be used as financing vehicles to enable the owners to transfer ownership to employees.

ESOPs must satisfy the qualification requirements of the Internal Revenue Code. The contributions or benefits provided cannot discriminate in favor of employees who are officers, shareholders, or highly compensated individuals. When an ESOP conforms to these and other standards, contributions are tax-deductible. As with certain tax-deductible pension funds, distributions from the plan are eligible for favorable tax treatment.

An ESOP can be used to shift ownership in the following way:

1. The firm sets up an ESOP.
2. Key employees purchase a percentage of the owners' stock.
3. The ESOP borrows the valuation amount, less the amount paid in item 2 above.
4. The ESOP buys the remaining stock.
5. The firm annually contributes enough cash to amortize the loan. The contributions are tax-deductible.

ESOPs are normally used to finance less than 50 percent of ownership. The remaining shares are purchased directly from the owners.

In considering ESOPs it is important to recognize that the firm may be required to buy back its stock from participants who receive distributions of stock from the ESOP. This can be very costly.

ESOPs can be used as financing vehicles to enable the owners to transfer ownership to employees.

Salary Continuation Plans

In some ownership transition plans the purchasers agree to pay all or a portion of the former owner's salary to his or her estate in the event of death before retirement. These arrangements can be funded with company-owned insurance on the owner's life. The company receives life insurance benefits tax-free, and is allowed a deduction for salary continuation payments, if in accordance with a prior agreement. Normally payments disbursed in accordance with a salary continuation plan are deducted from principal balance outstanding from the sale.

There are many types of life insurance plans that can be used to provide benefits to a former owner. The use of life insurance and trusts, particularly Retired Lives Reserves, is beneficial to the firm, but most owners do not want the bulk of their payments tied up until after their death.

Partnership Agreements

In a partnership each partner is personally liable for all the obligations of the business, including those incurred by the other partners. Continuation of the business in the event of the death, retirement, or withdrawal of a partner should also be considered.

Waiting until events such as death, disability, and retirement occur to determine the price and terms surrounding the liquidation of an equity interest will have the following disadvantages:

Disadvantages to the firm:

• There is no certainty that the ownership interest in question will not become part of a controlling interest sold to outsiders.

• Without an agreed-upon formula for price, the firm cannot effectively plan for funding its obligation to a withdrawing principal.

• Negotiations without formulas and without methods of funding can be protracted and sometimes bitter.

Disadvantages to the principals and their estates:

• Important negotiating leverage is lost once the principal is removed from an active role in the firm.

• If the principal was a minority owner, the firm may feel no strong need to acquire the interest unless on terms favorable to the firm. This can also lead to bitter negotiations.

• Without an agreed-upon formula for price, the principal cannot effectively plan for his or her retirement or estate.

• If the firm has not planned to fund the purchase, it may not be able to pay the price in a way that meets the needs of the principals.

• When the IRS audits estate tax returns, it will normally accept valuation formulas that have been made binding in an agreement signed during life. In the absence of these formulas, IRS may use its own, which could inflate the estate tax. There is no assurance that the amount the firm would be willing to pay would take into account the increased tax obligations of the estate.

For all these reasons, buy-sell agreements are often incorporated into ownership transition documents. These agreements typically define

Negotiations without formulas and without methods of funding can be protracted and sometimes bitter.

the events giving rise to a transition in form ownership and establish the price at which equity interests in the firm will be liquidated. Careful thought and planning are the keys to a successful buy-sell agreement.

Most architectural firms are owned by a relatively small number of individuals who are active in the day-to-day affairs of the firm. These firms usually distribute their earnings from compensation and have no viable arrangements for paying a return on investment to passive investors. Principals generally want the right to cash out their investment when they are no longer active in the firm and no longer receiving compensation. They also require assurance that they can withdraw funds immediately should death or disability occur.

In these closely held firms, current management usually doesn't want individuals who are no longer associated with the firm, or their estate representatives, to be able to participate in the affairs of the firm. Therefore, whenever a principal is no longer able to serve the firm, these firms would want to acquire the ownership interest, or they would want the remaining principals to do so if the firm is unable to fund such acquisitions. This situation may occur upon death, serious disability, or departure—voluntary or otherwise—including planned retirement.

If the departure occurs voluntarily because of personal reasons, other than planned retirement, or if the principal is asked to leave for committing an act detrimental to the firm, there is less reason for the firm to provide a favorable market for the liquidation of the principal's interest. The firm has good reason to require a penalty for early withdrawal, because if the valuation payment is too attractive, the plan may encourage people to leave the firm and perhaps even to compete with it.

In such situations, the firm may want only an option to purchase the interest rather than a definitive obligation to purchase. Creating this option will give the firm negotiating leverage concerning issues that may not have been addressed totally in the agreements between the parties regarding separation.

Serious disabilities create other problems. Principals who are seriously disabled for an extended time are often required to liquidate their investment in the firm, and firms are typically required to acquire that interest.

It is important that the agreements define "serious disability." A definition of serious disability is usually provided under disability insurance policies covering employees.

In the absence of insurance coverage, disability is usually defined as 'the inability to perform normal duties related to the firm'. Determination of whether this condition exists may be vested in doctors, whose decisions are made binding on all the parties. The agreement should also define the amount of time that may elapse before the disabled person is required to liquidate.

How Are Liquidations Funded?

The traditional sources for funding liquidations are:
• Firm reserves. These are the amounts set aside from earnings to

Principals generally want the right to cash out their investment when they are no longer active.

cover future contingencies.

- New capital from existing or new principals.
- Qualified pension, profit, or ESOP plans.
- Life insurance. The availability of this resource is dependent upon the firm's ability to pay premiums, the insurability of the individuals, and their expectation of working until their final days.
- Annuities purchased from insurance companies. The funding methods are chosen according to the specific situation involved. The firm must decide how much insurance it wants to buy if it can insure an event, and the level of reserves it needs to establish to cover uninsured events. Agreements regarding uninsured obligations need to allow for flexibility in payment. The firm will want to limit the cash flow expended should multiple liquidations occur during a short period of time.
- Borrowed funds. If the firm does not have adequate insurance or reserves to pay a fixed obligation, the only alternative is to borrow funds. Usually the money is borrowed from the liquidating principal in the form of an installment obligation loan, although the firm could borrow from a financial institution.

Security

The principals who are selling need provisions covering the contingency that the purchasers default on their obligations. The ability to foreclose and recapture the position being purchased, and/or the personal guarantees of the purchasers, are traditional forms of security.

If personal guarantees are not used, the participants may want to consider operating covenants. These are pledges from the remaining principals to govern the firm in the ordinary course until the obligation is retired. This would protect the sellers from a situation in which the remaining principals attempt to avoid obligations by starting a new firm.

The firm's obligations to principals for their interest in the firm may be either an amount that is fixed at the time the interest is acquired, or variable and contingent on the future success of the firm. Frequently, ownership transition plans have elements of both fixed and variable payments.

Fixed Purchase Obligations

The formula for determining value and the schedule for payment are stipulated in a plan with a stated or fixed purchase obligation.

Equal consideration should be given to predicting the timing and amount of obligations created by the plan, and identifying sources of repayment. The plan must assure that the firm can pay its obligations in a time frame that will not cripple the firm.

Variable and Contingent Obligations

Because of the problems of predicting the timing and amount of fixed obligations and then funding them, many firms use agreements that contractually require continued compensation and preclude liquidation for a fixed period. They may also make payment contingent on other situations. This contractual obligation may or may not be in addition to an amount necessary to retire the hard or excess asset portion of the investment.

These arrangements have several advantages to the firm:

• If the obligation is contingent, the risk the firm could not afford payment is reduced.

• Reduction of fixed obligations improves the financial statement of the firm.

• The selling principals have a vested interest in maintaining the viability of the firm.

• The payments can be structured to be tax-deductible to the firm, rather than treated as a reserve account. If the firm is a corporation, tax law problems regarding unreasonable accumulation of reserves and constructive dividends are minimized.

These arrangements have several disadvantages to the principals:

• For tax purposes, the payments are treated as ordinary income, not capital gain. Usually, the principals selling an interest back to the firm are able to treat it as capital gain.

• The payment is usually unsecured.

• The principals are gambling on the future health of the firm. If they leave the firm in good condition but their successors ruin it, they will lose the value that was present on the date of departure.

The plan must assure that the firm can pay its obligations in a time frame that will not cripple the firm.

Corporations

In both corporations and partnerships, the liquidation of the principal's interest may be made by direct sale to the organization (entity purchase), by sale between the owners (cross-purchase), or by a combination of the two.

Funds reserved for the liquidation of an interest will generally be taken from after-tax dollars.

A properly structured liquidation of the principals' interest in a corporation should yield the same tax consequences whether it is by means of an entity purchase or a cross-purchase.

The selling shareholders, who may be the principals' successors, will realize capital gain income in an amount equal to the difference between the sale price and the adjusted tax basis in the stock (which is most often its original purchase price, except in the instance of a shareholders' death, where the stock will acquire a tax basis equal to its value on the date of death).

Where an entity purchase is involved, it is important to comply with the redemption provisions of the Internal Revenue Code. Under some circumstances, where family members or relatives of the selling shareholder continue to own stock in the corporation, the redemption of stock by the corporation may be treated as a taxable dividend.

Partnerships

Structuring a complete liquidation of a partnership interest depends on the tax situation of each partner.

The selling partners usually prefer a cross-purchase of the partnership interest, since gains on sale (except for portions attributed to ordinary income items such as receivables) will be treated as a capital gain.

The redemption can be structured to generate ordinary income to the seller and a deduction for the partnership if the partnership purchases the interest.

Liquidation of partnership interests should be timed to avoid the bunching of income and deductions.

Partial Transfers

In cases where the principals decide to shift some of the risks and benefits of the business to younger principals without, for the time, liquidating their equity interest, there are other approaches.

Guaranteed payments are an accepted way of structuring a partial transfer in a partnership. Guaranteed payments provide a fixed and determinable return to the partners who wish to curtail or reduce their activities, and are calculated on a different basis from partnership income. Such a payment may take into account a fixed percentage return on the principal's share of the partnership's assets, as well as a specific rate for services performed by the principals.

Under the Internal Revenue Code, guaranteed payments are treated as income to the recipient and reduce the partnership income otherwise reportable by the remaining partners.

In corporations, a stock recapitalization coupled with an employment contract can achieve results equivalent to guaranteed payments. The contract can provide current compensation for services, and the recapitalization provides a return for the use of capital and freezes the principal's equity participation in the firm.

The federal income tax treatment of partial transfers in corporations will depend on the form of transaction. The serial redemption by a corporation of the stock interest of a shareholder will constitute a taxable dividend to the principals even though the equity interest in the corporation is reduced, unless the distribution qualifies as a "substantially disproportionate redemption of stock" under the Internal Revenue Code. Cross-purchases between stockholders can alleviate this tax burden, but this will require careful drafting by the corporation's counsel to avoid still other problems.

A serial liquidation of the interest owned by about-to-be-retired partners is a more flexible tax situation. If the partnership purchases a portion of a partnership interest, the selling partners may be able to defer a significant portion of the taxes until the tax basis in the partnership interest has been exhausted. Such would not be the case if the partners sold to the remaining partners instead of to the partnership entity.

Summary: Assemble the Right Team

This article presents basic guidance regarding the legal, financial, and tax problems involved in an ownership transition. The services of attorneys, accountants, bankers, insurance advisors, and perhaps manage-

Structuring a complete liquidation of a partnership interest depends on the tax situation of each partner.

"Guaranteed payments" are an accepted way of structuring a partial transfer in a partnership.

ment and personnel consultants will be required. It will be important to select the right team, and to work closely with it in ironing out the major issues and the myriad of details involved in an ownership transfer.

Reprinted from *Architectural Technology*, Spring 1984.

Valuing Your Firm

Richard Praeger

Internal self-evaluation starts with projected earnings, always on a net accrual basis. Net here means that salaries, bonuses, and fringe benefits for all personnel would be those acceptable during the projected period. Projected income must be based on current backlog and anticipated replenishment of backlog based on recent history. The earnings derived therefrom must also be related to recent history, and anticipated changes in overhead and contract conditions.

The projected earnings should be subjected to the type of questioning a knowledgeable acquisition team would give it. Of particular importance is the historical source of the anticipated backlog. If those responsible for immediate past success are interested in early retirement or perhaps are not on contract or not to benefit from the acquisition, the quality of the backlog is suspect. This is a principal strategic reason for the acquiring company to prefer stock acquisitions. Key personnel in the acquiree are then in a position of being affected by their own performance-based payouts. The more certain the acquiree's earnings, the stronger its position in demanding a larger down payment.

The emphasis in most negotiations will be on projected earnings.

The emphasis in most negotiations will be on projected earnings. To justify an acquisition, corporate management must present a statement to its board projecting improved earnings due to the acquisition. Many factors enter into the evaluation of a company, but each one directly or indirectly relates to the quality of potential earnings. Net worth, for example, supports a history of past earnings and husbanding of fiscal resources. Current assets indicate a company's ability to financially support its own internal growth. Backlog deals directly with immediate earnings prospects. Conservative allowance for bad debts or unrecoverable fees reduces the possibility of future surprise write-offs. Whether the geographical and technical market penetration is complementary or competitive with the parent relates to future earnings. The attitude, interests, reputation, and health of key personnel are of vital importance to future earnings in professional service firms.

A good projection of earnings plus enough information on potential acquiring companies to understand their negotiation position will provide the needed tools for self-evaluation.

Analyzing the Acquirer

In a stock transaction the upper figure will certainly be a fraction of the parent's price/earnings (P/E) ratio applied to projected earnings.

P/E ratios for all companies on the New York or American Exchange are listed with the daily quotations in the *Wall Street Journal* and other major newspapers. It must be a fraction as no company can justify an acquisition that would dilute its earnings. The size of the fraction depends on many factors. The acquisition itself involves initial costs for the parent as well as ongoing management costs. Auditing costs are almost always higher for a public traded company. As management costs are not proportional to size, the fraction should be lower for a smaller firm on these elements.

A proposed method for estimating the fraction is to develop "paper trial marriages." A combination that could convince a tough board of directors as being in the interest of its shareholders should approach the right fraction. It may not be satisfactory to the acquiree, but it would be unrealistic to expect considerably more.

A cash acquisition price can also be estimated by a trial marriage process though the extenuating factors are more complex. One must determine the availability of cash to the acquiring company. One with little long-term debt and strong current assets is in good position to consider cash acquisitions. The rate at which the acquiree's earnings would replenish cash in a given paper marriage will be a prime factor to a company's board. Short- and long-term interest rates will be an important consideration. The acquirer will expect considerable leverage in utilizing cash resources. As with stock, an increase in earnings per share is mandatory.

To determine realistic expectations with cash a number of trials can be used. One would be to compare a given dollar investment in the acquiree with a similar investment in the parent's own stock at a step-up of current market prices. The possible acquisition cited earlier of the company earning $4 million for $16 million cash resulted in earnings of $1.32. The same amount invested in a successful repurchase program of its own stock at say $10 a share (25 percent over a market of $8) would retire 1,600,000 shares and allowing for the same 10 percent interest and 50 percent tax rates, resultant earnings would be ($10 million minus $800,000) divided by 8,400,000 shares which equals only $1.095 per share. Thus a cash acquisition of an attractive new company at an even higher price could be aggressively pursued by an acquirer with cash resources.

In a cash acquisition, a professional services firm's assurance of continuity and growth potential of earnings within the framework of the larger corporation is difficult and complex. As the purchase involves primarily human resources, contracted backlog, and good will, the assurance of continuity requires in-depth interviews with employees and possibly clients and a structure of personal contracts and incentive plans tied to the acquisition agreement.

Other factors in a cash purchase include relative net worth of the acquirer and acquiree. As many publicly traded companies are selling below their own net worth per share, a cash acquisition above net worth would dilute the net worth per share of the acquirer. This would only be acceptable when it could be demonstrated that the new earnings would result in a growth of net worth over the original in a reasonable period of time.

Once a decision has been made to sell, a self-evaluation should prove most helpful.

Conclusion

Self-evaluation in a free market is only possible for the seller in relation to a potential buyer. Nevertheless, once a decision has been made to sell, and one or more potential buyers identified, a self-evaluation should prove most helpful. While it may eliminate some "dreams of glory," it could save all parties from the frustration of a courtship with no chance of consummation. It will certainly help the acquiree know his own company better. The trial paper marriage process should place the acquiree in a much more knowledgeable, realistic, and therefore improved bargaining position. By assuming the position of the acquiring company's management selling to its board of directors, the acquiree should feel more satisfaction in the terms of the acquisition and therefore the resulting marriage could be much smoother.

Better Valuation

In nearly 90 percent of buy-sell agreements that we review for clients, the purchase or redemption price for stock is based on book value. Nothing is further from the proper value than book value. No one will deny that book value based on generally accepted accounting principles developed over the years serves a useful purpose. It records what has happened in the past.

Because of a long tradition of usage, book value is understood by most businessmen, accountants, lawyers, and laymen. Yet, anyone contemplating a purchase or sale of all or a portion of a design firm must be concerned with the economic value, rather than historic book value. In addition, the historical balance sheet that your accountant puts together annually for the firm is deficient from a valuation standpoint. Book value is a starting point and must be adjusted to approximate your firm's true economic value. The following major items are common to the design profession:

1. Most assets are recorded at cost.

Each asset included within the financial statements is recorded at its historical cost. For example, the building that houses your office may have been purchased in 1970 for $200,000. On the financial statement, this asset may be carried at a depreciated value of only $75,000, depending on your firm's method of depreciation. Yet, the market value of this asset may be substantially higher. To use book value of this asset would potentially understate your firm's true economic value.

2. Some assets are omitted entirely.

It is common practice in the design profession to omit certain assets entirely. For example, maps, drawings, and technical libraries are notable items of value that are not included in book value. A price must be placed on these assets to properly value your firm.

3. Estimates are required.

Not all assets can be easily valued. Many items of value require estimates which will affect value. For instance, work-in-process and unbilled accounts receivable are large assets which affect the value of a design firm that must be estimated. Too often, work-in-process is omitted or undervalued by accountants.

4. Different accounting methods may be employed.

A wide variety of accounting methods may be employed which are proper and acceptable. Each method can have a tremendous effect on the value of your firm, even when applied consistently. Similarly, different

Anthony F. Dannible

Nothing is further from the proper value than book value.

design firms use different methods of accounting, making comparisons difficult:

a. Cash versus accrual. A large number of design firms use the cash method of accounting. This is because most closely held design firms are more interested in saving income tax than reporting income from professional service. A buy-sell agreement of a value based on a book value determined on the cash method will effectively eliminate substantial value. For example, the accounts receivable and work-in-process of the firm are not an asset using the cash method of accounting. For valuation purposes, the accrual method must be employed.

b. Depreciation variations. The method of depreciation used is heavily influenced by income tax reporting. Among the more common methods are the straight-line and declining balance. Both are acceptable for reporting purposes. However, the declining balance method accelerates the depreciation of fixed assets and reduces the book value faster. An economic appraisal should be taken.

Summary

In valuing your design firm, you must be concerned with real net tangible value. As outlined above, you can never afford to accept the book value shown in the financial statements prepared by your accountant as being the true value.

In valuing your design firm, you must be concerned with real net tangible value.

Common ESOP Misconceptions

O ver the last five years, the subject of employee ownership has been given more and more attention by government, private and public company management, and by the media. Yet many common apprehensions persist, based largely on misconceptions. Business owners often bypass the many advantages of shared ownership because of groundless fears. This article is planned to help sweep away the fears and open the door to the potential of shared ownership in solving some tough problems in design firms.

Owner Apprehensions

Giveaway. "I don't want to give away what I've spent years building" is a frequent response to the suggestion that broad employee ownership may produce business benefits. First, and emphatically, it's not a giveaway but an earned bonus, the financing for which is usually produced by increased productivity and lowered costs—in other words, higher profits. Virtually all studies in the area have demonstrated that labor costs go down, not up, if an employee stock ownership plan (ESOP) is properly installed, operated, and communicated. Second, a professional practice is not built solely by its owners. It must usually have had at least a few old, loyal, and dedicated employees who are core and key to the business success. Vesting schedules and other design mechanisms serve to increase the rewards of ownership for such key people.

Disclosure. "How I run this company is none of their damn business! I don't wish to share all management and operational decisions with the worker. He doesn't need to know and I don't want him to know all the facts!" Here, the owner is expressing concern about nonexisting requirements of disclosure in the event of implementing an ESOP. In real life and in accordance with regulations, management of an ESOP firm has no more requirement for sharing secrets than does a non-ESOP company. Management, including the board, shares only what good judgment and good management indicate will make the employee-owner more interested, more effective, and more productive.

True, if the firm falls on hard times and its value-per-share decreases, the employee participation statement will reveal that fact. But how better to combat the problem of reduced profitability than to communicate the need for improved effectiveness, reduced costs, and increased productivity to those who are in the best position to affect these

Harry J. Orchard

I don't want to give away what I've spent years building.

areas, the worker! We see this approach daily in public, non-ESOP companies such as Chrysler appealing to their workers, union and nonunion alike, to help reverse economic trends and return the company to profitability. Won't the employee-owner respond to such appeals more eagerly than the nonowner? He has more to lose and more to gain. Carry this thought one step further. If the value-per-share goes up, rather than down, isn't that "good news" logically impacted on productivity if everyone is an owner and knows it?

Dilution. "We own it all, including all the votes. We don't want to dilute our ownership nor our vote," say the owners of closely held private firms. Let's deal first with ownership dilution. If it's true that ESOP companies typically speed up growth and profitability after the ESOP is installed (and most studies confirm that they do), isn't the 70 percent or 80 percent owner of a larger and more profitable firm better off financially than he was as the 100 percent owner of the original smaller firm? In other words, his ownership value has increased. In addition, the owners, usually the most highly compensated employees, have the largest allocations of ownership within the ESOP trust.

Now let's talk about vote dilution, perhaps the biggest bugaboo (and least understood) of all objections to the ESOP. First, unless the ESOP is leveraged (and the vast majority are not), the stock owned by the trust isn't even required to be voting stock. In such a case, there is obviously no dilution nor can there be. However, a good case can be made that the ESOP with voting stock will be more meaningful to the employee than an ESOP with "second-class" stock. Even then, in the private company, there is no vote pass-through to the employee except in major corporate matters in those states requiring more than a majority vote of the stockholders in such matters. Actions such as merger or sale of the corporate assets, or discontinuance of operations, are examples of such major matters.

In other matters, the stock in the ESOP trust is voted by the trustee, at the direction of the ESOP Committee, which committee is appointed by the board and responsible to the board. In cases in which the vote is, or is required to be, passed through to employees, the usual result will be less than crucial, as most ESOPs, due to retirements, turnover, and effective design, never reach a majority ownership position unless that is the intent and design of the original owners who wish to transfer most or all ownership eventually to employees.

Potential Benefits

As can be seen, three objections, i.e., "It's a giveaway," "I don't want to have to tell the employee everything," and "I don't want to give up full control (or voting control)" are largely misconceptions not supported by the facts. If more private companies (as are the majority of design professional firms) were provided the same level of expert consultation and guidance in the employee ownership concept as these firms themselves provide to their clients in their individual areas of expertise, there probably

We don't want to dilute our ownership nor our votes.

would be more such firms installing employee ownership plans to accomplish one or more of the following:

• provide a qualified retirement plan for all employees;

• increase employee motivation and productivity;

• generate capital internally on a tax-deductible basis;

• provide a market for purchase of company stock for principal shareholders, thus providing liquidity for them.

As is the case with many ideas, the ESOP concept is often discarded without adequate investigation due to misunderstandings and misconceptions which are largely groundless. Thus, a great opportunity can be missed. Getting the full answers from qualified professionals can clear the path to tomorrow's growth to the benefit of owner and employees alike.

Index

420